A James Sprunt Reader

Two complete classic books by the Cape Fear's greatest historian

Tales and Traditions of the Lower Cape Fear

Tales of the Cape Fear Blockade

newly illustrated and with an additional short story,

A Colonial Apparition

plus the essay

"Stories of the Old Plantations"

by Dr. John Hampden Hill

edited by

Jack E. Fryar, Jr.

Published in the United States of America by Dram Tree Books.

Publisher's Cataloging-in-Publication Data
(Provided by DRT Press)

Sprunt, James.

A James Sprunt reader : two complete classic books by the Cape Fear's greatest historian. Tales and traditions of the Cape Fear River, Tales of the Cape Fear blockade, newly illustrated and with an additional short story, A Colonial apparition, plus the essay "Stories of the old plantations" by John Hampden Hill / edited by Jack E. Fryar.

p. cm.
Includes bibliographical references and index.
ISBN 978-0-9814603-6-9

1. Cape Fear River Valley (N.C.) —History. 2. North Carolina —History —Civil War, 1861-1865. 3. Wilmington (N.C.) —Description and travel. 4. United States —History —Civil War, 1861-1865 —Blockades. 5. Wilmington (N.C.) —History —Civil War, 1861-1865. 6. Plantations—North Carolina. I. Sprunt, James, 1846-1924. II. Fryar, Jack. E. III. Hill, John Hampden.

F262.C2 S68 2009
917.562—dc22

10 9 8 7 6 5 4 3 21
Dram Tree Books
P.O. Box 7183
Wilmington, N.C. 28406
(910) 538-4076
www.dramtreebooks.com
Potential authors: visit our website for submission guidelines

Editor's Note

I have always admired James Sprunt very much. When you think of all the good things that go along with the term, "Southern gentleman," Mr. Sprunt seems to embody most of them. That's not to say he didn't have his faults (who among us doesn't), and he was certainly a product of the times he lived in. Nevertheless, when taken as a whole, James Sprunt was an excellent example of what a "Southern gentleman" should be. When he was a teen, he served aboard a blockade runner here on the Cape Fear River. He owned Orton Plantation, and the Governor Dudley Mansion in downtown Wilmington. He and his family became the largest cotton exporters in the world. During the riots of 1898, when the mob marched on the Sprunt cotton compress on Wilmington's downtown riverfront to get at the blacks working for him, James Sprunt dismounted swivel guns from his yacht and put himself in front of the mob to protect his employees. He quite possibly saved those men's lives. Mr. Sprunt was a philanthropist (a community college in North Carolina still bears his name), and many charities benefited from his generosity, sense of civic duty and pride. Finally, James Sprunt was one of the best historians North Carolina has ever produced. His history of southeastern North Carolina was the first comprehensive history of the region ever written. While it borrows liberally from the work of other historians, the fact remains that it is still the single best history of the region ever produced. The James Sprunt Historical Series which he sponsored provided a means for serious contributions to the historical record of North Carolina to be shared with the citizens and scholars who call the state home. James Sprunt's legacy extends far beyond the stately walls of the plantation house at Orton he is most closely associated with. It has touched countless lives among the people who live in the place he loved so much along the Lower Cape Fear.

James Sprunt wrote four full-length books that I admire a lot, and which I consider to be representative of his contributions to the historical record of southeastern North Carolina. Through my company, Dram Tree Books, I have brought two of those books back into print. *Chronicles of the Cape Fear River: 1660-1916* remains the single best history ever written of the place Mr. Sprunt called home, while *Derelicts* is a fascinating look into the story of ships lost off the North Carolina coast and of the blockade runners who played such a big role in the war effort of the Confederacy. It is my great pleasure to bring the last two of those works by James Sprunt that I admire so much back into print in this volume. *Tales and Traditions of the Lower Cape Fear* was written as a tour guide for passengers aboard Captain John Harper's excursion boat, pointing out the places of historical significance along the Cape Fear River on their voyage from Wilmington to Southport. *Tales of the Cape Fear Blockade* recounts the thrilling exploits of the dashing blockade runners and their fast ships, who gambled their lives and freedom against the possibility of enormous profits to be made supplying the Confederacy with the goods it could not provide itself. As well, I have include in this anthology Dr. John Hampden Hill's essay on the plantations that once lined the Cape Fear River between Old Inlet and Wilmington, as plantation culture played such a big role in the development of the place Mr. Sprunt called home. Also included in the essay are Samuel Ashe's notes on Hill's work. Finally, just for fun, is a short story Mr. Sprunt penned, *A Colonial Apparition*. It's a ghost story, oddly enough, but in the telling of it, Sprunt gives a quick synopsis of much of the region's colonial history (besides which, it's also a fun tale).

Readers who compare Mr. Sprunt's original books with this volume will find that some original illustrations have been omitted. That's because some of the illustrations just did not reproduce well, or because the publisher had better images at our disposal to replace the original with. On the other hand, we've greatly expanded the over all number of illustrations from what Mr. Sprunt's original works contained. Hopefully we've struck a balance that will leave readers more than satisfied.

I hope you enjoy this, and I encourage you to seek out Mr. Sprunt's other work. It will become readily apparent why James Sprunt is widely considered the "grandfather of all Cape Fear historians."

Jack E. Fryar, Jr.
Dram Tree Books
Wilmington, N.C.
15 May 2009

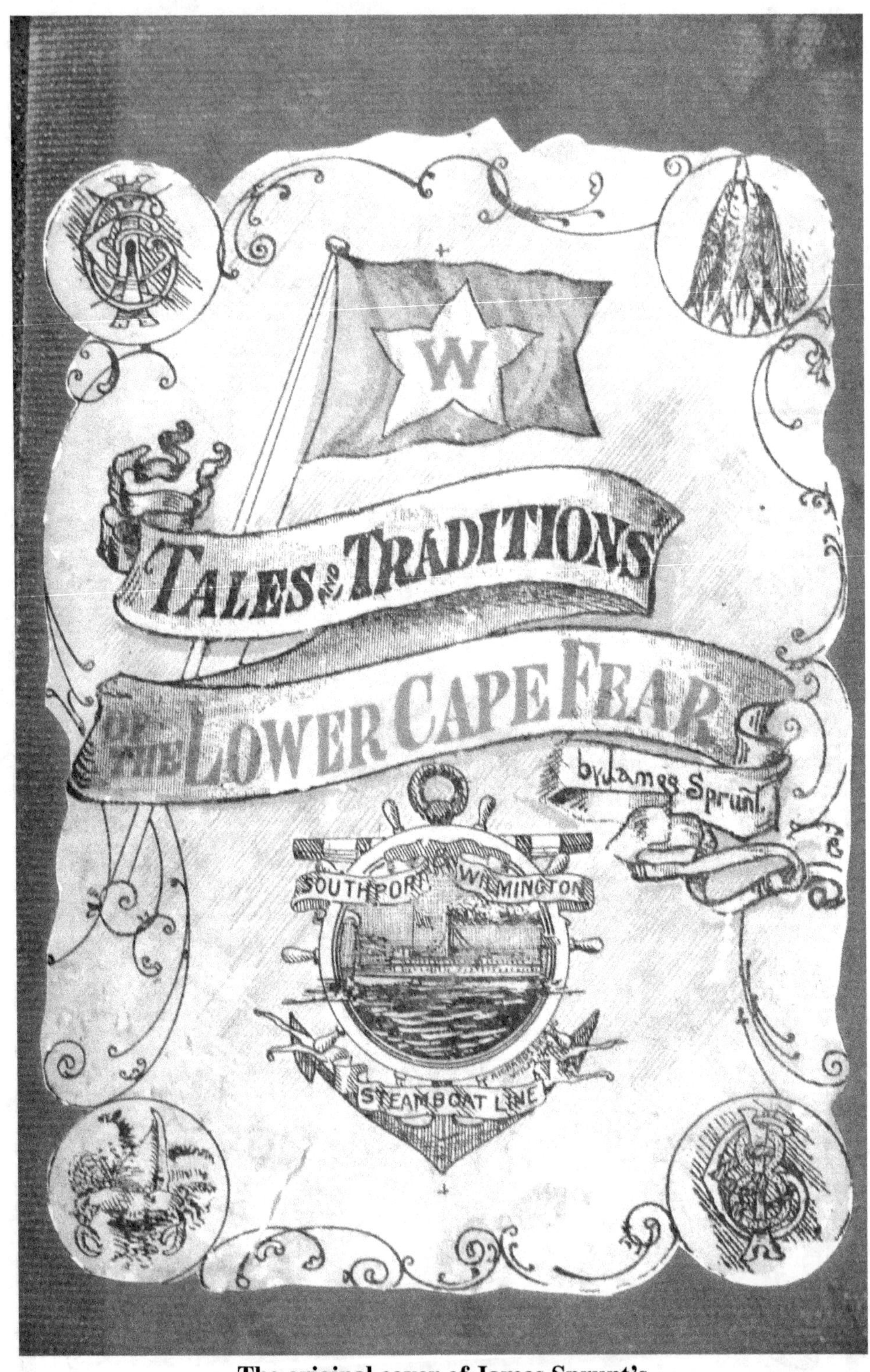

The original cover of James Sprunt's
Tales & Traditions of the Lower Cape Fear.

Tales & Traditions of the Lower Cape Fear

by

James Sprunt

The steamer **Wilmington** *on a leisurely cruise down the Cape Fear River.*

Captain John Harper

The Southport Steamer.

The steamer *Wilmington* is a model of marine architecture, combining spacious and comfortable passenger accommodations with the greatest speed attained by steam craft on the Cape Fear River. Her clean decks and tidy saloons afford the bracing outside air, or the restful seclusion which invites repose. The daily run to and from Southport is made in two hours, including all river landings; and the object of this little book is to interest and amuse the traveler by a concise description of Wilmington business enterprise and local scenery, contrasting the record of the present busy age with the history and traditions of long ago.

As we approach the gangway of this stately steamer, we are impressed with the quiet of the scene. We miss, most gratefully, the noisy roar of escaping steam, the confusing shouts, the imprecations and jostlings of the professional baggage-steamer, and all the other distasteful and offensive features of former days. We are promptly met by the American sailor and gentleman, who receives us courteously, and who welcomes us with unmistakable cordiality. His name is John W. Harper, and he is said to be the favorite skipper of North Carolina. When you have made the round trip in his charge you will not doubt his title to that honorable distinction. A successful steamboat captain should be competent, cool, cautious, patient, polite and amiable to the last degree; with an infinite reserve stock of never failing good humor. These attributes are possessed by Captain Harper, to an unusual extent, which combined with a large experience, inspire confidence and insure safety. He has been running boats up and down the river for twenty-two years, and he has made, during that time, more than thirteen thousand trips between Wilmington and Southport—equal to fifteen trips around the world. He was the pioneer of the regular summer excursions to the Cape Fear seacoast, by which thousands of weary people and sick babies from the up country and the city, oppressed with mid-summer heat, have been refreshed and strengthened by ocean breezes and salt water at a nominal expense. It is a matter of fact that salt sea air will often do more good to a sick, puny child than any of the medical remedies in the pharmacopoeia. Many anxious, worn-out mothers, have had reason to bless Captain Harper as the means under Providence of restoring to health their sick or feeble little ones. A beloved physician has often said that daily trips from Wilmington to Southport are even more beneficial to sick children than a residence on the seashore. The gliding motion of the boat soothes them, the clear, fresh air of the river invigorates and strengthens them, and the entire freedom from dust and grime which is so disagreeable and hurtful on railroad journeys brings grateful sensations of cleanliness and comfort to young and old alike.

"How happy they
Who from the toil and tumult of their lives
Steal to look down where naught but ocean strives."

The First Steamboat on the Cape Fear River.

Let us contrast the swift steamer *Wilmington* with the ridiculous example of former days—let us turn back for three-quarters of a century, when the town of Wilmington contained only a tenth of its present population, and recall an incident, related to the writer by our venerable townsman. Col. J.G. Burr, which created the greatest excitement at the time, and which was the occasion of the wildest exuberance of feeling among the usually staid inhabitants of the town—the arrival of the first steamboat in the Cape Fear River. A joint stock company had been formed for the purpose of having one built to ply between Wilmington and Smithville or Wilmington and Fayetteville. Captain Otway Burns, of Privateer *Snap Dragon* fame during the war of 1812, was the contractor. The boat was built at Beaufort, where he resided. When the company was informed that the steamer was finished and ready for delivery, they dispatched Captain Thomas N. Gautier, an old sea captain, and a worthy citizen of the town, to take command and bring her to her destined port. Expectations

Wilmington's first steamer, the **Prometheus**, *built by Otway Burns.*

were on tiptoe after the departure of the Captain; a feverish excitement existed in the community, which daily increased, as nothing was heard from him for a time, owing to the irregularity of the mails; but early one morning this anxiety broke into the wildest enthusiasm when it was announced that the *Prometheus* was in the river and had turned the Dram Tree. Bells were rung, cannon fired, and the entire population, without regard to age, sex, or color, thronged the wharves to welcome her arrival. The tide was at the ebb, and the struggle between the advancing steamer and the fierce current was a desperate one; for she panted fearfully, as though wind-blown and exhausted; ash could be seen in the distance, enveloped in smoke, and the scream of her high pressure engine reverberated through the woods, while she slowly but surely crept along. As she neared Market Dock, where the steamer *Wilmington* is at present moored, the old Captain, gorgeously arrayed in brilliant uniform, with cocked hat and epaulettes, made his appearance near the engine room, in full view of the excited crowd, and applying his speaking-trumpet, his symbol of authority, to his lips, bellowed to the engineer below, in a voice that sounded like the roar of some hoarse monster of the deep: "Give it to her, Snyder"; and while Snyder gave her all the steam she could bear, the laboring *Prometheus* snorted by amid the cheers of the excited multitude. In those days the river traffic was sustained by sailing sloops and small schooners, with limited passenger accommodations and less comfort. The schedule time to Smithville (now called Southport), was four hours, wind and weather permitting, and the fare was one dollar each way.

Settlement of Wilmington.

About the year 1730, some five years after the town of Brunswick was established fourteen miles lower down the river, a few settlers built their humble habitations on a bluff in the midst of the primeval forest now known as Dickinson Hill, nearly opposite the junction of the Northeast and Northwest branches of the Cape Fear River, which was then known as the Clarendon River. Their purpose was to find a safer harbor than the exposed roadstead of Brunswick, and to secure a larger share of the river traffic from the up country, which was then very profitable.

In a few months this hamlet increased to the proportion of a small village, without order or regularity, which was named New Liverpool.

In 1733 it was surveyed into town lots, although the inhabitants had no legal right to the land.

In the same year John Watson obtained a Royal grant of 640 acres of land on the East side of the Northeast branch of the river called the Cape Fear, in which was included the site of the village or town called New Liverpool, but latterly known as Newton.

In 1739, through the influence of the Colonial Governor, Gabriel Johnston, the name was again changed to Wilmington, in honor of Spencer Compton, Baron Wilmington, an influential English friend of the Governor. In 1760 King George II made the town a borough, with the right of sending a member to the Assembly.

Arthur Dobbs was then the Royal Governor, and he lived at Russelboro, which is now a part of Orton plantation.

In 1763, George III being King, additional rights were granted by the Crown, the corporate title being made "The Mayor, Recorder and Aldermen of the Borough of Wilmington."

In 1776 the corporate name was changed to that of "The Commissioners of the Town of Wilmington;" and this name was continued for one hundred years. The present corporate name, "The City of Wilmington," was acquired in the year 1866.

Sanitary.

Artificial drainage has in recent years carried the storm water from the city into the tributary streams of the Cape Fear, and if maintained in proper condition, is well designed to effectually quarter off the settlement. As a result malarial fever has greatly decreased in the last twenty years, and it may be truly said, although stigmatized forty years ago as the sailor's grave, and shunned by the people of the up country as an unsafe place in which to tarry all night during the summer and autumn, it has become exceptionally healthy. As an evidence of this, the death-rate for several years past has been much smaller than in the surrounding country; and compares favorably with the most favored towns of its size on the Atlantic coast, the annual death-rate being about seventeen to the thousand.

Drainage has not, and cannot, it is true, alter the malarial influence upon crews of vessels sleeping on the river in the months of July, August, September and October. This standing menace to the prosperity of our shipping, as evidenced by the scarcity of tonnage during these months, has been seriously considered for many years, and a remedy actually devised. The difficulty has been to impress the lesson of prevention, learned at such a cost, upon the interested parties. The State Board of Health has done much towards inculcating important advice upon the subject. For many years it has been known, as well by the people as by the doctors, that the fevers occurring among the vessels in our tide-water streams were preventable in a marked degree. Observations extending over a space of time marked by four or five generations demonstrated that the cause of sickness among sailors was due very largely to sleeping on board of vessels in the Cape Fear River particularly. This fact was so firmly established in the opinion of merchants in Wilmington, that $20,000 was subscribed to build a home for seamen, in which they might find a safe retreat from the effluvia of the river, and what is not exactly pertinent to the present subject, to escape also the abominable effluvia of low sailor lodgings. In this building ample provision was made for more sailors than ever visit the port of Wilmington at one time, and by the Christian benevolence of Capt. Gilbert Potter, one of the oldest citizens of our city, who had himself been a sea-captain, a house of worship, supplied by the yearly ministrations of a preacher, was provided, to throw around these "toilers of the sea" a beneficent influence.

Cape Fear Steamboats.

Before railroads were so numerous and the means of transportation limited, the Cape Fear River Steamboat Company enjoyed a large share of public patronage. The merchandise for the merchants of Western North Carolina, East Tennessee and portions of South Carolina, Georgia and Virginia was brought to this port by vessels, transferred to the river boats to Fayetteville, and then forwarded to destination by the slow, tedious and expensive means of transportation by wagons. Fayetteville in those days was a place of as much business and importance in a commercial point of view as any inland town in the country, and every citizen in the place took pride in seeing the place flourish and prosper. The merchants built steamboats and plank-roads, and in this way fostered the trade which from the position at the head of navigation was a natural outlet. But as soon as the railroad became the grand artery to receive and disperse everything as public and private interest directed, the river traffic decreased, and with its decline the plank-roads ceased to be profitable, and there was almost a total disappearance of the white-covered caravans that plied between the mountains and the Cape Fear country.

The Worths, Lutterlohs, Orrells and others had regular fleets on the Cape Fear. We now recall the steamers *Rowan*, *Henrietta*, *Chatham*, *Gov. Graham*, *Flora McDonald*, *A.P. Hurt* and *Gov. Worth*, commanded by captains Roderick McRae, A.P. Hurt, Sam Skinner, A.H. Worth; the steamers *Brothers*, *James R. Grist*, *Douglass*, *J.T. Petteway* and *Scottish Chief*, all of which boats were at times under the command of that whole-souled, jovial Scotchman, "Uncle Johnnie Banks"; the steamer *Sun*, Captain Rush; the steamer *Enterprise*, Captain Datus Jones; the *Fannie Lutterloh*, Captain Stedman; the *Kate McLaurin*, Captain Daily; the *Black River*, Captain Jesse Dicksey; the *John Dawson*, Captain Lawton; the *Hattie Hart*, Captain Peck; and other steamers and captains we cannot now recall. In these later days there has been employed in the river trade the steamers *Murchison*, the *North State*, the *Cumberland*, the *Juniper*, the *Cape Fear*, the *Wave*, the *J.C. Stewart*, the *Frank Sessoms*, commanded by captains Garrison, Smith, Green, Worth, McLauchlin and the Robesons.

Negro Head Point.

As the *Wilmington* lies at her wharf, near Market Dock, we see from her spacious upper deck Negro Head Point, which divides the waters of the Cape Fear into Northwest and Northeast branches. It is the Northern limit of the jurisdiction of the Board of Commissioners of Navigation and

Boaters at Point Peter, or Negro Head Point, where the Cape Fear splits opposite Wilmington.

Pilotage, and its name is derived from a melancholy incident in the time of slavery.

In the latter part of the year 1831, through the influence of Northern emissaries, an insurrection of Negro slaves occurred in Southhampton, Virginia, which spread rapidly into this State creating great and general excitement.

A number of helpless white women and children fell victims to the madness of the blacks, which so infuriated the whites that a race war seemed inevitable. All the approaches to the town of Wilmington were heavily guarded by the militia, and two companies of United States troops, numbering 170 men, from Fortress Monroe, remained on duty here for several months. The uprising was overcome and the leaders suffered death. Four were hanged near Giblem Lodge, on Princess Street; several others were shot, and, according to the barbarous custom of those days, their heads, after decapitation, were placed on poles in conspicuous places as a warning to others like minded.

At the intersection of Market and Front Streets, a few rods from the steamer's dock, stood the town market house, where the slave-trade was constantly carried on until 1863.

We draw a veil over the sad scenes enacted there, but we recall the fact that it was not until after the slave-traders of the North had received full value of their human merchandise from their Southern brethren that our neighbors began to realize the enormity of the institution.

And yet our people who were impoverished by its downfall would not, if they could, deprive the negro of his freedom.

With reference to the introduction of slavery into Carolina by the Colonial Governor, Yeamans, from Barbados in 1671, the late lamented George Davis said:

"This seems to be a simple announcement of a very commonplace fact; but it was the little cloud no bigger than a man's hand. It was the most portentous event of all our early history. For he carried with him from Barbados his negro slaves; and that was the first introduction of African slavery into Carolina.—"

If, as he sat by the camp-fire in that lonely Southern wilderness, he could have gazed with prophetic vision down the vista of two hundred years, and seen the stormy and tragic end of that of which he was then so quietly inaugurating the beginning, must he not have exclaimed with Ophelia, as she beheld the wreck of her heart's young love:

" 'O, woe is me! To have seen what I have seen, see what I see!' "

Hilton Park.

Just beyond Negro Head Point, on the Northeast branch, a beautiful wooded bluff may be seen. It is Hilton, named in honor of one of the three first explorers from Barbados who visited the Cape Fear in the year 1663,

Hilton Park was the site of Cornelius Harnett's colonial residence, seen at left just before being torn down. Later, it was a place where Wilmington citizens enjoyed picnics and other outings (below). Today it hosts the city's water treatment plant.

which became famous in Revolutionary history as the home of Cornelius Harnett, a prominent patriot of this section and a conspicuous, noted personage of his day. Until a few years ago his house, a neat Colonial structure, embowered by noble oaks, and subsequently owned by the Hill family, was our most interesting relic of Revolutionary times; but the estate passed into other hands, and this picturesque, historic home was demolished, to the shame of our people, who were offered the building, as a public gift, for the cost of its removal and preservation.

"A perfect woman, nobly planned," whose skill and virtues are of national reputation, and whose ancestors were always leaders on the Cape Fear, has happily devised, as President of the Society of Colonial Dames, the means of placing a public monument over the grave of this sturdy patriot whose dust long since mingled with its mother earth in old St. James' churchyard, ere his noble sacrifice of life to liberty was appropriately recognized.

Market Dock and Ferry.

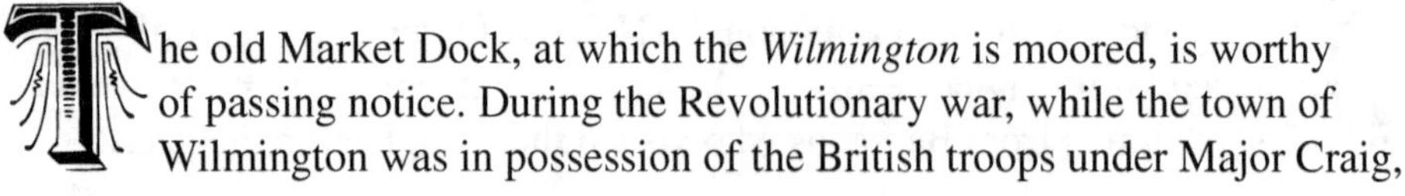

The old Market Dock, at which the *Wilmington* is moored, is worthy of passing notice. During the Revolutionary war, while the town of Wilmington was in possession of the British troops under Major Craig,

The old Market Dock, seen circled in this model of colonial Wilmington.

an American soldier in ambush on Point Peter or Negro Head shot with a long-range rifle a number of British troopers standing at Market Dock.

Also, more than a hundred years afterwards, when the Federal troops under Schofield and Terry reached the Brunswick side of Market Dock ferry on their way to Wilmington, the last stand of the Confederate troops was made near Market Dock; a detachment of light artillery having fired from this point upon the advancing Federals on the west side of the river and checked their progress. The Federals were in overwhelming numbers, however, and the artillerists soon followed Bragg's retreating forces before the invaders reached the town.

The Confederates had carefully removed from the west shore all boats and other means of transportation to the Wilmington side in order to retard the Federal advance. Consequently there was considerable delay in crossing the river, which was at last overcome by a demented Wilmington woman, who secretly obtained a small boat and paddled it across to the Federals, by means of which other craft was soon floated, and the town for a second time invested by a hostile army.

In the early morning of the 22d February 1865, a Confederate officer in command of the last battalion of infantry to leave Wilmington when evacuated by the Southern troops, was leading his men along Fourth Street on his way to rejoin General Hoke, who had passed up to the North East River the night previous.

Saddened and woefully depressed with the thought of leaving all his loved ones to the mercy of enemies, he called the next officer, and, giving him orders about the route to march, turned back from Boney Bridge to hurriedly bid adieu to all the dear ones. Passing down Red Cross to Front, hurried visits were made to several friends, but on reaching the intersection of Market and Front streets, the proximity of the enemy was apparent, for there were gathered the Mayor and Alderman of the city—John Dawson, W.S. Anderson, P.W. Fanning and others of the citizens who had there met to turn over the keys of the city to the captors. Around on every side were seen the results of the cannon-firing of the day previous, the window-panes in every house were shattered and artillery debris lay scattered around. Immediate passing events urged a very prompt retreat, and the officer hurried to his father's house to say good-bye and to receive their loving blessings and wishes for safety. Hastening through this distressing scene, he began his journey to rejoin his command, accompanied as far as Boney Bridge by his sister. The streets of Pompeii or Herculaneum when buried beneath the lava of Vesuvius were no quieter than those of Wilmington. Not a soul was to be seen on the streets, not a window-blind but was closed. Apparently even the dogs were affected by the prevailing distress. The mournful walk was continued, and the officer, parting with his sister, continued his march with feelings easily to be imagined, and soon rejoined his command about five miles out. This lady subsequently said that this was the loneliest walk of her life-time. She met no one between Boney Bridge and her father's residence, South of Market Street on Second Street.

Russellborough is most often associated with the colonial govrenors who lived on the Cape Fear River, though they also had homes in Wilmington. This model of Russellborough is based on site archaeology.

Colonial Governor's Residence.

A few steps from the *Wilmington*'s wharf is an unpretentious tobacconist's shop—a small brick building—which is said to have been the residence of the celebrated Colonial Governor, William Tryon, who was closely identified with the Cape Fear section of Revolutionary times, as will be seen further on. Higher up, on the corner of Third Street, may be seen the fine residence, which served as the headquarters of General Lord Cornwallis,

The Burgwin-Wright House, at the corner of Third and Market Streets in Wilmington. The house was used by British General Charles Lord Cornwallis as a hedquarters in April 1781.

commander of the British forces. It is now owned and occupied by Mrs. McRary. Immediately opposite stands an ancient residence of the deRosset family, which was used throughout the civil war nearly a hundred years later as headquarters of the Confederate Generals commanding this district.

Confederate States Cotton Press.

As we leave the wharf, on our passage down the river, we see a conspicuous relic of an extraordinary era in the foreign trade of Wilmington. It is the leaning, but unbroken, brick chimney of the Confederate States Cotton Press established here in the year 1864. This press was the first in Wilmington, and had a capacity of 500 bales a day. The wharves and marsh adjoining to the warehouses were piled with enormous quantities of cotton bales belonging to the Confederate Government, and hither came all the swift blockade-runners for cargoes which were laden with great rapidity; work went on day and night, as many as twenty steamers loading together. The entire plant, together with several thousand bales of cotton was destroyed by fire by order of General Bragg upon his evacuation of this place on the evening of February 21st, 1865.

The Dudley Mansion in downtown Wilmington as it looked in the early 1900s.

Historic Mansion.

On the East bank at a considerable elevation above the river is an historic residence. It was built and occupied by the first Governor of North Carolina elected by the people, Edward B. Dudley, a statesman of liberal and patriotic views, of commanding presence and of most amiable manners. His name should ever be held in grateful remembrance by our people, for he was a leader in every public and private work for the benefit and prosperity of Wilmington, and contributed $25,000 towards the building of the Wilmington & Weldon Railroad, of which he was the first President. He was a man of generous impulses and stainless integrity, beloved and honored by rich and poor, and by white and black alike. He served as a member of the Twenty-first Congress, to which he was elected in the year 1829, but declined re-election, because he said Congress was not the place for an honest man.

In May 1849, he entertained at this residence the distinguished Daniel Webster, who visited Wilmington as his guest. Mr. Webster was doubtless well cared for, as he wrote to a friend May 7th: "We are grandly lodged in the Governor's mansion."

In later years Cardinal Gibbons, with an Archbishop and twelve bishops were entertained here by Mr. Kerchner, who owned the place at that time.

The present owner and occupant has greatly enlarged and improved this property, at the foot of which may be seen the *(U.S. Monitor* Nantucket, *see next page)*

The monitor Nantucket.

United States Monitor Nantucket.

A battle-scarred survivor of the war between the States. This vessel took part in the bombardment of Fort Sumter and in other conflicts at sea. Her turret is indented by hostile shot and shell, and she is regarded as an interesting type of the old navy. The *Nantucket* is in charge of the Wilmington Division of North Carolina Naval Reserves, and is used as the school ship of this fine organization.

Old Ship-Yard.

The first and only sailing ship built at Wilmington was launched June 5th, 1833, by Mr. John K. McIlhenny, and named after his two daughters, Eliza and Susan. The work was done by Mr. Josh Toomer, the grandfather of the present generation of that name, under the direction of Mr. McIlhenny, at the saw mill of the latter upon the exact site of Kidder's mill. Mr. McIlhenny owned a rice mill and a saw mill, both of which were about the first erected at Wilmington.

The *Eliza and Susan* was a full-rig ship of 316 tons, built of the staunchest live oak, and of unusual strength. The oak came partly from Bald Head and partly from Lockwood's Folly. She was pine-planked and coppered. It is not certain what cargo she took out, but she came back loaded with salt. The commander was Captain Huntington, already in middle life at the time of the ship's first voyage. His son afterwards married Miss Brown of this place.

Long afterwards, while the *Eliza and Susan* was engaged in the whaling trade of the Pacific, Captain Thomas F. Peck, who had gone from Wilmington to the land of gold with the "forty-niners," saw the familiar Wilmington ship at anchor in San Francisco Bay. He was subsequently invited on board and served with a glass of Cape Fear River water, then highly esteemed as pure and wholesome, which had been kept in one of the reserve tanks for more than twenty years.

At right angles with the river and parallel with Queen Street Mr. McIlhenny cut a canal; at the head of this canal the ship was built. In launching her she stuck in the mud, and Colonel McIlhenny remembers as a boy seeing his father fume most vigorously about it. There were on the river about that time the *Enterprise*, the *Spray*, the *John Walker* and the *Henrietta*. Mr. McIlhenny and Governor Dudley owned the *Enterprise*, which was a very small boat, and was used by them for towing the rice flats from the different plantations. They lengthened her first ten or twelve feet, then afterwards gave her an additional length and ran her as a passenger boat from Wilmington to Smithville.

The old Dram Tree.

The *Spray* ran about 1853 or 1854, and was the fastest of them all. She was shaped something like a barrel, hooped up on the sides. She was the favorite steamboat plying between Wilmington and Smithville a few years before the war.

Mr. McIlhenny was awarded a contract by the Government to furnish timber for building the United States man-of-war *Pennsylvania*. No large ships were built here subsequently. Mr. B.W. Beery built some schooners and pilot boats, and afterwards Mr. Cassidy established the ship-yard now conducted by Captain S.W. Skinner, the only ship-yard in Wilmington.

The Dram Tree.

Looking ahead to the farthest point in view, we distinguish an object, the passing of which was signalized in "ye olden time" by the popping of corks or by other demonstration of a convivial nature. It is an old cypress tree, moss-covered and battered by the storms of centuries. Like a grim sentinel, it stands to warn the out-going mariner that his voyage has begun, and to welcome the in-coming storm-tossed sailor to the quiet harbor beyond. Its name is significant. It is called the Dram Tree, and it has borne this name for more than a hundred years. For further particulars see Captain Harper.

The old Marine Hospital once stood at Hospital Point.

Hospital Point.

We now pass Hospital Point, whereon was placed a pest house during the small-pox plague which followed Sherman's army. Many thousands of negro refugees fell victims to this dread disease. At low water may be seen the charred remains of several Confederate war vessels which composed Commodore Lynch's small and crippled fleet, and which were burned by the Confederates when Wilmington was evacuated after the fall of Fort Fisher.

This place is also known as Mount Tirzah, and it is the property of the Seamen's Friend Society of Wilmington. In 1835 the citizens of the town held a meeting to establish the Wilmington Marine Hospital for the benefit of sick seamen in this port for whom no provision up to that time had been made. Subscriptions were raised, a society formed, and the Mount Tirzah property of 150 acres and several houses standing thereon purchased from Governor E. B. Dudley for one thousand dollars.

The principal building, a house of two stories, was converted into a hospital and managed by the Marine Hospital Society until April 24th, 1855, when this property and the other assets of the Society were transferred to the Seamen's Friend Society, which undertook to carry on the work in conjunction with its own benevolent enterprise in the port of Wilmington. Later on the United States

Government established in the Southeastern part of the town a fine marine hospital, which provided greatly improved quarters and treatment for sick seamen, and which is now one of the most interesting features of the port of Wilmington.

The Mount Tirzah property is occasionally used by the City Government for the isolation and treatment of cases of infectious diseases.

Brunswick River, Mallory Creek, Clarendon Plantation.

On the West side is the mouth of the Brunswick River, still partly obstructed by Confederate torpedoes. Mallory Creek is some distance lower down. Near it is "Clarendon," a fine rice plantation, originally owned by Marsden Campbell and afterwards the property of William Watters, esq., a Cape Fear gentleman of the Old School, and a planter of large experience. It is now owned by Messers. Fred Kidder and H. Walters.

Old Town Settlement.

Passing Barnard's Creek on the east side, near which in the olden time were several valuable plantations, we come to Town Creek, where 800 colonists from Barbadoes, led by Sir John Yeamans, built a town in the year 1665 and called it Charlestown in honor of the reigning sovereign of England, King Charles II.

Sir John had been a loyal adherent of the deposed King, and was rewarded upon the Restoration with the order of Knighthood and a royal grant of lands in Carolina. He is said to have been the first British Governor of Clarendon, which extended originally from Albemarle to St. Augustine, Florida. The settlement did not prosper. In a few years the colonists abandoned it and removed, some to Charleston, S.C., others to Albemarle, in the North. Not a white man remained, and the river land continued in possession of the Indians for many years after.

Big Island, Rice Birds.

About a mile below Old Town is Big Island, a tract of nearly 300 acres of rich alluvial soil, which the first voyagers to the Cape Fear in 1668 named Crane Island, and which is charted by the United States Coast Survey as Campbell's Island. It was formerly a light-house station, but the light was discontinued during the late war and a battery erected in its place. There is a fortune in this island waiting for some enterprising truck farmer, as the State Geologist says it contains some of the richest lands in the South, that will never need fertilizing. Millions of fat rice birds roost here at night after preying upon the milky rice of the neighboring plantations during the day. It is estimated that these toothsome little pests devour 25 per cent of all the rice made on the Cape Fear. They appear every Fall together on the same day and depart during a single night when the rice gets too hard for them. The planters have never been able to protect their crops from the yearly ravages of these birds. Although a gang of boys and men are kept firing guns at them all day, a very small proportion of the immense droves is killed. For a dainty supper, a fat rice bird is perhaps the most delicious morsel that ever tickled the palate of an epicure.

A bob-o-link, known locally as a "rice bird"

First Navigators of the Cape Fear; King Watcoosa and His Daughters.

The first reference made in history to Big Island is in the report of the Commissioners sent from Barbadoes in October 1663, to explore the river Cape Fear.

After describing the voyage to the Cape, they say that the channel is on the East side by the Cape shore, and that it lies close aboard the Cape land, being 18 feet at high water in shallowest place in the channel, just at the entrance, but that as soon as this shallow place is passed, a half cable length inward, thirty and thirty-five feet water is found, which continues that depth for twenty-one miles, when the river becomes shallower until there is only twenty-feet depth running down to ten feet (where Wilmington now stands).

These bold voyagers brought their vessel some distance higher than Wilmington, and were much pleased with the land on the main river above Point Peter.

They found many Indians living on their plantations of corn, which were also well stocked with fat cattle and hogs stolen from the Massachusetts settlers of 1660 on the Cape opposite Orton Point. Game was very abundant, and fish was also plentiful. During an expedition higher up in a small boat, they killed four swan, ten geese, ten turkeys, forty ducks, thirty-six paraquitos and seventy plover.

They were attacked by Indians once; a display of fire-arms afterwards compelled the peaceful recognition of the natives. And when the ship reached Crane Island (now Big Island) on the return, Sunday, 29th November, 1663, they met the first ruler of the "Cape Fear Country," the Indian Chief Watcoosa, who sold the river and land to the Barbadians, Anthony Long, William Hilton and Peter Fabian.

A ludicrous incident which the virtuous Barbadians took very seriously occurred during their negotiations. The King, Watcoosa, accompanied by forty lusty warriors, made a long speech to them, which, although unintelligible to the white men, was undoubtedly of a peaceful nature, as he indicated by pantomime that he would cut off the heads of any of his people who attempted to injure them, and in testimony of his good-will, at the conclusion of his discourse he presented to the Barbadian Captain two very handsome and proper young Indian women, whom the voyagers were given to understand were the King's daughters. These guileless maidens of the Cape Fear, whom Hilton describes as the tallest and most beautiful women he ever saw, were not at all shy, but forced their way into the white men's boat and refused to leave it. Captain Hilton probably had a wife at home, and the thought of presenting these two beautiful girls in their native costume to his better half in Barbadoes must have appalled the stout-hearted explorer who had already faced so many lesser dangers. He loaded them with presents; he gallantly entreated them to call again, but they laughingly shook their heads, and pointing to the ship, indicated their purpose to remain with him for better for worse. What was the poor man to do? Worse still, thought the Captain, what will Mrs. Hilton do! He met the emergency as little George Washington did *not* do. He presented to the father a little hatchet, and he told him a lie. He promised to take the girls aboard in four days; but, alas! Their names do not appear later in the passenger list for the homeward voyage. It is said that for many years after, these disappointed maidens might be seen on the Cape lands shading their eyes as they gazed towards the Southern horizon, looking in vain for the return of the perfidious Hilton, who wisely remained at home when the colonists came to settle on Old Town Creek.

Cushing's Exploits.

Opposite Big Island, on the East side, is Todd's Creek, known as also Mott's Creek, which was the scene of Lieut. William B. Cushing's brave exploit June 23d, 1864. This gallant young naval officer perhaps accomplished more by personal valor than any other individual on either side during the war.

At half-past seven o'clock on the night of May 6th, 1864, the Confederate iron-clad *Raleigh*, which was built at the foot of Church Street, in Wilmington, proceeded down the river in company with several other smaller boats composing the puny fleet of Commodore Lynch, and under the command of Lieut. J.Pembroke Jones, C.S.N., crossed the New Inlet bar and attacked the blockading fleet. The Federals were taken by surprise, and after a feeble resistance took flight, the *Raleigh* having damaged one or two of the blockaders by her well-directed fire. The ram was too unwieldy for service at sea, however, and on the second day out Commodore Lynch ordered her back to the river. After crossing the Inlet she stuck on the Rip Shoal and sunk, where she still remains buried in the sand. Lieut. Cushing, then attached to one of the blockaders, the United States steamer *Monticello*, with his usual zeal and fearlessness, volunteered to attempt the destruction of the *Raleigh*, whose fate was unknown to the Federals. He also undertook a reconnaissance of the defences of the Cape Fear River for the information of the United States Government, which was then preparing an expedition for the capture of Wilmington.

William B. Cushing, USN

Notwithstanding the warning of his superiors that he was almost certain to be captured or killed in this adventure, he persisted in his scheme, and on the night of June 23d, 1864, left his vessel in the first cutter, accompanied by two subordinate officers and fifteen men, crossed the western bar and passed the forts and town of Smithville without discovery, but was very nearly run down by an outward-bound blockade-runner. He then proceeded fearlessly up the river, and with muffled oars steered his boat immediately under the guns of Fort Anderson.

As Cushing attempted to leave Fort Anderson the moon came out from the clouds and disclosed the party to the sentinels, who hailed and immediately opened fire. The fort was roused and the confusion general. Cushing boldly pulled for the opposite banks and swiftly disappeared along the other shore.

His next stopping-place was in this creek, up which he poled his boat until he came to the military road leading from Wilmington to Fort Fisher. Here he cut the telegraph wire and captured a courier from General Whiting with dispatches for Colonel Lamb at Fort Fisher. He then put one of his officers (Howorth) in the

Confederate's uniform and dispatched him in broad daylight to Wilmington for supplies.

Howorth returned a few hours after with a liberal supply of chickens, eggs and butter, which he had bought without attracting any suspicion. Cushing then waited for darkness, and it is said went in person and also in the courier's clothes to Wilmington, and proceeded to his aunt's house, corner of Eighth and Market streets, where he peeped through the window-blinds and recognized his Confederate kinsfolk, who were of course not made aware of his presence.

On the following day he made sketches of the fortifications around Wilmington and captured a boat-load of Confederates, from whom he learned the fate of the *Raleigh*, which he subsequently inspected in person. He next put his prisoners (six men) into a boat without oars or sails and sent them adrift to get home as best they could. Proceeding down the river, he carefully inspected the torpedo obstructions, and attempted the capture of the Confederate guard-boat near New Inlet. Here he met with formidable resistance, four boats having pursued him, and he was obliged to dash into the breakers on Carolina shoals to escape a large force of Confederates. He reached the blockading squadron safely after an absence of two days and three nights.

His subsequent destruction of the Confederate Ram *Albemarle* is doubtless one of the bravest examples of personal valour in military history.

John J. Hedrick, CSA

Cushing's Daring Visit to Fort Anderson.

At early dawn on Friday, February 17th, 1865, the Federal fleet in the river began to bombard Fort Anderson, while the troops under General Schofield attacked the land force and the lines extending westward. The bombardment was kept up all day long with great fury, but the firing ceased at sundown.

About eight o'clock that night the "Eutaw Band," attached to the 25th S.C. Regiment (Colonel C.H. Simonton commanding) came into the Fort and gave a serenade complimentary to the commanding officer (Colonel John J. Hedrick, 40th N.C. Regiment) and his officers. Colonel John D. Taylor was requested by Colonel Hedrick to return thanks to the band, and while he was doing so in a neat and appropriate speech, the officer of the day reported that a boat had been seen passing the Fort and going into the

John D. Taylor, CSA

cove on the north side of the Fort. Soon after the speaking the boat was seen pulling out into the river. Captain E.S. Martin had seen the boat going up the river and ordered that the heavy shot be withdrawn from several guns and grape-shot substituted; and when the boat was seen going down the river he ordered the guns fired at it. The boat responded with small arms, and the crew escaped and notified those in the Fort of their safe arrival at the fleet by a single rocket that shot up into the air, and the Confederates heard nothing more of it at that time.

On the 9th or 10th of March 1865, the same troops which were in the Fort the night above mentioned were at Kinston, N.C., resisting the advance of General Cox's command from New Berne to Goldsboro. The advance guard of General Cox was captured and one of the prisoners gave a Confederate officer a copy of the *New York Herald*, which contained an account of a visit made by Captain Cushing to Fort Anderson. He stated that he commanded the boat above mentioned, and had passed into the cove above the Fort, landed and gone into the Fort while Colonel Taylor was speaking. He had hidden himself under one of the guns (which was not in use) on the opposite side of the Fort, about 75 or 100 feet from the speaker, and heard the rest of his speech, which was reported in the account of this visit. The officer (Captain Martin) into whose hands the *Herald* came, having heard the speech of Colonel Taylor, recognized the report as accurate in every particular.

The account also described the escape of Captain Cushing from the Fort and of the boat from the fire of the Confederate guns, and his safe return to his vessel below the Fort.

Carolina Beach.

The next point of interest on the east side is the wharf of the New Hanover Transit Company, from which there is a short railroad connection of about two miles to the favorite seaside resort, Carolina Beach.

This place was long known to a few of our people as the finest and safest beach on the Atlantic coast, but generation after generation of our inhabitants

The "Shoo-Fly Train" took passengers from the steamer docks on the river side of Federal Point to the sands of Carolina Beach.

lived and died without having seen the beautiful foaming breakers curling over these hard white sands, which extend for five miles along this exquisite shore. Before the Wilmington and Wrightsville turnpike was thought of, and long years prior to the building of the Seacoast Railroad, Captain Harper undertook to bring in the steam yacht *Passport* thousands of excursionists from Wilmington and the interior to the health-giving breakers at such a trifling expense, that the humblest and poorest might enjoy the pleasures of surf-bathing, which had hitherto been the exclusive privilege of the rich, until the number has increased to forty and fifty thousand passengers annually.

The steamer *Wilmington* makes four or five trips daily, and the run occupies one hour from Wilmington to the beach.

Gander Hall.

Near this landing may be seen a fine grove of old oaks which many years ago sheltered an attractive estate, still known as Gander Hall. It was owned in the year 1830 by Captain James McIlhenny, of an honored and respected family on the Cape Fear. Captain McIlhenny was the victim of a well-known joke which gave the place its peculiar name. An extraordinary trade demand for goose-feathers at high prices led him to purchase in the upcountry a flock of geese which he intended to use for breeding purposes. He counted the increase before it was hatched, and anticipated with satisfaction large profits from the sale of feathers. The Captain selected the geese in person, and as he wanted white feathers, was careful to accept only the white birds. After waiting an intolerable time for the laying season to begin, he consulted a goose expert, and was informed, to his amazement, that his geese were all ganders.

Sedgeley Abbey.

Near Gander Hall are the ruins of "Sedgeley Abbey," which was the grandest colonial residence of the Cape Fear. It was of about the dimensions and appearance of the Governor Dudley mansion in Wilmington, and was erected about 170 years ago by an English gentleman of wealth and refinement, named Maxwell, who owned all the land as far as Smith's Island. The house was built of coquina, a rock made up of fragments of marine shells slightly consolidated by natural pressure and infiltrated calcareour matter, of which there are still large formations there. The cellar alone remains, having been cut out of the solid rock. The south wing of the building was standing until about 25 years ago, when it was demolished and the material burned for fertilizers by an unsentimental tenant, who might have gathered all the oyster-shells he desired which had been left by the Indians at a slightly greater distance. A beautiful avenue of oaks extended from the mansion on the east for 1,500 feet towards the ocean in full view, and a corduroy road, which may still be seen, was built through a bay and lined with trees to the river landing. Some weird traditions about the house and its lonely master have come down through the neighborhood negroes, who still regard the place with superstitious awe. It is said that several attempts were made many years ago to find some gold alleged to be buried there, and although the times chosen were on bright, clear days, the sky became suddenly overcast, the wind moaned through the roofless walls, and cries and groans were distinctly heard by the treasure-hunters, who did not tarry for further investigation.

First White Settlement.

A few miles below this interesting ruin may yet be seen indication of the first white settlement on the Cape Fear in 1661 by the enterprising New Englanders from Massachusetts, who might have prospered, but their greed led them to destruction. For a time they carried on a profitable and apparently peaceable intercourse with the native Indians, but when they sent Indian children North to be sold into slavery under the pretense of instructing them in learning and in the principles of the Christian religion, the red men were not slow to discern their treachery, and from that time, as Lawson says, "they never gave over till they had entirely rid themselves of the English by their bows and arrows."

The New Englanders left much cattle behind them, which the Barbadians four years later found in the possession of the Indians along the Cape Fear.

On this first attempt at a settlement on the Cape Fear River, Bryant, in his *Popular History of the United States*, page 272, says: "There were probably few bays or rivers along the coast, from the Bay of Fundy to Florida, unexplored by the New Englanders where there was any promise of profitable trade with the Indians. The colonist followed the trader wherever unclaimed lands were open to occupation. These energetic pioneers explored the sounds and rivers south of Virginia in pursuit of Indian traffic, contrasted the salubrity of the climate and the fertility of the soil with that region of rocks where they had made their homes, and where winter reigns for more than half the year. In 1660 or 1661, a company of these men purchased of the natives and settled upon a tract of land at the mouth of the Cape Fear River. Their first purpose was apparently the raising of stock, as the country seemed peculiarly fitted to grazing, and they brought a number of neat cattle and swine to be allowed to feed at large under the care of herdsmen. But they aimed at something more than this nomadic occupation, and a company was formed, in which a number of adventurers in London were enlisted, to found a permanent colony. Discouraged, however, either by the want of immediate success, or for want of time to carry out their plans, or for some less creditable reason, the settlement was soon abandoned."

Cape Fear Indians.

It is an interesting fact that the descendants of these Indians live in the same locality to the present day, and illustrate an unusual condition—an amalgamation of white, black, and Indian races. The Indian characteristics, however, predominate. The men are thrifty, industrious and peaceable; engaged principally in fishing during the shad season, and in cattle-raising upon the same range that was occupied two hundred years ago by their savage ancestors.

Large mounds of oyster-shells, many pieces of broken wicker pottery, arrow-heads, and other relics of the red men are still found on the peninsula below Carolina Beach. During the late war these remains of an Indian settlement were frequently unearthed by the Confederates engaged upon the intrenchments around Fort Fisher; and here are buried the last of the Corees, Cheraws and other small tribes occupying the land once inhabited by the powerful Hatteras Indians. They were allies of the Tuscaroras in 1711, and in an attack upon the English suffered defeat, and have now disappeared from the earth and their dialect is also forgotten. The Hatteras tribe numbered about 3,000 warriors when Raleigh's expedition landed on Roanoke Island in 1584, and when the English made permanent settlements in that vicinity eighty years later, they were reduced to about fifteen bowmen. The Cape Fear Coree Indians told the English settlers of the Yeamans colony in 1669 that their lost kindred of the Roanoke colony, including Virginia Dare, the first white child born in America, had been adopted by the once powerful Hatteras tribe and had become amalgamated with the children of the wilderness. It is believed that the Croatans of this vicinity are descendants of that race.

The Massachusetts settlers referred to the Cape Fear as the Charles River, which was applied, as was also the original name, Carolina, in honor of King Charles IX of France, during whose reign Admiral Coligny made some settlements of French Huguenots on the Florida coast, and built a fort which he called Charles Fort, on what is now the South Carolina coast.

The big house at the plantation that would bear the names of Lilliput and Kendal.

Lilliput.

Nearly opposite, surrounded by noble oaks, are the ancient estates of Lilliput and Kendal. The first record extant of Lilliput plantation is in a patent from the Lords' Proprietors, 6th November, 1725, recorded in the Secretary's Office of North Carolina, to Eleazar Allen. Mr. Allen was born at or near Charleston about 1692. He married Sarah, eldest daughter of Colonel William Rhett, about the year 1722. In 1730 he was recommended for one of the council of North Carolina by Governor Burrington, and appointed to that office by the Crown; but he does not appear to have assumed the duties until the 22d of November, 1735. He was appointed in that year with Nathaniel Rice, Roger Moore and Capt. James Innes, a Commissioner to fix the boundary line between North and South Carolina. He was made Receiver General of the Province of North Carolina from 1735 to 1748. During that time he experienced, in common with all the other public treasurers, great difficulty in collecting the quit rents due the Crown, for which he was held personally responsible by the British Government, and for the security of which he ultimately pledged his entire estate, including Lilliput.

An English gentleman who visited the Cape Fear in 1734 with thirteen other travelers, made special mention of Mr. Allen's residence, a beautiful brick house on Lilliput, adjoining Kendal, and also of his well-known hospitality. He says Mr. Allen was then speaker to the Commons, House of Assembly in the Province of South Carolina. Mr. Allen must have lived sumptuously and entertained lavishly, as among the items of personal property in his estate made known at his death, was twelve dozen cut-glass table basins, now known as finger-bowls.

On the death of Mr.Allen, 17th January, 1749, aged fifty-seven years, at Lilliput, where he was buried, this plantation became the property and residence for a time of Sir Thomas Frankland. It was subsequently sold to John Davis, Jr., in 1765.

Sir Thomas Frankland was a grandson of Frances, daughter of Oliver Cromwell, who upon the death of his brother, Sir Charles Frankland, in 1765, succeeded him as baronet. Sir Thomas was previous to that time an Admiral of the White in the British Navy, a post of great distinction. He married Susan, daughter of William Rhett, Jr. of Charleston. They have numerous descendants now living in England.

We find that, in 1789, Lilliput was in possession of the well-known McRee family of this section, and here was born the distinguished medical practitioner and diagnostician, Dr. James Fergus McRee, who afterwards lived and died in Wilmington.

Kendal.

The adjoining plantation of Kendal was originally owned by "King" Roger Moore, who bequeathed it 7th March, 1747, to his son, George Moore. "King" Roger also devised to other heirs two hundred and fifty negro slaves.

George Moore, of Moore Fields, as he was afterwards called, was remarkable for his great energy, good management and considerable wealth. The original proprietors of the Cape Fear plantations were men of extraordinary discernment and discretion. They first took up all the best land within easy access, laid out and built their plantation residence, and then provided themselves with a comfortable summer house on the Sound. Evidences of this method are still to be seen in the many Sound roads which converge into the old thoroughfare at the east landing of the Brunswick ferry near Big Sugar Loaf and opposite the site of old Brunswick. George Moore's summer place was a tract on the north side of the creek at Masonboro, now owned by the McKoy family. He was twice married, and his wives, with remarkable fidelity and amazing fortitude, presented him every Spring with a new baby, until the number reached twenty-eight. An interesting relic of this extraordinary family is preserved by Mr. Junius Davis. It is a book of Common Prayer, on the fly-leaf of which is inscribed the names and dates of birth of the entire family of twenty-eight children.

In common with the titled class in England, the Cape Fear planters held trade and trades-people in abhorrence, and kept themselves aloof from the commercial centres. They preferred to live on their plantations, and their social life betrayed a class distinction not at all in keeping with the democratic ideas of their descendants. In one respect, however, they greatly differed from the aristocracy of the Old Country—a generous and refined hospitality being universal and proverbial, and this excellent trait is still a striking characteristic of their successors on the river to the present day.

For personal reasons, to avoid the public parade of his numerous family through the town of Wilmington, it suited George Moore to cut a private road for his own use, from his plantation on Rocky Point to Masonboro sound, by which his faithful wife and her remarkable progeny traveled on horseback in their yearly journeys from the country plantations to the seashore.

Mr. Moore's method of transporting his household effects was unique, by which he employed the services of a large retinue of negro slaves; upon the head of one was placed a table; upon another a mattress; a third a chair, and so on, until fifty or more bearers were in line, when the cavalcade proceeded on foot towards Masonboro – an extraordinary and moving spectacle.

When corn was wanted at the summer place, one hundred negro fellows would be started, each with a bushel bag on his head. There is, said the late Dr. John H. Hill, quite a deep ditch leading from some large bay swamps lying to the west of the George Moore road. It used to be called the Devil's Ditch, and there was some mystery and idle tradition as to why and how the ditch was cut there. It was doubtless made to drain the water from those bays, to flood some lands cultivated in rice, which were too low to be drained for corn.

Kendal and Lilliput have been owned and cultivated for years past by Mr. Fred Kidder, a type of the Old School gentleman, one of the most prominent and industrious planters on the river, a worthy and honored successor of the distinguished settlers on the Cape Fear, described as gentlemen of birth and education, bred in the refinement of polished society, and bringing with them ample fortunes, gentle manners and cultivated minds.

A nineteenth century photo of the house at Orton .

Orton.

Among the venerable relics of Colonial days in North Carolina there is probably none richer in legendary lore, nor more worthy of historic distinction, than the old Colonial plantation of Orton on the Cape Fear. The name is doubtless taken from the old town or village of Orton, near Kendal, in the beautiful lake district of England, from whence the ancestors of the Moore family on the Yeamans side may have come to Barbadoes; the line of the Moore family being of Scotch Irish origin, as there is a Kendal Point and it is said an Orton plantation on that Island, which was the home of Sir John Yeamans, who afterwards settled upon the Cape Fear and was Governor of Clarendon.

Orton plantation was owned originally by Maurice Moore, the grandson of Governor Sir John Yeamans, and the son of Governor James Moore, of South Carolina, who came with his brother, Colonel James Moore, to suppress the Tuscarora Indian outbreaks in the Province of North Carolina in 1711. From him it passed to his brother, Roger Moore, known ever afterwards as "King" Roger. He was a man of lordly and distinguished bearing, and owned immense bodies of land in this part of the country, and was for many years a member of Governor Gabriel Johnston's Council. During his absence from home, in the early days of the settlement, his house at Orton was attacked, pillaged and burned by the Cree Indians, who lived on the Cape opposite the plantation. Some days afterwards "King" Roger, with a small force of neighbors and servants, seeing the Indians at play and bathing in the river near Big Sugar Loaf, marched up the river out of sight, crossed over, and taking the savages by surprise, exterminated the whole tribe. His tomb, a brick mound, is still in a good state of preservation in the old family burying ground at Orton. The spot, which has unfortunately in recent years been partly cleared, is described by the author of *Roanoke* as follows:

"I found myself in one of those spots which nature herself seems to have consecrated for her most holy rites. There was not a shrub, nor a blade of grass, within this sacred temple; there the garnish beams of the sun never penetrate, but even at noonday a deep, solemn twilight reigns. The oaks, whose multitudinous branches form a thick canopy above us, looked as if they had witnessed the flight of centuries; and from their limbs and trunks there streamed hoary and luxuriant flakes of moss sweeping almost to the ground, and looking like elfin locks whitened by the frosts of a thousand years. Within this druid temple there are old brick vaults, without a name and without a date; and here, because, perhaps, nature herself seems to have formed a cemetery for her favorite child—here, beneath one of these vaults and close by the banks of the old Cape Fear, are supposed to repose the ashes of Utopia. The scene and the recollections which it awakened threw me into a meditative mood, and seating myself on one of the vaults, and looking out on the broad but lovely expanse of waters before me, I remained, listening to the subdued murmur of the distant ocean."

This fine property was sold about the year 1860, with the slaves upon it, for one hundred thousand dollars; but the purchase money was never paid, and the estate deteriorated for more than fifteen years from inattention and decay. In 1876, a young English gentleman of education and refinement, named Currer Richardson Roundel (a nephew of Sir Roundel Palmer who afterwards became Lord Chancellor of Great Britain as Lord Selborne), came to Wilmington evidently suffering with some mental disorder. He was induced by the agents to buy Orton, which had been in the market for some time previous, and he undertook to reclaim it, but met with difficulties which he had not anticipated, and which so depressed him that he took his own life. The writer found him early on the morning of July 26th, 1876, in his room at the hotel in Wilmington stripped to the waist, and lying upon the floor in a pool of blood, the deadly pistol in one hand, the other hand pointing to a ragged hole in his forehead. He was dead. He was buried by kind and gentle hands in Oakdale near Wilmington.

The present beautiful residence, with its majestic columns and its white and glittering vestments, now occupied by Colonel K.M. Murchison, the proprietor,

Orton as it looked in 2004.

was built about the year 1725 by "King" Roger Moore, of brick brought from England, and was afterwards enlarged and improved by the late Dr. Fred J. Hill, a rice-planter, an intelligent gentleman, and a princely citizen, who was noted far and near for his elegant and refined hospitality.

Colonel Murchinson has brought the plantation up to its best production—about a hundred laborers are employed and many expensive permanent improvements have been adopted. He resides here with his family during the winter months, his home and principal business being in New York City.

These ten thousand acres include a fine game preserve, which is greatly enjoyed by the Colonel and his friends, to whom the pleasures of the chase are its principal attraction.

Born and reared on the upper Cape Fear of Scotch ancestors whose brain and brawn have ever infused new life and vigor throughout the business world, Colonel K. M. Murchison is honored; for out of nothing but a stout heart, an honest purpose and a good name, he has built up a fortune and achieved a reputation for integrity and usefulness among men who only acknowledge such as leaders.

He deserves well of Wilmington because he has given liberally of his means for the development of our trade and industries. When there was not a hotel in the place worthy of the name, and when it was said that this lack barred a class of visitors hitherto unknown, but greatly to be desired by the community, he came forward and fearlessly invested a large amount in a first-class hotel, of which we should all be proud, although it has not been properly appreciated. Were our citizens animated with a little of the public spirit of their forefathers, who gave three hundred and fifty thousand dollars to build and equip a Wilmington railroad, when the entire taxables were only three hundred thousand dollars, "The Orton" would always be filled to overflowing and such an enterprise receive its just reward.

Colonel Murchinson served throughout the war as Colonel of the 54th N.C. Troops, took part in the active Virginia campaigns, and upon the conclusion of peace returned to New York, where he has ever since been engaged in business.

Colonial Governor Tryon's Palace, Scene of the First Outbreak of the Revolutionary War.

About half a mile to the South of Orton House, and within the boundary of the plantation, are the ruins of Governor Tryon's residence, memorable in the history of the United States as the spot upon which the first overt act of violence occurred in the war of American Independence, and nearly eight years before the Boston Tea incident, of which so much has been made in Northern history; while this Colonial ruin, the veritable cradle of American liberty, is probably unknown to nine-tenths of the people on the Cape Fear at the present day.

This place, which has been eloquently referred to by two of the most distinguished sons of the Cape Fear, and direct descendants of Sir John Yeamans, the late Hon. George Davis and the Hon. A.M. Waddell, and which was known as Russelborough, was bought from William Moore, son and successor of "King" Roger, by Captain John Russell, Commander of His Britannic Majesty's sloop of war *Scorpion*, who gave the tract of about fifty-five acres his own name. It subsequently passed into the possession of his widow, who made a deed of trust, and the property ultimately again became a part of Orton plantation. It was sold March 31st, 1758, by the executors of the estate of William Moore to the British Governor and Commander-in-Chief, Arthur Dobbs, who occupied it and who sold it or gave it to his son, Edward Bryce Dobbs,

Sprunt's conjectural drawing of Russellborough.

Royal Gov. Arthur Dobbs

Captain in His Majesty's 7th Regiment of Foot or Royal Fusileers, who conveyed it by deed dated February 12th, 1767, to His Excellency William Tryon, Governor, etc. It appears, however, that Governor Tryon occupied this residence prior to the date of this deed, as is shown by the following official correspondence in 1766 with reference to the uprising of the Cape Fear people in opposition to the Stamp Act:

"BRUNSWICK, 19TH FEBRUARY,1766,
"Eleven at Night,

"Sir:—

"Between the hours of six and seven o'clock this evening, Mr. Geo. Moore and Mr. Cornelius Harnett waited on me at my house, and delivered to me a letter signed by three gentlemen. The inclosed is a copy of the original. I told Mr. Moore and Mr. Harnett that as I had no fears or apprehensions for my person or property, I wanted no guard, therefore desired the gentlemen might not come to give their protection where it was not necessary or required, and that I would send the gentlemen an answer in writing to-morrow morning. Mr. Moore and Mr. Harnett might stay about five or six minutes in my house. Instantly after their leaving me, I found my house surrounded with armed men to the number I estimate at one hundred and fifty. I had some altercation with some of the gentlemen, who informed me their business was to see Capt. Lobb, whom they were informed was at my house; Captain Paine then desired me to give my word and honor whether Captain Lobb was in my house or not. I positively refused to make any such declaration, but as they had force in their hands I said they might break open my locks and force my doors. This, they declared, they had no intention of doing; just after this and other discourse, they got intelligence that Captain Lobb was not in my house. The majority of the men in arms then went to the town of Brunswick, and left a number of men to watch the avenues of my house, therefore think it doubtful if I can get this letter safely conveyed. I esteem it my duty, sir, to inform you as Fort Johnston has but one officer, and five men in garrison, the Fort will stand in need of all the assistance the Viper *and* Diligence *sloops can give the commanding officer there, should any insult be offered to his Majesty's fort or stores, in which case it is my duty to request of you to repel force with force, and take on board his Majesty's sloops so much of his Majesty's ordnance, stores and ammunition out of the said fort as you shall think necessary for the benefit of the service.*

This model based on the Russellborough ruins shows what the mansion may have looked like. *(photo courtesy Jim McKee)*

"I am,sir, your most humble servant,
(Signed) *"WM. TRYON."*
'To the commanding Officer, either of the Viper
or Diligence *Sloops of War."*

The writer, who frequently enjoys the old-time hospitality of Orton, had often inquired for the precise location of the ruins of Governor Tryon's Russelborough residence, without success. But during a recent visit, and acting upon Colonel Waddell's reference to its site on the north of old Brunswick, the service of an aged negro who had lived continuously on the plantation for over seventy years was engaged, who, being questioned, could not remember ever having heard the name Russelborough, nor of Governor Dobbs, nor of Governor Tryon, nor of an avenue of trees in the locality described. He said he remembered, however, hearing when he was a boy about a man named "Governor Palace," who had lived in a great house between Orton and old Brunswick.

We proceeded at once to the spot, which is approached through an old field, still known as the Old Palace Field, on the other side of which, on a bluff facing the east, and affording a fine view of the river, we found hidden in a dense undergrowth of timber the foundation walls of Tryon's residence. The aged guide showed us the well worn carriage road of the Governor, and also his private path through the old garden to the river landing, a short distance below, on the south of which is a beautiful cove of white and shining sand, known, he said, in olden times, as the Governor's Cove. The stone foundation walls of the house are about two feet above the surface of the ground. Some sixty years ago the walls stood about twelve to fifteen feet high, but the material was unfortunately used by one of the proprietors for building purposes.

Russelborough's ruins as they appear today, at Brunswick Town State Historic Site.

The old servant pointed out a large pine tree near by, upon which he said had been carved in Colonial times the names of two distinguished persons buried beneath it, and which in his youthful days was regarded with much curiosity by visitors. The rude inscription has unhappily become almost obliterated by several growths of bark, and the strange, mysterious record is forever hidden by the hand of time.

A careful excavation of this ruin would doubtless reveal some interesting and possibly valuable relics of Governor Tryon's household. Near the surface was found, while these lines were being written, some fragments of blue Dutch tiling, doubtless a part of the interior decorations; also a number of peculiarly shaped bottles for the favorite sack of those days, which Falstaff called Sherris sack, of Xeres vintage, now known as dry sherry.

Ruins of Brunswick.

About a quarter of mile distant towards the South, and yet within the limits of this time-honored estate of Orton, are the ruins of the old Colonial town of Brunswick, once the chief seaport and seat of government of the Province of North Carolina. Its public buildings and substantial houses have long ago crumbled to their foundations, which still remain.

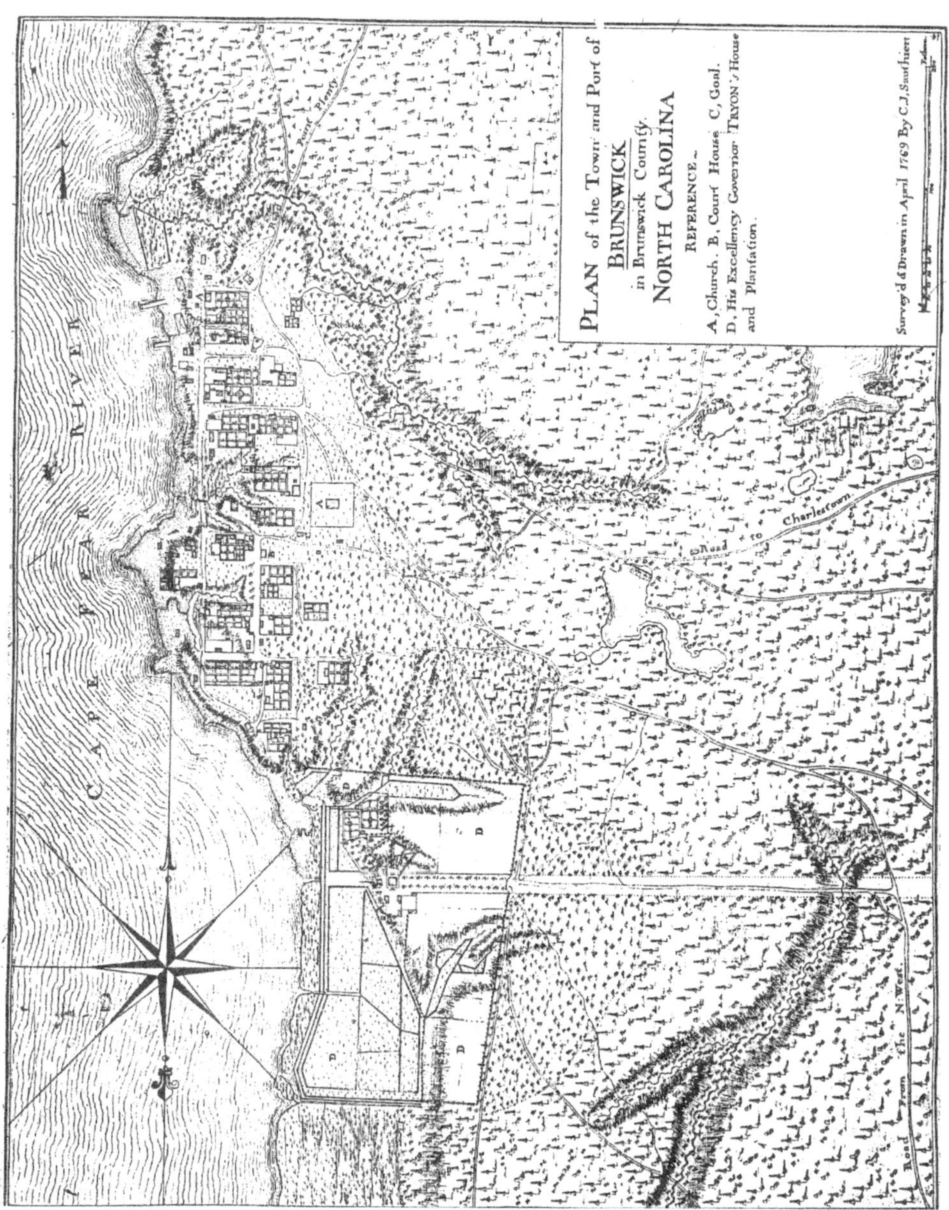

C.J. Sauthier's 1769 map of Brunswick.

The daily hum of traffic has long since ceased, and the busy feet that trod its now silent streets have mouldered into dust.

> *" No more for them the blazing hearth shall burn,*
> *Nor busy housewife ply her evening care,*
> *Nor children run to greet their sire's return,*
> *Or climb his knee the envied kiss to share."*

The glad voices of the village children, the merry ring of the blacksmith's anvil and the hearty yo-ho of the sailors in the bay have melted away into the silence of the dead, which is only broken by the hooting owl and the barking fox, or by the plaintive cry of the whippoorwill and the plunge of the osprey in the now peaceful waters of the Governor's Cove, while from across the narrow isthmus is heard the moaning of the lonely sea.

The ruins of St. Philip's Anglican Church, circa 1900.

Ruins of St. Philip's Church.

Within the boundaries of this forgotten town are the picturesque ruins of St. Phillip's Church, which was built by the citizens of Brunswick and principally by the landed gentry about the year 1740. In the year 1751 Mr. Lewis Henry deRosset, a member of Governor Gabriel Johnston's Council and subsequently an expatriated Royalist, introduced a bill appropriating to the church of St. Philip at Brunswick and to St. James' Church at Wilmington, equally, a fund that was realized by the capture and destruction of a pirate vessel, which, with a squadron of Spanish privateers, had entered the river and plundered the plantations. A picture ("Ecce Homo"), captured from this pirate, is still preserved in the vestry-room of St. James' Church in Wilmington.

St. Philip's Church was built of large brick brought from England. Its walls are nearly three feet thick and are solid and almost intact still, the roof and the floor only having disappeared. Its dimensions are nearly as large as those of our modern churches, being 76 feet 6 inches long, 53 feet 3 inches wide, standing walls 24 feet 4 inches high. There are 11 windows, measuring 15x7 feet, and 3 large doors. It must have possessed much architectural beauty and massive grandeur with its high pitched roof, its lofty doors and beautiful chancel windows.

Upon the fall of Fort Fisher, which is a few miles to the southeast of Orton, in 1865, the Federal troops visited the ruins of St. Philip's, and with pick-axes dug out the corner-stone, which had remained undisturbed for one hundred and twenty-five years, and which doubtless contained papers of great interest and value to our people. It is a singular fact that during the terrific bombardment of Fort Anderson, which was erected on Orton, and which enclosed with earthworks the ruins of St. Philip's, while many of the tombs in the church-yard were shattered and broken to pieces by the storm of shot and shell, the walls escaped destruction; as if the Power Above had shielded from annihilation the building which had been dedicated to His service.

This sanctuary has long been a neglected ruin, trees of a larger growth than the surrounding forest have grown up within its roofless walls, and where long years ago the earnest prayer and song of praise ascended up on high, a solemn stillness reigns, unbroken save by the distant murmur of the sea, which ever sings a requiem to the buried past.

In concluding his most interesting sketch of old Brunswick, in *A Colonial Officer and His Times*, the graceful and gifted author, Colonel Alfred Moore Waddell, says:

"Memorable for some of the most dramatic scenes in the early history of North Carolina as the region around Brunswick was (being the theatre of the first open armed resistance to the Stamp Act, and not far from the spot where the first victory of the Revolution crowned the American arms at Moores Creek Bridge, on the 27th of February, 1776), its historic interest was perpetuated when, nearly a century afterwards, its tall pines trembled and its sand-hills shook to the thunder of the most terrific artillery fire that has ever occurred since the invention of gun-powder, when Fort Fisher was captured in 1865. Since then it has again relapsed into its former state, and the bastions and traverses and parapets of Fort Anderson are now clad in the same exuberant robe of green with which generous nature in that clime covers every neglected spot. And so the old and the new ruin stand side by side in mute attestation of the

utter emptiness of all human ambition; while the Atlantic breeze sings gently amid the sighing pines, and the vines cling more closely to the old church wall, and the lizard basks himself where the sunlight falls on a forgotten grave."

Colonial Ferry and Inn.

The ruins of an inn and ferry-house attract attention at old Brunswick landing. This ferry to the landing at Big Sugar Loaf on the opposite side of the river, a distance of over two miles, must have been an exposed and dangerous passage during stormy weather. It was kept by Cornelius Harnett and connected with the only road to the northern part of the Province. This Colonial road is still used at the present day, an may be seen at the old landing place near Big Sugar Loaf.

It is interesting to recall the fact as stated by Doctor Brickell, a Dublin gentleman who visited this region in 1737, that the people on the Cape Fear were invariably comfortable and prosperous, and that they were also exceedingly hospitable and kindly. The planters cultivated rice, of which he says there were several sorts—"some bearded, others not so; besides there was the white and red rice, the latter the better." Indian corn was largely produced; fruits were plentiful; game abundant; cattle thrived and fattened in rich pastures; horse-racing, wrestling and foot-racing were favorite amusements. He says the women were well featured, brisk and charming in their conversation and as "finely shaped as any in the world;" that "they marry very young, some at thirteen and fourteen," and that "a spinster of twenty is reckoned a stale maid." The houses were full of healthy children.

Mr. Harnett entertained his patrons at the Inn with a liberal diet of beef, pork, venison, wild and tame fowl, fish of several delicate sorts, "roots" (vegetables, probably), several kinds of salads, good bread, butter, milk, cheese, rice, Indian corn, hasty pudding, rum, brandy, cider, persimmon beer, cedar beer, castena or tanpanan, Indian tea, etc.

Confederate Fortifications.

We now approach the ruins of Fort Anderson, Battery Hoke, Camp Wyatt (so named for the first victim of the war, private Henry A. Wyatt, of the 1st N.C. Regiment, killed at the battle of Big Bethel), Battery Buchanan, Fort Fisher and Mound Battery, famous as the gateway of the Southern Confederacy, and for months the only key to the outside world from which was replenished its scant supplies of army stores.

It has been well said by a prominent ex-officer of the late C.S. Navy that "the fall of Wilmington was the severest blow to the Confederate cause which it could receive from the loss of any port. It was far more injurious than the capture of Charleston, and but for the moral effect, even more hurtful than the evacuation of Richmond. With Wilmington and the Cape Fear open, the supplies that reached the Confederate armies would have enabled them to maintain an unequal contest for years; but with the fall of Fort Fisher, the constant stream of supplies was effectually cut off and the blockade made truly effective—not by the navy fleet, but by its captures on land."

Fort Anderson.

Fort Anderson and Orton House, the latter used as the headquarters of Captain E.S. Martin, Chief of Ordnance, were the last Confederate positions evacuated upon the river, and they were abandoned to superior force a month after Fort Fisher fell.

At nine o'clock on the evening of Sunday, January 15th, 1865, Fort Fisher, which had for years stubbornly resisted the bombardments and assaults of the Federal fleet and forces, was overcome. On Monday and Monday night, Fort Holmes, on Smith's Island, Forts Caswell and Campbell, on Oak Island, and Fort Pender (Johnston), at Smithville, were evacuated by the Confederates. On Friday of the same week, the garrisons of these forts were assembled at Fort Anderson under command of General Hebert. He was soon relieved in command by General Johnson Hagood, who commanded until Fort Anderson was evacuated.

After the capture of Fort Fisher, the Federals were employed in getting their monitors and gun-boats over the shoals called the Rip, near New Inlet, into the river. This was a tedious process. The heavy guns and turrets were slowly removed to lighten the draft, and these were afterwards replaced for an assault upon Fort Anderson, the last stronghold of the weary, half-starved, but devoted band of Southerners, who calmly awaited their death-blow. The Federal fleet then remained with General Terry's command in and about Fort Fisher in front of General Hoke's line, and made no demonstration until Friday, February 17th, 1865, when General Schofield's corps of 20,000 men having arrived, landed at Fisher, and were transferred to Smithville. Terry then attacked Hoke's line on the east side of the river, and Schofield moved up from Smithville and assaulted Fort Anderson from the rear, while the Federal fleet opened on the Fort from the river.

The bombardment and land attack on Fort Anderson continued all day Friday, Saturday and Saturday night, until Sunday morning, February 19th, about two o'clock, when the Fort was evacuated, and the Confederate troops fell back behind Town Creek, burning the bridges over the creek. Schofield attacked them

Sunday and Monday. On Monday afternoon, about four o'clock, the Confederates retreated towards Wilmington, which they entered on Monday night, February 20th, 1865.

Terry and Schofield followed on the 22d and took possession of Wilmington, the Confederates having moved towards North East river during the night of the 21st February.

Sherman, spreading desolation in his track, had already reached Fayetteville and messengers were sent to him by Schofield on board the steam tug *J. McB. Davidson*, which was the first boat to ascend the Cape Fear after the fall of Wilmington; she was commanded by Captain Marshall, and her Chief Engineer was Mr. Price, both of whom were subsequently lost at sea.

A Colonial Fort.

 short distance below Fort Anderson, on a bluff called Howe's Point, are the remains of a Colonial fort, and behind it the ruins of a residence, in which, tradition says, was born in 1730 one of the greatest heroes of the Revolutionary War (General Robert Howe), the trusted and honored lieutenant of Washington. He was the son of Job Howe, an educated and wealthy planter on the Cape Fear, who left, in 1748, a plantation to each of his five sons.

It is said that Robert's estate was on Old Town Creek, and that he resided there. It is also stated that he lived for a time at Kendal, and that on the 12th of May, 1776, the British Generals Cornwallis and Clinton landed with a troop of nine hundred men and ravaged General Howe's plantation. Mr. Reynolds, the present intelligent owner and occupant of the Howe place behind the Colonial fort, who took part in building Fort Anderson, says that his father and his grandfather informed him forty years ago that this fort was erected long before the War of the Revolution as a protection against buccaneers and pirates; that his great-grandfather lived with General Howe on this place during the war and took part in a defence of this fort against the British, who drove the Americans out of it; that the latter retreated to Liberty Pond, about a half mile in the rear, pursued by the British; that a stand was made at this pond, the Americans on the west and the enemy on the east

side, and that the blood which flowed stained the margin of the beautiful sheet of water which still bears the name of Liberty Pond; and that the Americans again retreated as far as McKenzie's Mill Dam, behind Kendal where the British abandoned the pursuit and returned to their ships of war.

Since the foregoing was written, Mr. Reynolds' statement with reference to General Howe's residence has been fully corroborated by the well-known Cape Fear skipper, Captain Sam Price, now eighty-six years old. He remembers distinctly, and has often visited the house known as General Howe's residence, which he says was a large three-story frame building on a stone or brick foundation, on the spot already described just below Old Brunswick, long and still known as Howe's Point.

Fort Fisher.

Colonel William Lamb, who was in command of Fort Fisher, in his admirable report of its defence, says that "the capture of Fort Fisher, N.C., on the 15th of January 1865, was followed so quickly by the final dissolution of the Southern Confederacy, that the great victory was not fully realized by the American people. The position commanded the last gateway between the Confederate States and the outside world. Its capture, with the resulting loss of all the Cape Fear river defences and of Wilmington, the great importing depot of the South, effectually ended the blockade-running."

William Lamb, CSA

General Lee, feeling the importance of the situation, sent word to Colonel Lamb "that Fort Fisher must be held or he could not subsist his army."

Description of Situation.

The indentation of the Atlantic Ocean in the Carolina coast known as Onslow Bay, and the Cape Fear River, running south from Wilmington, form the peninsula known as Federal Point, which during the Civil War was called Confederate Point. Not quite seven miles north of the end of this peninsula stood a high sand-hill called the "Sugar Loaf." Here there was an intrenched camp for the army of Wilmington under General Braxton Bragg, the Department Commander, that was hid from the sea by forest and sand-hills. From this intrenched camp the river bank, with a neighboring ridge of sand-dunes, formed a covered way for troops to within a hundred yards of the left salient of Fort

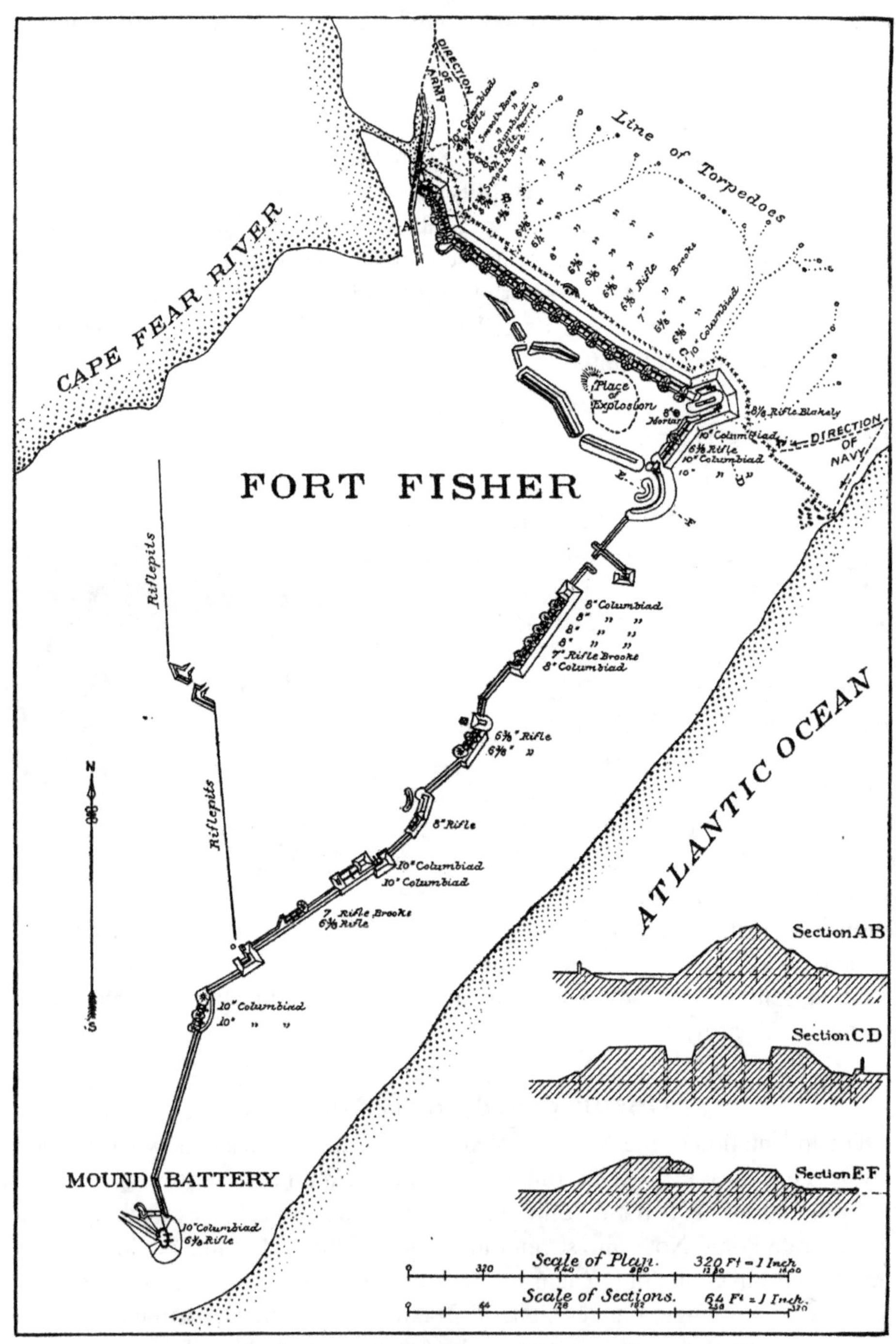

A diagram of the Confederate fortifications at Fort Fisher.

Fisher. Between the road and the ocean beach was an arm of Masonboro Sound, and where it ended, three miles north of the fort, were occasional fresh water swamps, generally wooded with scrub growth, and in many cases quite impassable. Along the ocean shore was an occasional battery formed from a natural sand-hill, behind which Whitworth guns were carried from the fort to cover belated blockade-runners or to protect more unfortunate ones that had been chased ashore.

"About half a mile north of the fort there was a rise in the plain, forming a hill some twenty feet above the tide on the river side, and on this was a redoubt commanding the approach to the fort by the river road. Thus nature, assisted by some slight engineering work, had given a defence to Confederate Point which would have enabled an efficient commander at the intrenched camp, co-operating with the garrison of Fort Fisher, to have rendered the Point untenable for a largely superior force at night when the covering fire of the Federal navy could not distinguish between friend and foe."

The plans of Fort Fisher were Colonel Lamb's, and as the work progressed were approved by Generals French, Raines, Longstreet, Beauregard and Whiting. It was styled by Federal engineers "the Malakoff of the South." It was built solely with the view of resisting the fire of a fleet, and it withstood uninjured, except as to armament, two of the fiercest bombardments the world has ever witnessed. The two faces to the works were 2,580 yards long. The land face was 682 yards long, and the sea face 1,898 yards long.

The interior of the land face fortifications at Fort Fisher.

The Land Face of Fort Fisher.

At the land face of Fort Fisher the peninsula was about half a mile wide. This face commenced about one hundred feet from the river with a half bastion, and extended with a heavy curtain to a full bastion on the ocean side, where it joined the sea face. The work was built to withstand the heaviest artillery fire. There was no moat with scarp and counterscarp, so essential for defense against storming parties, the shifting sands rendering its construction impossible with the material available.

The outer slope was twenty feet high and was sodded with marsh grass, which grew luxuriantly. The parapet was not less than twenty-five feet thick, with an inclination of only one foot. The revetment was five feet nine inches high from the floor of the gun chambers, and these were some twelve feet or more from the interior plane. The guns were all mounted in barbette on Columbiad carriages, there being no casemated gun in the Fort. Between the gun chambers, containing one or two guns each, there were twenty heavy guns on the land face; there were heavy traverses exceeding in size any known to engineers, to protect from an enfilading fire. They extended out some twelve feet or more in height above the parapet, running back thirty feet or more. The gun chambers were reached from the rear by steps. In each traverse was an alternate magazine or bomb-proof, the latter ventilated by an air chamber. The passage ways penetrated traverses in the interior of the work, forming additional bomb-proofs for the reliefs for the guns.

As a defense against infantry, there was a system of sub-terra torpedoes extending across the peninsula, five to six hundred feet from the land-face, and so disconnected that the explosion of one would not affect the others; inside the torpedoes, about fifty feet from the berme of the work, extending from river-bank to seashore, was a heavy palisade of sharpened logs nine feet high, pierced for musketry, and so laid out as to have an enfilading fire on the centre, where there was a redoubt guarding a sally-port, from which two Napoleons were run out as occasion required. At the river end of the palisade was a deep and muddy slough, across which was a bridge, the entrance of the river road into the port; commanding this bridge was a Napoleon gun. There were three mortars in the rear of the land face.

The sea face earthworks at Fort Fisher.

The Sea Face of Fort Fisher.

The sea face for one hundred yards from the northwest bastion was of the same massive character as the land face. A crescent battery intended for four guns joined this, but it was converted into a hospital bombproof. In the rear a heavy curtain was thrown up to protect the chambers from fragments of shells. From the bomb-proof a series of batteries extended for three quarters of a mile along the sea, connected by an infantry curtain. These batteries had heavy traverses, but were not more than ten or twelve feet high to the top of the parapets, and were built for richochet firing. On the line was a bomb-proof electric battery connected with a system of submarine torpedoes. Farther along, where the channel ran close to the beach, inside the bar, a mound battery sixty feet high was erected, with two heavy guns which had a plunging fire on the channel; this was connected with the battery north of it by a light curtain. Following the line of the works, it was over one mile from the mound to the northeast bastion at the angle of the sea and land faces, and upon this line twenty-four heavy guns were mounted. From the mound for nearly one mile to the end of the Point, was a level sand-plain scarcely three feet above high tide, and much of it was submerged during gales. At the Point was Battery Buchanan, four guns in the shape of an ellipse commanding the Inlet, its two 11-inch guns covering the approach by land. An advanced redoubt with a 24-pounder was added after the attack by the forces on Christmas, 1864. A wharf for large steamers was in close proximity to these works. Battery Buchanan was a citadel to which an over-powered garrison might retreat and with proper transportation be safely carried off at night, and to which re-inforcements could be sent under the cover of darkness.

A diorama of the fight at Fort Fisher's "Bloody Gate."

The Fort Fisher Fight.

General Whiting, in his official report of the taking of Fort Fisher on the night of the 15th of January 1865, after an assault of unprecedented fury, both by sea and land, lasting from Friday morning until Sunday night, says:

"On Thursday night the enemy's fleet was reported off the fort. On Friday morning the fleet opened very heavily. On Friday and Saturday, during the furious bombardment of the fort, the enemy was allowed to land without

molestation and to throw up a light line of field-works from Battery Ramseur to the river, thus securing his position from molestation and making the fate of Fort Fisher, under the circumstances, but a question of time.

"On Sunday, the fire on the fort reached a pitch of fury to which no language can do justice. It was concentrated on the land face and front. In a short time nearly every gun was dismounted or disabled, and the garrison suffered severely by the fire. At three o'clock the enemy's land force, which had been gradually and slowly advancing, formed in two columns for assault. The garrison, during the fierce bombardment, was not able to stand to the parapets, and many of the re-inforcements were obliged to be kept a great distance from the 10,000 men on shore and 600 heavy guns afloat, killing and wounding almost as many of the enemy as there were soldiers in the fort, and not surrendering until the last shot was expended."

The garrison consisted of two companies of the 10th North Carolina under Major Reilly; the 36th North Carolina, Colonel William Lamb, ten companies; four companies of the 40th North Carolina; Company D of the 1st North Carolina Artillery Battalion; Company C, 3d North Carolina Artillery Battalion; Company D 13th North Carolina Artillery Battalion, and the Naval Detachment under Captain Van Benthuysen.

General Whiting had been assigned to no duty by General Bragg, although it was his right to have commanded the supporting troops. He determined to go to the fort and share its fate. The Commander, Colonel Lamb, offered to relinquish the control, but General Whiting declined to take away the glory of the defense from him, but remained with him and fought as a volunteer. It is related that during the fight, when one hundred immense projectiles were being hurled per minute at the fort, General Whiting was seen "standing with folded arms, smiling upon a 400-pound shell, as it stood smoking and spinning like a billiard-ball on the sand not twenty feet away until it burst, and then moved quietly away." During the fight General Whiting saw the Federal flags planted on the traverses. Calling on the troops to follow him, they fought hand to hand with clubbed muskets, and one traverse was taken. Just as he was climbing the other, and had his hand upon the Federal flag to tear it down, he fell, receiving two wounds. Colonel Lamb, a half-hour later, fell with a desperate wound through the hip. The troops fought on. Lamb, in the hospital, found voice enough, though faint unto death, to say: "I will not surrender;" and Whiting, lying among the surgeons near by, responded: "Lamb, if you die, I will assume command, and I will never surrender."

After the fort was captured and General Whiting was made prisoner, he was taken to Fort Columbus, on Governors' Island, and there died, March 10th, 1865.

The fearless defender of the last stand at Fisher, Major James Reilly, remained not far from the scene of his exploits until his death, November 5th, 1894.

Colonel William Lamb still survives, and since the war has resided continuously at his home in Norfolk, Virginia, where he is engaged in business.

Another prominent officer of the Cape Fear, Colonel George Tait, a gallant Scotchman from Bladen county, who volunteered at the outbreak of the war and remained in active service to the end, is also living in Norfolk. Always beloved and honored as a soldier and a gentleman, he has in his declining years the comforts and respect achieved by an honorable, active and successful business life.

Craig's Landing.

From the deck of the steamer *Wilmington* the watchful tourist may espy near Craig's Landing a weather-beaten little cottage of very humble aspect. This unpretentious building was the residence of the Commandant of Fort Fisher and his little family during the war. It is worth preserving, because one of the sweetest little flowers of Confederate womanhood graced its rough interior, and encouraged by her noble self-sacrificing spirit the gallant defenders of the Lost Cause. She, too, has crossed over the river, and rests under the shade of the trees. Like a gentle exhalation she has passed away, but the memory of her devoted life of faith and fortitude, her loving and tender sympathy for the sick and wounded, will live as long as the story of Fisher is told.

Col. Lamb's cottage at Craig's Landing.

By the courtesy of our friend who was her worthy husband, we are permitted to copy the following sketch published some months ago in the *Southern Historical Papers* of Richmond:

The Heroine of Confederate Point.

In the Fall of 1857, a lovely Puritan maiden, still in her teens, was married in Grace Church, Providence, Rhode Island, to a Virginia youth, just passed his majority, who brought her to his home in Norfolk, a typical ancestral homestead, where, beside the 'white folk,' there was quite a colony of family servants, from the pickaninny, just able to crawl, to the old, gray-headed mammy who had nursed "ole Massa." She soon became enamored of her surroundings and charmed with the devotion of her colored maid, whose sole duty it was to

Sarah Chaffee "Daisy" Lamb and daughter.

wait upon her young missis. When the John Brown raid burst upon the South and her husband was ordered to Harper's Ferry, there was not a more indignant matron in all Virginia, and when at last secession came, the South did not contain a more enthusiastic little rebel.

"On the 15th of May, 1862, a few days after the surrender of Norfolk to the Federals, by her father-in-law, then Mayor, amid the excitement attending a captured city, her son Willie was born. Cut off from her husband and subjected to the privations and annoyances incident to a subjugated community, her father insisted upon her coming with her children to his home in Providence; but, notwithstanding she was in a luxurious home, with all that parental love could do for her, she preferred to leave all these comforts to share with her husband the dangers and privations of the South. She vainly tried to persuade Stanton, Secretary of War, to let her and her three children with a nurse return to the South; finally he consented to let her go by flag of truce from Washington to City Point, but without a nurse, and as she was unable to manage three little ones, she left the youngest with his grandparents, and with two others bravely set out for Dixie. The generous outfit of every description which was prepared for the journey and which was carried to the place of embarkation, was ruthlessly cast aside by the inspectors on the wharf, and no tears or entreaties or offers of reward by the parents availed to pass anything save a scanty supply of clothing and other necessaries. Arriving in the South, the brave young mother refused the proffer of a beautiful home in Wilmington, the occupancy of the grand old mansion at "Orton," on the Cape Fear River, but insisted upon taking up her abode with her children and their colored nurse in the upper room of a pilot's house, where they lived until the soldiers of the garrison built her a cottage one mile north of Fort Fisher on the Atlantic beach. In both of these homes she was occasionally exposed to the shot and shell fired from blockaders at blockader-runners.

"It was a quaint abode, constructed in most primitive style, with three rooms around one big chimney, in which North Carolina pine-knots supplied heat and light on winter nights. This cottage became historic and was famed for the frugal but tempting meals which its charming hostess would prepare for her distinguished guests. Besides the many illustrious Confederate Army and Navy officers who were delighted to find this bit of sunshiny civilization on the wild sandy beach, ensconced among the sand-dunes and straggling pines and black-jack, many celebrated English naval officers enjoyed its hospitality under assumed names; Roberts, afterwards the renowned Hobart Pasha, who commanded the Turkish navy; Murray, now Admiral Aynsley, long since retired, after having been rapidly promoted for gallantry and meritorious services in the British navy; the brave but unfortunate Burgoyne, who went down in the British iron-clad *Captain* in the Bay of Biscay; and the chivalrous Hewitt, who won the Victoria Cross in the Crimea and was knighted for his services as Ambassador to King John of Abyssinia, and who, after commanding the Queen's yacht, died lamented as Admiral Hewitt. Besides these, there were many genial and gallant merchant captains, among them Halprin, who afterwards commanded the *Great Eastern* while laying ocean cables; and famous war correspondents, Hon. Francis C. Lawley, M.P., correspondent of the *London Times*, and Frank Vizitelly, of the *London Illustrated News*, afterwards murdered in the Sudan. Nor must the handsome and plucky Tom Taylor be forgotten, the purser of the *Banshee* and the *Night Hawk*, who, by his coolness and daring, escaped with a boat's crew from the hands of the Federals after capture off the fort, and who was endeared to the children as the "Santa Clause" of the war.

"At first the little Confederate was satisfied with pork and potatoes, corn-bread and rye coffee, with sorghum sweetening but after the blockade-runners made her acquaintance the impoverished store-room was soon filled to overflowing, notwithstanding her heavy requisitions on it for the post hospital, the sick and wounded soldiers and sailors always being a subject of her tenderest solicitude, and often the hard-worked and poorly-fed colored hands blessed the little lady of the cottage for a tempting treat.

"Full of stirring events were the two years passed in the cottage on Confederate Point. The drowning of Mrs. Rose Greenough, the famous Confederate spy, off Fort Fisher, and the finding of her body, which was tenderly cared for, and the rescue from the waves, half dead, of Professor Holcombe and his restoration, were incidents never to be forgotten. Her fox-hunting with horse and hounds, the narrow escape of friendly vessels, the fights over blockade-runners driven ashore, the execution of deserters and the loss of an infant son, whose little spirit went out with the tide one sad summer night, all contributed to the reality of this romantic life.

"When Porter's fleet appeared off Fort Fisher, December, 1864, it was storm-bound for several days, and the little family, with their household goods, were sent across the river to Orton, before Butler's powder-ship blew up. After the Christmas victory over Porter and Butler the little heroine insisted upon coming back to her cottage, although her husband had procured a home of refuge in Cumberland County. General Whiting protested against her running the risk, for on dark nights her husband could not leave the fort; but she said, 'if the firing became too hot, she would run behind the sand-hills as she had done before,' and come she would.

"The fleet re-appeared unexpectedly on the night of the 12th of January 1865. It was a dark night, and when the lights of the fleet were reported, her husband sent a courier to the cottage to instruct her to pack up quickly and be prepared to leave with children and nurse as soon as he could come to bid them good-bye. The garrison barge with a trusted crew was stationed at Craig's Landing, near the cottage. After midnight, when all necessary orders were given for the coming attack, the Colonel mounted his horse and rode to the cottage, but all was dark and silent. He found the message had been delivered, but his brave wife had been so undisturbed by the news that she had fallen asleep and no preparations for a retreat had been made. Precious hours had been lost, and as the fleet would soon be shelling the beach and her husband have to return to the fort, he hurried them into the boat as soon as dressed, with only what could be gathered up hastily, leaving dresses, toys and household articles to fall into the hands of the foe. Among the articles left was a writing desk, with the following unfinished letter, which after many years has been returned. It is such a touching picture of those old Confederate days that consent has been given to its publication:

The Cottage: January 9th, 1865.

My Own Dear Parents:

I know you have been anxious enough about us all, knowing what a terrible bombardment we have had, but I am glad that I can relieve your mind on our behalf and tell you that we are all safe and well, through a most merciful and kind Providence. God was with us from the first, and our trust was so firm in Him that I can truly say that both Will and I feared no evil."

"I staid in my comfortable little home until the fleet appeared, when I packed up and went across the river to a large but empty house, of which I took possession; a terrible gale came on which delayed the attack for several days, but Saturday it came at last in all its fury; I could see it plainly from where I was; I had very powerful glasses, and sat on a stile out doors all day watching it—an awful but magnificent sight.

"I kept up very bravely (for you know I am brave, and would, if I thought I could, whip Porter and Butler myself), until the last gun had ceased and it began

to get dark and still. I was overcome at last and laid my head on the fence and cried for the first and last time during it all. I then got my carriage and rode to a fort near by to learn the news, but my heart failed as I approached it, and I returned to the house and waited a dispatch, which I received about 11 o'clock, saying all was well, I was quite touched with a little incident which occurred during the day; the little ones looked very grave and thoughtful; at last Dick came to me in the midst of the tearing and awful thundering and said: 'Mamma, I want to pray to God for my papa'. He knelt down and said his little earnest prayer; then jumped up, exclaiming and dancing about: 'Oh, sister, I am so glad! I am so glad! Now God will keep care of my papa'!

The shelling was even more terrific on Sunday, and I, not knowing how long it might continue, concluded to go to Fayetteville, and started Sunday noon in a small steamer, with the sick and wounded, to Wilmington, where I was obliged to stay for several days in great suspense, not able to get away and not able to hear directly from Will, as the enemy had cut the wires—and then a martyr to all kinds of rumors—one day heard that Will had lost a leg, etc., etc.; but I steadfastly made up my mind to give no credit to anything bad. At last I heard again that we had driven our persecutors off, and I returned again to the place where I went first, and the next day Will came over for me and took me to the fort, which I rode all over on horseback, but we did not move over for nearly a week. The fort was strewn with missiles of all kinds—it seemed a perfect miracle how any escaped—the immense works were literally skinned of their turf, but not injured in the slightest; not a bomb-proof or a magazine—and there are more than one—touched; the magazine the enemy thought they had destroyed was only a caisson; the men had very comfortable quarters in the fort—pretty little white-washed houses—but the shells soon set fire to them, making a large fire and dense smoke, but the works are good for dozen of sieges—plenty of everything; particularly plenty of the greatest essential—brave hearts. Our beloved General Whiting was present, but gave up the whole command to Will, to whom he now gives, as is due, the whole credit of building and defending his post, and has urged his promotion to Brigadier-General, which will doubtless be received soon, though neither of us really care for it.

We expect the Armada again, and will give him a warmer reception next time. The fort, expecting a longer time of it, was reserving their heaviest fire for nearer quarters. Butler's gallant troops came right under one side of the fort, but our grape and canister soon drove them off, and not Porter's shell, which did not happen to be falling that way at that time; they left their traces sufficiently next morning.

The 'gallant fellow' who stole the horse from the inside of the fort was doubtless so scared he didn't know much where he was. The true statement of the thing is, that an officer, unauthorized by Will or the General, sent a courier outside the fort with a message to some troops outside, and soon after he left the fort was attacked and killed by a Yankee sharp-shooter hidden under a bridge. The poor body fell and the horse was taken, and the flag spoken of, in the same way, was shot from the parapet and blew outside, when it was taken. When any of them see the inside of the fort, they will never live to tell the tale.

Ah, mother! you all, at home peacefully, do not know the misery of being driven from home by a miserable, cruel enemy! 'Tis a sad sight to see the sick and aged turned out in the cold to seek a shelter. I cannot speak feelingly because of any feeling myself, as God is so good to us, and has so favored us with life, health and means, and my dear, good husband has provided me a comfortable home in the interior, where I can be safe.

Will has worried so much about you, dear mother, thinking you would be so anxious about us. He often exclaims, when reading some of the lying accounts: 'How that will worry Ma'!

How is my darling Willie? We do so want to see our boy. I think Will will have to send for him in the Spring. Kiss the dear one dozen of times for his father and mother.

Though it was a very unpleasant Christmas to me, still the little ones enjoyed theirs. Will had imported a crowd of toys for them, and they are as happy as possible with them.

I have not heard from my dear home since last August, and you can imagine how very anxious I am to hear, particularly of dear sister Ria. Is she with George? Do write me of all the dear ones I love so much. How I would love to see you all, so much, and home!

I forgot to tell you of the casualties in the fight. Ours were only three killed; about sixty wounded; they were all.

Gen. Butler's powder ship, the **USS Louisiana.**

Butler's Powder Ship.

In the course of his admirable address to 5,000 ex-Union soldiers at Steinway Hall, New York City, on May 3d, 1878, our silver-tongued orator of the Cape Fear, Colonel Alfred M. Waddell, said:

"While it may be difficult to determine in what engagement of the war the severest concentrated fire of small arms occurred, there can be no doubt as to the place where the power of heavy artillery was exhibited in its most terrific form. The bombardment of Fort Fisher was by far the most frightful that has ever happened since the invention of gun-powder. All the testimony taken before the 'Committee on the Conduct of the War' goes to establish this fact; but, in addition to this, and to the universal admission on the Confederate side, there was still stronger evidence which was given in my presence the day after the capture of the fort by a competent and disinterested witness. The siege of Sebastopol is admitted to have been the greatest bombardment in history up to that time. An English officer, however, who had run the blockade, and who was present at Fort Fisher under an assumed name, was giving an account of it after his escape, and, as preliminary to his remarks, said what he had seen at Sebastopol was the merest child's play compared to what I have witnessed in the last two days. It was simply inconceivable and indescribable in its awful grandeur. I had no conception until now of what an artillery fire could be.' You remember, perhaps, that there was no cessation for more than forty-eight hours, and there were, besides the other projectiles, as many as twenty-five 11-inch shells in the air at the same instant throughout the whole time. Fifty thousand shells were expended by the fleet. During the continuance of the fire it would have been impossible for any living thing to remain on the parapets which faced the sea for a mile, and when the assaulting column was formed there was, along that whole front, but a single gun remaining, and that could only be fired once before the fort was reached, and that long, desperate hand-to-hand struggle began. A month before this the celebrated powder-ship explosion occurred, which was intended to blow down this solid earthwork, a mile in extent, with forty-feet traverses every few yards. The best incident of this huge joke was related to me by a distinguished officer of the navy several years ago. The night after the explosion of the powder-ship some of our pickets on the beach were captured and carried on board the Admiral's ship. Among them was a very solemn-looking fellow, who sat silently and sadly chewing tobacco. As there was intense curiosity among the officers of the fleet to know the result of the remarkable experiment, one of them asked the solemn-looking 'Reb' if he was in the fort when the powder-ship exploded; to which he replied in the affirmative, but without exhibiting the least interest in the matter; whereupon the officers gathered around him and began to ask questions:

"You say you were inside the fort?"

"Yes; I was thar."

"What was the effect of the explosion?"

"Mighty bad, sir—powerful bad."

"Well, what was it? Did it kill any rebels or throw down any of the works?"

"No, sir; hit didn't do that."

"Well, what did it do? Speak out."

"Why, stranger, hit waked up pretty nigh every man in the fort!"

The Rocks: Closure of New Inlet.

Beginning at Battery Buchanan, a long line of heavy masonry, known as the Rocks, will doubtless interest the traveler. This sea-wall is one of the best planned and most successful engineering feats in the South. In the year 1761, during a heavy storm, the Atlantic Ocean broke across the narrow sand beach which divided the sea from the river some seven miles above the mouth, which from that time became known as the New Inlet, and which caused a rapid shoaling of the old channel, there being then two outlets instead of one as formerly.

"The Rocks" sealing off New Inlet.

The Cape Fear River, from its mouth nearly to Wilmington, is properly a tidal estuary of about thirty-eight square miles. The river and its branches drain an area of about eight thousand square miles. The amount of fresh water passing out at the mouth, though large, is insignificant when compared with the tidal flow which alternately fills and empties this great reservoir. The mean fresh water discharge of the river does not exceed 9,000 cubic feet per second, while the tidal flow at the entrance averages about 175,000 cubic feet per second. This is the real force which creates and preserves the channel across the shifting sands of the coast at the mouth of the river. No demonstration is needed to prove the importance of concentrating this force. It is also apparent that such a force would be most efficient in preserving a passage across a bar and shoals which are in a position sheltered from the prevailing winds and heaviest storms of the coast. This we have at the natural mouth of the river, which is wholly sheltered from northerly, northeasterly, and, in a great measure, from easterly winds by its position in the bay, protected by Cape Fear and Frying Pan Shoals.

Congress was accordingly petitioned by our people to appropriate the necessary means for increasing the depth of water on Cape Fear bar and river;

and after careful surveys and estimates by the Corps of Engineers U.S.A., it was decided to undertake the entire closure of New Inlet under the direction of Colonel W.P. Craighill. This important and difficult work was begun in 1875. A continuous line of mattresses composed of logs and brushwood sunk and loaded with stone, was laid entirely across the New Inlet from October 1875, to June 1876. This was the foundation of the dam. The work was continued from year to year by piling small stone rip-rap on and over this foundation, bringing it up to high water, and then covering it with heavy granite stones on the top and slopes to low water. The closure was completed successfully in 1881 and was the occasion of much rejoicing in Wilmington, for its failure would have completely ruined the port of Wilmington, which depends for its life upon deep water and successful competition with Norfolk and Charleston.

The length of the dam from Federal Point to Zeke's Island is one mile, but the extension of Zeke's Island jetties to Smith's Island makes the line much longer. The Rock foundation of this wall is from 90 feet to 120 feet wide at the base, and for three-fourths of the line the average depth of the stone wall is 30 feet from the top of the dam. In some places it is 36 feet deep. The stone used in this gigantic structure would build a solid wall eight feet high, four feet thick and one hundred miles long. The cost of the work was $480,000—a small sum when the magnitude and difficulty of the undertaking is considered.

Battery Lamb & Confederate Salt Works.

Passing Battery Lamb, a Confederate work on Reeves' Point, we come to Walden's Creek, upon which were established, in war times, large Confederate Salt Works for the supply of this indispensable article to the soldiers of the South.

The salt-water was carried in lighters from New Inlet to this creek and evaporated by artificial heat, producing a fine white salt at a small expense. These Salt Works lined the coast from Cape Lookout, and many were owned by speculators who made large fortunes in Confederate money from their product. Nearly all of them were demolished from time to time by the Federal blockaders which threw shells in the woods every day where tell-tale smoke indicated the location of salt pans. But as soon as the demoralized darkies who attended them could be brought back from a seven-mile stampede, the plucky owners would begin to lay out another plant.

It is also noteworthy that the bricks which were used in the original construction of Fort Caswell were made on the banks of Walden Creek.

Snow's Marsh & Dredging Steamer Cape Fear.

Farther down is Snow's Marsh, through which the ship channel runs. This tortuous course has for years perplexed and discomfited navigators on account of the shifting sands and shoaling water which made it at times almost impassable to large vessels. For a long time this trouble baffled the engineers, but in 1895 Major W.S. Stanton, Corps of United States Engineers, undertook to protect the channel by a training dike or wall of brushwood bound in bundles by heavy wire, which has proved highly effective. The bundles were 22 feet long and 2 feet in diameter, piled to a height of half tide between piles driven 15 feet into sand and mud, 8 feet apart, in two rows, 5 to 6 feet apart. Should this means prove permanently effective, a more substantial wall may be built later.

Another helpful contrivance of Major Stanton's is the U.S. dredging steamer *Cape Fear*, which he designed especially for this service and which began a most successful work in June 1895. She is fitted with sand-pumps of great strength and capacity, which lift and deposit in the bins on board about 500 cubic yards of sand per hour. This steamer is invaluable to the work now under the direction of Colonel D. P. Heap, U.S. Engineers, for the deepening of the river and bar.

The total expenditure of money upon our river and harbor improvement from the year 1829 to 1895 was $2,427, 584.46, and Congress has just appropriated the further sum of $195,000 for the continuance of the work.

Price's Creek Light House & Confederate States Signal Station.

We see on the Western side the old ante-bellum lighthouse and keeper's residence on Price's Creek, which were used during the Civil War as a signal station—the only means of communication between Fort Caswell at the western bar and Fort Fisher at the New Inlet via Smithville, where the Confederate General resided.

The Confederate States Signal Corps frequently rendered some very efficient service to the blockade-runners after they had succeeded in getting between the blockaders and the beach, where they were also in danger of the shore batteries until their character became known to the forts.

As the signal system developed, a detailed member was sent out with every ship, and so important did this service become that signal officers, as they were called, were occasionally applied for by owners or captains of steamers in the Clyde or at Liverpool before sailing for Bermuda or Nassau to engage in running the blockade.

The first attempt to communicate with the shore batteries was a failure, and consequently the service suffered some reproach for awhile, but subsequent practice with intelligent, cool-headed men, resulted in complete success, and some valuable ships with still more valuable cargoes, were saved from capture or destruction by the intervention of the Signal Service, when, owing to the darkness and bad landfall, the captain and pilot were alike unable to recognize their geographical position.

Price's Creek lighthouse in 2004.

To Mr. Frederick Gregory, of Crowells, N.C., belongs the honor of the first success as a signal operator in this service. Identified with the corps from the beginning of the blockade, and with the Cape Fear at Price's Creek Station, which was for a long time in his efficient charge, he brought to this new and novel duty an experience and efficiency equaled by few of his colleagues and surpassed by none. It was well said of him that he was always ready and never afraid—two elements of the almost unvarying success which attended the ships to which he was subsequently assigned. It was my good fortune to be intimately associated with Mr. Gregory for nearly two years, during which we had many ups and downs together as shipmates aboard and as companions ashore. He was one of the few young men engaged in blockade-running who successfully resisted the evil influences and depraved associations with which we were continually surrounded. Unselfish and honorable in all his relations with his fellows, courageous as a lion in time of danger, he was an honor to his State and to the cause he so worthily represented.

Another gallant Confederate deserving honorable mention was Leo Vogel, an officer under Maffitt on the corvette *Florida*, and subsequently with us on the *Lillian*. Patriotic, brave, generous, he was a noble type of Southern chivalry, an honor to his flag and country. Of charming physique and pleasing address, his modesty and good breeding were in striking contrast with the occasionally disgraceful conduct of others who were most discreditable to the South. For some time after the war Captain Vogel was identified with the Charleston and

Florida Steamboat Company, commanding for many years the steamer *Dictator*, until he was placed in charge of the magnificent steamer *St. Johns*, the most palatial boat ever constructed for the Florida business. While with this Company Captain Vogel numbered his friends and acquaintances by the thousands, and now that he has a steamer on the St. John's, they never fail to avail themselves of a trip with him up this beautiful river. He is said to be one of the attractions of the "Land of Flowers."

Wilmington and Charleston Mail Boats.

The ruined light-houses at Big Island, Orton Point and Price's Creek remind us of the days long ago, when passengers and mails from the great North and South were transported between Wilmington & Weldon Railroad with Charleston and the South. The names of these steamers, which were of the best design in those days, were *Wilmington*, *Gladiator*, *North Carolina*, *Vanderbilt* and *Dudley*. The average passage between Wilmington and Charleston was about seventeen hours, but it was done under exceptionally favorable conditions in twelve hours. The boats were about 190 feet long, draft 10 to 12 feet, and in consequence of the lack of water on the bar, they had often to wait for a tide.

The Company's office and landing pier was just north of the Champion Compress, where the Atlantic Coast Line warehouses now stand. John A. Taylor, esq., Col. James T. Miller and Captain Benjamin Lawton were agents of the line at different times; the last named acted in that capacity when the boats were sold upon the completion of the Wilmington and Manchester Railroad, now the Wilmington, Columbia and Augusta Railroad.

In 1851, the remains of the lamented statesman, John C. Calhoun, were brought from the North by the Wilmington and Weldon Railroad, and conveyed to the present Custom House wharf, from which they were transported by the *Nina*, a special steamer, sent from Charleston with the Committee from that city on board. The *Nina* was draped in deep mourning.

On another occasion the famous singer, Jenny Lind, known also as the Swedish Nightingale, was a passenger during the most tempestuous voyage ever encountered by these boats—a very destructive storm prevailed along the coast. The *diva* was under the management of P.T. Barnum, and the troupe consisted of sixty persons. The great singer persisted in remaining on deck during the entire trip, while the others kept below, indifferent to everything but the fact that they were distressingly sea-sick.

The quarantine station once existed in the Cape Fear River opposite Southport.

The Cape Fear Quarantine Station.

The following excellent editorial by Doctor Robert D. Jewett is taken from the *North Carolina Medical Journal* of April 5th, 1896:

The Cape Fear River is the only marine gateway of importance by which epidemics may gain an entrance into North Carolina; and while vessels never pass up the river more than two or three miles above Wilmington, the whole State is, of course, deeply and directly interested in the efforts to prevent the introduction of infectious diseases at this port. As the poison gaining an entrance through a slight peripheral lesion passes along the lymph and circulatory channels and makes the whole organism sick, so one case of contagious disease gaining entrance through this port, away down in the southeastern corner of the State, may spread along the avenues of travel and endanger the welfare of the whole Commonwealth. And as this applies to one State it applies to the whole country; therefore the whole country is directly interested in stopping the poison at the gateway. The watchers at the port of New York protect Chicago as truly as they do New York, and those at New Orleans. And since the quarantine at a port of entry is intended as a protection for the whole country, it is not just that one State or city should be burdened with the expense of conducting it.

For a number of years the quarantine at the mouth of the Cape Fear has been under the control of a Quarantine Board, consisting of the State. We speak of it as a Station, but it was so only nominally, for there was no plant for the disinfection of vessel and crew, and no hospital for the care of the sick or the detention of suspects. The disinfection of vessels was accomplished by burning in their holds a quantity of sulphur, while disinfection of the crew's clothing was probably never done. The fact that we have so long escaped the introduction of contagious diseases is therefore due, apparently, rather to Divine beneficence than to our own care and watchfulness.

The Quarantine Board have long felt the great need of a well-equipped station, and with the co-operation of the City Produce Exchange succeeded in getting passed by the Legislature of 1893 a bill appropriating $20,000 for this *purpose, provided the city of Wilmington would appropriate $5,000. The city refused to do its part, and the station remained unequipped.*

In February, 1893, a bill was passed in Congress granting to the Marine Hospital Service the control over all quarantines; but provided that whenever a local quarantine station complied with the minimum requirements of the United States laws, as determined by periodical inspections by officers of the Marine Hospital Service, that station should not be interfered with. The State Board of Health seeing that the effort to equip the station and keep it under the State control had failed, turned the station over to the Marine Hospital Service. An inspection was made and an appropriation of $25,000 immediately secured for building and equipping the station with modern apparatus.

Plans were devised in the office of the Supervising Architect and the contract to build the station awarded. Dr. J.M. Eager, who has had several years experience in Marine Hospital Service at Cincinnati, Key West and New Orleans, besides several details for special quarantine duty, was detailed to take command of the station, and will make an efficient officer.

The new station is located on the east side of the channel of Cape Fear River about one and one-eighth miles north of Southport. The station is to be built on a pier 600 feet long, with gangways, dock and ballast crib. The head of the pier will extend into the channel in 20 feet of water. The general plan of the pier will be in the shape of a cross, the front of which will extend towards the shoals. The Disinfecting House will be provided with the most approved scientific appliances for the mechanical and chemical cleansing of infected vessels. A sulphur furnace will be provided, with which 10 per cent, per volume strength of sulphur dioxide of gas can be evolved, a result not otherwise obtainable except by the liberation of liquefied sulphur dioxide. This gas will be conducted in the holds and other parts of the vessels by means of a hose. Apparatus will also be provided for disinfection by live steam, and tanks for the storage of disinfecting solutions with appliances for their application. There will be buildings for a hospital, surgeon's quarters and attendants' quarters.

A special landing for contagious patients, to be taken to the hospital without contact with other parts of the station, will also be provided. At present the station is being conducted for inspection only. Should any infected vessel arrive at Southport quarantine before completion of the station, it will be remanded to United States quarantine station, Blackbeard Island, Sapelo, Georgia, for proper treatment.

The inspection of vessels is always made by daylight except in cases of vessels in distress. All persons on vessels having had small-pox on board, must be vaccinated or show satisfactory evidence of recent vaccination, or of having had small-pox, or detained in quarantine for not less than fourteen days, and all effects and compartments liable to convey infection, disinfected. No fees are charged for United States quarantine. Pilots who have boarded infected vessels are subject to the same treatment as members of the crew.

When a vessel is held for disinfection, the passengers and all of the crew are removed if cholera has occurred, save those necessary to care for the vessel. The sick are placed in hospital. Those especially suspected are carefully isolated. The others are segregated in small groups, and no communication is allowed between these groups – those being especially capable of conveying infection are not permitted to enter the barracks until they are bathed and furnished with sterile clothing. No material capable of conveying infection is taken in barracks, especially food. All hand-baggage is disinfected. All cargo liable, are disinfected. The water-tanks or casks are chemically cleaned and afterwards filled with water known to be absolutely pure, or with water recently boiled.

After completion of all disinfection all persons are detained in quarantine for a time sufficient to cover the period of incubation of the disease for which quarantine is practiced—this for yellow fever is five days; for typhus, not less than twenty; for small-pox, not less than fourteen. No alien lepers are allowed to land. The quarantine laws will be rigidly enforced here as soon as the station is equipped."

Benjamin Smith

Southport, Governor Smith, Cape Fear Pilots.

Near the mouth of the beautiful Cape Fear River, on its right bank, is a pleasant little town. It is fanned by the delicious sea breezes; huge live-oaks gratefully shade its streets. In its somber cemetery repose the bodies of many excellent people. Its harbor is good. It is on the main channel of the river. From its wharves can be seen, not far away, the thin white line of waves as they break on the sandy beach. But the ships to and from its neighbor, Wilmington, pay little tribute as they pass and repass. Its chief fame is that it contains the Court House of the county of Brunswick. Its name is Smithville."

Thus wrote the Hon. Kemp P. Battle, in his beautiful tribute to the memory of the first benefactor of the State University, Benjamin Smith, who had served in his youth as Aid-de-Camp of Washington, who had behaved with conspicuous gallantry under Moultrie, when he drove the British from Port Royal, who had roused to enthusiasm, by an address full of energy and fire, the entire male population of Brunswick county to follow his lead against their country's enemy, who was elected fifteen times to the Senate, and who, in 1810, became Governor of the Commonwealth. Philanthropist, Patriot, Soldier, Statesman, he came at last, in poverty and wretchedness, to a pauper's end. For him, in 1792, this charming little town was named. It was previously known as Fort Johnston, a fortification named for the Colonial Governor, Gabriel Johnston, having been established here about the year 1745 for the protection of the Colony against pirates which infested the Cape Fear.

The old garrison is still one of the sights of this healthful seaside resort. The town, or city as it is gravely called by its dignified inhabitants, is now known as Southport, and, to the credit of its virtuous citizens, it is also known as a dry town, in the sense that no intoxicants are permitted to be sold within its jurisdiction.

Smithville was a centre of busy military life during the war between the States. Here were the headquarters of the Confederate General commanding the post, and here the homes of about sixty hardy pilots whose humble sphere was

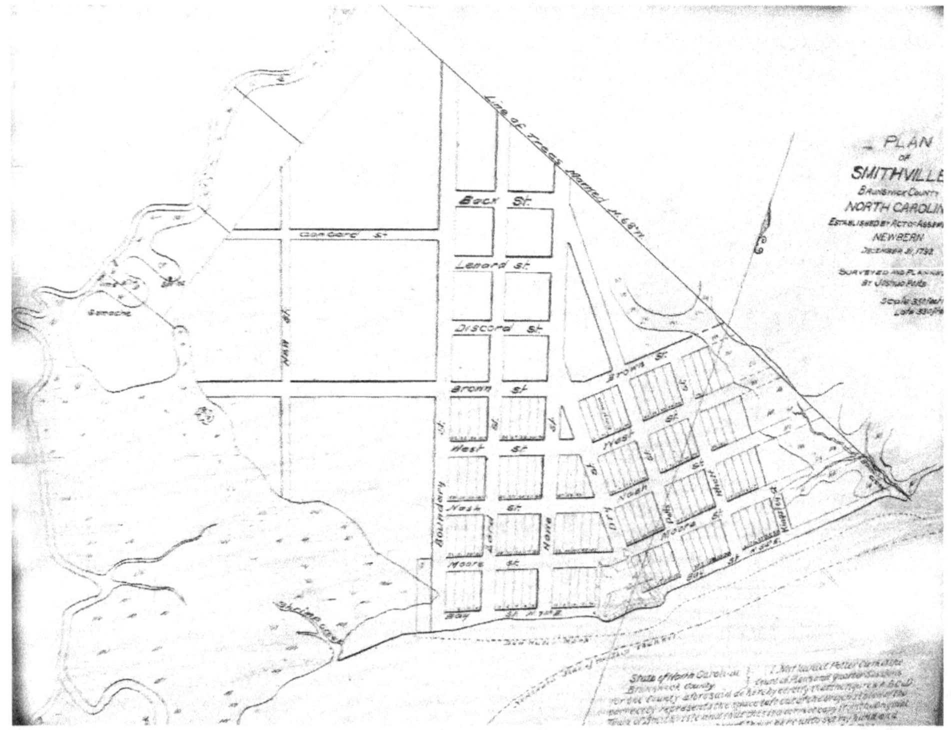

An early plan of Smithville.

suddenly exalted to the dignity of the most important and responsible officers of the swift blockade-running steamers, which braved the dangers of a hostile fleet and crept in every night under cover of the darkness.

The Cape Fear pilots have long maintained a standard of excellence in their profession most creditable to them as a class and as individuals.

The writer, for eight years a member of the Board of Commissioners of Navigation and Pilotage, having ample means of observation at home and abroad, believes that our pilots would compare most favorably with any organization of the kind elsewhere in all the essential qualifications of this noble calling.

The story of their wonderful skill and bravery in the time of the Federal blockade has never been written because the survivors are modest men, and time has obliterated from their memories many incidents of this extraordinary epoch in their history.

Amidst the impenetrable darkness, without lightship or beacon, the narrow and closely-watched inlet was felt for with a deep sea lead as a blind man feels his way along a familiar path; and even when the enemy's fire was raking the wheel-house, the faithful pilot, with steady hand and iron nerve, safely steered the little fugitive of the sea to her desired haven. It might be said of him as it was told of the Nantucket skipper, that he could get his bearings on the darkest night by a taste of lead.

Bald Head, Pirates.

Bald Head, upon which now stands the friendly lighthouse, an emblem of peace and good will to men, was once the scene of barbarous atrocity. In the early days of the colony, and after the abandonment of the river settlements by the whites, the Cape was in great disrepute on account of the savage barbarity of the Indians, who decoyed vessels ashore, and who after plundering the ships, fiendishly mutilated and murdered the unfortunate sailors who fell into their hands.

It was also for years after, the rendezvous of pirates—as many as twenty piratical vessels, under the black flag, skull and cross bones, having anchored at one time in the now peaceful harbor of Southport. These preyed upon the shipping between Charleston and the West Indies; and they were commanded by the notorious pirate chiefs, Stede Bonnett and Richard Worley. The infamous Edward Teach, known as Blackbeard, also used these waters in his nefarious undertakings. He commanded a ship of forty guns and his squadron consisted of six vessels. The depredations of these sea robbers became so alarming that Governor Spotswood, of Virginia, appealed to the British naval officers on that station to send a force into Carolina waters and capture those desperate pirates.

The lifesaving station on Bald Head Island according to Sprunt.

Two sloops of war were at once fitted out and a brave British officer, Lieutenant Maynard, placed in command, who sailed from James River, November 1718, and overtook Teach in Pamlico. As Maynard approached Teach, the pirate swore at him with the most horrid imprecations, saying that he would neither give nor take quarter. Maynard's ship unfortunately grounded, giving Teach the advantage, and the pirate's first broadside killed twenty of his men. Maynard saw that the situation was desperate, and promptly determined to fight hand to hand to the death. Teach immediately laid his ship alongside and boarded and the slaughter began. The deck was soon slippery with blood. Not a man on either side escaped unhurt; nearly all the pirates were killed or desperately wounded. Maynard and Teach fought hand to hand with their dirks. At last the pirate fell and the gallant Maynard, having ordered the pirate's head severed from his body, placed it at the end of his bowsprit and returned to Virginia.

On Bald Head is now established, in striking contrast with those dreadful times, a well-equipped Life Saving Station, with a sturdy crew of brave hearts and strong arms, always alert for signals of distress at sea.

The honored and lamented George Davis has eloquently referred to this point, as follows:

"Looking then to the Cape for the idea and reason of its name, we find that it is the Southermost point of Smith's Island, a naked, bleak elbow of sand, jutting far out into the ocean. Immediately in its front, are the Frying Pan Shoals pushing out still further twenty miles to sea. Together they stand for warning and for woe: and together they catch the long majestic roll of the Atlantic as it sweeps through a thousand miles of grandeur and power from the Arctic towards

the Gulf. It is the play-ground of billows and tempests, the kingdom of silence and awe, disturbed by no sound save the sea-gull's shriek and the breaker's roar. Its whole aspect is suggestive, not of repose and beauty, but of desolation and terror. Imagination cannot adorn it. Romance cannot hallow it. Local pride cannot soften it. There it stands to-day, bleak and threatening and pitiless, as it stood three hundred years ago, when Grenville and White came near unto death upon its sands. And there it will stand bleak and threatening and pitiless until the earth and the sea shall give up their dead. And as its nature, so its name, is now, always has been and always will be the 'Cape of Fear.'"

Fort Caswell.

The work at Fort Caswell at the mouth of the Cape Fear River was commenced by the Government in the year 1826. Major George Blaney of the United States Engineer Corps, was in charge of it for several years until his death at Smithville (now Southport), in 1836 or 1837. He was born in Boston, Massachusetts, and was an accomplished officer. His remains were brought to Wilmington, and the Wilmington Volunteers, a uniformed Company, and the only one then existing in the town, formed at the Market dock to receive them, and escorted them to the old burial-ground adjoining St. James' church, where they were interred with military honors and where they still repose.

The main sallyport at Fort Caswell.

Major Blaney's assistant in building the fort was Mr. James Ancrum Berry, a native of Wilmington, a natural engineer, the bent of whose mind was strongly mathematical, who was thoroughly competent for the position he held and who took great pride in the work. So much so, indeed, that he had a small house erected on the riverfront of the fort and resided there with his family for a year or two until the encroaching waters rendered his habitation untenable, when he returned to Smithville. He died suddenly in 1832. He was hunting with the late Mr. John Brown, and while crossing a small stream on a log he lost his footing, his gun came in contact with the log and was discharged, the contents entering his brain, killing him almost instantly. He was an honorable gentleman, high-toned and chivalric, and was greatly mourned.

It is probable that Captain A.J. Swift, son of the distinguished Chief of the Engineer Corps, General Joseph Swift, succeeded Major Blaney. It is known, however, that he had charge of the works at the mouth of the river for quite a long time, and it is believed they were finished under his supervision.

Captain Swift was regarded as one of the ablest engineer officers in the Army, and, though dying quite young, left behind him a reputation second to none in that branch of the service.

Fort Caswell, named in honor of Richard Caswell, first Governor of the State, was in the charge of United States Sergeant James Reilly at the beginning of the Civil War, who surrendered to a large force of Confederates under Colonel J.J. Hedrick, of Wilmington.

It is a remarkable fact that, notwithstanding its exposed position to the Federal fleet, no general engagement occurred at Caswell during the four year's war. The fort was of great service, however, in defending the main bar and the garrison at Smithville, although the fighting was confined to an occasional artillery duel with the United States blockading fleet.

The ruins are very interesting and are of a totally different character from the earthworks at Fort Fisher. It is understood that the War Department will restore and reinforce this once formidable fortification.

We learn from the *Literary Digest* of April 25th, 1896, that, with practical unanimity, the House of Representatives passed the Fortifications Appropriation Bill without a division, and in the form recommended by the Appropriations Committee, on April 14th. The bill carries a total of $5,842,337, of which $1,885,000 is for the construction of gun and mortar batteries and fortifications, and $1,729,000 for armament of fortifications. In addition to the total direct appropriation carried by the bill, the Secretary of War is authorized to enter into contracts to the total amount of $5,542,276 for materials and construction of fortifications and armament, making the aggregate amount appropriated and authorized $11,384,613.

Evacuation and Explosion of Fort Caswell.

The defences of Oak Island were composed of Forts Caswell and Campbell, the latter a large earth fort, situated about one mile down the beach from Fort Caswell; Battery Shaw, and some other small works, all under the command of Colonel Charles H. Simonton. With Colonel Simonton were the following members of his staff: Captain E.S. Martin, Chief of Ordnance and Artillery; Captain Booker Jones, Commissary; Captain H.C. Whiting, Quartermaster, and Captain Booker, Assistant Adjutant General.

Fort Fisher fell about nine o'clock Sunday night, January 15th, 1865, and by midnight orders had been received at Fort Caswell to send the garrisons of that fort and Fort Caswell down the beach and into the woods before daylight in order to conceal them from the Federal fleet. The troops were immediately withdrawn from the forts, and under cover of darkness marched away. Orders were also received to spike the guns in those two forts and destroy the ammunition as far as possible. Accordingly, during Monday, the 16th of January, the Chief of Ordnance and Artillery (Captain E.S. Martin) was employed with the ordnance force of the forts in carrying out this order, preparing to burn the barracks—large wooden structures built outside and around Fort Caswell—and blow up the magazines.

About one o'clock, A.M., Tuesday, January 17th, the order came to evacuate and blow up the magazines, when Colonel C.H. Simonton, Lieutenant Colonel John D. Taylor and Captain Booker Jones, who had remained up to this time, departed, leaving Captain Martin to destroy the barracks and forts. The buildings without the fort and the citadel within were at once set on fire, and were soon blazing from top to bottom. Trains had been laid during the day to each of the seven magazines at Fort Caswell and the five magazines in Fort Campbell, and under the lurid glare of the burning buildings the match was applied to the trains. The magazine in Fort Caswell contained nearly one hundred thousand pounds of powder, and when it exploded the volume of sound seemed to rend the very heavens, while the earth trembled and shook, the violence of the shock being felt in Wilmington, thirty miles distant, and even at Fayetteville, more than one hundred miles away. The sight was grand beyond description. Amidst this sublime and impressive scene the flag of Fort Caswell was for the last time hauled down and carried away by the officer above mentioned, who, with his men, silently departed—the last to leave the old fort, which for four long years of war had so gallantly guarded the main entrance to the river.

War Department Records: Forts Johnston and Caswell.

Since the foregoing sketches of Forts Johnston and Caswell were in type I have received the following official particulars from the Honorable the Secretary of War, which will doubtless be found valuable and interesting:

Fort Caswell, at the mouth of Cape Fear River, North Carolina, was commenced in the year 1826, the first appropriation for its construction being under Act of Congress approved March 2d, 1825. It was reported as about completed by Captain Alexander J. Swift, United States Engineers, October 20,

1838, at a total cost of $473,402. From 1838 to 1857, for preservation of site, repairs, etc., at Fort Caswell, and some repairs at Fort Johnston, the sum of $69,422.09 was expended, making a total to 1857 of $542,844.09. It was named Fort Caswell by War Department Order No. 32, of April 18th, 1833.

Fort Caswell was an inclosed pentagonal work, with a loop-holed scarp wall, flanked by caponniers, was constructed for an armament of 61 channel-bearing guns, mounted en-barbette, and a few small guns for land defense. Capacious defensive barracks called a citadel occupied a large part of the parade.

Upon its evacuation by the Confederate forces in January 1865, an attempt was made to blow it up. All the scarp wall of the southeast face was overturned by a mine exploded in the scarp gallery of that face; a portion of the scarp wall of north and west fronts was badly shattered by the explosion of a magazine on the covered way near the northwest salient, and the citadel on the parade of the work was burned.

It is now in a dilapidated condition—its armament consists of seven 10-inch and four 8-inch Columbiads and one 9-inch Dahlgren guns all en-barbette and not mounted.

New works are contemplated for the site of this fort, but their details are not published.

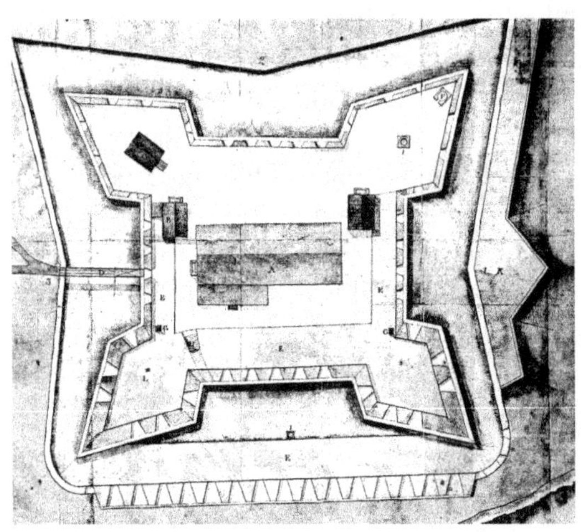

Original plan of Fort Johnston.

Fort Johnston, N.C.

*The erection of the original fort was provided for by an Act of the Colonial Assembly held at New Berne April 20th, 1745 (page 94 of the Laws of North Carolina). It recited that, 'Whereas from the present War with France and Spain, there is great reason to fear that such parts of this Province which are situated most commodious for shipping to enter, may be invaded by the enemy; and whereas the entrance of Cape Fear River, from its known depth of water and other conveniences of navigation may tempt them to such an enterprise while it remains in so naked and defenceless a condition as it now is: Therefore, for the better securing of the Inhabitants of the said river from any insult and invasion,' etc. *** That the 'Fort or Battery shall be called Johnston's Fort, and shall be large enough to*

Fort Johnston's Garrison House in 2004.

contain at least Twenty-four Cannon, with Barracks and other conveniences for Soldiers.'

This was before the opening of New Inlet. This opening, which was caused by a violent equinoctial storm in 1761, increased in importance, so as to form a new mouth for the Cape Fear River, deepening from 6 feet at low water in 1797 to 10 feet at low water in 1839, had a marked effect upon that river, diminishing the depth of water upon the main bar entrance from 15 feet in 1797 to 9 feet in 1839. Prior to the opening of New Inlet, and even until 1839, Baldhead channel was the natural and main entrance to the river. From 1839 to 1872 both the Rip (western channel) and New Inlet were the main entrances, and the use of Baldhead was discontinued. Since 1872 and the closure of the New Inlet, Baldhead has again become the main channel.

As a result of work carried on under the supervision of the Corps of Engineers in 1894 the depth of the channel at mean low water was from Wilmington, 20 miles, to Snow's Marsh 18 feet, except where shoaling had occurred at the lower extremity of Liliput Shoal, where the depth was 16.5 feet; at Snow's Marsh Shoal 14 feet; on the inner shoals at the bar 16 feet by a crooked channel and 14.3 feet by a straight course, and on the outer bar 16.6 feet.

For the original depth of water, see old maps in the office of Lieutenant-Colonel D.P. Heap, Corps of Engineers, in the Post Office building at Wilmington. For historical sketches of the work of improving that river, &c., see report of Captain C.B. Phillips, Corps of Engineers, pages 321-331, of Annual Report of the Chief of Engineers for 1876; report of Captain W.H. Bixby, Corps of Engineers, pages 1,004-1,011 of Annual Reports of the Chief of Engineers for

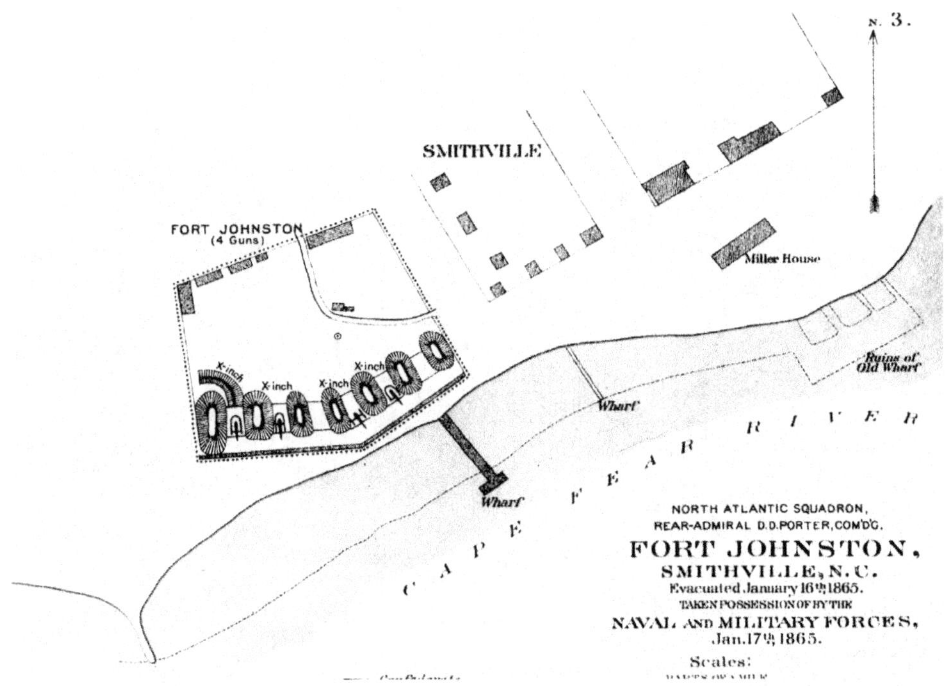

Fort Johnston, previously known as Fort Pender during the Civil War.

1886; various reports of Mr. Henry Bacon in the Annual Reports of the Chief of Engineers from 1876 to 1890, and an article on the subject published on pages 236-246 of Volume XXIX, (July, 1893, number) of the Transactions of the American Society of Civil Engineers, in a paper entitled 'The Improvement of the Harbors on the South Atlantic Coast of the United States.' The printed annual reports of the Chief of Engineers may be seen in Colonel Heap's office.

In a report made by Acting Assistant Surgeon, S.S.Boyer, U.S. Army, on this fort, published on pages 92-94 of Circular No.4, War Department, Surgeon General's Office, December 5th, 1870, a report on Barracks and Hospitals, with descriptions of Military Posts, he states: 'This fort receives its name from Gabriel Johnston, who was Governor of the Province of North Carolina from 1734 to 1752. It was erected by the British soon after France declared war against England, in 1744. Since that period it has been garrisoned at irregular intervals." * * *

There is no fort built upon the reservation. During the late civil war it came into the possession of the rebels, and they constructed some minor works upon it, which have since been removed by United States troops.

By reference to American State Papers, Military Affairs, Vol. I, pages 95-101, 224,237, etc., Mr. Sprunt will find information that may be of use to him in relation to the construction by the United States of a new work on the site of the old fort, finished about the year of 1809. etc. The new work consisted of a simple epaulement of concrete (some of it yet remains) and an enclosure of planks; within the enclosure there was a block house, lately destroyed, to the regret of this Department, a powder magazine, and quarters for officers of brick; and a barracks, a guard-house and a store-house of wood.

The terreplein of the battery was ten feet below the parade and site of the buildings. The battery could receive eleven or twelve guns. The block house was square and of two stories, the upper projected three feet, forming a machicoulis defense of the approach to the lower story. The distance from the block house to the battery was about one hundred yards. This battery was provided with loop holes and embrasures above.

There is a drawing on file entitled 'Fort Johnston and part of the town of Smithville, N.C., 1802,' which shows a large pentagonal work. Whether this represents the fort erected about 1745 or one erected later, is not shown by an examination of the records.

This is about all the information than can be ascertained from the records and maps of this office relative to these two forts, in reference to the inquiries of Mr. Sprunt.

Wild Pigeons, Wreck of Spanish Ship, Probable Murder, Treasure Trove.

During the early part of the century, about the year 1812, great numbers of wild pigeons frequented Bald Head, where there was an immense roost. General Swift, then in command of Fort Johnston, says in his memoirs that some of these flocks were miles in extent and that the sound of their wings was like that of a roaring wind. Many were killed by sportsmen.

In November, 1803, a large Spanish ship called the *Bilboa*, was cast away on Cape Fear in a storm. The crew, numbering twenty men of villainous aspect, were arrested by Lieutenant Fergus, at Fort Johnston, and confined in the block house (which still exists), under suspicion of having murdered their captain and mate at sea. They told the improbable story that their officers had died at sea, and that they, being ignorant of navigation, had let the ship drive before the wind until she fetched up on Bald Head. They all had silver dollars tied in their sashes around their waists, and they said there was a great deal more on the wreck. The pilots and others made search for this treasure but did not recover it. For fifty years afterwards, these silver coins were occasionally washed up by the sea, and the pilots living on the island were always on the alert for specie on the beach after a severe storm.

The sailors were sent to Charleston for trial, and in the absence of testimony against them, were discharged.

Cape Fear lifesavers rescue passengers and crew of a ship lost off the coast.

Life-Savers.

About a mile from Fort Caswell, facing the dangerous middle-ground upon which many a gallant ship has met her doom, is situated the Oak Island Life-Saving Station, the crew of which patrol the beach south of main bar, while their fellow life-savers of the Cape Fear Station on Bald Head watch the white line of breakers for miles to the north.

A visit to either of these well-equipped stations will greatly interest those who are not already familiar with the drill and appliances of this humane institution. They were established upon our dangerous coast some years ago mainly through the instrumentality of our member of Congress, Colonel Alfred M. Waddell, who has said with reference to the service:

"It is a hard life, a most trying and hazardous employment, the pecuniary compensation for which, as to the surfmen, is small, and as to the keepers, who have great responsibilities, totally inadequate, being only $200 a year. If you have ever been in the breakers, as I have, even in ordinary weather and in a good boat, you can appreciate the value of calm, steady nerves, courage, strength and self-possession.

"But when a howling tempest is raging, and the waves leap heavenward (with the thermometer perhaps at zero), the men who launch a life-boat in the surf, and pull out into the hell of waters to save their fellow-beings, must be made of such stuff as heroes are made of."

A Run to Sea.

Old Baldy lighthouse

Perhaps the air is balmy and the trip to-day includes a run to sea. We swiftly pass Fort Caswell on the starboard side, with Bald Head Light House close aport. Soon the long ground-swell of the majestic ocean tells us we have crossed the bar. Ahead we hear the dong, dong of the restless bell buoy, a weird but welcome warning to incoming strangers that dangerous shoals are near. Far off in the dim horizon, also in nearer view, white-winged merchantmen speed on their voyage up and down the coast. A trail of smoke marks the track of a distant steamer. Sea gulls, which Coleridge likened to human souls in the mist and darkness, sail past us with a grace and beauty of flight that is not of earth, but that comes alone from Him who marks the sparrow's fall and who holds the ocean in His fist.

Away to the southwest are the blackfish shoals, where many a seasick amateur has longed to be at home. Exposed to the fury of every storm on the edge of the dangerous Frying Pan, we see the faint outlines of the good Light Ship as she plunges to her mushroom anchors and buries her head in the foam.

"Alone on the wide, wide sea, so lonely 'twas that God Himself scarce seemed there to be."

We are now about ten miles out. Beneath us many fathoms deep reposes a gallant and ill-fated ship, the Cuban steamer *Virginius*. It is a sad but o'er true tale, and it may interest the sympathizers of Cuba Libre.

Captain Fry and the Cuban War.

In the year 1841, a winsome, honest lad, who had determined to join the navy of his country, and who had been thwarted in his purpose by the friends at home, made his way alone from Florida to Washington, and demanded his right to speak with the President, which was not denied him.

The former blockade runner **Virginius.**

Mr. Tyler was so pleased by the youthful manliness of the little chap, who was only eight years old, that he invited him to dine at the White House on the following day. The favorable impression was confirmed on that occasion. The young Floridian was the observed of all observers; members of the Cabinet and their wives, members of Congress and officers of the navy had heard of the little lad's story, and all united in espousing his patriotic cause.

The President, won by his ardor, as well as by his gentlemanly and modest behavior, granted the boy's request and immediately signed his warrant as a midshipman in the United States Navy.

The subsequent record of Captain Joseph Fry, the Christian gentleman, the gallant sailor, the humane commander, the chivalrous soldier, is known to readers of American history. Of heroic mould and dignified address, he was

"A combination and a form indeed,
Where every god did seem to set his seal,
To give the world assurance of a man."

When the Civil War came, it found him among the most beloved and honored officers in the service. The trial of his faith was brief and bitter. He could not fight against his home and loved ones, much as he honored the flag which he had so long and so faithfully cherished. He was a Southron, and with many pangs of sincere regret he went with his native State for well or woe.

His personal bravery during the war was wonderful; he never performed deeds of valor under temporary excitement, but acted with such coolness and daring as to command the admiration of superiors and inferiors alike. He was severely wounded at the battle of White River, and while on sick leave was ordered, at his own request, to command the Confederate blockade-runner *Eugenie*, upon which the writer made a voyage. On one occasion the *Eugenie* grounded outside of Fort Fisher, while trying to run through the fleet in daylight. The ship was loaded with gun-powder—the Federal fleet was firing upon her—the risk of immediate death and destruction to crew and ship was overwhelming. Fry was ordered by Colonel Lamb to abandon the vessel and save his crew from death by explosion. He accordingly told all who wished to go—as for himself, he would stand by the ship and try to save the powder, which was greatly needed by the Confederate Government. Several boatloads of his men retreated to the fort; a few remained with Fry, the enemy's shells falling thick and fast around them. In the face of this great danger, Fry lightened his ship, and upon the swelling tide brought vessel and cargo safely in.

Later on he commanded the steamer *Agnes E. Fry*, named in honor of his devoted wife. In this ship he made three successful voyages, after which she was unfortunately run ashore by her pilot, and lies not far distant from the *Virginius*. Captain Fry was then placed in active service during the remainder of the war in command of the Confederate gun-boat *Morgan*, and was highly complimented by his General, Dabney H. Maury, for conspicuous bravery in action.

After the war his fortunes underwent many changes. Several undertakings met with varying success or failure. At last he went to New York in July 1893, where he hoped to secure employment in command of an ocean steamer. There he was introduced to General Quesada, agent of the Cuban Republic, who offered him the command of the steamer *Virginius*, then lying in the harbor of Kingston, Jamaica. He accepted the offer, and received a month's pay in advance, one hundred and fifty dollars, two-thirds of which he sent to his needy

***The Spanish warship* Tornado *which captured* Virginius.**

family, and reserved the remainder for his personal outfit. The *Virginius*, originally named *Virgin*, was built in Scotland in 1864, and was especially designed for a blockade runner in the Confederate service. She made several successful trips between Havana and Mobile. Being shut up in the latter port, she was used by the Confederates as a dispatch and transport steamer. For a time after the war, she was used by the Federal Government in the United States Revenue Service, but proving unsatisfactory, owing to her great consumption of coal, was sold at public auction by the United States Treasury Department to an American firm. The owners in 1870 took out American papers in legal form, and cleared her for Venezuela. From that time she was used in conveying volunteers and supplies to Cuba; and while engaged in this business under the American flag, recognized by American consuls as an American vessel, she was overhauled at sea on the 31st of October, 1873, by the Spanish man-of-war *Tornado*, and declared a prize to the Spanish Government. Fry never dreamed of greater danger—he occupied the same position he had assumed while running the Federal blockade and the same as in the recent cases of the *Commodore* and the *Bermuda*. He was a merchantman, carried no guns, made no armed resistance and flew the American flag. Notwithstanding all this, a drum-head Court-Martial was held on board the *Tornado* on the second day afterwards, the unfortunate victims condemned as pirates and sentenced to immediate execution at Santiago de Cuba, where the Spanish war ship had arrived. Even then Captain Fry and his crew, who were nearly all Americans, expected release through the intervention of the United States authorities. Vain hope! The American Consul protested, but without avail, and the butchery of these brave men began. We read from the newspaper accounts of the dreadful scene that the victims were ranged facing a wall. Captain Fry asked for a glass of water, which was given him by the friendly hand of one of his own race. He then walked with firm, unfaltering steps, to the place assigned him, and calmly awaited the volley which ended his noble life.

A touching scene occurred on the march to execution. When the brave man passed the American Consulate, he gravely saluted the bare pole, which should have borne the flag, once and again, so dear to his heart, but which had failed him in his extremity.

Although the firing party was only ten feet away, says the published account, Fry was the only one killed outright. Then ensued a horrible scene. "The Spanish butchers advanced to where the wounded men lay, writhing and moaning in agony, and placing the muzzles of their guns in the mouths of their victims, shattered their heads into fragments. Others were stabbed to death with knives and swords."

Fifty-three victims had suffered death—ninety-three more were made ready for execution; the bloody work was to be resumed, when an unlooked-for intervention came. The news had reached Jamaica, and it found in the harbor the

British man-of-war *Niobe*, under command of Captain Sir Lambton Lorraine, who, true to her name (goddess of tears) and to his instincts and honor as an Anglo-Saxton, needed no orders to speed to the rescue. Leaving in such haste that many of his men were left behind, he steamed with forced draught to Santiago. Before the anchor reached the bottom of the harbor the *Niobe*'s drums had beat to quarters and the well-trained gunners were at their stations. Commander Lorraine ignored the customary formalities; precious lives were trembling in the balance; moments were vital. Before the Spanish General was made aware of his arrival, Lorraine stood before him, and demanded that the execution be stayed. To Burriels' unsatisfactory response the brave Commander returned answer that in the absence of an American man-of-war, he would protect the interest of the Americans. Brave words, Captain Lorraine! All honor to you for them! Still the Spaniard hesitated—he had tasted human blood, but his thirst was not satisfied. Again the gallant Britisher demanded an unequivocal answer, and report says, confirmed it by a threat that he would bombard the town as he had in Honduras for the protection of the Anglo-Saxon. His prompt, decisive action arrested the bloody work, and eventually saved the lives of the remainder of the *Virginius*' crew.

On his return to England, some months later, Sir Lambton was detained some days in New York. The city authorities, animated by his gallant conduct, tendered him a public reception, which was modestly declined. Virginia City, Nevada, desiring to testify its appreciation of his noble humanity, forwarded to him a fourteen-pound brick of solid silver, upon which was inscribed his name and the incident, with the legend, "Blood is thicker than water," signifying also, in Western eulogy, "you'r a brick."

A tardy recognition of the rights of American possession was made later by the Spanish Government, and the *Virginius* delivered to an American man-of-war. While towing the unfortunate craft off Cape Fear and bound for a Northern port, the *Virginius* sprang a-leak, or some say, was scuttled, and found her grave in the ocean-depths beneath us.

Cape Fear Privateers In the War of 1812 and 1861.

The war against Great Britain was declared on the 18th of June 1812, and the United States were very successful on the high seas in several naval engagements, but it was the privateers which were fitted out under letters of marque that did the most damage. They severely distressed the enemy's commerce, and during the first seven months of the war captured about five hundred of their merchantmen and took nearly three thousand prisoners. The prizes taken by those "skimmers of the seas" were generally carried into the port nearest the scene of action, and sold with whatever cargoes they had, and immense sums were realized. Several were brought into Wilmington, having been captured near the coast; and it was not long before the port became a rendezvous for vessels of that character. They would appear suddenly in the river, remain a few hours, sometimes a day or two, and then mysteriously disappear, returning again with a prize they had succeeded in capturing.

Privateer Otway Burns (above), and his ship, the **Snap Dragon** *(below)*

Tradition reports that on one occasion two of them came in together—the *Snap Dragon*, under the command of Captain Otway Burns, who had at that time a considerable amount of local notoriety; and the *Kemp*, commanded by Captain Almida, each accompanied by a merchant vessel they had captured. In due time the vessels and cargoes were sold, but when the proceeds of the sale were to be divided a dispute arose between the two officers, each claiming that the larger portion should belong to him as he was more instrumental in securing the prize than the other. The quarrel waxed hot, and it was feared that they would come to blows at any moment, when the fiery Burns put an end to the discussion by challenging his antagonist to meet him on the sea and fight it out yardarm to yardarm. The challenge was promptly accepted; each vessel got under way immediately, and sailed for the appointed place of meeting; but while maneuvering for position, a fleet of the enemy's merchantmen, under convoy of a ship of war, hove in sight, and effectually put a stop to the contemplated duel. Adjourning their quarrel to another time (but which was never renewed), they dashed into the fleet and succeeded in capturing two or three ships with valuable cargoes, and brought them safely into port, a much better result in every way than trying to send each other to the bottom on a mere question of dollars and cents.

As showing how profitable the business was to all engaged in it, it is remembered that on one occasion a youth, in fact, a mere boy, who was a son of a citizen of Wilmington, volunteered on one of the ships, and was gone but one week, and his portion of the prize money amounted to more than six hundred dollars. He never tried it again, however, owing to the fact that a cannon-ball from one of the enemy's guns passed through his hat and slightly scalped him on its passage. He was not seriously hurt, but sufficiently so to quash any further desire on his part to become a privateersman.

In addition to the *Kemp* and *Snap Dragon* already mentioned, the waters of the Cape Fear were frequently vexed by two other craft of similar character—the *Saratoga*, the name of whose commander is not now attainable and the *General Armstrong*, Captain Sinclair, of the naval force of the United States. Quite an amusing incident is remembered in connection with Captain Sinclair, though at the time it occurred it came very near being a serious matter to him. While lying in this port, he received orders to discharge his crew and dismantle his ship which he proceeded at once to do, and carried his light spars and rigging, ammunition and fire-arms, which latter he stacked muzzle upwards, to a building which then stood on the southeast corner of Market and Second streets, while he occupied the rooms above as an officer and bed-room. This arrangement continued undisturbed for some time, but one night during the prevalence of a violent thunder-storm, a loud explosion startled the inhabitants of the town, who rushed to the spot and found that the lightning had struck the building in which Sinclair had deposited so much combustible matter, and completely destroyed it. A rigorous search was made for Sinclair, but he could not be found, and it was finally given up upon the supposition that he had been blown to pieces; but at daylight, as two of his intimates were still searching amid the ruins, one of them finally remarked: "It is no use searching any longer; old Sinclair has gone to h— at last." A smothered voice that seemed to issue from beneath their feet was heard exclaiming: "That's a lie; come here, Jacobs, and help me out." It was Sinclair in the flesh; he had been stunned by the explosion, but with the exception of a few bruises was not seriously injured. He was soon extricated from the debris under which he had been covered, and after a few remarks about the lightning, which were more emphatic than polite, he and his chums disappeared from view and were seen no more until the following day. What finally became of him we have no means of ascertaining.

When the war between the States commenced, the entire common navy was in possession of the Federal authorities, and the Confederates had no other resort than to enlist armed ships under letters of marque. Very soon quite a number of small vessels were put in commission, and reached the high seas by running the blockade; and in less than a month more than twenty prizes were taken and run into Southern ports. These vessels sailed from Charleston, Mobile, New Orleans and Wilmington, two having been fitted out in this port. It will be remembered that the *Savannah*, a schooner of fifty tons, ran the blockade at Charleston in 1861, captured one brig , but was herself soon after captured by the United States ship *Perry*, and her officers and crew were sent to Philadelphia, where they were tried for piracy, and condemned to be executed, which was only prevented by an announcement from President Davis to Mr. Lincoln that if they were executed he would surely retaliate by the execution of an equal number of United States prisoners then in the hands of the Confederate authorities. This brought the Government at Washington to their senses, and the men were subsequently exchanged as other prisoners of war. The steamers *Sumter*, *Nashville*, *Florida*, *Alabama* and *Shenandoah* were fitted out by the Confederate Government; and by this little fleet millions worth of merchandise was captured, and the foreign trade of the enemy nearly driven from the ocean. But this is a matter of general history, and our business just now is with that which is more local.

The first vessel fitted out as a privateer in Wilmington was the steam tug *Mariner* during the summer of 1861. She was owned by a company of which the late Joseph H. Flanner was president, and was armed with one twenty-four pounder forward and two nine pounders aft, and was under the command of Captain B.W. Beery. She made a cruise on the coast of North Carolina, captured one, perhaps two, vessels, and sent them into New Berne, when she returned to Wilmington. She was afterwards used during the spring and summer of 1862 by the Confederate States Government as a guard boat on the Cape Fear River, and was under command of the late Captain Joseph Price, a Wilmington boy, who was well known and greatly esteemed by our citizens. She then made one trip through the blockade to Nassau and back to this port, but was captured on the next outward trip.

The United States Government tug *Uncle Ben* came to Wilmington in April, 1861, and was taken possession of by the Confederate States Government. When the iron-clad *North Carolina* was built, the engines of the tug were taken out and used for that ship, the hull was sold and bought by a Mr. Power, of the firm of Power, Low & Co., who were engaged in the blockade business at that time. She was rigged as a schooner and armed with one twenty-pound Parrott gun and two nine-pound smooth bore guns. She went to sea as a privateer, cruised in the West Indies for some months, capturing three or four vessels, but only succeeded in getting one into port, owing to the rigid blockade. She was finally sold in Nassau and was lost on Hatteras in the Winter of 1865. After the seizure of the *Uncle Ben* by the Confederate authorities, her name was changed to *Retribution*, and she was commanded by Captain Locke, of Nova Scotia, her first officer being Captain Joseph Price, of Wilmington. These two were the only privateers fitted out in Wilmington during our late Civil War. They did not accomplish very much, and much could not have been expected of them, for they were ordinary tug boats improvised for the occasion, and not suited to the hazardous business in which they were employed. But they did some damage, nevertheless, and those who managed and had charge of them are justly entitled to praise for the skill and intrepidity they displayed under very embarrassing and adverse conditions.

Blockade-Runners.

The blockade runner Hope *captured by Union blockaders.*

This narrative would be incomplete without a more extended reference to blockade-running on the Cape Fear during the Civil War, in which this writer, then a lad of sixteen years of age, was engaged as purser on the steamers *North Health*, *Lilian* and *Susan Beirne*. The beach for many miles North and South of Bald Head is marked still by the melancholy wrecks of swift and graceful steamers then employed in this perilous enterprise. Some of the hundred vessels engaged in this traffic ran between Wilmington and the West Indies with the regularity of mail-boats, and some, even of the slowest speed, eluding the vigilance of the Federal fleet, passed unscathed twenty, thirty and forty times, making millions for their fortunate owners. One little beauty, the *Siren*, a fast boat, numbered nearly fifty voyages. The success of these ships depended, of course, in a great measure, upon the skill and coolness of their commanders and pilots. It is noteworthy that those in charge of Confederate naval officers were never taken; but many were captured, sunk or otherwise lost through no fault of the brave fellows who commanded them. There were also cases of contemptible and ludicrous cowardice on the part of officers who dearly loved to brag on shore of the perils they had passed and the dangers they had braved. Such an one commanded for a time a noted and most successful blockade-runner. He was a good navigator, but when shots from the enemy's guns fell near him, he fled ingloriously from the bridge and locked himself in his cabin, leaving his chief officer and never-failing chief engineer to extricate the ship, which their cooler heads and braver hearts accomplished with safety to all on board. The unworthy commander would then, with unspeakable audacity, relate to his admiring friends from Fort Fisher a clever story of how he had eluded the pursuing blockaders.

The names of some of the wrecks referred to may interest the traveler. The *Beauregard* and the *Venus* lie stranded on Carolina Beach; the *Modern Greece* near New Inlet; the *Antonica* on Frying Pan Shoals; the *Ella* on Bald Head; the *Spunky* and the *Georgiana McCall* on Caswell Beach; the *Hebe* and the *Dee* between Wrightsville and Masonboro. Two others lie near Lockwood's Folly bar, and others whose names are forgotten lie half buried in the sands where they may remain for centuries to come.

The loss of the *Georgiana McCall* is associated with a horrible crime—the murder of her pilot. When the ship was beached under the fire of the blockaders, Mr. Thomas Dyer did not leave with the retreating crew who sought safety ashore; he seems to have been left behind in the rush. It was known that he had a large amount of money in gold on board, and it was thought that he remained to secure it. A boat returned for him, but found his bloody corpse instead. His skull was crushed as by a blow from behind; there was no money on his person. Another man was found on board, but unhurt, who professed ignorance of his fellow. This person was the watchman, and it is said that he carried ashore a large amount of money. He was arrested on suspicion;, but there was no proof. He still lives on the river, but the cause of poor Dyer's death will probably never be known until the Great Assize.

Maffitt's Experience.

We conclude our blockade-runner's reminiscences with a few extracts from his *Tales of the Cape Fear Blockade*, published originally in the *Southport Leader*.

[Experiences of Captain John Newland Maffitt, C.S.N., in running the blockade at Wilmington.]

We are ready to depart; friends bid us farewell with lugubrious indulgence of fears for our safety, as the hazards of blockade-running had recently increased in consequence of the accumulated force and vigilance of the enemy. Discarding all gloomy prognostications, at dusk we left the harbor of Nassau. Before break of day Abaco light was sighted, a place of especial interest to Federal cruisers as the turning-point for blockade-runners. At the first blush of day we were startled by the close proximity of three American men-of-war. Not the least obeisance made they, but with shot and shell paid the early compliments of the morning.

The splintering spars and damaged bulwarks warned us of the necessity for traveling, particularly as nine hundred barrels of gun-powder constituted a

John Newland Maffitt

portion of our cargo. A chance shell exploding in the hold would have consigned steamer and all hands to Tophet. We were in capital running condition and soon passed out of range. Tenaciously our pursuers held on the chase, though it was evident that the fleet Confederate experienced no difficulty in giving them the go-by. In the zenith of our enjoyment of a refreshing sense of relief, the old cry of "sail ho"! came from aloft. The look-out announced two steamers ahead and standing for us. A system of zigzag running became necessary to elude the persistent enemy. Our speed soon accomplished this object. In about three hours the Federals faded under the horizon, and our proper course for the Cape Fear was resumed. Those who needed repose retired for the indulgence. My relaxation from official cares was of brief duration, as a gruff voice called out: "Captain, a burning vessel reported aloft, sir." Repairing on deck, by the aid of a spy-glass I could distinctly see, some four miles ahead, a vessel enveloped in smoke. Though not ourselves the subjects of charity, nevertheless we were human, and as seamen cherished the liveliest sympathy for the unfortunate who came to grief on God's watery highway. Regardless of personal interest, your true Jack Tar scorns the roll of Pharisee and prides himself upon the Samaritan proclivities that fail not to succor the sufferer by the wayside.

Increasing our speed, we quickly ran quite near to the burning vessel. She proved to be a Spanish barque, with ensign at half-mast. Out of her fore hatch arose a dense smoke. Abaft were clustered a panic-stricken group of passengers and crew. Among them several ladies were observed. An ineffectual effort had been made to hoist out the long boat, which was still suspended by the yard-arm stay tackles.

Sending an officer aloft to keep a sharp look-out that we might not be surprised by the enemy while succoring the unfortunate, the chief mate was dispatched in the cutter to render such assistance as his professional intelligence might suggest. He found the few passengers, among whom were four ladies, much calmer than the officers and crew; the latter, in place of endeavoring to extinguish the fire, which had broken out in the forecastle compartment, were confusedly hauling upon the stay-tackle in a vain effort to launch the long boat. Our mate, with his boat's crew, passed the jabbering, panic-stricken Spaniards, and proceeded at once to the forecastle, which he instantly deluged with water, and to the astonishment of all hands, speedily subdued the trifling conflagration, which proved to have resulted from the burning of a quantity of lamp-rags that had probably been set on fire by one of the crew, who carelessly emptied his pipe when about to repair on deck. The quantity of old duds that lay scattered about Jack's luxuriously furnished apartment supplied abundant material for raising a dense smoke, but the rough construction of the vessel in this locality fortunately offered nothing inflammable, and the great sensation, under the influence of a cool head, soon subsided into a farce.

The mate, who was much of a wag, enjoyed the general perturbation of the passengers, particularly on ascertaining that three of the ladies hailed from Marblehead, and were returning from a visit to an uncle who owned a well-stocked sugar plantation near Sagua Le Grande, in Cuba. A Spanish vessel bound to Halifax had been selected to convey them to a British port convenient for transportation to New York or Boston, without risk of being captured by Confederate buccaneers, whom, according to Cuban rumors, swarmed over the ocean and were decidedly anthropophageous in their proclivities.

A hail from the steamer caused our mate to make his adieus, but not before announcing himself as one of the awful Southern slave-holders they had in conversation anathematized. They could not believe that so kind and polite a gentleman could possibly be a wicked 'rebel.' 'But I am, ladies, and also a slave-owner, as is your uncle—farewell.' Instead of manifesting anger at the retort, they laughed heartily and waved their handkerchiefs in kind adieu, utterly unsuspicious of having received kindness and courtesy from a blockade-runner. We made the best of speed on our way to Wilmington.

The following day, our last at sea, proved undisturbed and pleasant. At sunset the bar bore west-northwest seventy miles distant. It would be high at half-past eleven, the proper time for crossing. Sixty miles I determined to dash off at full speed, and then run slowly for disentangling ourselves from the fleet.

None but the experienced can appreciate the difficulties that perplexed the navigator in running for Southern harbors during the war. The usual facilities rendered by the light houses and beacons had ceased to exist, having been dispensed with by the Confederate Government as dangerous abettors of contemplated mischief by the blockaders.

Success in making the destined harbors depended upon exact navigation, a knowledge of the coast, its surroundings and currents, a fearless approach, and *banishment of the subtle society of John Barleycorn. Non-experts too often came to grief, as the many hulks on the Carolina coast most sadly attest.**

Under a pressure of steam we rushed ahead, annihilating space and melting with excited fancy hours into minutes. Our celerity shortens the distance, leaving only ten miles between us and the bar. With guiding lead, slowly and carefully we feel our way.

'Captain,' observed the sedulous chief officer, as he strove to peer through the hazy atmosphere, 'it seems to me from our soundings that we should be very near the blockaders. Don't you think so?'

'I do,' was my response. 'Hist! there goes a bell—one, two, three, four, five, six, seven, half-past eleven—a decidedly good calculation, and it is high water on the bar. By jove! there are two directly ahead of us, and I think both are at anchor. Doubtless others are cruising around these indicators of the channel.'

I ordered the helm put hard a-starboard, directing the wheelman to run between the two blockaders, as it was too late to steer clear of either. Through a bank of clouds huge grim objects grew distinctly into view and necessity forced me to run the gauntlet, trusting against hope that our transit would not arouse their vigilance. They were alert vessels, for a sparkling, hissing sound was instantly followed by the fiery train of a rocket, succeeded by the dreadful calcium light, with a radiance brilliant, though brief, as to illuminate distinctly an area of miles.

'Heave to, or I'll sink you' ! shouted a gruff, imperious voice, so near that we could fancy his speaking trumpet projected over the steamer. 'Ay, ay, sir' ! was the prompt response, and to the horror of all on board, I gave the order in a loud tone: 'Stop the engine' !

Then was heard the boatswain's whistle, the calling away of cutters and the tramping of boat's crews. Our impetus had caused the steamer to nearly emerge from between the Federals.

Back your engines, sir, and stand by to receive my boats,' said the same stern voice. Affirmatively acknowledging the command, I whispered loud enough for the engineer to hear me: 'Full speed ahead, sir, and open wide your throttle valve.' The movements of the paddles for a moment deceived the Federal Commander into the belief that we were really backing, but speedily comprehending the maneuver, with very fierce execrations, he gave the order to

---

*Captain Maffitt's reference to the necessity of exact navigation on the part of masters of blockade runners during the war, recalls to us a story told by Mark Stevenson, one of the signal corps boys, about a wonderful landfall made in the *Boston* by an old friend and shipmate, Captain John W. Carrow, who said that meridian observation made him a few miles to the westward of Raleigh, and that while he was trying to reach the capital, a yankee came along and picked him up. - J.S.

fire. Drummond lights were burned, doubtless to aid the artillerists, but so radiated the mist as to raise our hull above the line of vision, causing the destructive missiles to play havoc with the sparse rigging instead of shattering our hull and probably exploding the nine hundred barrels of gunpowder with which General Johnston afterwards fought the battle of Shiloh. It certainly was a miraculous escape for both blockader and blockade-runner. We paused not recklessly, but at the rate of 16 knots an hour absolutely flew out of the unhealthy company who discourteously followed us with exploding shells and for some time kept up such a fusillade as to impress us with the belief that the blockaders had inaugurated a 'kilkenny cat muddle,' and were polishing off each other, a supposition I subsequently learned was partially correct.

The breakers warned us of danger, and the smooth water indicated the channel, through which we passed in safety, and at one o'clock in the morning we anchored off the venerable village of Smithville (now Southport). Then came the mental and physical reaction, producing a feeling of great prostration, relieved by the delightful realization of having passed through the fiery ordeal in safety and freedom.

'If after every tempest came such calms,
May the winds blow till they have weakened death,
And let the laboring barks climb hills of seas
Olympus high! and duck again as low
As hell's from heaven.'

After sunrise we proceeded in all haste to Wilmington, where our cargo was quickly discharged. Having obtained our return cargo, in company with two other blockade runners, I started for Nassau, and although the sentinels of the bar presented me with affectionate souvenirs in the way of shot and shell, they did but little damage. My companions came to grief, thereby adding to the prize fund that was shared by the Government with the officers of the blockade squadron.

Mrs. Maffitt adds: *"On the 10th of May 1862, Captain Maffitt arrived in Nassau on the steamer* Gordon, *and was there presented with a communication from Captain Bullock, Confederate Navy Agent in Europe, requesting him to take immediate charge of the gunboat* Oreto, *afterwards christened the* Florida, *which he had dispatched to Nassau, and hasten to sea. Fully appreciating the necessity for prompt action, Captain Maffitt surrendered the* Gordon *and took charge of the* Oreto, *being confirmed in the command by the Secretary of the Navy. He retained command of the* Florida *until April or June of 1864, when the state of his health compelled him to apply for detachment, which being granted, Captain Barney became his successor. At this time the* Florida *had been run into the harbor of Brest, France, for needed repairs. Captain Maffitt writes: 'The demand on my physical ability had been excessive, nor had I entirely recovered from the effects of yellow fever, which still clung to me, and was militating against my general usefulness. Consulting a distinguished physician in Paris, he pronounced my heart affected by tropical disease, and after putting me through a course of severe treatment, started me off for Sweden, not to rest, but to travel for my health."*

Shortly afterwards Captain Maffitt went to England, took command of a blockade-runner, *Lilian*, of which Mr. James Sprunt, the compiler of these notes, was the purser, and returned to the Confederacy through the port of Wilmington. He was then ordered to relieve Captain Cooke at Plymouth, N.C., from the command of the *Albemarle*, which had been so wonderfully constructed and gallantly handled by Captain Cooke in the attack on the *Southfield* and *Miami*. From this duty Captain Maffitt was soon relieved and ordered to the command of the *Owl*, one of the blockade-runners purchased from England by the Government. The 21st of December 1864, found him on board the *Owl* at Wilmington, receiving her cargo of 750 bales of cotton. With three other blockade-runners in company, he started for the bar. He escaped the Federal sentinels "without the loss of a rope-yarn," though one of his companions came to grief through an accident to machinery. Their destination was St. George, Bermuda, which they reached in safety, finding several steamers loaded and anxiously awaiting news from the Federal expedition under General Butler against Fort Fisher. Through a Halifax steamer, the Northern papers apprised them of the failure of the expedition, and in company with six other steamers and many gallant spirits, the *Owl* started on her return to Dixie, all cheered by the (to them) joyful news.

In the meantime another expedition against Fort Fisher had been fitted out under General Terry and Admiral Porter, which had been successful, and the river was in possession of the Federals.

Communicating with Lockwood's Folly, where they reported all quite and Fisher intact, Captain Maffitt steamed for the Cape Fear. At eight o'clock it was high water on the bar, and the moon would not rise before eleven. Approaching the channel, he was surprised to see but one sentinel guarding the entrance. Eluding him, he passed in. Some apprehension was excited by a conflagration at Bald Head and non-response to his signals, but as Fort Caswell looked natural and quiet, he decided to anchor off the Fort Wharf. He was immediately interviewed by the Chief of Ordnance and Artillery, E.S. Martin, and another officer, who informed him of the state of affairs and that the train was already laid for blowing up Fort Caswell. Gunboats were approaching, and in great distress Captain Maffitt hastily departed. The solitary blockader pursued him furiously for some time, and far at sea he heard the explosion that announced the fate of Caswell. As his cargo was important and much needed, Captain Maffitt determined to make an effort to enter the port of Charleston, although he had been informed that it was more closely guarded than ever before.

The rest of the story is told in Captain Maffitt's inimitable style:

The history of the five steamers in whose company I sailed from the harbor of St. George's is briefly told. Captain Wilkinson, the late gallant commander of the Chickamauga, *was too experienced and keen a cruiser to be caught in a trap. Convinced from observation that there was 'something rotten in the State of Denmark,' he judiciously returned to Bermuda. The remaining three were decoyed into New Inlet by the continuance of the Mound Light, and became easy prey under the following circumstances: First, the* Stag, *with several English officers on board as passengers, deceived by Admiral Porter's cuteness, crossed the bar, and, as was customary, anchored under the mound, there to abide the usual visit of inspection of the boarding officer of Fort Fisher. Waiting some little time without receiving the official call, the Captain naturally concluded it had been deferred until daylight. He therefore directed the steward to serve the entertainment that had been elaborately prepared to celebrate their safe arrival in the Confederacy. The gastronomic hidalgo flourished his baton of office and escorted his guests to the festive board. In shouts of revelry and with flowing bumpers, the jocund party huzzahed for Dixie, and sang her praises in songs of adulation that made the welkin ring, and aroused the sea mews from their peaceful slumbers. A pause from exhaustion having occurred in their labor of justice to the luxurious repast gave to an English captain a desired opportunity of the joyful occasion. Mysteriously rapping to enjoin attention, in the silence that followed, he solemnly arose. At a wave of his dexter, the steward, all alertness, replenished the glasses.*

"Gentlemen," said the captain, "after a successful voyage, fraught with interesting incidents and excitements, we have anchored upon the soil of battle-worn, grand old Dixie. We come, not as mercenary adventurers, to enlist under the banner of the Confederacy, but, like true knights errant, to join as honorable volunteers, the standard of the bravest lance in Christendom, that of the noble, peerless Lee (cheers, hear, hear). In gaining this Palestine of our chivalrous aspirations we have successfully encountered the more than ordinary perils of the sea, in storm, the lingering chase, and hazards of the blockade. Through all vicissitudes there was a mind to conceive, a hand to guide, a courage to execute. Gentlemen, I propose the health and happiness and speedy promotion of the officer who merits these commendations—our worthy commander."

Mingled with vociferous applause, came the customary hip ! hip ! Huzzah ! Hip ! huz—

The half uttered huzzah froze like an icicle on the petrified lips of the orator, who

'With wild surprise,
As if to marble stuck, devoid of sense.
A stupid moment, motionless stood.'

as the apparition of a Federal midshipman appeared upon the cabin stairway.

"Who commands this steamer?" was the Federal's interrogatory.

"I am that unhappy individual," groaned the commander, as reminiscences of a long confinement came painfully to his mind.

"You are a prize to Admiral Porter's squadron, and I relieve you of all further responsibility. Gentlemen, as parolled prisoners, you are at liberty to finish your repast."

The withering enunciation of capture blighted like a black frost the hopeful blossoms that had, under the inspiring influence of the sparkling Epernay, bubbled into poetic existence. One by one the lights soon faded in this banquet hall deserted, their last glimmer, falling mournfully on the debris of the unfinished congratulatory repast. Ere an hour elapsed two more unfortunates, lured by the channel lights, entered and likewise anchored off the mound, and became a prey to Admiral Porter's fleet.

My cargo being important, and the capture of Fort Fisher and Cape Fear cutting me off from Wilmington, I deemed it my duty to make an effort to enter the harbor of Charleston, in order to deliver the much-needed supplies.

I had been informed that the blockade of that port was more stringently and numerically guarded than ever before since the inauguration of hostilities. The Owl*'s speed was now accommodated to the necessary time of arriving off the bar, which was 10 p.m. Throughout the day vigilant steamers were seen along the shore inspecting inlets and coves regardless of their want of capacity for blockade purposes. This spirit of inspection and watchfulness was most assiduous, as if an order had been issued to overhaul even the coast gallinipers to see that aid and comfort in the shape of muskets and pistols were not smuggled into the needy Confederacy. Occasionally one of these constables of the sea would fire up and make a dash after the* Owl*; a little more coal and stirring up of the fire-draft was sufficient to start the blockade-runner off with such admirable speed as to convince the Federal that he was after the fleetest steamer that ever eluded the guardians of the channel-ways.*

"Seasonably making the passage, 9 o'clock p.m., found us not far from the mouth of Maffitt's channel. Anticipating a trying night and the bare possibility of capture, two bags were slung and suspended over the quarter by a stout line. In these bags were placed the Government mail not yet delivered, all private correspondence, and my war journal, including the cruise of the Florida*, besides many other papers. An intelligent quarter-master was ordered to stand by the bags with a hatchet, and the moment capture became inevitable, to cut adrift and let them sink.*

When on the western tail-end of Rattlesnake Shoal, we encountered streaks of mist and fog that enveloped stars and everything for a few moments, when it would become quite clear again. Running cautiously in one of these obscurations, a sudden lift in the haze disclosed that we were about to run into an anchored blockader. We had bare room with a hard-a port helm to avoid him some fifteen or twenty feet, when their officer on deck called out: 'Heave to, or I'll sink you'! The order was unnoticed, and we received his entire broadside, that cut away turtle-back, perforated forecastle and tore up bulwarks in front of our engine-room, wounding twelve men, some severely, some slightly. The quarter-master stationed by the mail-bags was so convinced that we were captured that he instantly used his hatchet, and sent them, well moored, to the bottom. Hence my meager account of the cruise of the Florida. *Rockets were fired as we passed swiftly out of his range of sight, and drummond lights lit up the animated surroundings of a swarm of blockaders, who commenced an indiscriminate discharge of artillery. We could not understand the reason of this bombardment, and as we picked our way out of the melee, concluded that several blockade-runners must have been discovered feeling their way into Charleston.*

After the war, in conversing with the officer commanding on that occasion, he said that a number of the steamers of the blockade were commanded by inexperienced volunteer officers, who were sometimes over zealous and excitable, and hearing the gun-boat firing into me, and seeing her rockets and signal lights, they thought that innumerable blockade-runners were forcing a passage into the harbor, hence the indiscriminate discharge of artillery, which was attended with unfortunate results to them. This was my last belligerent association with blockade-running. Entering the harbor of Charleston, and finding it in the possession of Federals, I promptly checked progress and retreated. The last order issued by the Navy Department, when all hope for the cause had departed, was for me to deliver the Owl *to Frazier, Trenholme & Co., in Liverpool, which I accordingly did.*

The Blockade Runner Don.

One of the most distinguished Commanders of the blockade running steamers was Captain Roberts (so-called) of the twin screw steamer *Don*, a quick, handy little boat, admirably adapted to the trade. I had the pleasure of knowing him personally through frequent intercourse with his signal officer, a fine young fellow, named Selden, from Virginia, and we were much impressed with the superior bearing and intelligence of this remarkable man, who afterwards became famous in the war between Russia and Turkey as Hobart Pasha, Admiral-in-Chief of the Turkish Navy.

"Captain Roberts" was really the Honorable Augustus Charles Hobart Hampden (son of the Earl of Buckinghamshire), Post Captain in the Royal Navy, and for a time Commander of Queen Victoria's yacht *Victoria and Albert.* He had seen service in the war between Emperor Nicholas, France and Great Britain in 1854, under the great Admiral Sir Charles Napier, when he commanded *HMS Driver*, and after the general order "Lads sharpen your cutlasses" boarded the Russian warships before Cronstadt, stormed the seven forts which guarded the entrance to that harbor, and sailed up the Neva even to St. Petersburg itself. Having made several runs into Wilmington during his absence from England on leave, he returned home, and, fretting under the dull routine of service ashore, accepted the command of the entire Turkish Navy at the outbreak of the war with his old antagonists, the Russians. He died in 1886 Admiral-in-Chief of the Turkish Navy, and was buried in the English cemetery at Scutari. Following is his own account of adventures in blockade-running to Wilmington:

"We left the quay at Wilmington cheered by the hurrahs of our brother blockade-runners, who were taking in and discharging their cargoes, and steamed a short distance down the river, when we were boarded to be searched and smoked. This latter extraordinary proceeding, called for perhaps by the existing state of affairs, took me altogether aback. That a smoking apparatus should be applied to a cargo of cotton seemed almost astounding. But so it was ordered, the object being to search for runaways, and strange to say, its efficacy was apparent, when, after an hour or more application of the process (which was by no means a gentle one) an unfortunate wretch, crushed almost to death by the closeness of his hiding-place, poked with a long stick till his ribs must have been like touch-wood, and smoked the color of a backwood Indian, was dragged by the heels into the daylight, ignominiously put into irons and hurled into the guard-boat. This discovery nearly caused the detention of the vessel on suspicion of our being the accomplices of the runaway; but after some deliberation we were allowed to go on.

"Having steamed down the river a distance of about twenty miles, we anchored at two o'clock in the afternoon near its mouth. We were hidden by Fort Fisher from the blockading squadron lying off the bar, there to remain till some time after nightfall. After anchoring we went on shore to take a peep at the enemy from the batteries. Its commandant, a fine, dashing young Confederate officer (Colonel Lamb), who was a firm friend to blockade-runners, accompanied us round the fort. We counted twenty-five vessels under weigh; some of them occasionally ventured within range; but no sooner had one of them done so than a shot was thrown so unpleasantly near that she at once moved out again.

"We were much struck with the weakness of Fort Fisher, which, with a garrison of twelve hundred men, and only half finished, could have been easily taken at any time since the war began by a resolute body of five thousand men making a night attack. It is true that at the time of its capture it was somewhat stronger than at the time I visited it, but even then its garrison was comparatively small and its defences unfinished. I fancy the bold front so long shown by its occupiers had much to do with the fact that such an attack was not attempted till just before the close of the war. The time chosen for our starting was eleven o'clock, at which hour the tide was at its highest on the bar at the entrance of the river. Fortunately the moon set about ten, and as it was very cloudy, we had every reason to expect a pitch-dark night. There were two or three causes that made one rather more nervous on this occasion than when leaving Bermuda.

"In the first place, five minutes after we had crossed the bar we should be in the thick of the blockaders, who always closed nearer in on the very dark nights. Secondly, our cargo of cotton was of more importance than the goods we had carried in; and thirdly, it was the thing to do to make the double trip in and out safely. There were also all manner of reports of the new plans that had been arranged by a zealous Commodore lately sent from New York to catch us all. However, it was of no use canvassing these questions, so at a quarter to eleven we weighed anchor and steamed down to the entrance of the river.

"Very faint lights, which could not be seen far at sea, were set on the beach in the same position as I have before described, having been thus placed for a vessel coming in; and bringing these astern in an exact line, that is, the two into one, we knew that we were in the passage for going over the bar. The order was then given: 'Full speed ahead,' and we shot at a great speed out to sea.

"Our troubles began almost immediately; for the cruisers had placed a rowing barge, which could not be seen by the forts, close to the entrance, to signalize the direction which any vessel that came out might take. This was done by rockets being thrown up by a designed plan from the barge. We had hardly cleared the bar when we saw this boat very near our bows, nicely placed to be run clean over, and as we were going about fourteen knots, her chance of escape would have been small had we been inclined to finish her. Changing the helm, which I did myself, a couple of spokes just took us clear. We passed so close that I could have dropped a biscuit into the boat with ease. I heard the crash of broken oars against our sides; not a word was spoken.

"I strongly suspect every man in that boat held his breath till the great white avalanche of cotton, rushing by so unpleasantly near, had passed quite clear of her.

"However, they seemed very soon to have recovered themselves, for a minute had scarcely passed before up went a rocket, which I thought a very ungrateful proceeding on their part. But they only did their duty, and perhaps they did not know how nearly they had escaped being made food for fishes. On the rocket being thrown up, a gun was fired uncommonly close to us, but as we did not hear any shot, it may have been only a signal to the cruisers to keep a sharp lookout.

"We steered a mile or two near the coast, always edging a little to the eastward, and then shaped our course straight out to sea. Several guns were fired in the pitch-darkness very near us. (I am not quite sure whether some of the blockaders did not occasionally pepper each other.) After an hour's fast steaming we felt moderately safe, and by the morning had a good offing.

"Daylight broke with thick, hazy weather, nothing being in sight. We went all right till half-past eight o'clock, when the weather cleared up, and there was a large paddle-wheel cruiser (that we must have passed very near to in the thick weather) about six miles astern of us. The moment she saw us she gave chase. After running for a quarter of an hour it was evident that, with our heavy cargo on board, the cruiser had the legs of us, and as there was a long day before us for the chase, things looked badly. We moved some cotton aft to immerse our screws well; but still the cruiser was steadily decreasing her distance from us, when an incident of a very curious nature favored us for a time.

"It is mentioned in the book of sailing directions that the course of the gulf stream (in the vicinity of which we knew we were) is in calm weather and smooth water plainly marked out by a ripple on its inner and outer edges. We clearly saw, about a mile ahead of us, a remarkable ripple, which we rightly, as it turned out, conjectured was that referred to in the book. As soon as we had crossed it we steered the usual course of the current of the Gulf Stream, that here ran from two to three miles an hour. Seeing us alter our course, the cruiser did the same; but she had not crossed the ripple on the edge of the stream, and the course she was now steering tended to keep her for some time from doing so. The result soon made it evident that the observations in the book were correct; for until she, too, crossed the ripple into the stream, we dropped her rapidly astern, whereby we increased our distance to at least seven miles.

"It was now noon, from which time the enemy again began to close with us, and at five o'clock was not more than three miles distant. At six o'clock she opened a harmless fire with the Parrott gun in her bow, the shot falling far short of us. The sun set at a quarter to seven, by which time she had got so near that she managed to send two or three shots over us, and was steadily coming up.

"Luckily, as night came on, the weather became very cloudy, and we were on the dark side of the moon, now setting in the West, which occasionally breaking through the clouds astern of the cruiser, showed us all her movements, while we must have been very difficult to make out, though certainly not more than a mile off. All this time she kept firing away, thinking, I suppose, that she would frighten us into stopping. If we had gone straight on, we should doubtless have been caught, so we altered our course two points to the eastward. After steaming a short distance, we stopped quite still, blowing off steam under water, not a spark or the slightest smoke showing from the funnel; and we had the indescribable satisfaction of seeing our enemy steam past us, still firing ahead at some imaginary vessel.

"This had been a most exciting chase and a very narrow escape; night only saved us from a New York prison. All this hard running had made an awful hole in our coal-bunkers, and as it was necessary to keep a stock for a run off the Bahama Islands, we were obliged to reduce our expenditure to as small a quantity as possible. However, we were well out to sea, and after having passed the line of cruisers between Wilmington and Bermuda, we had not much to fear until we approached the British possessions of Nassau and the adjacent Islands, where two or three very fast American vessels were cruising, although five hundred miles from American waters. I am ignorant, I confess, of the laws of blockade, or indeed if a law there be that allows its enforcement and penalties to be enacted, five hundred miles away from the ports blockaded. But it did seem strange that the men-of-war of a nation at peace with England should be allowed to cruise off her ports to stop and examine trading vessels of all descriptions, to capture and send to New York, for adjudication vessels on the mere suspicion of their being intended blockade-runners so near to the shore that on one occasion the shot and shell fell into a fishing village, and that within sight of an English man-of-war lying at anchor in the harbor at Nassau. Surely it is time that some well-understood laws should be made, and rules laid down, or such doings will sooner or later recoil on their authors.

"Having so little coal on board, we determined on making for the nearest point on the Bahama Islands, and luckily reached a queer little island called Green Turtle Quay, on the extreme North of the group, where was a small English colony, without being seen by the cruisers. We had not been there long, however, before one of them came sweeping round the shore and stopped unpleasantly near to us; even though we were inside the rock, she hovered about outside, not a mile from us.

"We were a tempting bait, but a considerable risk to snap, and I suppose the American captain could not quite make up his mind to capture a vessel (albeit a blockade-runner piped full of cotton) lying in an English port, insignificant though that port might be. We had got a large white English ensign hoisted on a pole, thereby showing the nationality of the rock, should the cruiser be inclined to question it. After many longing looks she steamed slowly away, much to our satisfaction. Goals were sent to us from Nassau the next day, which having been taken on board, we weighed anchor, keeping close to the reefs and islands all the way. We steamed towards that port, and arrived safely, having made the in-and-out voyages, including the time in unloading and loading at Wilmington, in sixteen days.

"To attempt to describe at length the state of things at this unusually tranquil and unfrequented little spot is beyond my powers. I will only mention some of its most striking features. Nassau differed much from Wilmington, inasmuch as at the latter place there was a considerable amount of poverty and distress, and men's minds were weighed with many troubles and anxieties; whereas at Nassau everything at the time I speak of was *couleur de rose.* Every one seemed prosperous and happy. You met with calculating, far-seeing men who were steadily employed in feathering their nests, let the war in American end as it might; others, who in the height of enthusiasm for the Southern cause, put their last farthing into Confederate securities, anticipating enormous profits; some men, careless and thoughtless, living for the hour, were spending their dollars as fast as they made them, forgetting that they 'would never see the like again.' There were rollicking captains and officers of blockade-runners, and drunken, swaggering crews; sharpers looking out for victims; Yankee spies and insolent, worthless free niggers—all these combined made a most heterogeneous, though interesting, crowd.

"The inhabitants of Nassau, who, until the period of blockade-running, had with some exceptions, subsisted on a precarious and somewhat questionable livelihood gained by wrecking, had their heads as much turned as the rest of the world. Living was exorbitantly dear, as can well be imagined, when the captain of a blockade runner could realize in a month a sum as large as the Governor's salary. The expense of living was so great that the officers of the West India regiment quartered here had to apply for special allowance, and I believe their application was successful. The hotel, a large building, hitherto a most ruinous speculation, began to realize enormous profits. In fact, the almighty dollar was spent as freely as the humble cent had been before this golden era in the annals of Nassau.

"As we had to stay here till the time for the dark nights came round again, we took it easy, and thoroughly enjoyed all the novelty of the scene. Most liberal entertainment was provided free by our owner's agent, and altogether we found Nassau very jolly; so much so that we felt almost sorry when 'time' was called, and we had to prepare for another run. In fact, it was pleasanter in blockade-running to look backwards than forwards, especially if one had been so far in good luck.

"All being ready, we steamed out of Nassau harbor, and were soon again in perilous waters. We had a distant chase now and then—a mere child's play to us after our experience—and on the third evening of our voyage we were pretty well placed for making a run through the blockading squadron as soon as it was dark. As the moon rose at twelve o'clock, it was very important that we should get into port before she threw a light upon the subject.

"Unfortunately, we were obliged to alter our course or stop so often to avoid cruisers that we ran our time too close; for, as we were getting near to the line of blockade, a splendid, three-quarter size moon rose, making everything as clear as day. Trying to pass through the line of vessels ahead with such a bright light shining would have been madness; in fact, it was dangerous to be moving about at all in such clear weather, so we steamed towards the land on the extreme left of the line of cruisers, and having made it out, went quite close inshore and anchored.

"By lying as close as we dared to the beach, we must have had the appearance of forming part of the low sand hills, which were about the height and color of the vessel, the wood on their tops forming a background, which hid the small amount of funnel and mast that showed above the decks. We must have been nearly invisible, for we had scarcely been an hour at anchor, when a gun-boat came steaming along the shore very near to the beach; and while we breathlessly watching her, hoping she would go past, she dropped anchor alongside of us, a little outside where we were lying—so close that we not only heard every order that was given on board, but could almost make out the purport of the ordinary conversation of the people on her decks. A pistol shot would have easily reached us. Our position was most unpleasant, to say the least of it. We could not stay where we were, as it only wanted two hours to daybreak. If we had attempted to weigh anchor, we must have been heard doing so. However, we had sufficient steam at command to make a run for it. So, after waiting a little to allow the cruiser's fires to get low, we knocked the pin out of the shackle of the chain on deck, and easing the cable down into the water, went ahead with one engine and astern with the other, to turn our vessel round head to seaward.

"Imagine our consternation when, as she turned, she struck the shore before coming half round (she had been lying with her head inshore, so now it was pointed along the beach, luckily in the right direction, *i.e.*, lying from the cruiser). There was nothing left to us but to put on full speed, and if possible force her from the obstruction, which after two or three hard bumps we succeeded in doing.

"After steaming quite close to the beach for a little way, we stopped to watch the gun-boat, which, after resting for an hour or so, weighed anchor and steamed along the beach in the opposite direction to the way we had been steering, and was soon out of sight. So we steamed a short distance inshore and anchored again. It would have been certain capture to have gone out to sea just before daybreak, so we made the little craft as invisible as possible, and remained all the next day, trusting to our luck not to be seen. And our luck favored us, for although we saw several cruisers at a distance, none noticed us, which seems almost miraculous.

"Thus passed Christmas day, 1863, and an anxious day it was to all of us. We might have been landed in a dismal swamp, and we would have been obliged to go into Wilmington for our cargo of cotton.

"When night closed in we weighed anchor and steamed to the entrance of the river, which, from our position being so well defined, we had no difficulty in making out. We received a broadside from a savage little gunboat quite close in shore, her shot passing over us, and that was all. We got comfortably to the anchorage about half-past eleven o'clock, and so ended our second journey in.

"It is not my intention to inflict on my readers any more anecdotes of my doings in the D—n, suffice it to say that I had the good luck to make six round trips in her, in and out of Wilmington, and that I gave her over to the chief officer and went home to England with my spoils.

"On arriving at Southampton, the first thing I saw in the *Times* was a paragraph headed 'The capture of the 'D—n.' Poor little craft ! I learned afterwards how she was taken, which I will relate, and which will show that she died game.

"The officer to whom I gave over charge was as fine a specimen of a seaman as can well be imagined, plucky, cool and determined, and by the way, he was a bit of a medico, as well as a sailor; for by his beneficial treatment of his patients we had very few complaints of sickness on board. As our small dispensary was close to my cabin I used to hear the conversation that took place between C— and his patients. I will repeat one:

C.—'Well, my man, what's the matter with you?'

Patient.—'Please, sir, I've got pains all over me.'

C.—'Oh, all over you are they; that's bad.'

"Then, during the pause, it was evident something was being mixed up, and I could hear C—say: 'Here, take this and come again in the evening.' (Exit patient.)

" Then C—said to himself: I don't think he'll come again; he has got two drops of the croton. Skulking rascal, pains all over him, eh?'

"I never heard the voice of that patient again; in fact, after a short time we had no cases of sickness on board.

"C—explained to me that the only medicine he served out, as he called it, was croton oil; and that none of the crew came twice for treatment.

"Never having run through the blockade as commander of a vessel (though he was with me all the time and had as much to do with our luck as I had), he was naturally very anxious to get safely through. There can be no doubt that the vessel had lost much of her speed, for she had been very hardly pushed on several occasions. This told sadly against her, as the result will show.

"On the third afternoon after leaving Nassau she was in a good position for attempting the run when night came on. She was moving stealthily about waiting for the evening, when suddenly, on the weather, which had been hitherto thick and hazy, clearing up, she saw a cruiser unpleasantly near to her, which bore down under steam and sail, and it soon became probable that the poor little D—n's twin screws would not save her this time, well and often as they had done so before.

"The cruiser, a large, full-rigged corvette, was coming up hand over hand, carrying a strong breeze, and the days of the 'D—n' seemed numbered, when C—tried a ruse worthy of any of the heroes of naval history.

"The wind, as I said, was very fresh, with a good deal of sea running.

"On came the cruiser till the 'D—n' was almost under her bows, and shortened sail in fine style. The moment the men were in the rigging, going aloft to furl the sails, C—put his plan into execution. He turned his craft head to the wind, and steamed deliberately past the corvette at not fifty yards distance. She with great way on, went nearly a quarter of a mile before she could turn.

"I have it from good authority that the order was not given to the marines on the man-of-war's poop to fire at the plucky little craft who had so fairly out-maneuvred the cruiser, for out-maneuvred she was to all intents and purposes.

"The two or three guns that had been cast loose during the chase had been partially secured, and left so while the men had gone aloft to furl the sails, so that not a shot was fired as she went past. Shortly after she had done so, the cruiser opened fire with her bow guns, but with the sea that was running she could do no harm, being without any top weights.

"The 'D—n' easily dropped the corvette with her heavy spars astern, and was soon far ahead, so much so that when night came on the cruiser was shut out of sight in the darkness.

"After this the 'D—n' deserved escape, but it was otherwise fated.

"The next morning when day broke she was within three miles of one of the new fast vessels, which had come out on her trial trip, flying light alas! She had an opportunity of trying her speed advantageously to herself. She snapped up the poor 'D—n' in no time and took her to the nearest port.

"I may mention that the 'D—n' and her captain were well known and much sought after by the American cruisers. The first remark that the officer on coming aboard her was: 'Well, Captain Roberts, so we have caught you at last !' and he seemed much disappointed when he was told that the captain they so particularly wanted went home in the last mail.

"The corvette, which had been chased and beaten by the 'D—n' the day before, was lying in the port into which she was taken. Her captain, when he saw the prize said, 'I must go on board and shake hands with the gallant fellow who commands that vessel!' and he did so, warmly complimenting C—on the courage he had shown, thus proving that he could appreciate pluck and that American naval men did not look down on blockade-running as a grievous sin, hard work as it gave them to put a stop to it. They were sometimes a little severe on men who, after having been fairly caught in a chase at sea, wantonly destroyed their compasses, chronometers, etc., rather than let them fall into the hands of the cruiser's officers.

"I must say that I was always prepared, had I been caught, to have made the best of things, to have given the officer who came to take possession all that they had fairly gained by luck having declared on their side, and to have a farewell glass of champagne with the new tenant at the late owner's expense. The treatment received by persons captured engaged in running the blockade differed very materially.

"If a *bona fide* American man-of-war of the Old School made the capture, they were always treated with kindness by their captors. But there were among the officers of vessels picked up hurriedly and employed by the Government a very rough lot, who rejoiced in making their prisoners as uncomfortable as possible. They seemed to have only one good quality, and this was that there were among them many freemasons, and frequently a prisoner found the advantage of having been initiated into the brotherhood.

"The 'D—n' crew fell into very good hands, and till they arrived at New York were comfortable enough; but the short time they spent in prison there, while the vessel was undergoing the mockery of a trial in the Admiralty Court, was far from pleasant. However, it did not last very long—not more than ten days; and as soon as they were free most of them went back to Nassau or Bermuda ready for work.

"C— came to England and told me all his troubles. Poor fellow! I am afraid his services were not half appreciated as they ought to have been, for success, in blockade-running, as in everything else, is a virtue, whereas bad luck, even though accompanied with pluck of a hero, is always more or less a crime not to be forgiven."

Pilots in a Storm.

We have referred to the hard life of these toilers of the sea, who often win their bread at the risk of their lives.

Before the recent change in the method of boarding inward-bound vessels, pilotage business was open to general competition, and as about sixty licensed men depended upon their profession for a living, many of them took their lives in their hands and cruised in frail boats and heavy weather for fifty and a hundred miles at sea, searching for vessels in need of their assistance.

We illustrate some of the hardships to which they were exposed by the following thrilling story of the great storm in 1877 by Colonel Waddell, which will doubtless be read with interest:

"On April 12th, 1877, one of the most terrific storms that ever visited the North Carolina coast began and lasted for three days, culminating on the 15th off Cape Fear. It was fearfully destructive to life and property, wrecking many ships with their crews and cargoes, and burying them beneath the waves. One large three-masted vessel broke up and parts of her drifted into Smithville Bay, a prize for the wreckers, which not only illustrated the force of the storm, but was a curiosity in the strength of its structure.

"All her bolts," said one who examined pieces of the wreck, "are brass, four, six and even eight feet long; the knees are solid iron and the outside planking six inches through and of stout pine."

There were two Smithville pilot-boats, the *Mary K. Sprunt* and the *Uriah Timmons*, cruising off the coast at the time the storm commenced, and finding it impossible to make a harbor, they were compelled to stand off and try to weather it out.

The *Mary K. Sprunt* had a crew of five men, viz: Christopher Pinner, Robert Walker, Charles Dosher, Jr., Thomas Grissom and Lawrence Gillespie, the cook. They were brave and skilful men, but after a desperate struggle, in which all that the most skilful seamanship could accomplish had been exhausted, she went down with all on board. On the 28th, the body of Tom Grissom was found by the pilot-boat *H. Westerman*, floating at sea, about nine miles out, and the pilots also found the *Mary K. Sprunt* lying on the bottom, in eleven and a half fathoms, her white sails torn into ribbons, shining up through the blue depths and undulating with the motion of the restless sea.

The *Uriah Timmons* had a crew of four men, C.C. Morse, Julius Weeks, Joseph Thompson, Jr., and Joseph Arnold, and of these Arnold was the youngest, hardly twenty years of age. Every precaution was taken upon the approach of the storm, and with only enough canvas to steer by, she faced it. All day and night of the 12th, she leaped and rolled and dived like a cork on the waves, while the storm increased in fury every hour. Day dimly dawned on the 13th over a howling waste of waters, whose billows heaved her skyward, leaving great chasms, down whose sides she rushed headlong as if to certain destruction. A gray mist shrouded sky and sea, and the storm-fiend shrieked with that unearthly voice which once heard, is never forgotten. Cowering before the blast, licked from stem to stern by the tongue of the hungry sea, groaning and sobbing as she strained up the watery heights or slid down the hissing gulfs, the little ship drove on. Although carrying but thirteen yards of canvas, the jaw of the boom was eating into the foremast like a famished animal. With the advancing day, the fury of the gale increased. It seemed as if the spirit of an angry god walked the waters and was lashing the elements in his wrath. A mountainous wave, leading the host of billows, would rush toward the little vessel, and toppling as if to fall upon and crush her, would lower its crest, and gliding beneath her trembling timbers, lift her almost clear in the air and toss her, toy-like to another billow, while the multitudinous ocean roared with rage.

The crew of the *Timmons*, brave and hardy mariners as they were, and accustomed to storms on the broad water from childhood, stood appalled at the surpassing terrors of this awful scene.

Lashed in the cockpit, with vise-like grip upon the wheel and drenched to the skin, sat Julius Weeks, who had been there thirteen hours. At last, towards afternoon, to the utter dismay of all on board, the jib-halyard parted, and flying down the stay, the jib hung, bag-like, below the bowsprit, and instantly the sea, like a ravenous beast, fell upon it and held it down as if devouring it. The brave boat struggled hard to lift her bow, thus weighed, from the waves, and with a mighty effort succeeded. Again the sea seized and held the bellying jib, and again the gallant boat, struggling, raised it clear, but with weakening power. The pilots now realized that, unless immediately released from this new and frightful danger, the *Timmons* could not hold her head up, but must founder after a few more struggles; but, feeling assured that an attempt to reach the jib-stay would result in certain death, as no man could ever remain on the bow-spirit, even if he could reach it, they were stricken with despair. "We are lost," exclaimed one; "unless we can cut that jib-halliard, we are certainly gone! A man can't live there, but it is our only hope."

Who should do this desperate deed? They hurriedly agreed to decide the matter by lot, and were about to proceed to do so, when Joe Arnold, who was now at the wheel, shouted: "Hold on, men! You are all married and have families; I am a single man; let me try it, and if I go overboard it will be all right," and surrendering the wheel, the brave boy drew his sheath-knife, and putting it between his teeth, started forward. It was impossible to keep his footing, and so he crawled cautiously along the deck (there is no railing to a pilot-boat), holding on as best he could. His companions watched him with the eagerness of men whose only hope of life hung on his steadiness of nerve and physical strength. If he reached the bowsprit in safety, the sea would certainly beat him off, for every time the little craft plunged, the waves seemed to leap up to meet her. For the first time since childhood fervent prayers rose to the lips of these men, who had "followed the sea" all their days without thinking of Him whose presence they now realized as they had never realized it before, and tears flowed freely down their bronzed faces. Joe reached the foremast, and just then the *Timmons* rolled nearly on her beam-ends. He threw his arms around the mast and held on. The storm was now indescribably fierce and terrific. As the vessel slowly recovered herself, he loosened his hold and crawled towards the bowsprit. He reached it, got astride of it, locked his arms around it, drew a long breath, and then with a rush, the Timmons buried her head and Joe disappeared in the seething waters.

The crew held their breath in an agony of suspense, while their eyes strained towards the boiling foam which engulfed him. In a moment the staunch craft, as if conscious of the heroic effort for her relief, and stimulated by it to renewed exertion, bounded forward and upward through the dashing waters. And on the bowsprit, which was pointing skyward, the crew saw Joe straightening himself into a sitting position, the knife still held in his clenched teeth, and preparing to crawl still further out. Again and again this scene was enacted, each plunge and rise finding the hero nearer the object at which he aimed, while the crew fairly ached with the intensity of their emotions.

He reached it at last, and watching the most favorable opportunity, released his right arm, snatched the knife from his teeth, and with a swift and powerful stroke cut the jib-halliard through, as the trembling vessel started down another sea, restored the knife to its place, again clasped the bowsprit in his arms, and again disappeared, but only for a moment, for the *Timmons*, now relieved of the weight which held her down, sprang out of the threatening gulf as with new life inspired. It was a great relief, but the tempest was still at its height, and now both Joe and the crew realized that the most hazardous part of this heroic enterprise was still before him, namely getting back to the deck again. It was not like coming down from aloft. He had to repeat the desperate performance backward.

Slowly, and still astride the bowsprit, and still alternately plunged in the sea and lifted high in the air, he began the fearful task. Every instant was a crisis, every moment threatened to be his last; but slowly and steadily he approached the deck.

Finally he reached it, slid along the foremast, clasped it as before, and at last, crawling, laid himself down exhausted amid his awe-struck companions.

The storm still howled, the sea was still awful, and night was coming on—another night of horrors—but the *Timmons* carried her head free, and a feeling akin to confidence was beginning to take place of despair in the breasts of the crew.

They passed in the gloom of the starless night upon that wild waste of waters, clinging to the hope that with the coming of another the storm would pass. And their hope was not in vain. Gradually the violence of the wind abated, although the sea leaped frantically, and by the next morning had ceased to be alarming. They looked eagerly for the land, gave more sail, and in a few hours recognized points which assured them that they were off Georgetown, S.C. With grateful hearts they steered for the bar and entered the bay in safety, with no other damage to the *Timmons* than the loss of her boats, sails and rigging, a foremast rubbed almost in two and some strained timbers.

Joe Arnold still lives and pursues his calling, and he will be greatly astonished if he ever sees this account of his heroism, for he is modest and does not think he did anything worth talking about.

Homeward Bound.

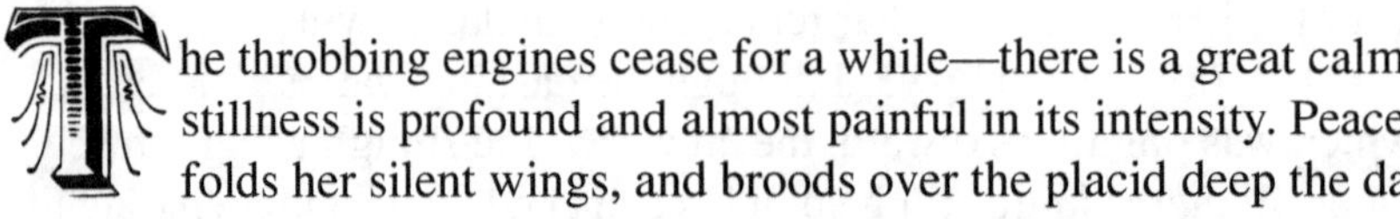

The throbbing engines cease for a while—there is a great calm—the stillness is profound and almost painful in its intensity. Peace gently folds her silent wings, and broods over the placid deep the day is waning, and as we view the majestic grandeur of the scene, our hearts respond to the prophetic vision of the lonely exile on Patmos, who saw beyond the barrier of his mortal life the walls of jasper, and the city of pure gold, where there shall be no more sea.

The sun is sinking in the Western ocean, bathed in a sea of glory, "The image of Eternity, the throne of the Invisible." Ever changing clouds of silver, of amber, of gold, reflect the beauty of the Better Land, which eye hath not seen, nor the heart of man conceived. "A realm where the rainbow never fades—where the stars are spread out like the islands that slumber on the ocean, and where the beautiful beings who now pass before us like shadows, shall remain forever in our presence."

Above the sighing pines the crescent queen of night is shining, tinging with quivering yellow rays the silent shadowy river. Weary nature seems to sleep. Our steamer's head is toward the ancient city whose honored name she bears. The anchor lights are gleaming in the harbor—the warning whistle tells us that the time to part has come; like

"Ships that pass in the night, and speak each other in passing,
Only a signal shown and a distant voice in the darkness:
So on the Ocean of Life we pass and speak one another,
Only a look and a voice, 'then darkness again and silence."

J.S.

Men of the Past.

If a man die shall he live again?" was the inquiry of the Patriarch centuries ago, and inspiration answers in regard to the spiritual and our own knowledge and experience to that of the natural life, and each in the affirmative, for there really is no death. A man's good and great actions survive after he himself has departed, and keep him in continued remembrance, not only by his contemporaries, but by posterity, for his name and the story of his life exists forever and is held up as a beacon light and an example to incite future generations to noble deeds and lofty enterprises. Michaelangelo, Titian, Raphael, and other great masters still live though long since passed away, and speak to us to-day through their works, and the majesty of their deeds in words, of "living light;" and they will live forever. And so with others the world over; they are found in every country, and among all peoples, and monuments are erected to commemorate their deeds, and poetry and song embalm their memories in the hearts of a grateful people. There are heroes in every walk in life, even the humblest, and who well deserve the plaudits of the world, but whose names do not appear upon the scroll of fame, whose lives are an example for others, and who have benefited the world by acts of heroism unknown beyond the limits of their own contracted surroundings.

Within the grandest sacred building of the British Kingdom may be seen this inscription upon the tomb of its renowned architect and builder: "Beneath lies Christopher Wren, architect of this church and city, who lived more than ninety years, not for himself but for the public. Reader, do you seek his monument? Look around you!" A modest and unassuming statement, yet how grand and beautiful in its simplicity, and how well intended to excite emotion. He lived not for himself, but for the public, and that noble virtue was illustrated years ago by the people of the then small town of Wilmington to their great detriment, and to the ruin of many, while others have reaped the benefit of their generous and unselfish public spirit. In 1835 it was determined to build the Wilmington & Weldon Railroad, and books were opened for subscription to its stock. The citizens of Wilmington, in their individual capacity, subscribed to a greater amount of the stock than the value of the entire property of the town listed for taxation, an act unprecedented in our history and never equaled so far as is known. They were determined that the road should be built, and it was done; but very many of them beggared themselves in the effort, while others received all the benefit of the sacrifices they had made. It is painful to recall the fact that nearly all the early friends of that great undertaking have passed away and are well-nigh forgotten, and in many cases their very graves are undistinguishable from those of the multitude sleeping around. Is it not a reflection upon our people that neither marble nor bronze should have been erected to mark the spot where their ashes repose?

In the following list are some of the names of the most active friends of that enterprise, who undertook the great work for the public good; also some of the names of others who acted well their part in later years, and deserved a place in the memory of our Wilmington people:

Edward B. Dudley, Governor, and first President of the Wilmington & Weldon Railroad.

James Owen, Member of Congress, and second President of the Wilmington & Weldon Railroad.

Alexander McRae, Civil Engineer and third President of the Wilmington & Weldon Railroad.

P.K. Dickinson, mill owner, successful merchant.

Alexander Anderson, merchant and Mayor of the town.

O. G. Parsley, mill owner and large real estate holder, Bank President, Railroad President, Mayor, and a man of great firmness and integrity.

Asa A. Brown, Editor of the *Chronicle*.

Aaron Lazarus, prominent merchant.

Thomas H. Wright, Physician and President Bank of Cape Fear.

Wm. B. Mears, Lawyer and Planter and eminent citizen.

E.P. Hall, Merchant and President State National Bank.

F.J. Hill, Physician and Planter.

Wm. A. Wright, Lawyer, prominent and useful citizen.

Joseph H. Watters, prominent planter and citizen.

John McRae, Merchant, and first Mayor of Wilmington.

Henry Nutt, Father of the improvements on Cape Fear River, and foremost in public spirit.

Edward Kidder, originator and promoter of Clarendon Water Works, mill owner, and the first to utilize saw dust for fuel, friend of popular education.

Gilbert Potter, mill owner, successful merchant.

James S. Green, first Secretary and Treasurer of the Wilmington & Weldon Railroad, until his death, 1862.

Wm. A. Williams, dry goods merchant.

Robert H. Cowan, Sr., planter.

John Wooster, dry goods merchant and turpentine distiller.

James F.McRee, physician, planter and botanist.

James H. Dickson, physician of great attainments.

Z. Latimer, wealthy merchant.

Wm. J. Harriss, prominent physician.

Christopher Dudley, for many years Post Master of the city.

Wm. C. Lord, Collector of the Port, sound judgment and great business qualifications.

John Hill, physician, Cashier and President Bank of Cape Fear.

R.W. Brown, a good merchant and esteemed for his probity.

Geo. W. Davis, merchant, and familiar with all matters of business.

J.W.K. Dix, prominent merchant.

John C. Latta, merchant and Christian gentleman.

Isaac Northrop, large mill owner.

Talcott Burr, Jr., distinguished journalist.

James T. Miller, Mayor of the town and Chairman County Court.

T.C. Worth, generous hearted merchant.

Rt. Rev. Bishop Atkinson, Bishop of the Diocese of North Carolina.

Cyrus S. VanAmringe, a gifted young business man.

C. L. Grafflin, incorporator and first Superintendent of Navassa Guano Company.

T. Savage, Cashier Commercial Bank.

E.T. Hancock, merchant of prominence.

H. R. Savage, Cashier Cape Fear Bank.

W.T. Daggett, successful merchant.

Daniel B. Baker, prominent lawyer.

W.M. Parker, merchant and prominent in religious circles.

N. Green Daniel, a thorough merchant and faithful friend.

N.N. Nixon, the largest peanut planter of his day.

Daniel L. Russell, planter and politician.

Eli Murray, merchant, possessing many good traits.

R.H. Cowan, accomplished scholar and orator.

C. D. Myers, inspector and Captain in C.S.A.

John A. Taylor, a public spirited citizen and successful man of business.

Rev. Dr. Drane, the beloved Rector of St. James.

W.A. Berry, physician, and scholar.

Dougald McMillan, large and prominent planter.

F.J. Cutlar, physician, and a most estimable gentleman.

Samuel Davis, long associated with our newspapers.

Robert Strange, the able jurist, accomplished scholar and chivalrous gentleman.

W.S. Anderson, jeweler and alderman.

R.S. French, Judge, and ornament of the bar.

Eli W. Hall, a notable citizen and lawyer.

Wm. McRae, Brigadier General, Confederate Army.

S.H. Morton, prominent merchant.

D.R. Murchison, successful merchant, endowed with great boldness and sound judgment.

W.L. Smith, successful insurance agent and Mayor of the City.

Isaac B. Grainger, Bank President of great attainments.

J.L. Hathaway, a prosperous and conservative merchant.

Levi A. Hart, prominent citizen, proprietor Foundry Works.

Thomas L. Colville, inventor, master machinist.

W.H. McRary, a successful merchant.

John C. Bailey, Iron Founder and machinist.

John Dawson, Mayor and merchant.

James Anderson, merchant.

J.C. Walker, a skillful physician and amiable gentleman.

James M. Stevenson, inspector and Captain in C.S.A.

James Dawson, successful banker.

Robert B. Wood, architect, builder and honored citizen.

Geo. R. French, a prosperous merchant and philanthropist.

Frank Brown, active merchant.

Wm. S. Ashe, Member of Congress and President Wilmington & Weldon Railroad.

Robert G. Rankin, prominent merchant, a gallant Captain of Artillery.

C.S.A., who fell in the last battle of the war, pierced by three bullets; his garments showed eleven bullet holes.

Rev. Father Murphy, who died at his post during the yellow fever epidemic, beloved by all.

Rev. John L. Pritchard, the faithful pastor and loving friend.

J.A. Engelhard, Editor of Journal and Secretary of State.

Thos. D. Wallace, President Wilmington & Manchester Railroad.

Alexander Sprunt, British Vice Consul and merchant.

S.D. Wallace, President Wilmington & Weldon Railroad and Bank Cashier.

W.L. Saunders, Secretary of State and Historian.

Geo. Davis, lawyer, statesman and beloved citizen.

A.L. Price, Founder of the *Wilmington Journal.*

Edwin E. Burruss, banker, a warm-hearted and genial friend.

R.R. Bridgers, President Wilmington & Weldon and Wilmington, Columbia & Augusta Railroads.

George Chadbourn, mill owner and President National Bank.

John L. Holmes, prominent lawyer.

Donald MacRae, President Navassa Guano Company, and a successful financier.

P.W. Fanning, Grand Master of Masons and sterling citizen.

M. London, a prominent member of the bar.

E.A. Anderson, a skilful physician and an honor to the profession.

A.H. VanBokkelen, the friend of Confederate soldiers, one of our fore-most citizens.

Will, Geo. Thomas, an accomplished physician and a prominent citizen.

John C. Heyer, successful merchant and honest man.

Thomas F. Wood, "the beloved physician" and botanist.

Robert E. Calder, one of the noblest of Wilmington's sons.

F.J. Lord, Spanish Vice Counsul and an honest man.

Julius A. Bontiz, the progressive editor.

T.D. Love, a gallant Confederate soldier.

B.R. Dunn, Engineer of Roadway, Atlantic Coast Line.

B.F. Mitchell, a most worthy citizen, grain merchant.

L.C. Jones, Superintendent of the Carolina Central Railroad.

O.G. Parsley, Jr. once an active business man, and subsequently Post Master of the City.

Geo. Sloan, Superintendent of the Wilmington Compress and Warehouse Company.

Jos. Price, Harbor Master and gallant soldier.

J. Francis King, prominent physician.

F.W. Potter, physician, and Superintendent of Health.

G. H. Kelly, weigher and inspector.

J.J. Hedrick, merchant, and a brilliant officer of the Confederacy.

Henry Flanner, druggist and soldier.

R.E. Heide, Danish Vice Consul and merchant.

W.P. Elliott, identified with the trade of the Upper Cape Fear.

M.M. Katz, dry goods merchant.

L.B. Huggins, successful merchant.

Wm. G. Fowler, coal merchant.

L. Vollers, merchant.

Edward Savage, a prominent merchant, and afterwards Colonel in the Confederate army.

Thomas J. Southerland, liveryman and Captain in C.S.A.

James F. McRee, Surgeon Confederate States army.

E.S. Tennent, physician, notably allied to our Wilmington people, who fell at Secessionville, S.C., a Confederate soldier.

A.H. Cutts, an experienced and trusted railroad officer.

G.A. Peck, hardware merchant and excellent citizen.

T.F Toon, Colonel C.S.A., a friend of the sailor.

Hugh Waddell, a notable lawyer and eminent citizen.

James A. Willard, merchant.

F.A. Newbury, merchant.

Robert Morrison, coal dealer.

Alfred A. Moffitt, merchant and a good man.

Willie Meares, a beloved young man.

W.H. Lippitt, prominent druggist.

Frank Darby, lawyer.

Junius D. Gardner, bank officer.

Alexander Johnson, excellent merchant and citizen.

John Judge, experienced accountant and merchant.

H.B. Eilers, excellent citizen and Christian gentleman.

M.J. DeRosset, Sr., prominent physician.

James Fulton, editor of the *Journal*.

Joshua G. Wright, prominent lawyer.

Thomas Loring, newspaper editor.

J.C. Abbott, General U.S. Army, large mill-owner.

M.J. DeRosset, brilliant scholar and noted physician.

Joshua Walker, physician, amiable gentleman.

William B. Giles, honored and beloved Christian gentleman.

Richard A. Bradley, prominent mill owner.

John Hampden Hill, prominent planter, eminent citizen and physician.

Wm. N. Peden, a prominent citizen for fifty years.

S.M. West, an upright merchant.

Gaston Mears, Colonel C.S.A.

Louis H. DeRosset, a gifted business man.

Joseph S. Murphy, accountant and successful merchant.

John E. Lippitt, successful merchant.

Hugh W. McLaurin, expert accountant, and others whose names are not at this moment remembered.

Among the younger men, who have passed away in recent years, and who had developed many good traits and bid fair to be classed among the prominent men of our city, we recall L.P. Davis, T.C. DeRosset, J.B. Willard, L.S.F. Brown, John H. Daniel, Edwin A. Northrop, Jas. McR. Cowan, John MacRae, Thos. J. Sinclair, Duval French, Louis J. Poisson, Norwood Gause, James Elliott, Herbert Perdew, Murray Grant, William Grant.

It may be appropriate and a matter of interest to some to recall in connection with the "Men of the Past" the name of Thomas Godfrey, son of the inventor of the Quadrant and the author of the first dramatic work written in America. He died in this city and was buried in the old graveyard adjoining St. James' Church in August, 1763. While living here he wrote his tragedy *The Prince of Parthia.*

Men in the Present.

Business, in every age of the world, has been the chief pioneer in the march of man's civilization. Blessings everywhere follow its advancing footsteps. It brings humanity into friendly and harmonious intercourse. It removes local prejudices, breaks down personal antipathies and binds the whole family of mankind together by strong ties of association and of mutual and independent interests. It brings men together where towns and cities are built, it leads them to venture upon the high seas in ships and traverse continents on iron pathways, and wherever we go, whether abroad or at home, it is business that controls the great interests of the world, and makes mighty the affairs of men.

Wilmington has six lines of railroads; the Wilmington & Weldon Railroad to the North; the Wilmington, Columbia & Augusta Railroad to the South; The Cape Fear and Yadkin Valley Railroad to the West; the Carolina Central Railroad along the Southern tier of Counties in the State to the West; the Wilmington, Newbern & Norfolk Railroad along the Eastern tier of Counties in the State to the North; and the Wilmington Sea Coast Railroad to the Atlantic Ocean.

Steamship Line direct to New York, also to Georgetown, S.C.; Steamboat lines on the Cape Fear River to Fayetteville; on Black River to Point Caswell; and on the lower Cape Fear River to Carolina Beach and Southport.

Ocean steamers during the fall, winter and early spring to Liverpool, Bremen and other ports in Europe.

Sailing vessels to the nearby rivers, and estuaries; also to all coast-wise and foreign ports when required.

Steam tugs for deep water towing, and harbor and river towing.

Eminent Citizens.

The record of the past and of the present would be incomplete without a grateful reference to the lives of a few of our eminent citizens who having served long and faithfully their day and generation, have now retired from the activities of a well-spent life and await with Christian calmness and an abiding faith the summons to their reward. Six of them are octogenarians, whose shining examples as Christians, as patriots, as men of affairs, our youth would do well to emulate. We distinguish them by the good they have done in public and private life, and by their long and faithful devotion to the best interest of our city and commonwealth. When they have passed away may coming generations honor and revere the memory of Mr. John S. James, Dr. A.J. DeRosset, Mr. Alfred Martin, Mr. Alfred Alderman, Dr. John D. Bellamy, Col. James G. Burr and others whose names have long been, and happily are still, household words in Wilmington.

Atlantic Coast Line.

The most prominent and remarkable of Wilmington industries is that of the busy, thriving Atlantic Coast Line Company. The development of this splendid organization of forces was largely due to the industry, intelligence and wealth of the late Mr. W.T. Walters, of Baltimore; and its continuous prosperity, in the face of almost general depression in railway properties, to the superior skill and foresight of its present executive staff, at the head of which is Mr. Harry Walters, the only son of its projector.

The annual meeting of stockholders of 1895 was marked by a melancholy incident—the presentation of resolutions of respect to the memory of the dead President by the greatest of North Carolinians, who too, alas, was soon to pass away.

Mr. George Davis said: "The fortunate soldier who makes a wilderness and calls it peace, will ever be the world's hero, and the theme of its glowing praise; but of those who are to live when the soldier has passed by, surely he who devotes his life with a broad charity and an untiring energy to build up the waste places which the soldier has made, ought not to be without the grateful remembrance of those whom his labors have benefited. Such, in a great measure, is the life history of William T. Walters. And that mind must be incapable of sound discrimination which withholds its commendation, because in benefiting others he also benefited himself. Those of us who remember the country between Charleston and Richmond, when it was first awakened by his touch, and who look upon it now, will need no aid to invoke our grateful remembrance.

His keen sagacity to discern where great possibilities lay dormant, and the courage to grasp and fix them, the ability to command great resources and to weld and organize them, never losing sight of details until the whole were moulded into one consistent plan, and then the energy and resolution which moved on as resistless as fate, until the work was done—these lifted him up to the level of those merchant princes of old who sat at the board of kings and propped the revenues of empires. He was no gilded youth, dallying with opportunities and catching them only when they fell into his hands. He made his opportunities and utilized them for himself and that after all, was the great lesson of his life."

The system comprises fifteen Southern roads, with an aggregate of 1,540 miles of track, extending from Richmond and Norfolk on the North, to Charleston, Columbia, and Denmark on the South. The company owns and employs 180 locomotives, 3,800 freight cars, and 135 passenger coaches. The number of employees varies between 4,800 and 5,300 men.

The fastest railway journey ever made in the South was completed over the Coast Line in 1894, from Jacksonville to Washington, 780 miles, in fifteen hours and forty-nine minutes, by a special train for the accommodation of the Knights of Pythias. The actual running time was fifty-three miles an hour. This was done via the Wilson Short Cut, "the fly in the amber" from a Wilmington point of view, by which we lose the through connection of former days, and which has probably proved as unprofitable to the Company, as it has been injurious to Wilmington.

Colonel Warren G. Elliott, President of several railroads included in the system, was elected to this most important position on the death of Hon. R.R. Bridgers. Colonel Elliott is a man of broad and liberal views, familiar with the laws governing transportation lines, and thoroughly conversant with the administrative department. He is admired for his genial and social qualities as well as for his bright intellect and business knowledge. Probably no other stranger who ever cast his lot in Wilmington has gained so quickly and so generally the friendship esteem and cordial good-will of our people.

Major J.R. Kenly's reputation as manager of this great system extends beyond the sea. Endowed with an active and discerning mind, he readily comprehends the most difficult problems and with rapidity arrives at conclusions. From the minutest details he is familiar with all that pertains to executive control of the myriads of forces which play their parts in this grand aggregation. Secure in the assurance of his power to wield and weld this force into a harmonious whole and to direct the whole for the best interest of his system, he impresses everyone strongly with his thoughtful, serious face and courteous demeanor, which so often characterize the man who is born to lead in the great business of life.

Captain John F. Divine, General Superintendent, one of the oldest officials of the line, has ever been faithful and devoted to the interests of the companies he has served for so many years. His long experience has given him a thorough knowledge of the requirements for successfully and economically operating railroads. He has long enjoyed the reputation of being better informed as to the cost of construction and equipment than any one in the South. Captain Divine is one of our most esteemed citizens, kind and considerate, charitable and benevolent, and always willing to lend a helping hand in the up-building of his city and State.

Mr. W.A. Riach, the General Auditor, has long experience in his profession. A gentleman of education and refinement, an expert accountant, trained under the most favorable conditions in his native Scotland, he retains the confidence and esteem of not only the great corporation which he so ably represents, but of our entire community. His superior traits of heart and mind in works of Christian benevolence have been recognized and honored by our best people.

The enormous increase in the freight business of this system has been developed under the able management of the Traffic Manager, Mr. T.M. Emerson, who brought to this field the skill and experience of a well-trained and far-seeing mind. Nothing short of a genius in railroad affairs could have held the lead in Southern traffic management that Mr. Emerson has sustained for five years past. Always alert, with an intellectual penetration not excelled in his profession, this Argus of the hundred eyes suffers nothing to escape him that would under his skilful direction subserve the interest of his employers. His tranquil countenance never betrays the workings of his attempt to cut rates, will soon find it a hopeless task.

Mr. Horace M. Emerson, Assistant General Freight and Passenger Agent, is steadily building a reputation which is already second to none in his line of duty. Affable, courteous, persuasive, he exemplifies superior tact, which, with a tenacity of purpose, effects results simply unattainable by heroic measures.

Mr. James F. Post, Jr., Treasurer, has a thorough knowledge of the intricate and voluminous transactions which give life and strength to large corporations, and that he has performed his duties acceptably is well attested by his ability to give general satisfaction. His promotion from a subordinate place to the responsible position he now fills, reflects credit on his financial knowledge and capabilities. He takes great interest in education, and for many years has served as Chairman of School District No. 1. He has served as Alderman, and is active in city affairs. And last, but not least, is a faithful and consistent member of the Methodist Church, having served his people as Superintendent of the Sunday School. Mr. Post is generally liked by his associates and friends.

Mr. E. Borden, Superintendent of Transportation, is eminently fitted for the place. The variety and completeness of his work, the methods of its arrangement, the necessary orders and instructions to guide, command our respect and admiration. He might be termed a specialist in his branch of railroading, having given more attention to this particular line, and this enables him to lend a helping hand to those occupying other positions, dependent on his prompt movement of trains. He has been wonderfully successful, and stands high with his Company. Mr. Borden is quite and unassuming and possessed of many superior traits of character.

Alexander Sprunt & Son.

The Champion Compress and Warehouse Company's plant adjoins to that of the Atlantic Coast Line. This corporation was chartered by the State of North Carolina in 1879, and the entire capital stock is owned by the proprietors, who have long controlled it and whose export business alone has fostered and sustained it.

The property includes 120,000 square feet of warehouse and dock space, with storage capacity of twenty thousand bales of cotton. Two of the largest Morse Compressors of ninety inch cylinders, are kept going from the beginning to the end of the cotton season. Their capacity is 3,000 bales in twenty-four hours, and more than a million bales of cotton have been pressed by them during the past fifteen years, with scarcely a break of serious consequence. The plant is said to be the most convenient and complete of its kind in the United States. The warehouses are protected from fire by a thorough system of automatic sprinklers, which have never failed in any emergency. The proprietors, Alexander Sprunt & Son, were the pioneers of the steam foreign trade in Wilmington,

Sprunt's cotton compress.

having previous to the charter of their first steamer, *Barnesmore*, in 1881, been largely engaged in the naval stores trade, by sailing craft, and their business kept steady pace with the development of navigation by river and harbor improvement under the direction of United States Engineers. The *Barnesmore*'s draft was 13 feet and her cargo 3,458 bales of cotton. The *Jeanara* took last year 11,250 bales of cotton on 18.5 feet of water. The firm has frequently loaded as many as five large steamers simultaneously, and the present class of boats employed by them average a capacity of 10,000 bales. The firm's direct agencies extend from Barcelona and Genoa, on the Mediterranean, in the South, to Helsingfors, in the Gulf of Finland, and Moscow, in central Russia, in the North of Europe. They have also an office and staff in Liverpool and in Ghent.

"The Orton."

The Orton Hotel, in the center of the picture.

The advantages and attractions of Wilmington, North Carolina, as a Winter Resort are being more widely recognized every year. Its location, directly on the Atlantic Coast Line, only eighteen hours from New York, renders it a desirable resting-place for both Northbound and Southbound tourists. It is just half-way between Jacksonville and New York City.

The climate of Wilmington is excellent; there is not a more healthful Winter Resort in the United States. The Orton is one of the best Hotels in the South—containing all modern comforts and conveniences, including excellent beds, dainty, well-prepared food, electric lights, Otis elevator and return call-bell system.

This establishment was built and is owned by a prominent North Carolinian, a resident of New York, who has sustained robust health and fine spirits by a Winter residence near Wilmington on his historic Colonial plantation, Orton, where he keeps a well-stocked game preserve.

The table of "The Orton" Hotel in Wilmington is supplied with rice-fed poultry from this old farm, which in flavor and tenderness cannot be equaled at any other hostelry North or South.

Worth & Worth.

This well-known firm was established by Dr. T.C. Worth, who came to Wilmington in 1852, and conducted successfully a large shipping business. He was joined in 1853 by his brother, B.G. Worth, Esq., and the firm style changed to T.C. & B.G. Worth. At that time all merchandise from the North for the interior of this State, and also for a part of South Carolina and Tennessee was brought by fast sailing packets from Philadelphia, New York, Boston and Baltimore to Wilmington, and transhipped in part by rail, but mostly by river steamboats to the country. An immense business was done by forwarding merchants here, who charged 20 per cent on the freight for their service, and the wharves of Wilmington were lined for a mile or more with the beautiful white-winged schooners, sometimes two or three abreast. River property was valuable in those days, as the following incident will show: A small wharf below Market street, which would not realize more than two hundred dollars a year now, was being rented at public auction, and the veteran crier, Mr. M. Cronly, surprised by the lively competition of responsible bidders, which reached sixteen hundred dollars, came to a full stop and said: "Gentlemen, please understand that I am not *selling* this wharf, I am only renting it for one year !"

Worth & Worth's Wilmington dock.

Messrs. T.C. & B.G. Worth were also largely interested in the river steamboats plying between Wilmington and Fayetteville and were agents of the Cape Fear Steamboat Company. The Worths built the *Flora McDonald, A. P.*

Hurt and *Governor Worth.* The *Hurt* still survives. We recall the names of a few of the sailing vessels regularly engaged in our trade at that time: *Damon, Charles E. Thorn, Alfred F. Thorn, Repeater, Regulus, Aloric, Venus, DeRoset, John, Ned, Ben, Alba, Mary Powell, A. Denike, Belle, David Duffield, Myrover, Lilly, David Faust, Wm. L. Springs, E.S. Powell, Enchantress.* There was also quite a fleet of small sailing craft styled "corn crackers," which brought corn in bulk and in bags from the Eastern counties, Hyde county being the centre. Three of these sprightly little schooners bore peculiar, and at times when off their schedules, strangely inappropriate names: *We're Here, I'm Coming, So Am I.*

In 1862 Dr. T.C. Worth died, and after several changes of the firm name it became Worth & Worth, the present partners being Messrs. B.G. Worth, D.G. Worth, and C.W. Worth. The house has always ranked highest in the commercial ratings of Wilmington, and its members are eminent in public and social life, especially and notably so in their liberal support of the cause of Christian benevolence.

The writer, who received his early training from one of the leaders of business affairs in Wilmington, Mr. David G. Worth, would fain pay his tribute in this connection to the virtues and excellence of his former employer. The records of Wilmington do not contain a more patriotic citizen, a more upright merchant, a more consecrated life, a more devoted friend, than David Gaston Worth. In early youth he acquired from his distinguished father-the late Governor Jonathan Worth—those traits of heart and mind which, fitly joined together, make up the life and character of the gracious Christian gentleman. Of remarkable intellectual discernment and superior business penetration, he daily illustrates with characteristic modesty a broad charity and a noble purpose which our youth would do well to emulate.

The Clyde Steamship Company.

Adjoining the Champion Compress and Warehouse Company's dock is the wharf of the Clyde Steamship Company. Their steamers run between New York and Wilmington, N.C., and Georgetown, S.C., bringing large quantities of freight South of Wilmington and the interior, and taking lumber, cotton, naval stores and many other products to New York, Canada, Northwest and points in Europe. The steamers consist of Steamship *George W. Clyde*, 1574 tons; Steamship *Delaware*, 1272 tons; Steamship *Pawnee*, 858 tons; Steamship *Croatan*, 827 tons; Steamship *Oneida*, 752 tons, forming a fleet of fast, able steamers, with good passenger accommodation. General office is at 5 Bowling Green, New York, and the Traffic Manager of the line is Mr. Theo. G. Eger. The company is ably represented here by Mr. H.G.

The Clyde Steamship docks (above), and the steamer **SS Cherokee** *(below)*

Smallbones, as Superintendent, who has been long and favorably known in Wilmington.

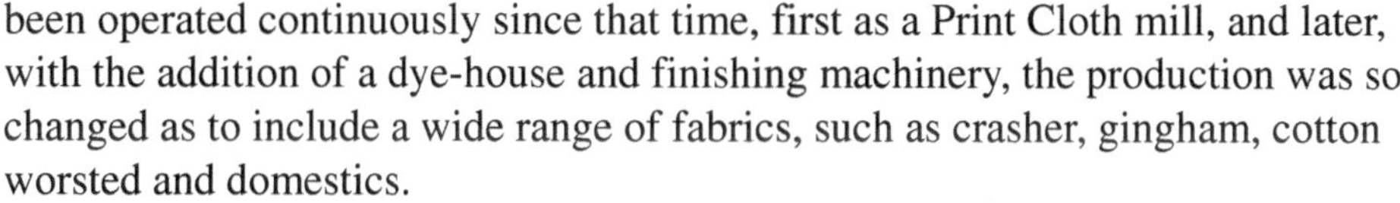

The Wilmington Cotton Mills.

The Wilmington Cotton Mills was incorporated in the year 1874. It has been operated continuously since that time, first as a Print Cloth mill, and later, with the addition of a dye-house and finishing machinery, the production was so changed as to include a wide range of fabrics, such as crasher, gingham, cotton worsted and domestics.

At the present time the mill is making domestics and napped goods almost exclusively. The product is sold in the North and Northwest, in the principal markets, and to the largest buyers in the country, thus meeting successfully severe competition and demonstrating the fact that in Wilmington there are no serious obstacles to continued expansion of textile industries.

The mill employs about two hundred people, and pays to employees about $4,000 per month; uses 2,000 bales of cotton a year; runs 7,000 spindles, 286 looms and dyeing and finishing machinery.

Much of the machinery was added during 1894 and 1895, and during 1896 a new weave building has been completed which will add greatly to the production of the plant and to its efficiency. Plans are now being made for increasing the dyeing and finishing departments.

The officers of the corporation are: President, Hugh MacRae; Vice President, David G. Worth; Secretary and Treasurer, Donald MacRae; Superintendent, J.W. Hawkins; Directors—Matt J. Heyer, B.G. Worth, Clayton Giles, D.G. Worth, D. MacRae and Hugh MacRae.

Patterson Sowing Co.

This is perhaps the most extensive house in the naval stores trade in the United States. Their business connections extend throughout the great Northwest and Canada, and their foreign agencies are in every port abroad where the rosin and turpentine demand justifies the expense. They have branches in Canada, New York, Wilmington, Charleston, Savannah, Brunswick, and probably in other places.

The firm is managed in New York by a former Wilmingtonian, Mr. E.S. Nash, and the agent here is his brother, Mr. H.K. Nash.

Mr. Patterson has been long and favorably known as a merchant and capitalist of superior ability and a gentleman of extraordinary social qualities.

J.H. Sloan, Cotton Buyer.

Conducts a large business in Charlotte and has an agency in Wilmington under the efficient charge of Mr. A.H. Brenner. Mr. Sloan was a member of the late firm of Walker, Fleming & Sloan, and he has long experience in the trade.

This firm employs foreign steamers in their cotton export trade from Wilmington to ports abroad and represents the well-known cotton merchants G.H. McFadden & Bro., of Philadelphia.

The Seaboard Air Line.

Controlling over one thousand miles of railway, and having one of its termini in the city of Wilmington, has been one of the principal factors in promoting the prosperity of the city. The Carolina Central Railway Company, constituting that part of the Seaboard Air Line which reaches Wilmington, succeeded the Wilmington, Charlotte & Rutherford Railroad Company, which was projected and partly constructed prior to the war. It traverses the prosperous and fertile tier of counties on the Southern border of the State, and has a length of 287 miles, extending to the foot of the Blue Ridge Mountains. It is intersected 110 miles west of Wilmington by the main line of the System, the latter reaching from Portsmouth to Atlanta and placing our city in easy reach of both the North and the South.

First-class passenger service, with quick schedules, is operated, and all Southern, Western and Northwestern points are of easy access to travelers. This is also the case as to Northern and Western cities. A large number of visitors, some for a short stay, and some spending the summer, come from the interior for the benefit of the salt water bathing, the good service affording a comfortable trip from Georgia, Alabama and other Southern States. Transfers to trains to the beach or boat for the river to Southport are made without expense, and without trouble.

A large freight business is handled in and out of Wilmington, both local and to distant points. Excellent freight connections guarantee prompt movement, and the consolidation of the several roads now comprising the serviceable route to and from all the great markets of the North and West.

Attention is especially called, however, to the strenuous efforts being made by the Seaboard Air Line towards advertising the resources of the South, in the benefits of which Wilmington will share in proportion to its endeavors in the same direction. Mr. E. St. John, Vice-President and General Manager, became convinced immediately after assuming charge of the Line, a little over a year ago, that the prosperity of the Southern country, and consequently of the railroads traversing it, was largely dependent upon augmenting its populace with the same class of industrious, thrifty and intelligent farmers by whom the West had been built up and he organized a special department under his immediate direction, in the interests of immigration. Thorough knowledge of the wants to be filled and a wide experience in the management of a large system of railroads in the West, outlined a policy which is beginning to bear fruit, and promises to build up the waste places in the South putting in cultivation the fertile fields now idle, which should be yielding abundant harvests. A publication in the interest of intending settlers is published monthly, and can be had free of charge from any agent. In addition a handsome, illustrated pamphlet, with carefully prepared description of the lands along the Line, can be had by addressing (with four cents for postage) Mr. George L. Rhodes, General Agent, Portsmouth, Virginia, who gives this department his personal supervision.

The interests of the Seaboard Air Line at Wilmington are in charge of Mr. Thomas D. Meares, General Agent. The offices of the line are in Portsmouth, Va. the following being a list of the general officers:

E. St. John, Vice-President and General Manager; V. E. McBee, General Superintendent; H.W.B. Glover, Traffic Manager; Geo. L. Rhodes, General Agent; Charles R. Capps, General Freight Agent; T.J. Anderson, General Passenger Agent.

Mr. Thomas D. Meares, the Wilmington Agent, is a conspicuous representative of an old and honored family of the Cape Fear. His fine courtesy, his frank and manly qualities and his recognized business ability have won him many friends in social, political and professional life. Elected an Alderman of the city some years ago, his official acts have been marked by singleness of purpose—the promotion of the public good. He believes in the benefits of advertising, and has already accomplished much by that means for the development of Eastern North Carolina and for the Railway system which he so ably represents.

Navassa Guano Company of Wilmington.

As early as 1804, Humboldt had described deposits of guano on the Islands of the Pacific ocean off the coast of Peru. The increasing demand and large exportation of this article from these Islands stimulated search for new localities, and in 1856 deposits were discovered in the West Indies, including the Island of Navassa. This Island was purchased by a party of enterprising Americans and placed under the protectorate of the United States Government, and has the distinction of being the only foreign possession of this Government outside of Alaska. Immediately upon obtaining possession of this Island the projectors cast around for a suitable location for the establishment of a plant to utilize the valuable deposits found there, and Wilmington was selected as the most available point in the South for the distribution of their manufactured product.

On the 5th day of August 1869, letters patent were issued by Governor Holden, of North Carolina, to Robert R. Bridgers, George W. Grafflin and Francis W. Kerchner, creating them a body politic and corporate to be known as Navassa Guano Company of Wilmington, for the purpose of manufacturing fertilizers and chemicals, mining and working the necessary ores, and such other things as may be incident to the manufacture and sale of fertilizers and chemicals. This Company was promptly organized, its capital stock subscribed for, officers elected and a site, known as Meares' Bluff, on the Cape Fear River, about four miles above Wilmington, secured. The erection of their plant was rapidly pushed forward, and as soon as practicable the Company began the work of manufacturing commercial fertilizers. The Navassa Guano Company has developed into one of the largest and most successful organizations engaged in this important industry, and is to-day one of the best known industrial enterprises

The Navassa Guano Company fertilizer plant.

ever originated in the South, attesting the foresight of the gentlemen who conceived this idea. This plant was established and in successful operation long before the deposits of phosphate were known or exploited around Charleston, and before a single factory had been established at that centre. The plant is well located, being situated on the banks of the Cape Fear River, where vessels from all parts of the world can proceed to discharge their cargoes of materials; in addition, they have most excellent terminal facilities connecting all the important railroads which centre at Wilmington. They procure their material from all parts of the United States, and import from South America, the West Indies, Italy and Germany. Their plant is thoroughly equipped with all modern devices and appliances for the economical manufacture of high grade fertilizers, and their enormous warehouses occupy something over six acres of floor space.

The Navassa Guano Company claims the distinction of being the pioneer in the fertilizer industry in the South, which since the establishment of their factory, has developed into enormous proportions, giving employment to thousands of people, utilizing thousands of tons of what was formerly waste products, and representing an investment of about $40,000,000.

The Wilmington, Newbern and Norfolk Railway.

The Wilmington, Newbern and Norfolk Railway was completed and in operation between Wilmington and Jacksonville, North Carolina, a distance of fifty miles, by February 1st, 1891, under the charter of the Wilmington, Onslow and East Carolina Railroad. Subsequently it was extended thirty-eight miles northward from Jacksonville to Newbern, namely, under the charter of the East Carolina Land and Railway Company; which extension was completed in the latter part of July 1893. Under legislative authority the two roads were consolidated by purchase of the East Carolina Land and Railway Company's Railroad, franchises, etc., and the entire line is, and has been since February 1894, owned and operated by the Wilmington, Newbern and Norfolk Railway Company.

The railway is of standard gauge, 4'9", namely, and is laid with 56-pound steel rails. The Company has four locomotives, eight passenger cars, three baggage cars and sixty-four freight cars. It also operates a steamer on New River between Jacksonville and Marines, a distance of eighteen miles, the latter point being within about three miles of the mouth of the river. Semi-weekly trips are also made by this steamer to Tar Landing, about seven miles north of Jacksonville, on New River.

In addition to the shipping facilities afforded by the Company at Jacksonville, it has also constructed wharves on New River at Glenoe Stock Farm, seven miles below Jacksonville, and at Moore's Landing, on the west bank, and Marines, on the east bank of New River, eighteen miles below Jacksonville.

At Jacksonville it has numerous sidings running into the property of the Parmele-Eccleston Lumber Company, one of the largest and most completely equipped lumber-milling establishments in the South.

At Newbern the Company has a large and commodious wharf and warehouse on the Neuse River at its Newbern terminal, and an attractive and roomy passenger station and warehouse.

At Wilmington the Wilmington, Newbern and Norfolk Railway Company has a fine terminal property on the Cape Fear River at the south end of the city, on which is a wharf five hundred feet in length along the river, with a depth of water varying at mean low tide from 12.5 feet at the extreme northern end of the wharf to 17 feet at the southern end. At this wharf vessels of large tonnage can load and unload directly from the cars and the Company's tracks alongside the wharf, which tracks are capable of holding fourteen freight cars suitably placed for discharging or receiving cargo to and from vessels.

At Surry and Wooster streets, just above the Wilmington Cotton Mills, this railway has another warehouse and operates a valuable wharf property, now occupied, in part, by the United States River and Harbor Improvements Department under a lease. The Company has also leased for forty years the freight line of the Wilmington Street Railway Company, operated by steam dummy along the water-front on the Cape Fear River, and connecting the Wilmington, Newbern and Norfolk Railway on the south with the Cape Fear and Yadkin Valley, the Wilmington, Columbia and Augusta Railroad, the Wilmington and Weldon Railroad, and the Carolina Central Railroad, near the extreme north end of the city.

The general offices of the Wilmington, Newbern and Norfolk Railway are at the foot of Orange Street, in the Power House of the Wilmington Street Railway. Its principal passenger station and warehouse is at Kidder street, in the south end of the city.

The property of this railway company is in all particulars well constructed and equipped. At Newbern it connects with the East Carolina Despatch, thus giving it a through line connection with Norfolk, Baltimore, Philadelphia, New York and other Northern cities.

This railway is almost entirely owned by Mr. Thomas A. McIntyre, of the firm of McIntyre & Wardwell, Produce Exchange, New York City, who is its President. The other officers of the Company are: Vice-President and General Manager, H.A. Whiting, of Wilmington, North Carolina; Traffic Manager and Auditor, J.W. Martenis, of Wilmington; Treasurer, William A. Nash, President Corn Exchange Bank, New York City; Secretary, C.M. Whitlock, of Wilmington;

Cashier and Purchasing Agent, A.J. Howell, Jr. of Wilmington; Engineer of Roadway, W.G. Furlong, of Wilmington; Master Mechanic, George E. Branch, of Wilmington.

Robinson & King.

This well-known and strictly reliable firm has long been identified with the naval stores trade of Wilmington. The senior member has served repeatedly as President of the Produce Exchange, and is thoroughly conversant with all the details of his business. Consignments from the interior will receive prompt personal attention. Orders from the North and West and from abroad, could not be placed in better hands. They make a specialty of the Tar business.

Boney & Harper.

This firm, the largest in the grain and feed trade of Wilmington, was established by Mr. G.J. Boney in 1884; two years later he associated with him Captain J.T. Harper, who was previously engaged in the steamboat business. The firm possess ample means, and valuable modern machinery, with all needful appliances in the manufacture of hominy and corn meal, which are their principal staples. The capacity of their mills is about two thousand bushels per day. They hold an extensive trade with North and South Carolina, and their well-earned reputation for fair dealing has been established throughout that district. The senior partner was elected President of the Produce Exchange twice, and is one of the most active and intelligent traders of Wilmington. His public acts in political and business life have been rewarded by the recognition and respect of our entire community.

Captain Harper, the junior partner, has established for his own account in Southport, one of the most complete general stores in the State. It is regarded as a model in its various modern appliances for convenience and comfort.

Wilmington Compress and Warehouse Company.

The Wilmington Compress and Warehouse Company was organized in 1874. Operations were immediately commenced with a small Baldwin Press on the present site of the Wilmington, Columbia & Augusta Railroad freight warehouse. The following year a change was made to the present location, north of the Carolina Central Railroad, where the capacity of the plant was increased by the erection of a Tyler Compress. Unfortunately during the season of 1876, the Baldwin Press broke down, at which time there were twenty-eight vessels in port, loading and waiting for cargoes of cotton. In 1877 the Company was chartered, the Tyler Press was sold, improvements made and a more powerful Hydraulic Compress purchased. Recently another Compress of same make has been added.

The plant now consists of two Compresses, five separate warehouses for the storage capacity of 10,000 bales of cotton and a wharf-front of over a thousand feet, and a depth of water sufficient for the largest steamers coming to this port.

The officers are: H.G. Smallbones, President: Walter Smallbones, Secretary and Treasurer.

Atlantic National Bank.

The Atlantic National Bank was organized in April, 1892, the last installment on the capital stock being paid during October of the same year. This bank does not pay interest on its deposits. Since the first year has paid semiannual dividends of three per cent, and has increased its surplus account each year, having now a surplus of some $50,000 undivided profits.

The President says: "Those who organized the Atlantic Bank determined to pay no interest on deposits, and to do business only on security as far as possible. As the patrons of Wilmington banks had not been accustomed to seeing banks conducted in this way the business of the bank was very small to begin with, but the volume of business increased steadily and at the end of the first year, the bank had accumulated profits at the rate of about twelve per cent, per annum of the capital employed. Its stock will readily sell at about thirty per cent, premium, though it pays only six per cent, per annum in dividends, besides paying all taxes. The bank makes a specialty of always being able and willing to supply all customers with money at the minimum rates on approved security." This institution employes twelve salaried officers and clerks J.W. Norwood is President and W.J. Toomer is Cashier.

Powers, Gibbs & Co.

Located at Almont, on the North East River, within sight of Wilmington, is the extensive Fertilizer Works of Powers, Gibbs & Co. The plant is fully equipped, with a capacity of 25,000 tons per annum, the product being high grade fertilizers. The capital employed in the business is $200,000. Mr. Powers, the Wilmington managing partner, has established a large business and sustains it with characteristic skill and energy. His employment of many laborers contributes much to the material prosperity of Wilmington.

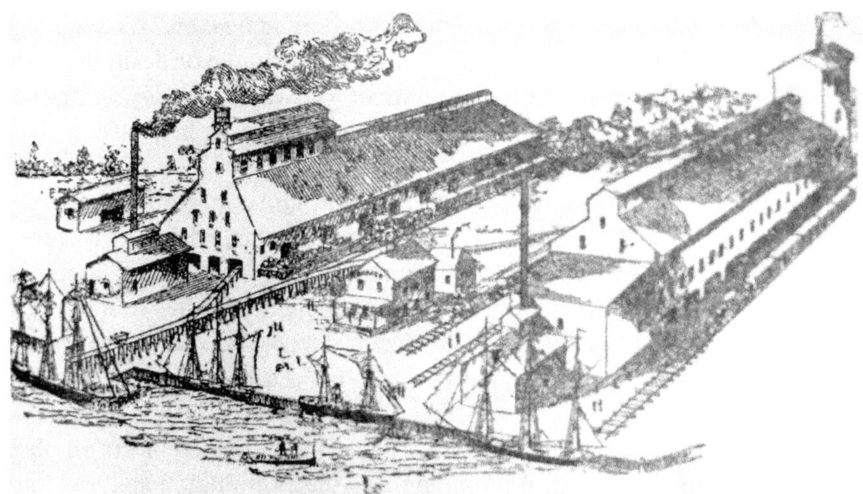

The Powers, Gibbs & Co. fertilizer operation.

Murchison & Co.

The firm of Murchison & Co. Bankers, receives money on deposit, subject to check, discounts business paper for depositors, and does a very large collection business. Their facilities for banking in all departments are unsurpassed. The principals have been identified with Wilmington for more than forty years, and they are rated in wealth at one million dollars and upwards. Confidence, caution and conservatism has been the rule of their businccss lifc.

The junior partner and Wilmington manager, Mr. Henry C. McQueen, has been long bred to the business of this widely-known firm. He is endowed with a well-balanced judicial mind and versed in all branches of business. He was selected years ago as a member of the Board of Audit and Finance and still holds that honorable position in the municipal government. He has also served as President of the Wilmington Produce Echange, and is known to our community as an honest Christian gentleman.

The Wilmington Street Railway Co.

The Wilmington Street Railway Company was incorporated under an act of the General Assembly of North Carolina, February 10th, 1887, and by an amendment in 1891 it was allowed to use electricity as a motive power in place of horses, and was also empowered to sell electric current for the production of arc and incandescent lights for power and heat and for such commercial and other purposes as might be found profitable or desirable.

The electric system of the Wilmington Street Railway Company was put into operation early in 1892. The Company possesses also an exclusive franchise upon especially favorable terms.

In January 1896, an additional line of track was laid connecting its Castle Street branch on the south along 6th, Orange and 9th streets, with the Princess Street branch north of the centre of the city; thus forming a complete loop. Its railway property, therefore, embraces at present about 5.25 miles of track in its passenger line completely equipped with electric motive power; it also owns a freight line 1.5 miles in length most advantageously located along the water-front of the Cape Fear River; which line is well constructed, with 60-pound steel T-rails, and is operated by a steam dummy. This freight line connects all the steam railways which centre in Wilmington, *viz*; the Wilmington and Weldon Railroad, the Wilmington, Columbia and Augusta Railroad, these two constituting a part of the Atlantic Coast Line system; the Carolina Central Railroad, forming a part of the Seaboard Air Line system; the Cape Fear and Yadkin Valley Railway, and the Wilmington, Newbern and Norfolk Railway; between these several roads the freight line of the Wilmington Street Railway Company is used to transfer passengers, cars and freight. This freight line has recently been leased to the Wilmington, Newbern and Norfolk Railway Company for a term of forty years upon advantageous terms.

The Company's power house is situated at the corner of Orange and Water streets on the river-front; it is a commodious, two-story brick building, equipped with electric generating apparatus of considerably more than the capacity required at present. All parts of the building and carsheds are protected by an automatic sprinkler system. The Company also owns a wharf on the Cape Fear River at the foot of Orange Street, from which vessels can be loaded directly and unloaded from and into cars.

The officers of the Company at present are as follows: President, H.A. Whiting, Wilmington, North Carolina; Vice-President, B.F. O'Connor, New York City; General Manager, M.F.H. Gouverneur, Wilmington, North Carolina; Secretary and Treasurer, J.W. Martenis, Wilmington, North Carolina.

J.C. Stevenson & Taylor.

The above firm is a native product, both having been born in New Hanover county. The senior received his education in the common schools before the late war, and the junior since the war. The senior was in business for many years as a retailer, and was at one time the proprietor of four establishments, retail groceries, the junior a clerk at that time. At the age of 22 Mr. Taylor was admitted to a partnership, which was about ten years ago, since which time all of the retail stores have been sold out, and the business has gradually gravitated towards an exclusive wholesale business, which now extends over nearly every county in the State of North Carolina and a large number of counties in South Carolina. They are now represented on the road by five traveling salesmen, and are daily in touch with the trade, and have superior facilities for handling a large volume of business. Their quarters are in the central part of the city, extending entirely through the block from Front to Water street, with a warehouse on the riverside, where they receive from the boats and pack the celebrated "Cape Fear" brand of mullets, so popular throughout the State. They are classed among the largest dealers in molasses in the South, and keep constantly on hand a large stock of all grades of molasses and syrups.

These gentlemen, having worked up from the retail trade, are capable of giving wholesome advice as to how to buy a stock, what to buy, what not to buy, and are well versed in the science of trade-winning.

McNair & Pearsall.

This firm began business in July 1888. They are strictly wholesale grocers, making specialties of coffee, rice, molasses and salt; although they carry a line of nearly everything kept in an establishment of the kind. They are agents for the King Powder Company, of Cincinnati, Ohio. They are also in the Commission business for the sale of cotton and naval stores.

Hilton Lumber Co.

The Hilton Lumber Company manufactures rough and dressed lumber, mouldings, boxes and shingles from the North Carolina pine and cypress. The Company has the most improved mills, with four large dry kilns, five planning machines and one shingle machine. Some 70 hands are employed and the capacity is ten million feet of lumber a year.

D.L. Gore.

D.L. Gore is a wholesale grocer and commission merchant, and has an extensive trade with the merchants and farmers in the adjoining counties of North and South Carolina. He is also a large dealer in peanuts, shipping in quantities to Southern and Western States.

His remarkable success, achieved by habits of thrift, economy and never-failing energy, proves him to be a man of superior ability. He is reckoned among the wealthy merchants of Wilmington.

J.A. Springer & Co.

J.A. Springer & Co. wholesale and retail dealers in coal for domestic, steam, foundry and blacksmithing purposes, established this business in 1873. The retail yards for supplying the city trade are located on Water Street near the foot of Chestnut Street. The wholesale depot is at the Seaboard Air Line yards, where large stocks of Anthracite coal are handled for rail shipments to interior points in North Carolina, South Carolina and Georgia. All the coal is brought from Philadelphia and New York by vessels and discharged directly into bins and oftentimes direct into cars for through shipment. Special attention is given to coaling steamships with the celebrated Pocahontas coal received direct from the mines by rail.

R.W. Hicks.

The well-known house of R.W. Hicks, wholesale grocer and commission merchant, has been in existence for fifteen years; for ten years previous Mr. Hicks was with Messrs. E. Murray & Co. He carries a full line of groceries and his business amounts to several hundreds of thousand dollars a year. The building he occupies is well adapted to his business, containing more floor space than any other in the city in the same line of trade. He invites all friends to call when visiting the city, whether on business or pleasure.

Roger Moore.

Roger Moore's place of business is in the three story brick store, 104 North Water Street, Wilmington, N.C., and warehouse nearly in rear of same, with wharves in front for storage of brick, shingles, laths, etc. He manufactures brick largely, and has always on hand for sale besides a large stock of his own make, re-pressed brick for fronts, round cornered brick, for windows, doors, etc. He also deals largely in fire brick, clay, best brand of Portland Cement—Stettiner his leading brand. Laths, shingles, sawed Cypress and riven Cypress, 4, 5 and 6 inches wide; Longman & Martinez prepared Paints, Oils, &c. Roofing Felt, Sheathing Paper, M.B. Coating Paint for Roofs, Nails, Caps, etc. Aluminite, one of the best wall plasters known; Muresco, of delicate tints, for finishing walls, and a most durable substitute for white-washing at a low price. Also Agricultural Lime and Land Plasters.

S.P. McNair.

In 1881, Mr. S.P. McNair came to Wilmington and established himself in the wholesale grocery and general commission business. The success of his undertaking has been marked from the beginning, and his house is well and favorably known throughout the territory in which he operates. He possesses superior facilities for handling consignments, being a member of all exchanges where fluctuations of markets are recorded; thus keeping abreast with the times, he can dispose of the same to advantage.

B.F. Keith Company.

The B.F. Keith Company are not only wholesale grocers and commission merchants, but are also manufacturers of Colly Mill water, ground meal and shingles. This Company deals in flour, molasses, rice, sugar, coffee, salt, fish, tobacco and pea-nuts. Their trade in groceries extends through North Carolina and a part of South Carolina. Their shingle trade is with the West India Islands.

Seamen's Friend Society.

This Society was organized fifty-three years ago for the purpose of improving the social, moral and religious condition of seamen. As a means to secure these ends, there has been erected on Front and Dock streets a Seamen's Home and a Seamen's Bethel, where seamen are properly cared for and attended, and where the ministrations of the Gospel can be secured. Services are conducted at the Bethel every Sunday afternoon commencing at 3 o'clock.

Any person contributing Two Dollars annually is a member of the Society, or by paying Twenty Dollars at any one time is a member for life. The officers of the Society are: George Harriss, President; George R. French, Vice-President; W.J. Woodward, Secretary and Treasurer; and the Directors, James Sprunt, John Cowan and Rev. Dr. Robert Strange.

Vollers & Hashagen.

Vollers & Hashagen are engaged in the brokerage and commission business, in provisions, flour and grain. Being provision-packers and millers agents, their goods are received in car-load lots and disposed to

The Seamen's Friend Society hospital.

jobbers under the most favorable advantages. Having trackage room and their warehouses located in close proximity with the tracks of the Atlantic Coast Line, there is a saving of the expense in drayage or storage. For years they have represented Messrs Armour, of Chicago, for the sale of their goods at this point, and they handle on commission flour from the Michigan Mills, which is asserted to be of the best grades of flour on the market.

Clarendon Water Works.

The Clarendon Water Works, located at Hilton, were built in 1880-81, at a cost of $200,000. There are three Worthington pumps, with a daily capacity of 3,000,000 gallons, the system pumping to stand-pipe and direct into the mains. The fire pressure is 100 pounds. There are one hundred and five public hydrants, fourteen and half miles of mains. The source is the Cape Fear River, which Professor Nichols, of Boston Institute of Technology, says "is a more potable water than is usually furnished American cities." The rates charged are comparatively low, both for domestic and manufacturing purposes.

William S. Rankin & Co.

The firm of Williams, Rankin & Co., wholesale grocers and commission merchants, Nos. 16 and 18 North Water Street, are successors of the long-established and well known firm of Williams & Murchison. Their facilities for business are excellent and their correspondence extensive. Mr. Rankin is one of the best trained wholesale grocers in Wilmington, and can always be found at work. He never takes a holiday, and if ample means, skill and industry count for anything, this firm should do a thriving business.

Peregoy-Jenkins Co.

The Peregoy-Jenkins Company, a corporation existing by special act of the Legislature of North Carolina, succeeded the Peregoy Lumber Co. August 1st, 1895. This Company manufactures and dresses into flooring, ceiling, partition, siding, casings, mouldings, etc., etc., from twelve to fifteen million feet of North Carolina pine and cypress per annum. Besides, they have capacity for making about six million sawed cypress shingles. Their plant is equipped with all the latest improved machinery, and consists of band saw mill, planning mill and dry kilns. Everything is up to date, well arranged and strongly constructed. They have a large frontage on deep water, the largest vessel having no difficulty in reaching their dock, and ample side-tracks from the railroads terminating at Wilmington. About 100 hands are employed. W. Edwin Peregoy is President and Treasurer, and J. Wilcox Jenkins Secretary.

Wilmington Savings and Trust Company.

J. Pembroke Jones

The Wilmington Savings and Trust Company was organized in January 1888. The most prominent promoters were Messrs. H. Walters, D. O'Conner, J.W. Atkinson, B.F. Hall, F. Rheinstein, Pembroke Jones and G.R. French. The institution has grown steadily in deposits and in favor in the community since its organization. During the panic of 1893 the Bank would no doubt have been compelled to suspend business during that year, but for the fact that Mr. H. Walters, of the Atlantic Coast Line, guaranteed all depositors against any loss and provided funds in Baltimore to pay all depositors in full. Since that time the growth of the Bank in deposits and prosperity has been much more rapid than at any previous time in its history. The deposits now exceed $200,000, the surplus account $5,000, and the stock sells readily at 20 per cent, premium. The policy of the Directors of this Company is to strengthen the Bank financially in every conceivable way. J.W. Norwood is President, H. Walters Vice-President and George Sloan Cashier.

Cape Fear Lumber Co.

One of the largest manufacturers of kiln-dried North Carolina pine lumber in the rough is the Cape Fear Lumber Company. Having a double band mill, about twenty million feet of lumber can be made each year. Recently the Company was re-organized by electing E.C. Gates President, and Bradley L. Eaton Secretary and Treasurer, both residing in New York; and John A. Arringdale, Vice-President and General Manager, who resides here. The entire product of these mills is handled in New York City and Eastern markets, and is shipped mostly by water.

Elevator and Fertilizing Warehouse

The Wilmington Compress and Warehouse Company own the Elevator and Storage Warehouses, which are separated from their cotton warehouses by the saw mills of J. H. Chadbourn & Co. Here guano, kainit, salt an other products in bulk are received from vessels and stored in bins. This plant is fitted with Hunt's patent elevator and engine, the most rapid method known for discharging cargo in bulk, vessels frequently discharging two hundred and fifty tons in ten hours, the material being dumped in a hopper, thence loaded in cars and dropped from elevated railroad into the bins below.

S.H. Fishblate.

The attractive clothing and furnishing store of S.H. Fishblate may be mentioned as one of the largest and most complete emporiums of its kind in the State. The proprietor came to this city in 1869 and began business on Market Street. In 1879 he moved to his present quarters, Nos. 22 & 24 North Front street, where he carries the largest stock in his line in the State. He is sole agent for Dunlap's celebrated hat, pearl shirts and Strouse & Bros'. "high art" clothing. Mr. Fishblate is public-spirited and progressive, and has been prominent in municipal affairs for many years, serving on the Board of Aldermen for six terms and Mayor for four terms. He recently resigned this high office, and now devotes his entire time to his business, which he intends shall make his name even more widely known than through the channels of political ambition.

Hall & Pearsall.

Some of our best citizens have been given to us by the old county of Duplin, which was also the home of both members of the above firm—Messrs. B.F. Hall and Oscar Pearsall. The senior member is one of the many Duplin county veterans of four year's service in the Confederate Army, for which the junior member was ineligible on account of his youth. But now, thirty years after the war, they are both veterans among the mercantile firms of this city.

The business was established at No. 3 South Water Street in the year 1869 by J.J. Edwards and B.F. Hall. Increasing trade called for larger room, and about the year 1873 they bought and occupied the large brick building on the same street, in which they did a prosperous business till the death of Mr. Edwards in the year 1876. On his death the firm name was changed to Hall & Pearsall, Mr. Pearsall having been admitted a partner the year previous.

Under the favorable conditions then existing the new firm continued to do a prosperous and increasing business in the old stand until the year 1892, when they moved into the store and offices (which they still occupy) in the large new building on the corner of Nutt and Mulberry streets. And in order to utilize the large property owned by them on the river-front between the depots of the A.C. Line and the Seaboard Air Line, a large wharf was extended to deep water, with a commodious dock on each side, and on the property two large warehouses were built and connected by private lines with the different railroad depots of the city.

In this shipping depot, called "Waterland," they carry a large stock of heavy goods, such as salt, meats, flour, molasses, fish, bagging, ties, nails, iron, etc., which they are able to ship either by water or rail at the least expense of handling. In their store and offices on Front Street they exhibit samples of their heavy stock, together with a full line of light goods, selected chiefly with reference to the requirements of the country trade.

The firm owns a large storage depot on Point Peter, at the junction of the Cape Fear and North East rivers, where their receipts of naval stores and produce of that class are handled by competent men employed for the purpose.

Wilmington Refrigerator and Ice Works.

W.E. Worth & Co., proprietors of the Wilmington Refrigerator and Ice Works, have the most extensive and complete plant of the kind in the State. At their large Ice Factory, with a capacity of forty tons per day, they manufacture hygienic ice, as near absolutely pure as can be made artificially. They give special attention to orders for one hundred and two hundred pounds. And ice by the car-load is loaded direct from the Ice House to the cars without being exposed to either the sun or air, thus avoiding loss in leakage thereby. Undoubtedly their facilities for doing a general ice business, in all its details, are unsurpassed, and the quality of the ice is the very best. They solicit orders. The managing partner, Mr. William E. Worth, one of the most honored names in the State, has long experience in this business. He is, perhaps, without any exception, "the greatest hustler in Wilmington," and it is said one must be an early riser to get ahead of him. Besides his management here, he is interested in the same line of business at Goldsboro, Rocky Mount and Greensboro, and is Director in several companies organized for the material development of the State.

Armour Packing Company.

This is a branch of Armour Packing Company, of Kansas City, the largest Packing House in the world. All kinds of fresh and cured meats, in refrigerator cars, owned and operated by the company, are received almost daily. A large cold storage room, for the purpose of keeping beef, pork, mutton and sausage fresh and sweet, is kept at a temperature of 38 degrees all the year round.

A large stock of all kinds of dry, salt and smoked meats constantly on hand. Hams and breakfast bacon, including the famous "Gold Band" brand, "White Label," and "Helmet" pure leaf lard, and Helmet brand canned meats. Ships, railroads and commissaries supplied with barrel beef, and pork, oils and tallow. All orders filled promptly from this branch. Pure animal fertilizers sold in any quantity. Correspondence solicited.

L.P. MacKenzie is Manager of the branch at Wilmington, N.C.

Wilmington Iron Works.

This corporation has been identified with Wilmington industries for more than half a century. The firm was originally Polley & Hart, then Hart & Bailey, then Burr & Bailey, from which it was changed a few years ago to the Wilmington Iron Works. Mr. H.A. Burr and Mr. E.P. Bailey, the proprietors, need no introduction, being well-known as technical and practical engineers, honored citizens and energetic thrifty business men. They describe their works as architectural and general foundry, machine shops, wood work, sash, doors, &c. Copper stills, machinery supplies. Agency of leading houses in belting, Engines, Gins, &c, located at Nos. 19 and 21 South Front Street.

Powell & Co.

Powell & Co., Purveyors, have their Parlor Market at the City market. Everybody knows Sam Powell, and Sam knows everybody's appetite, and just how to meet it more than half way with a delicious, juicy steak, an artistic bundle of lamb chops, a roast that brings the smile of satisfaction to the most chronic dyspeptic and—well, just ask Sam what you want, and if he don't produce it instantly, you may as well wait, as you will not find it elsewhere. Special attention given to ship supplies. Powell & Co. get their supplies direct from the great stock centre of America, and if there is anything good to be had Sam is not the man to be without it.

Cape Fear & Yadkin Valley Railway.

Fifty years ago Fayetteville controlled nearly all the inland trade of North Carolina, with a large part of portions of Tennessee and Virginia. The merchants of Wilmington were accumulating fortunes in plying a vast and lucrative business with the West Indies; and the Cape Fear River transportation of molasses, sugar, salt, iron, coffee and the goods of the Northern markets to Fayetteville, the head of navigation, was immense. Canvas-topped wagons, drawn by two, four and six horses, with jingling bells, traversing hundreds of miles from across the Blue Ridge, winding over the red hills of the rugged country about the Pilot and the Sauratown Mountains—creaked slowly and heavily on, to the shout of driver and the crack of whip, towards Fayetteville, the Mecca of trade, the El Dorado of marvelous riches in merchandise. These wagons, all laden, were driven into town in long lines, grouping themselves about the different places of business whence came the hum of traffic all day and often far into the night. But the "iron horse" was more powerful than the road-wagon, and for this cause Fayetteville lost most of her back country trade.

In 1852, a charter was granted for the Western (Coal Fields) Railroad, extending from Fayetteville West, through the counties of Cumberland, Moore, Harnett and Chatham, which, with the large amount of stock taken therein by the State, and by the aid of liberal subscriptions from the county of Cumberland, the town of Fayetteville and individual stock-holders, was built to Egypt, progressing no farther than that point when the outbreak of the war suspended all further operations. Imperfectly worked as they were, the coal mines of Egypt and the Western Railroad, with its facilities for transportation, proved of incalculable service to the Confederate Government in the struggle of four years which ensued.

As far back as 1815 the immense advantages of opening to the markets of the world the rich territory of the Upper Yadkin Valley by connection with Fayetteville as the head of navigation on the Cape Fear River had attracted the attention of leading men in the Legislature, and such connection by canal was favorably reported and even undertaken, but the obstacles opposing themselves proved insurmountable to the crude progress of that day, and the work was abandoned.

Later, in the late 40's and early 50's, Edward Lee Winslow, George McNeill, H.L. Myrover, T.S. Lutterloh, A.A. McKeithan, D.A. Ray, Jonathan Worth, G. Deming, John H. Hall, Duncan G. McRae, Alexander Murchison, Daniel McDiarmid and others, under charter, built the Fayetteville & Western Plank Road in order to reach the rich and productive sections of Western Carolina. These public-spirited men went to work to tear away the veil which had so long covered their eyes and blinded them to their interests, and relieve from the bondage in which the people of the productive region of Western Carolina had been kept by bad roads. This means of transportation was some relief, giving a quicker and more healthful circulation through the arteries of trade. But these roads were not adapted to the wants and conditions of the people, and the attention of all was directed to the feasibility of building the Western Railroad.

A Cape Fear & Yadkin Railroad boarding pass.

Whilst all who based their conclusions upon a knowledge of the country to be penetrated by the Western Railroad rested in a full conviction of its vast importance and of its ultimate final triumph, yet there was a number whose minds were closed against such conviction, and who, with triumphant air, proclaimed its uselessness and prophesied its failure. These evil declarations and ill-timed prophecies were not the fault of the country which was to be reached, or for any want of great and mighty resources within it, but only the misfortune of ignorance on the part of the prophets and their own utter want in this behalf, of any resources whatever. That any one born in North Carolina could have permitted himself to doubt or declare disbelief in the importance and success of a railway communication through the great Yadkin Valley, furnishes only melancholy evidence of the inexplicable conclusions to which human judgment will arrive. That this Valley should have been so long neglected was a riddle and a wonder. That it should now in the meridian of this enlightened century and the noon-tide of human enterprise and progress, find resistance, or indifference, or aught else than active, restless and united zeal for its development, baffles all human reason.

By the public spirit and energy of Messrs. John D. Williams, E.J. Lilly and John M. Rose and others of Fayetteville, the mists of prejudice and ignorance had to yield to the sunlight of truth.

For fourteen years the Western Railroad, although first in importance to the agricultural and commercial interests of the State had been neglected, and, indeed, lost sight of. It presented only an isolated line, without any outlet, either North or South, East or West.

But in 1879 this great proposed system of State internal improvement and material development demanded recognition and received it at the hands of the General Assembly, which by an Act ratified February 25th, 1879, authorized the consolidation of the Western Railroad with the Mount Airy Railroad, and changed the name of the Corporation to that of Cape Fear & Yadkin Valley Railroad Company.

In 1883, at the next General Assembly the State surrendered her interest in the Road, with some needed concessions, to a Company of private citizens, who went to work building wisely and vigorously.

Immediately after the new management of the Railroad, this Company entered into a contract with the Directory of the Fayetteville & Florence Railroad for the extension over its graded road-bed of the Cape Fear & Yadkin Valley to Maxton and continuing on to the State line. Simultaneously the work of construction was pushed Westward, and in 1884 trains were running into Greensboro and the Southern extension was completed to Maxton.

In 1883, a contract was made with the Directors of the Southern Pacific Railway for grading, track-laying and equipping that Road from the State line to Bennettsville, South Carolina, which work was completed in December, 1884. There was little pause in the work of extension, and in 1888 the Road was completed to Mount Airy—"the beautiful village lying under the shadow of the towering chain of the Blue Ridge." In the meantime branch roads were completed to Millboro' and Madison.

In 1890, the line was extended from Fayetteville to Wilmington, the eastern terminus. The Company immediately made their terminal facilities at Point Peter first-class, with ample accommodations for the handling of freight and passengers to the city wharves of the Company.

The work of construction was formed by the North State Improvement Company, incorporated in 1883, of which the late Mr. John D. Williams was President, and all cheerfully bear witness to the fidelity with which the work was done.

The Cape Fear & Yadkin Valley Railway crosses the chief water-ways of the State and forms a direct line through some of the finest regions of the three geological divisions of North Carolina—bisects it from northwest to southeast, aiming to make final connection by the shortest route with the great railway highway at Cincinnati and combining finally that most admirable feature of railroading which reaches out and penetrates the undeveloped back country, with its own seaport for an outlet, with all its advantages to hundreds of miles of interior of its shipping, diversified manufactures and commerce.

It will be noted that the Cape Fear & Yadkin Valley Railway system—conceived in the days of the wealth and prosperity of the tide-water and Upper Cape Fear section—lays the steel rail upon the disused old rut of this remunerative traffic, and its long trains bound with the swift life of steam power over the route of the slow-toiling wagon caravan; from the seacoast to the mountains, through some of the best settlements and most fertile counties of the State, it will move still onward, signalizing the wisdom which had seized upon what nature had blazed out for a great highway of commerce.

This railway is an enduring monument of the enterprise of John D. Williams and E.J. Lilly, of Fayetteville; George W. Williams, of Wilmington, K.M. Murchison, of New York, John M. Worth, of Ashboro, W. A. Lash, of Walnut Cove, Charles P. Stokes, of Richmond, Virginia, W. A. Moore, of Mount Airy, J. Turner Morehead, of Leaksville, Robert T. Gray, of Raleigh, D.W.C. Benbow and Julius A. Gray, of Greensboro, and richly deserved all the benefits and prosperity which it should have conferred on them.

Unfortunately, the Cape Fear & Yadkin Valley Railway became embarrassed on account of its original debt of construction, bondholders became exacting for their annual interest; and, although the management avoided making any outlays of money, not absolutely necessary to be made, and the operating expenses were conducted with prudence and strict economy, the Company was forced into the hands of a receiver. General John Gill was appointed, and is at present serving in this position.

The truth is emphatic that whether in war or in peace—in the rapid transmission of troops and munitions of war to the protection of the largest seaport in the State, and therefore the most likely to be assailed, or in the commercial interchange of the products of the West for those of foreign countries, the Cape Fear & Yadkin Valley Railway is of vital importance to our State, and as such the bondholders must conclude, governed by an enlightened policy, and disregarding the sectional prejudices attempted to be excited, that it is unwise to entertain terms looking to the disposal of its divisions and thus dismembering the main line.

Upon a review of the increasing popularity of the Road, with its present connections and its increased revenue, the people of the Cape Fear section indulged the confident belief that it is destined to succeed and prosper in despite of the obstacles and difficulties it has encountered.

The energy and zeal with which Captain W.E. Kyle, General Freight and Passenger Agent, has labored for the success of the Cape Fear & Yadkin Valley Railway amid many difficulties, the fidelity he has evinced in his sphere, and his warm co-operation in all efforts to promote the progress of his Road, entitles him to the highest commendation.

Captain T.C. James, the Agent of the Cape Fear & Yadkin Valley Railway at Wilmington, by his steadiness and attention to business, his courtesy to the patrons of his line, his zeal in the discharge of his duty, his uprightness of purpose and integrity of character, has gained him the confidence of our citizens.

Holmes & Watters.

This well-known enterprising firm of young men, "native and to the manner born," needs no introduction on the Cape Fear, for their fathers and grandfathers and great-grandfathers were eminent men in its history, and the race is not dying out. The partners, Gabriel Holmes and Joseph H. Watters, served their time as grocer clerks in the fine store which they have occupied for years as principals, and they are familiar with all the details of a business which now commands, perhaps, the most extensive retail trade in Wilmington, and a large share of the wholesale business in their line. The firm stands high financially and socially, and they attend strictly to their business.

Sneed & Co.

Invite an inspection of their stock of furniture, carpets, and matting, house-furnishings and window-shades. They are also large mattress manufacturers, and claim to be the cheapest furniture house in North Carolina. Their place of business is Nos. 114 and 116 Market street.

J.W. Murchison.

One of the most prominent hardware dealers in the State, carries a large stock of general supplies in his line, which he offers at close prices. He has the benefit of ample means and long experience in the trade, having been engaged in the business for many years, and he is generally recognized as one of the most industrious and deserving merchants in Wilmington. Call on him for agricultural implements, builders' hardware, turpentine distillers'

Murchison's store

supplies, fishing tackle, sporting goods, pistols, guns, ammunition, table and personal cutlery, and all the domestic et ceteras usually found in a first-class hardware store.

Mr. Murchison and his efficient staff are the embodiment of politeness and attention. His establishment is in the heart of the city, next to the Orton Hotel.

The National Bank of Wilmington.

This bank was incorporated in June 1894, with a capital of $100,000. The building occupied by this bank is on the Northwest corner of Front and Princess streets, and was built by a former banking institution for this express purpose, is three stories with basement, imposing in architectural design, and admirably arranged for the safe and expeditious transaction of business.

The surplus and profits is $12,000. It is the State and County depository, and transacts a general banking business. Solicits accounts of out-of-town customers and offers every facility of first-class banking.

Mr. John S. Armstrong, the President, is a financier of ability, and to him is due much of the credit of establishing this bank.

Messrs. Jas. H. Chadbourn, Jr. and William Calder, the Vice-Presidents, are ever alive to the best interests of the bank, to which much of their attention is given, which has resulted in making many friends and considerable business.

Mr. F.R. Hawes, the Acting Cashier, is a young man of recognized ability, thoroughly understands the business and is generally liked by the commercial people.

The directors of the bank are John S. Armstrong, Jas. H. Chadbourn, Jr., William Calder, William Gilchrist, Gabriel Holmes, C.W. Yates, George R. French, Hugh MacRae, J.G.L. Geischen, Chas. E. Borden.

Kidder's Saw Mill.

This establishment is the oldest, and perhaps the most extensive of its kind in Wilmington. It was owned first about the year 1834 by Captain Gilbert Potter, who operated it successfully under his own name, and who subsequently took in partnership his son-in-law, the late Mr. Edward Kidder.

The firm of Potter & Kidder was succeeded by Kidder & Martin, and after many years the name was changed to that of Edward Kidder & Sons. For more than half a century it was guided and controlled by the late Mr. Edward Kidder, honored and respected as one of Wilmington's foremost public-spirited citizens, the father of the present proprietor, Mr. George Wilson Kidder.

The present firm, Edward Kidder's Son, sustains the high reputation of its past history and controls a large trade with the West Indies.

Wilmington Steam Laundry.

Is owned and operated by Harper & Pennington, fully equipped with all modern appliances for cleansing wearing apparel, and other cotton, silk or woolen fabrics in the most approved manner at moderate charges. This establishment illustrates the Darwinian theory "the survival of the fittest" inasmuch as it outlived all competitors and secured the confidence of the public. A glance at their methods and neatly attired employees gives assurance of accuracy, carefulness, neatness and dispatch.

S. & W.H. Northrop.

The business of this firm was established many years ago by Isaac Northrop, now deceased, father of the present proprietors. These gentlemen, who were brought up in the lumber business, have a large experience in this trade and have successfully conducted it for a period of many years.

Their mill, drying kilns and yards are conveniently situated on the river in the Southern part of the city, and everything connected with their plant is thoroughly equipped with the latest improved methods, to save expense and expedite business.

They are large exporters of all kinds of lumber.

Both members of this firm take an active part in everything that pertains to the lumber interest of Wilmington and the material development of the city.

Carolina Cooperage and Veneer Co.

This Company was organized June 1, 1894, for the purpose of manufacturing oil, spirits of turpentine and syrup barrels, also crates, baskets and all the various packages for truckers. All these goods are manufactured from North Carolina timber and are superior in make and finish to any imported stock. In the manufacture of barrels they have patented machinery of a capacity of a barrel per minute. Their extensive plant, which occupies a whole block, located between the Atlantic Coast Line and the Seaboard Air Line depots, is complete in all its details. R.M. Nimocks, of Fayetteville, is President, and E.M. Wells is Manager.

W.F. Ketchum.

anufacturer and dealer in buggies, wagons, carts, drays, etc., at corner Second and Princess streets, solicits orders, guaranteeing excellent work and satisfactory prices.

California Fruit Transportation Co.

Some ten years ago the California Fruit Transportation Company began its career with fifty-five of their celebrated cars, carrying fruit and vegetables from Mississippi, Tennessee and Southern Illinois to Chicago for F.A. Thomas & Son, and were operated by Messrs. Thomas & Son.

The usefulness and great success of these cars made it apparent that the new fields just then opening in California demanded such facilities, and to market its fruits successfully in Eastern markets, 200 cars were built and put into the service. From that time the demand has so increased that the Company has now 1,000 cars in service, transporting fruits from and to all sections of the United States.

In 1892 there was a demand for California fruits across the water, and the Company, ever alive to the fruit industries, made arrangements to carry California fruits to Liverpool, England, using and fitting up the White Star Line steamers *Majestic* and *Teutonic*. Liverpool, however not proving a desirable market, the Company turned its attention to London, and arranged to put California fruits into that city in fourteen days. By the use of special export trains across the Continent, transferring at New York, St. Louis and St. Paul, carrying the fruit in cold storage and delivering into the London market in perfect condition, the fruit has always sold for good prices.

In this section of North Carolina the California Fruit Transportation Company is building up an industry which is assuming immense proportions. During the year 1892 this Company moved from Wilmington and intermediate stations to Goldsboro, on the line of the Wilmington and Weldon Railroad, to Northern and Eastern markets, 43 cars with 7,465 crates, of 32 quarts each, or 238,880 quarts of strawberries. This year (1896) they have moved 290 cars from this section

Strawberry pickers bring in the crop for California Fruit Transportation Co.

with 81,000 crates, or 2,602.000 quarts, of berries and 1,300 packages of vegetables.

The vegetable and strawberry business is on the increase, not only in this section, but in all parts of the Southern States, and it is through the energy of A.S. Maynard, Southern Agent, and his able assistant, C.W. Woodward, backed by their Company through its General Manager, H.A. Thomas, that, with a good refrigerator service, this Line has been able to accomplish these good results and give such general satisfaction to the growers.

The officers of the California Fruit Transportation Company are; F.A. Thomas, President; E.R. Hutchins, Vice-President; H.A. Thomas, General Manager, and W.H. Hubbard, Secretary and Treasurer. The general offices are located at No. 904, "The Rookery Building," Chicago, Illinois.

Mr. H.A. Thomas, the General Manager, is a gentleman of pronounced ability, who has successfully operated this Line from the beginning and established a business of so large proportions. He is always actively engaged in working for the material advancement of shippers of fruits and vegetables.

Mr. A.S. Maynard, the Southern Agent, is a leading spirit in Transportation circles, ever on the alert, polite and considerate to all, and ever alive to the development of his Company and the progress of its patrons.

Mr. Charles Worth Woodward, Assistant Southern Agent, has all his life been engaged in the ice business, and having had the experience so necessary to a full realization of the importance of proper refrigeration, is an acquisition to the corps of able officials. He is becoming one of the prime factors in the growth and prosperity of the California Fruit Transportation Company.

S.L. Alderman.

The photographer, has his gallery at No. 119 1/2 Market Street. His work is executed in the best style, and he carries in stock, for sale, views of Wilmington and vicinity. He invites all lovers of art and those desiring photographs to call at his gallery.

J.H. Boatwright & Son.

Insurance Agents, represent fire, life, boiler, accident, bond and liability Insurance. Their office is at No. 124 North Water Street. Telephone No. 73.

R.F. Hamme.

More familiarly known as "Hamme the Hatter," can be found at his old stand, No. 26 North Front Street. For seasonable and fashionable hats he excels.

George Darden.

Watchmaker and Jeweler, Front Street, deals in watches, clocks and jewelry. He makes a specialty of repairing fine complicated watches, clocks and jewelry, and re-setting precious stones, and gold and silver-hand soldering. Mr. Darden is chief inspector of watches for the Wilmington, Newbern & Norfolk Railway, and division inspector for the Sea Board Air Line.

Southerland & Cowan.

Proprietors of the large livery and sales stables, located at 108 and 110 North Second Street, between Princess and Chestnut, are prepared to give prompt attention to all calls day or night. They have first-class equipages and polite drivers. Special attention given to boarding horses-box stalls, and careful grooming for trotting horses. Hacks and baggage line to all trains going and coming. These gentlemen have on hand everything in the harness and horse-dressing line. Their telephone is No. 15.

H.C. Prempert's Sons.

Messrs. Arthur and Al. G. Prempert comprising the firm, are practical barbers and hair-cutters. Their work is done in the latest and most approved styles. They can be found at No. 11 South Front Street.

Sol. Bear. *(Established 1853)*

Long and favorably known to the trade, has his extensive establishment on Market, between Front and Water Streets. He offers at wholesale dry goods. Retail, carpets, oil cloth, mattings, house-furnishing goods, etc.

D. McEachern.

Mr. Duncan McEachern has a good name to start with; he comes of that sturdy race of Scotch ancestors who settled on the Upper Cape Fear, and who brought with them strong arms, honest hearts and the principles of an abiding faith in God, which govern these faithful people. Mr. McEachern has an extensive up country business, originally built up by Woody & Currie, whom he succeeded. He is a factor and general commission merchant, attentive to his business, and thoroughly reliable in every respect.

McEachern's docks on the Wilmington riverfront.

P. Heinsburger, Jr.

Book-seller and Stationer, also dealer in fine pictures, fancy goods, wedding presents, dolls, toys. All kinds of musical instruments, base-ball goods and hammocks, and agent for Williams' Typewriter. He can be found at 107 Market Street.

H.E. Bonitz.

Architect and Superintendent, has his office at 129 Market Street. He has displayed untiring energy and superior talent, and is gaining quite a reputation for artistic work and faithful execution of work entrusted to him.

Divine & Chadbourn.

These progressive young merchants occupy the store formerly "Daggett's Old Stand." No. 23 Market Street. They carry a full line of paints, oils, glass, sash, doors and blinds. Machinery and burning oils, copper paints and paints for exposure to salt atmosphere a specialty. They deal in the best and are fast gaining a large local business, as well as an extensive out-of-town trade.

James D. Dry.

Proprietor of the Steam Cleaning and Dyeing Establishment, No. 16 North Second Street. He is prepared to do a superior quality of dyeing on ladies' dresses and gentlemen's suits, Surah silks and kid gloves. Dry cleaning and fine dyeing given prompt and careful attention.

Richards & King.

Photo-Engravers and Designers, are ready to execute promptly and reasonably all commissions in their line of work. The illustrations and designs of this book have been prepared by them and testify to their capabilities.

Both of the partners are alert, industrious, thrifty and courteous, and business entrusted to them will always receive prompt and careful attention.

H.A. Tucker & Bro.

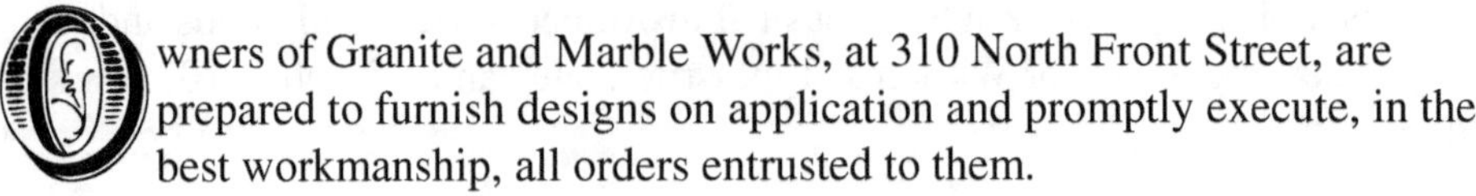

Owners of Granite and Marble Works, at 310 North Front Street, are prepared to furnish designs on application and promptly execute, in the best workmanship, all orders entrusted to them.

M.P. Taylor, Jr. & Co.

Proprietors of the Bicycle Parlors, corner Second and Market streets, keep on hand the following Wheels. The Solid Sterling—built like a watch; Tribune—a gentleman's mount; Monarch—king of bicycles; Dayton—a wheel of beauty; Eclipse—the strong wheel; Marvel, Defiance, Apollo, at prices ranging from $35 to $100. All kinds of repairing, enameling and vulcanizing. New wheels to rent exclusively to the white trade. They also deal in Electric Fans.

R.H. Grant.

Plumber and Gas Fitter, No 119 North Front Street. Sanitary plumbing a specialty. Full stock of plumbing and gas fitting on hand. Bath-tubs, ranges, globes, hose, slate mantels, grates and stoves. Hot water, steam-heating and tin-roofing.

A.D. Brown.

Successor to Brown & Roddick, has been established in business in this city for over a quarter of a century. He is located in a well-arranged building (No. 29 North Front Street), adapted to the requirements of his trade, which is known as the Dry Goods and Carpet House of Wilmington.

J. Hicks Bunting.

The Druggist, can be found in the Young Men's Christian Association Building, on North Front, between Grace and Walnut streets. He carries a full line of drugs etc. and gives prompt and careful attention to filling prescriptions.

The Real Estate Investment Company of Wilmington, North Carolina.

Has a paid-up capital of $75,000. It owns and has fully paid for 80,000 acres of land in Hyde and Tyrrell counties, including the celebrated tract known as **HYDE PARK** which Prof. Holmes, the State Geologist, who personally surveyed it, says is "very valuable for agricultural purposes, unequaled as a cattle range, unexcelled as a game preserve, as many as 26 deer having been started in a single day. The standing and buried timber is also of great value."

The Company also hold options on all state lands and invites correspondence of persons seeking investments. Thomas W. Strange President, William H. Sprunt Secretary and Treasurer.

W.N. Cronly, Notary Public, Wilmington, N.C. by Appointment of His Excellency Governor Carr.

May be seen in all business hours at the Office of Alexander Sprunt and Son, prepared to attest contracts or any other legal writings within the purview of his commission.

The Diamond Steamboat and Wrecking Company.

The Diamond Steamboat and Wrecking Company was incorporated several years ago, supplying a want the requirement of which had been very seriously felt by the commercial interests of the port of Wilmington. This Company owns the splendid tug *Marion*, two powerful hoisters, pile-divers, diving apparatus and all the appliances necessary for towing, loading and unloading vessels, building wharves, executing operations under the surface of the water, and, in fact, are thoroughly equipped to do all kinds of work that the name of the Company indicates Captain Edgar D. Williams is Manager.

Jas. H. Chadbourn & Co.

The oldest firm without change in Wilmington, if not in the State, and one of the most prominent and successful. Their saw mill is fully equipped with the best methods and processes of manufacturing lumber known to modern science, and the best of experienced skill is brought to bear in every department. Their lumber yard commands a large general trade and their special orders attest the high standing of their carefully selected material.

The original members of the firm James H. Chadbourn and George Chadbourn, came here in early life, and by strict economy, attention to business, sobriety and industry, made a reputation for business integrity and Christian benevolence. Mr. George Chadbourn died in 1891. His munificent gifts for church and other purposes were evidences of his true merit.

Although the firm is still continued under the name of James H. Chadbourn & Co. the milling lumber and shingle business is conducted under the corporate name of the Chadbourn Lumber Company, the officers being James H. Chadbourn, President; J.H. Chadbourn, Jr. Secretary and Treasurer, and W.H. Chadbourn, Manager.

Press Notices.

"There is in addition to the traditional features much historical information in these papers here presented in attractive form. The book is clearly printed illustrated, handsomely bound and will make an valuable addition to the library." —Morning Star (Wilmington).

"Mr. Sprunt has related the incidents of early Colonial history and the later events of the Civil War in his usual graphic manner, and the book will prove interesting reading to all who take pride in our history, and will be a valuable reference book to the student" —Southport Leader.

"Our thanks are due to the author, Mr. James Sprunt, of Wilmington, N.C. for a copy of a really charming little publication entitled "Tales and Traditions of the Lower Cape Fear," giving the past, present and possible future of that section. The name and reputation of the author, afford the best evidence of the attractiveness and real value of the work." —The Robesonian (Lumberton).

"James Sprunt, Esq., of Wilmington, has put forth an exceedingly attractive little paper back book—not such a very little one, either, for it is of about 300 pages—entitled "Tales and Traditions of the Lower Cape Fear, 1661-1896." Its style is delightfully fresh and chatty, and a glance shows that the volume is not confined to the telling of tales, but is in a sense a history of the historically interesting lower Cape Fear section." —Charlotte Observer.

"Captain J.W. Harper's picture, and that of his fine steamer, very appropriately are in the first place of the book, and to-day no pleasanter trip can be made than on this steamer, which is commanded by the universally popular Captain John W. Harper" —Newbern Journal.

"Tales and Traditions of Lower Cape Fear is a very charming book. The writer of this note has a special fondness for persons and things of the olden time, and more and more as the years goby that are fast numbering him among them. This book then that brings to him most vividly the things that he has seen, the persons he has known, the very many things of which he has heard and not a few of which he has never conceived—all true, all interesting, all valuable, as history rescued from the oblivion into which it has almost disappeared is most highly prized. It is not a book to devour, but a book to luxuriate upon at leisure. How delightful on the broad piazza of a summer home, the broad ocean stretching out before one, while the cooling breeze refreshes the fevered brow, and the low murmur of the waves as they lash the shore soothes and calm the care worn spirit to read of the scenes which were almost in full view of the spot where one is sitting. In view, indeed, of the very spot where lay, the Federal fleet when Fort Fisher fell, and fall in sight of the course over which the fleet blockade-runners sped when pursued by their foes.

A charming book it is. The author has spared no pains to obtain the facts, and in this and in presentation of them he gives full credit to those who have imparted them. In general the style, as is appropriate, is simple without the least attempt at ornament, but again as occasion requires, there are passages of elevated thought and rhythmic expression that add zest to the feast of which the reader is partaking. The book is well printed by Messrs. LeGwin Bros." —North Carolina Presbyterian.

"Tales and Traditions of the Lower Cape Fear, 1661-1896," by Mr. James Sprunt, of this city, is a really interesting, instructive and valuable contribution not only to the history and romantic incidents of this section but to North Carolina history.

It contains much to entertain, and shows how diligent explorer and a competent writer can gather forgotten and practically lost material, and so utilize it as to make it a positive source of pleasure and profit. The little volume contains over 20 pages, and is dedicated to the memory of the late Hon. George Davis in apt, fellcitous phasing that says not a word too much. The "little guide book" was prepared in six weeks, but it is well done and deserves many readers. Such a book has been long needed, and we are glad that Mr. Sprunt has taken the time to prepare it and so well" —Dr. Kingsbury in Wilmington Messenger.

In Diversity of Products,
In Healthfulness,
In Mildness and Equability of Climate,
In Nearness to Markets,
In Schools, Churches, and Other Needs of an Advanced Civilization, and
In All That Goes to Make Life Worth Living,
The Territory of The
ATLANTIC COAST LINE
IS PREEMINENT.

• •

Here are some of the Staple Crops of the different sections of this area:

All Vegetables and **Small Fruits**
Peaches, Pears,
Grapes, Figs,
And
Other Fruits,
Wheat,
Corn,
Oats,
And
Other
Grains,
Tobacco,
Cotton,
Peanuts,
Hay,
Rice,
Potatoes

The policy of the Atlantic Coast Line is to foster all developments along its line. **IT IS THE GREATEST TRUCKING ROAD IN AMERICA,** and it provides every facility for getting farm, garden and orchard products to the Northern markets in best possible condition, in shortest time and at lowest rates.

In no part of the country is there a greater abundance of game and fish than in the eastern counties of North and South Carolina.

NORTHERN FARMERS ARE INVITED to write for information in detail about the territory of the Atlantic Coast Line, which extends from **RICHMOND AND NORFOLK TO COLUMBIA AND CHARLESTON.**

T.M. EMERSON, Traffic Manager.
H.M. EMERSON, Ass't Gen'l Freight Agent.
Wilmington, N.C.

"Stories of the Old Plantations"

by

Dr. John Hampden Hill

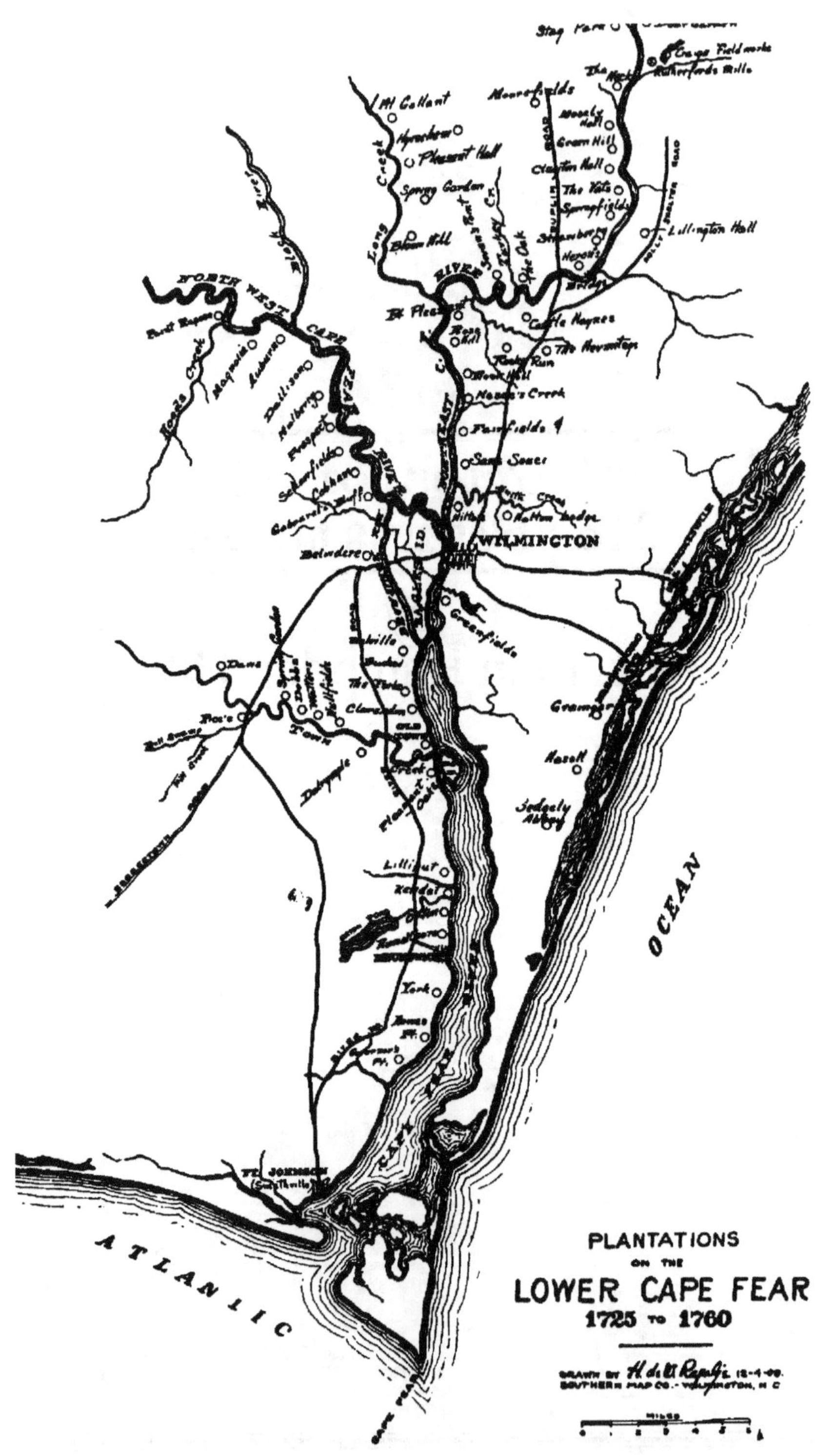
PLANTATIONS
ON THE
LOWER CAPE FEAR
1725 TO 1760
WILMINGTON
ATLANTIC
OCEAN
NORTH WEST CAPE FEAR RIVER
Pleasant Hall
Spring Garden
Lillington Hall
Castle Haynes
The Hermitage
Sans Souci
Belvidere
Greenfields
Clarendon
Lilliput
York
Sedgely Abbey
CAPE FEAR

(The following was written by Dr. Hill about 1845. It was never printed in book form. The original manuscript is owned by Thomas W. Davis, well-known attorney of this city, and was loaned for use in this volume of Biographical Sketches of Wilmington Citizens.)

When Sir John Yeamans was governor of the Island of Barbadoes, he fitted out a small vessel, and sent her under the command of a Captain Hilton, on a voyage of discovery. Hilton, according to instructions, located along the shores of the mainland, until he discovered the mouth of the Cape Fear River, which he entered and ascended with his vessel as far as the junction of its two main branches, now known as the North West and the North East. Here he anchored and proceeded with a small boat to ascend, selecting the North East branch as the most inviting for farther exploration. Several points attracted the attention and admiration of the adventurers, to which they attached names more or less characteristic, and it is somewhat remarkable that even at this remote time, many of those places retain the names given them by the first white men who had passed that way. Such for instance, the first attractive point on the right bank of the River as they ascended was named Hilton, in compliment to the commander of the party. Without encountering any unusual adventures, so far as tradition relates about the highest point which they reached was a place called Stag Park, named so by them, on the West bank of the stream. The tradition is that they saw a herd of deer on a handsome bluff, which overlooks the stream at this point. Standing amidst a magnificent park of forest trees, they gazed with startled amazement at these new intruders into their sylvan retreat, little knowing that they were the forerunners of far more formidable persecutors, than their red skinned contenants of the forests. Meeting with some obstruction to his farther ascent, Hilton with his party, returned to their vessel, and after exploring a short distance up the North West branch, from the banks of which they were assailed by some Indians, they set sail for Barbadoes, to make report of their discovery.

Sir John Yeamans himself afterward visited the Cape Fear, and brought a colony with him and made a settlement on the West Bank of the River, near the mouth of a stream which he named Charles River, now known as the Old Town Creek. Finding this location unhealthy and otherwise unsuitable, Yeamans soon abandoned it, and sailing farther South, he settled with his colony at the junction of the Ashley and Cooper rivers, when he founded the city of Charleston, naming it after his Sovereign and patron Charles II.

Not designing to follow the progress of Yeamans with his colony, we will return to the Cape Fear, of whose early traditions the writer has undertaken at the solicitations of some much valued friends to narrate (so far as his memory serves) some imperfect sketches. After this section began to be visited and settlements made by emigrants from Europe and the other provinces, amongst the earliest places that attracted attention was Stag Park. It was first located and patented by George Burrington, then governor of the Province of North Carolina. This Governor Burrington was a very worthless and profligate character, so much so that on one occasion being at Edenton, he was presented by the Grand Jury of Chowan County, for riotous and disorderly conduct on the streets with a party of rowdy companions. Of such material as this, did our English rulers make governors for the guardianship of the lives and fortunes of their loyal subjects in these provinces. After having disgraced himself in America, Burrington returned to England, where still pursuing his profligate habits, he not long after lost his life in a street brawl, in the city of London. Before that event he had contracted a debt to a Mr. Strudwick, for which he mortgaged the Stag Park estate of ten thousand acres, and a large body of land which he owned in what was known as the Hawfields in Orange County. Mr. Strudwick sent his son Edmund to look after his property thus acquired in this country. The tradition was that this gentleman had fallen into disfavor with his friends on account of having married an actress in the City of London, which was the cause of his coming to settle in America. His residence was divided between Stag Park and the Hawfields. He left a son whom the writer has only heard mentioned as Major Strudwick and as quite an influential citizen of Orange County, where he chiefly resided. He married a Miss Shephard of Orange, by which marriage there were several sons and daughters, of whom the late Mr. Samuel Strudwick of Alabama was the eldest. This gentleman was a successful planter and acquired a large estate. Of high intelligence and remarkable for his fine conversational talent, Dr. Edmund Strudwick of Hillsboro, is well-known as one of the ablest physicians of the State, and especially eminent as a surgeon. Betsy, the elder daughter married Mr. Paoli Ashe, and was the mother of the Hon. Thomas Ashe, one of the Associate Justices of the Supreme Court of North Carolina, and a gentleman distinguished alike for professional ability and great worth and purity of character.

Stag Park was sold about the year 1817 for division among the heirs and purchased by Ezekiel Lane, Esq., for $10,000. This gentleman, we will have occasion to mention farther on. The next place descending the North East is the Neck, the residence of Governor Samuel Ashe, who together with his brother, General John Ashe, were among the most prominent and influential characters in the Cape Fear region both before and after the Revolutionary War. Governor Ashe held with distinction the position of District Judge up to the time of his election as Governor of the State. His oldest son, John Baptiste Ashe, was also elected Governor , but died before he could be inducted into office. There were two other sons of Governor Ashe, Samuel and Thomas. The latter was the grandfather of the present Judge Ashe, already spoken of, and the former will be mentioned farther on. There was still another son named Cincinatus, who with some other youths of the Cape Fear gentry, volunteered as midshipmen on board a privateer fitted out at Wilmington, and commanded by a Captain Allen, an Englishman. The vessel went to sea and was supposed to have been sunk by a British ship, or foundered in some other way, as she was never more heard of. The writer remembers when he was a child, an old lady, a Mrs. Allen, entirely blind, the window of an English Captain, who lived with the families of the North East, first with one and then another, with whom she was always a welcome guest and treated with much respect and consideration.

Still below the Neck and within the precinct known as Rocky Point was Green Hill, the residence of General John Ashe. This gentleman did more probably than any man in the Province, towards rousing the spirit of resistance against what was called British oppression. He was the prime mover and leader of the party which resisted the then governor in his attempt to enforce the Stamp Act. And when the war of the Revolution did break out, he raised a regiment at his own expense, so ardently were his feelings enlisted in the cause.

But the history of General Ashe's services, is or ought to be known well to the people of the Cape Fear. But it may not be known that he died in obscurity, and the place of his interment cannot be pointed out. The story is that on a visit to his family at Green Hill, in feeble health, he was betrayed by a faithless servant to a party of soldiers sent out from the garrison at Wilmington for his capture. Taken to Wilmington, he was confined in Craig's bull pen as it was called. Here his health became so feeble that he was released on parole and attempted to get to his family at Hillsboro. But he reached no farther than Sampson Hall, the residence of Colonel John Sampson, in the county of that name. Here he died and was buried and there is neither stone nor mound to mark the spot. General Ashe left a son who also had served in the war of the Revolution. This was Major Samuel Ashe. He was an active politician of the Democratic Republican party and represented for many years the county of New Hanover in the legislature.

Of the three daughters of General Ashe, one of them married Governor Joseph Alston of South Carolina, another married Mr. John Davis, and the third Mr. William H. Hill, the most talented man of the family, with the most brilliant promise of distinction when he died at the early age of thirty-six. This Green Hill property is now owned by the estate of the late Major John Walker. The Ashe family in early times, after the Revolution, differed in politics with the generality of the Cape Fear gentry. The Governor and his sons with the exception of Colonel Samuel Ashe were leaders of the Republicans or Jeffersonian faction, whereas the large majority of the gentry and educated class were Federalist of the Hamilton school. After the adoption of the Federal Constitution and a Republican form of government established, there is no doubt but that a good deal of feeling and prejudice existed against what was called too much liberty and equality. And the practice of some of the old Republicans was not always consistent with their professed principles. A little anecdote which the writer remembers to have heard will illustrate this. One day there came to the Neck a plain country man to see Governor Ashe on business. His errand was not finished before the Governor's dinner hour arrived. He was invited in, but seated at a side table, and helped from that at which the Governor and family dined. The man took no umbrage, quietly ate his dinner and made no remark. It chanced that sometime afterwards the Governor was traveling to his summer residence in the up country, when night overtaking him, he stopped before a house on the roadside, and sent in his servant to know if he could get a night's lodging. He was invited in, and hospitably welcomed. When supper was ready, he was shown to a side table and then helped. The Governor at once recognized his visitor at the Neck, and very sensibly took the rebuke in good part.

The next place of note, and adjoining Green Hill to the West was a Moseley Hall, the residence of the Moseley family, and one of prominence in colonial times. One of them, Sampson Moseley, Esq., was a member of the King's council, and Surveyer General of the Province. But the writer does not know that any of the male members of the family survived the Revolution, or that any of their descendants whatever are left. They were nearly allied by blood to the Lillingtons. One of the daughters of the family married a Mr. Carlton Walker, and left one son, John Moseley Walker, who died soon after coming of age, and the estate passed to his half brothers and sisters. This was a large and quite a valuable place, and was said to have been handsomely improved, but all that the writer remembers to have seen were the remains of what were said to have been fine old avenues.

Crossing Clayton Creek, we come to the next place below, known in old times as Clayton Hall, the residence of a Mr. Clayton, a Scotch gentleman who died leaving no descendents, though I believe the Prestons of Wilmington were his nearest of kin. This property, which at one time was regarded as the best plantation in New Hanover County, was purchased by Colonel Samuel Ashe. Colonel Ashe when I knew him was about the only survivor of the olden times, on the North East River. He had been a soldier in the war of the Revolution, had entered the army when he was but seventeen years old, and served through the years of the war, was at the siege of Charleston, and was there made prisoner. Colonel Ashe was a gentleman of commanding appearance, tall and erect with prominent features, deep sunken but piercing eyes, of fine manners and bearing, of remarkable colloquial powers, and his manner and style of narration most engaging. Especially was he fond of anecdotes and incidents relating to the olden times most interesting and seemed almost inexhaustible. It was at the old Clayton Hall Mansion that he located the scene of his Tom Martin story and as it will serve to illustrate some of the characteristics of those old times, I will endeavor to relate it as well as my memory serves. At that time the old place was uninhabited, and the young gentry folks of the neighborhood held their dancing assemblies, there arrived at his Father's at the Neck, two strangers, one of them an elderly man, the other much younger. The older man turned out to be a Methodist preacher, the younger man anything else as subsequent events soon proved, and it seemed a strange chance that should have brought two such dissimilar characters to be fellow travelers. They were hospitably received and entertained, and soon made to feel at ease. The Colonel goes on to relate that towards evening he and his cousin Samuel, Major Ashe, retired to their rooms to dress for the evening party. They had not long been thus engaged when the Colonel discovered that his hair was sadly in want of a tonsure, and remarked to his cousin Sam that he wished very much that he could have the services of a barber, when just at that moment, the young stranger stepped into the room and hearing the Colonel's wish, at once offered his services protesting that he could dress his hair as well as any barber. The Colonel said that he had a very fine suit of hair, which in those days was worn quite full, and was reluctant to trust its dressing to an unskilled hand. The young fellow, however, insisted strenuously in his efforts to make himself useful that the Colonel no longer objected, and the volunteer barber soon exhibited by his dexterous handling of the scissors and comb that he had not overrated his skill, and in a very short time had performed the task as well as any professional barber. When the hair dressing was completed, his cousin Major Ashe stepped up to the Colonel, and whispered in his ear, "Cousin Ashe, this fellow is certainly a barber." Having finished their toilet they felt some hesitancy about inviting the young man to the party, but were reluctant to do so as he was an entire stranger, and each one departed on his way to meet at the dance. The Colonel to go through by Green Hill to take one of his cousins as his partner for the evening. When he got there, he found the young lady ready and waiting for him, and they passed on across the creek. As they approached the old Clayton mansion, their ears were regaled with some very delightful strains of music, which sounded like the human voice accompanied by some instrument. On reaching the house, they beheld the stranger who a little while before had been left at the Neck, promenading up and down the ball room performing a plaintive air on the violin accompanying it with his voice, and as the different couples arrived they were highly entertained and wondered who the stranger could be. The Colonel said he had hardly gotten in the room, when Major Ashe who had preceded him, came up and whispered, "Cousin Sam, he is surely a music master." By this time the party had all assembled and ready to begin the dance. At that time their assemblies were always opened with the old fashioned contra dance, which has now, I believe become obsolete, and each gentleman was expected to take as his partner for the first set, the lady whom he had brought with him. As soon as the couples were all arranged, occupying in two lines the whole length of the ball-room, the music struck up, a negro fiddler from one of the neighboring plantations. The first couple led off, and as the figure was not well understood, there was much awkwardness and confusion. When the stranger came forward and said if any lady would condescend to take him as a partner, he would take the fiddle and play at the same time going through with the figures, and then call out and direct the dance, so that there should be no more confusion. They were all glad to accept his services, and one of the ladies having consented to dance with him, he immediately struck up a lively air, and led off with his partner, going through the evolutions of the dance, never missing a step or a note. He then called out the next couple calling the figures and so on until the set was completed much to the gratification of the whole party. About this time said the Colonel, Major Ashe came up and remarked, "Cousin Sam, he is most assuredly a dancing master."

With such an acquisition as this young stranger proved to direct the dance and furnish music so superior, the frolic went on merrily. When the ladies retired just before supper was announced, the young men as was the custom kept up the fun, dancing Scotch jigs, and doing various feats of agility, and the stranger entered heartily into their merriment and proved himself equal to any of them, and on being bantered by someone, he proposed for a small wager that he would do a trick that none of them could perform. With that, taking an ordinary sized dining table, and placing it in the middle of the room, he took the fiddle and squatting down, placed a shilling piece under each ham, and commencing a lively air, he sprang nimbly across the table, first on one side and then the other, keeping time with the music, and never missing a note, and holding on to the shilling pieces where he had placed them. Presently Major Ashe came up and whispered, "Cousin Sam, this fellow is undoubtedly a mountebank." After this the young men began to be quite familiar with the stranger, and a plot was arranged among them that each one should invite him in turn to the side board to drink. But Colonel overhearing their plot, and not approving it, informed him of it. The stranger replied that he was aware of their design and would take care of himself and never declining to take wine with any of them, he soon had them all very lively, while he, himself kept very cool. And so the party passed off very quietly, the ladies all declaring it the pleasantest assembly they had ever attended, and gave full credit to the stranger for having contributed so large a share towards the entertainment of the evening. He remained in the Rocky Point and North East neighborhood for a considerable length of time, being hospitably welcomed at the hospitable mansions of all the gentry, ready at all times to join in the sports of the young people, and being full of anecdote proved no unwelcome companion at the fireside of the elders. The name of the hero of the old Colonel's story was Tom Martin. After becoming familiar with the Colonel he related his history as follows. He was a son of a Virginia planter, and his father had sent him to Petersburg with a wagon load of tobacco to sell for him, that after disposing of the tobacco, and having his pockets well filled, he unluckily fell in with a party of gamblers, and was enticed by them into a gambling hell. Here having engaged in play, he was very soon swindled out of all the money for which he had sold the tobacco. He then staked the horses and wagon and lost them. Finally, he staked the negro boy who had gone to market with him, and he also soon went, as money, horses and wagons had gone. So having lost all he had to venture, he was ashamed and afraid to return home to meet the anger and reproaches of his father, and falling in with a company of strolling play actors, he joined them and for some time traveled with them. It was while with these people probably that he picked up his mountebank tricks. He finally became tired of this sort of life and wandering in pursuit of other adventures, he arrived as has been stated among the North-Easters. The old Clayton Hall mansion left for a long time untenanted went to decay and there was nothing left of it when the writer can remember but the foundation. He can remember an old vault which stood to the North of the Creek, in which it was said, the remains of Mr. Clayton rested. After Colonel Ashe came in possession of the place he built immediately on the bank of the creek, so that you could stand at one end of his piazza and fish. The spring out of which they got their drinking water flowed from the base of a rock, which formed the bank of the creek, and when the tide was up the Spring was overflowed.

It was a great treat to visit the Colonel and hear him talk of old times. His memory was remarkable and his style of narration uncommonly good. He seemed familiar with the genealogy of every family that had ever lived on the Cape Fear, and their traditions. It is much to be regretted that some one who had the capacity could not have chronicled his narratives as they were related by himself. Colonel Ashe removed from Rocky Point, when he was pretty well advanced in years to a place which he owned on the Cape Fear in the neighborhood of Fayetteville where he lived several years. His only male descendant in the state I believe is Samuel C. Ashe, Esq., of Raleigh. Colonel Ashe on his removal sold the Clayton Hall Estate to Dr. James McRee, who retired from the practice of medicine in Wilmington, and made his residence here, where he carried on planting operations with fair success. He abandoned the old settlement and built what is known as the Sandridge, and renamed the place, calling it Ashemoore in compliment to the two families so long known and distinguished in the Cape Fear region. Dr. McRee had acquired a higher reputation than any physician of his day in the Cape Fear region or even in the whole state. The writer enjoyed the privilege of having been his pupil, and of his lifelong friendship, and to speak of him in such terms as he esteemed him as a noble gentleman and physician, might seem like extravagant eulogy.

The next place on the river is the Vats. Here the river changes its course making a pretty sudden bend, and a prominent point of rocks jutting into the stream gives the name of Rocky Point to all that portion of country lying West, as far as the Wilmington and Weldon Railroad. This place was first located by Colonel Maurice Moore, one of the earliest pioneers of the Cape Fear section. It is related that Colonel Moore and Governor Burrington, both of them exploring in search of rich lands happened to reach this place about the same time. As they stepped on shore from their boats each claimed possession by right of prior location and occupation. But the Colonel stoutly resisted his Excellency's pretensions and by dint of strong will held the property. The arbitrary spirit exhibited on this occasion rather strikingly illustrates what was said to have been characteristic of the Moore family, especially that branch of it. The lands of this place was very rich and it continued in the Moore family for several generations. It was finally sold by Judge Alfred Moore to Mr. Ezekiel Lane, a most worthy gentleman, who laid here the foundation of quite a large estate acquired by farming alone. Commencing with small means, he became the largest landowner in the county of New Hanover, and mostly composed of these Rocky Point lands. The next two places adjoining and to the South of the Vats were Springfield and Strawberry, owned by, and the latter place the residence of Mr. Levin Lane, a son of Mr. E. Lane, a planter like his father and a most worthy and highly respected gentleman.

Let us return to the Vats and cross the river by the ferry there, and traveling eastward by the New Bern road, about four miles, we come to Lillington Hall, the residence of General Alex Lillington. It would seem to have been a singular selection for a gentleman to have made for residence. Just on the border of the great Holly Shelter pocoson or dismals and quite remote from the other gentry settlements. But in those days stock raising was much attended to, and here immense tracts of unoccupied lands furnished pasturage and fine range.

Colonel Lillington was nearly allied to the Moseleys of Moseley Hall, and came to reside on the Cape Fear about the same time with them. He was an ardent Whig and Patriot and taking up arms early in the revolution, he soon distinguished himself as a bold and sagacious leader. On the attempt of the Scotch settlers about Cross Creek to move on Wilmington for the purpose of co-operating with the British force intended to invade and subjugate North Carolina, General Lillington speedily organized the militia of New Hanover and Duplin and marched rapidly in the direction from which the enemy approached. Selecting a position on Moores Creek, where it was crossed by a bridge, he threw up intrenchments and awaited the approach of the Scots. On the arrival of General Caswell, the superior in command, he approved of Lillington's plans and arrangements for meeting the enemy. The result of the battle which ensued is well known to history, and its success was by his contemporaries mainly attributed to Lillington's prompt movements and skillful arrangements. The Lillington Hall mansion was a quaint old structure of ante-revolutionary date, and standing alone, there was no house that approached in size or appearance in that wild region. When the writer visited there while a youth, there was quite a library of rare old English books, which would be highly prized at this day. At that time it was owned and occupied by Mr. Samuel Black, a highly respectable and worthy gentleman who had married the widow of Mr. John Lillington, youngest son of the General. This place like all the residences of the early gentry has gone out of the family, and into stranger hands.

As there is no other place of note on the East side of the River, we will recross the ferry at the Vats, and following the roads leading West to where it crosses the main county road we come to Moore's Fields. This was the residence of George Moore, Esq., one of the most prominent gentlemen of his day, both before and after the Revolution. I remember the old mansion as it stood, but much dilapidated. Not a vestige of it left now. There had been raised near the house two mounds for rabbit warrens, and a fish pond. Mr. Moore was the father of a numerous progeny. He was twice married. His first wife was a Miss Mary Ashe, a sister, I believe, of Governor Ashe. His second wife was a Miss Jones. There is extant an old copy of the church of England prayer book, in the possession of one of his descendants (Dr. Win. H. Moore) in which is recorded the birth and names of his children by these marriages, and they were twenty-seven (27). From these or the survivors, for many of them must have died during infancy, have sprung many of the families of the Cape Fear region, some of whose descendents are still living there, among whom can be mentioned the Hon. George Davis who has no superior if any equal here or in any part of the state. Also the Hon. Thos. S. Ashe, one of the lineal descendants of this old stock. There was one of the grand-daughters, Miss Sallie Moore, who was reputed to be the greatest beauty of her day. Her father William Moore removed to the State of Tennessee where she was heard of, still living a few years since. George Moore, of Moore Fields, as he was familiarly called, was remarkable for his great energy and good management, a man of considerable wealth, owning many slaves. He had a summer residence on the sound to reach which he crossed the North East River at the Vats Ferry, and from a mile or two from the East of it he had made a perfectly straight road, ditched on each side twenty miles in length. This road, though no longer used can still be traced. It is related that when corn was wanted at the summer place one hundred negro fellows would be started, each with a bushel bag on his head. There is quite a deep ditch leading from some bay swamps lying to the West of the Country road. It used to be called the Devil's ditch and there was some mystery and idle tradition as to why and how the ditch was cut then. It was doubtless made to drain the water from these bays to flood some lands cultivated in rice, which was too low to be drained for corn.

Proceeding Westward, a mile or two along the road leading from Rocky Point to Long Creek and turning to the left after crossing Jumping Run, you come to Mount Gallant, where resided Col. John Pugh Williams, a prominent gentleman of his time during and after the Revolution. What may have been the improvements on the place I know not, as there was no appearance of any that are in my recollection. Colonel Williams had three daughters, each of whom married gentlemen of distinction. One of them married John Hayward, Esq., who so long held the office of Treasurer of North Carolina. Another, the late Alfred Moore, of Brunswick, a gentleman of fine talents and achievements. The third married Captain Hall, also of Brunswick. There are still living on the Cape Fear and about Raleigh many descendants of these three ladies. Passing by the main road, leading South from Rocky Point depot of the Wilmington and Weldon Railroad, about two miles, there stood to the right of the road and in sight in the midst of a large clearing a brick house. This was Hymeham, built many years before the Revolutionary War by Henry Hyme. Mr. Hyme was a gentleman of high standing of his day. He died before the war and having never married, he left his Estate to his nephew, Mr. Henry Watters. This gentleman being a minor at the time of his Uncle's death, during the time intervening before his coming of age Hymeham was rented out, before and after the Revolution, and used as a roadside inn or tavern as they were called in those days, and kept by a German named Dr. Keiser. He was employed as trainer of horses of the neighboring gentlemen. Racing being a favorite pastime with them by which they exhibited their striking English characteristics. This man afterwards lived and kept an inn at Fayetteville, where his three daughters married gentlemen of good standing and position. Mr. Watters, after coming of age, settled at Hymeham, and married the daughter of William Hooper, one of the signers of the Declaration of Independence. When the writer was a boy at school, at Hillsboro, he knew this lady, as she took notice of and was kind to the down country boys, as we were called. The impression left on my mind is that she was the perfect ideal of a refined and elegant gentlewoman. Mr. Watters resided for several years at Hymeham until he and the writer's Father exchanged plantations. Mr. Watters taking in exchange for Hymeham, Forceput, a rice plantation two miles above Wilmington on the West side of the North East river. Mr. Watters' only son, Henry, by the marriage with Miss Hooper died soon after completing his course at University, where he displayed very promising talents and some essays of his on file in the archives of the Dialectic Society are said to be very excellent.

By the purchase of considerable tracts of land adjoining Hymeham, my father made a large estate of it and under his judicious management, it became very abundant and productive. Delighting in society, he saw and entertained a great deal of company and being especially fond of having his young relatives about him, the house was seldom without guest. At that time the range was very large and fine for stock, and the woods and fields abounded with game. Christmas with its festivities and pastimes was always observed, and was the season for the assembling of large numbers of friends and relatives. The days were passed by the gentlemen in hunting deer, with which the woods abounded, and dancing for the young people at night while the elder gentlemen had their game of whist. It was on the occasion of one of these Christmas hunts that a memorable and authenticated tradition is remembered of a famous shot that was made by one of the sportsmen, a friend and near neighbor of my father's Mr. Samuel Swann. Among the invited guests was a Mr. Avery, a friend of my father's and I think a merchant of Wilmington. He having no experience in woodcraft, but quite anxious to see the game and have a shot, was put in charge of Mr. Swann, an experienced sportsman to place him at a stand and to stand with him. The hunt began by driving the Park drive, so named because of its near vicinity to Hymeham and where game could almost always be found. Soon after reaching the old dogwood, Mr. Swann's favorite stand, the dogs were heard to give tongue and it was evident that the chase bore in the direction of the two standers. Presently they discovered five deer coming directly for them and when they got within easy range they stopped and stood with their heads turned back in the direction of the dogs. Mr. Avery with gun in hand, stood motionless with admiration. Mr. Swann whispered to him, "Why don't you shoot?" "Oh, they look so beautiful," replied Mr. Avery. Mr. Swann could resist the temptation no longer but raising his gun, fired and brought down all five of them.

The occasions were attended with feasting and cheer, and were nowhere so agreeable as at Hymeham. The old house was built, I suppose, in Old English style with very thick walls and quite commodious with many conveniences about it. The purpose of those early settlers seemed to be for permanency and there were many such structures erected by them. But, alas! Their expectations have not been realized as not one of these estates remain in the hands of any of the descendants of their founders, and the old structures that they took pride in raising have either fallen to decay or been destroyed by fire, and the crumbling material carried away to be used in humble structures as though a ruthless fate had decreed that not a vestige should be left to remind succeeding generations of the former prosperity. And may it not be apprehended that such may be the fate of our social institutions since the tendency seems to be to ignore anything like pride of ancestry or place.

Colonel Thomas Hill, was the youngest of four brothers, the sons of William Hill and Margaret Moore, daughter of Nathaniel Moore, Esq. They were married at Orton in Brunswick County on the 29th of September 1757. The writer may, he hopes without the imputation of vanity, be indulged in making some allusions to his father as he remembers him. A gentleman of fine appearance, of dignified thorough genial deportment, of manly and courteous bearing, extremely sensitive. Fond of having his young kinspeople around him and ever ready to counsel and aid them when in the pursuits of honorable aims and enterprises. And Hymeham was the favorite home and resort of many young relatives. No man could ever have been more loved or revered by his immediate family, and in my visions of the past are always associated my noble father, and kind and indulgent mother with dear old Hymeham. The old place has long since passed into the hands of strangers, who have destroyed fine old avenues, and respected no ancient landmarks and the old house has been burned, and its very foundations torn up and removed. The sad fate of all these old places and the descendants of those who once loved them so fondly are all scattered abroad.

We will now pass on our way, visiting in memory and talking of these old places. About a mile to the South of Hyemham stands, or did stand, for it also has been destroyed by fire, Pleasant Hall, a comfortable and convenient house of a story and a half with brick basement. This was in the times I write of, the residence of Mr. Wil. Davis, a first cousin of my father's their mothers being sisters. Mr. Davis was a gentleman of ardent and rather fiery temperament, which as I have heard was sometimes displayed in the warm contests, with his friends in discussing the politics of the day, which ran high. He being a Republican of the Democratic order, while the majority of his friends and relatives were Federalists. Mr. Davis married Miss Margaret Moore, daughter of

George Moore, Esq., of Moore's Fields. This lady survived Mr. Davis many years and continued to reside at Pleasant Hall, where she exercised the most unbounded benevolence and kindness to many relatives in reduced circumstances. Her house was always full and was proverbial as the home of the sick, the halt and the blind. The writer very well remembers two blind ladies who found a home and were kindly cared for by this excellent lady. One of them the widow of a deceased brother with five children. The other, the blind Mrs. Allen already mentioned, who mostly lived here, though frequently a guest at Hymeham.

At the death of Mrs. Davis, Pleasant Hall came into the possession of the writer, as a part of the inheritance left him by his father. Here he resided a few years most happily, until he felt the great calamity of life in the loss of his beloved wife. This property not being very productive, it was sold, and the writer purchased Lilliput, in Brunswick County, in 1837, where he resided and planted rice until the close of the war. Leaving Pleasant Hall and going South about a mile, we come to the river again, near the banks of which and within less than a mile of each other, there was erected many years before the Revolutionary war, two large and massively built brick houses by two brothers, Messrs. Samuel and John Swann. These places were called respectively the Oak and Swann Point. The Oak was the residence of Mr. Samuel Swann, Swann Point of his brother John, who was commonly designated as Lawyer John Swann. The two mansions must have been, and probably were, the finest and most stately in the whole Cape Fear region, and seem to have been designated for the occupancy of large families or the entertainment of numerous guests. The two brothers Swann removed, I think from the Albemarle and Pamlico sections to the North East and were connected and associated with the Lillingtons and Ashes. Of Mr. Swann of the Oak, I don't remember to have heard any tradition. He left but one son, Colonel Samuel Swann, a high toned chivalric gentleman, very greatly admired and beloved by his friends, especially by young men of his associates. Colonel Swann was killed in a duel fought with a person, whom he did not recognize as on a footing with him in society, but nevertheless, waived the distinction that he might vindicate the character of a person whom he had introduced into society as a gentleman and whose reputation had been assailed by his antagonist, a Mr. John Bradley. The place of combat was in the rear of the old St. James churchyard (the usual place of settling such affairs at that day) and resulted in Bradley shooting Swann through the head. I have heard a tradition that Colonel Swann had expressed a determination not to kill Bradley, but to shoot him, in some not vital spot (he being a very expert marksman, while Bradley was quite inexpert). Swann did shoot Bradley just where he had said he would, and as Bradley fell, he fired and the ball took effect as related. A number of Colonel Swann's friends had assembled to entertain him with a handsome collation, feeling no apprehension as to what might be the result. When his lifeless body was brought to them, there was great commotion. This affair created quite an excitement at the time, and it was a long time before the prejudice wore off against Bradley and his family, by Swann's numerous family connections. It was said of Colonel Swann, however, that he was apt to be rash and overbearing, and it was probable that the reputation of his supposed friend was not worthy of the sacrifice that had been made in its defense. Colonel Swann left but one son, Mr. Samuel Swann, who killed the five deer at one shot. I think there are none of his male descendants bearing his name. The old Oak's house was burned down about the year 1816, and the place was sold to Major Duncan Moore, who had the house rebuilt very handsomely, but he never occupied it, as he died in the year 1818.

In former times the main county road leading to Wilmington passed through the Oak plantation and the river was there crossed by a ferry. It was here that Cornwallis crossed with his army on his march towards Virginia. I will relate a little incident which occurred at the time, told me by an old gentleman, who was a boy then staying at the Oak. The advanced guard composed of part of Carlton's light horse crossed first. As soon as they got over, some of them were sent out to scout and forage. The troops in advance soon espied a couple of horsemen on one of the long reaches of the road, which will be remembered by anyone who has passed that way. The troopers immediately gave chase. The men seeing that they were pursued, turned and fled as fast as their horses could carry them. One of them leaped his horse over the ditch and escaped in the woods. His companion, whose horse could not be made to take the leap was captured and sent back to the ferry. No sooner there, than he was dragged from his horse and relieved of his booty, which was forthwith appropriated by one of the troopers. This little incident reminds us of similar scenes related by our Confederates, as occurring on the capture of some well shod Yankees. About this time there was a British vessel lying at anchor in the stream, brought there probably to assist in transporting the army across the river. A shot was fired from her deck without any warning being given the family and passed entirely through the walls of the Oak house. This wanton act was hardly sanctioned by Lord Cornwallis, who was reported to have been quite humane towards private citizens. The writer remembers to have seen where the breach was made in the walls, which had been repaired.

We will pass now a short mile to the West and come to Swann Point. This was also a fine old house, built of brick, but somewhat smaller than the Oak. It had been abandoned as a residence when the writer first saw it, and had fallen greatly to decay. This was the residence of John Swann, Esq., a lawyer and standing high in his profession. He was employed to codify the laws of the Province. John Swann's father, Samuel Swann, was the Codifier of the laws of North Carolina. Swann's Point was a large and valuable estate. The old house was so located as to command a fine view of the river to the South, while a long avenue led from the North through a rich forest. There is a deep Neck called Belahaemea formed by the river on one side and Turkey Creek on the other, which was fine outlet and range for stock of all kinds, and was a great resort for deer. It was the favorite place for driving of all the country round. With the river on one side, and creek on the other, bounded by swamps and the high land between interspersed with bays, the drives were short, and you could drive all day and not lose your dogs as they would quickly chase the deer, either to the river or to the creek, and return to you. It was to Belahaemea neck that those Christmas hunts from Hymeham were made and almost always good sport was found. Mr. Swann died, leaving no children and willed his property to his grand nephew, John Jones on condition that he should adopt the name of Swann. This gentleman who was noted for his enterprise and industry, did not reside at Swann Point many years, but removed to a fine rice plantation which he cleared on the North West called Lynas, a few miles above Wilmington, where he made the largest crop of any planter on the river. He left two sons, the late Messrs. John and Fred Swann, most estimable gentlemen and a daughter, the late Mrs. Judge Toomer, a most amiable and excellent lady.

We will now pass down the old Swann Point avenue to the county road, and traveling West, we soon reach and cross Turkey Creek, and come to that famous plantation Spring Garden, the residence of Frederick Jones, Esq., noted in his day as being the most industrious and successful farmer in all the country around. Mr. Jones was a Virginian, induced to settle on the Cape Fear by Mr. Swann, whose niece he had married. Besides the son, who had assumed the name of Swann, there were five daughters, one of whom married Mr. John Hill of Fair Fields. She was the mother of the late Drs. Fred J. and John Hill. Another married Michael Sampson, Esq., of Sampson Hall. The remaining three married three brothers, Scotch gentlemen by the name of Cutlar. Only one of these left children, Dr. Roger Cutlar, who was the father of the late Dr. Fred J. Cutlar of Wilmington, eminent in his profession and for his purity of character. From this good old Spring Garden stock also comes the writer's best esteemed and most worthy friend, DuBrutz Cutlar, Esq.

We will now retrace our steps across Turkey Creek, and pass over the river at the Oak, and going through what was called Lashiers Legeres Neck avenue, come to Castle Haynes. Lashieres Legeres, a deep neck formed by the river on one side and Prince George Creek on the other was like Belahaema, another great resort for deer and famous hunting grounds. Castle Haynes was the residence of Mr. Haynes, of whose history the writer has heard but little, except that he was the ancestor of the Waddell family, among whom I have heard related the tradition of his sad death by drowning. It is said that he was ill of a fever, and while in delirium, he arose from his bed and rushed to the creek which was near by, plunged in and was drowned before assistance could reach him.

This Mr. Haynes left an only daughter who married Colonel Hugh Waddell. From that union sprung the family of that name, so long respectably known on the Cape Fear.

Turning East from Castle Haynes and crossing the county road, we come to the Hermitage, the residence of the Burgwin family. The founder of this family was Mr. John Burgwin, an English gentleman, in olden times an opulent merchant, and between Wilmington and Bristol in England, he carried on an extensive commerce. He must have had fine taste, as displayed by the manner in which the grounds around the Hermitage were laid off and improved. Its fine avenues and handsomely arranged pleasure grounds surpassed every thing in the whole country round. Mr. George Burgwin, who occupied the Hermitage after his father's death, was also a gentleman of good taste and devoted much attention to the decoration of the place, and kept it up in a handsome condition.

Mr. George Burgwin reared a numerous and highly respectable family. His oldest son, Captain John Burgwin of the United States Army was killed in battle in the Mexican war, and his grandson, General George B. Anderson, died of a wound received at the Battle of Antietam. (This place has also passed out of the family and there is little left of it to tell of its former attractiveness.)

We will turn now Westward and crossing the County road at a short distance, come to Rocky Run, where lived Dr. Nathaniel Hill. In earlier times this place was the residence of Mr. Maurice Jones, whose daughter Dr. Hill married. Of the history of this gentleman, the writer never heard much. But a tradition worth relating will illustrate his firmness and self possession and presence of mind. He was a great woodsman, and in the habit of still hunting. On one occasion he was creeping to shoot a deer, which was feeding at a dogwood tree (the berries of which deer are very fond), when feeling that something was dragging at one of his legs, turned his head and saw that it was a large rattle snake, which had struck and fastened his fangs in the buckskin leggings, which all huntsmen wore at that day. He deliberately crawled on, dragging the snake as he went, getting within proper range he fired and killed the deer, then turning killed the snake. Dr. Nathaniel Hill was sent to Scotland when he was quite young, where he was placed with an apothecary. Having completed a full term at this business, he entered the Medical College at Edinboro, where he remained until he had completed his medical course. Returning home before he was quite of age, he entered actively in the practice of his profession at Wilmington. Full of energy and earnestness, with remarkable sagacity and decision, he very soon acquired the confidence of the community. His reputation was established and not surpassed in the whole Cape Fear region. After a laborious and lucrative practice of twenty-five years, Dr. Hill retired with an independent estate at Rocky Run, where he had built a commodious and comfortable house before the prime of life was over, and in the full vigor of manhood he took up his abode, and for many years dispensed a liberal hospitality to a large circle of friends and relatives.

On the first day of January of each year, being Dr. Hill's birthday a numerous party of friends and relatives always assembled at Rocky Run to celebrate the event "with feasting and good cheer." And then it was that those fine deer hunts came off, which were so skillfully conducted that they were invariably successful. The standers were judiciously placed, and the bringing down of the game depended on their skill as marksmen. In the management of these hunts, the guests whether old or young were invariably placed at the best stands, the doctor taking the chances as they might arise for himself. He always carried a flint and steel single barrel, silver mounted gun, and it was not often that he failed to bring down the deer coming fairly by him within one hundred yards. Many a day of sport has the writer enjoyed with this noble old gentleman, at his fine old seat. Most systematic and punctual in his habits, invariably as we arose from the breakfast table (eight o'clock in winter), the driver was waiting with horses and dogs eager for the drive, and as punctually we returned by two o'clock, the dinner hour, as the family were never kept waiting.

The old Rocky Run mansion was destroyed by fire many years since and the place has shared the fate of all the others on the North East and fallen into stranger hands.

The next two places below on the river were Rose Hill, the residence of the Quince family and Rock Hill of the Davises, two rather inconsiderable and inferior rice plantations. The Quinces were among the earliest of the gentry settlers on the Cape Fear. I have heard an old story related about a Mr. Parker Quince, somewhat characteristic I presume of himself and his times. It seems that he was a merchant and quite a trafficker. In sending an order for goods on one occasion to London, from whence most all importations were made, a dozen cheeses were included and several gross of black tacks. Instead of the cheeses, there were sent a dozen English chaises, and for the tacks there were sent an immense number of black jacks as they were called, a kind of small japanned tin drinking mug. His correspondent apologized for not completing the order as to the crops as he had bought all that could be found in the shops of London. Mr. Quince either spelled very badly or wrote illegibly, probably a little of both.

There was one of the Quinces who for some family reason or other, adopted the name of Hazell. William Serninza Hazell. He was much esteemed and the intimate friend of many gentlemen of his day. When party politics ran high between the old Federalists and Republicans, he edited a paper called *The Minerva,* advocating the principles of the Federal party, and was well sustained and caressed by his friends. He must have been a man of fine literary taste judging from the number of old volumes of the best English literature, with his name and coat of arms inscribed in them, which I have come across in the old libraries. Rock Hill was handsomely located on a bluff commanding a fine view of the river. It was in old times the residence of Mr. Jehu Davis, and more lately of Mr. Thomas J. Davis, his son. The name of Davis both in early and later times on the Cape Fear has always been associated with all that was highly respectable and honorable, and it has been most eminently sustained in the person of Hon. George Davis of Wilmington, and the late Bishop Davis of South Carolina.

Proceeding further down, but not immediately on the river, was once a place known as Nesces Creek, on a creek of that name, which before the Revolution was the residence of Arthur Mabson, Esq., a gentleman noted for his great energy and industry, by which he had accumulated a considerable estate, but died the first year of the war at the early age of forty. This place was long ago abandoned and I don't suppose there is a vestige of its improvement left.

Crossing Nesces Creek, and going on a mile or so farther, we come to where once stood Fairfields, also gone totally to ruin. Here lived Mr. John Hill, a gentleman of note in his day, frequently representing the County in the legislature. He had been a soldier in the Revolution. Entered the army while quite young and served with General Green in the Southern campaign.

Passing on, we come to Sans Sowei. Of the early history of this place the writer knows nothing. For many years past, it has been the residence of the late Mr. Arthur Hill.

Crossing Smith's Creek, we come to Hilton, the place named for the first adventurer who explored the river, Captain Hilton. This was the residence of Cornelius Harnett, Esq., and the old mansion erected by him is still standing, and is the only one left of all the old places on the river. It is not surprising that this point should have attracted the admiration of those who first beheld it, and gave it its name. A fine bluff near the junction of Smith's Creek with the river, it has a commanding and extensive view up and down the stream. Although much out of repair, the grounds mutilated by the deep cut of a railroad passing through them, it is still the most attractive spot near the city of Wilmington.

Cornelius Harnett was about the most noted and conspicuous personage of his day in the whole Cape Fear region. No man more entirely commanded the confidence and admiration of the community in which he lived. Notwithstanding that, Hilton was not within the corporate limits of the town of Wilmington, yet in such high estimation was Mr. Harnett held that by a special ordinance he was invested with all the rights and privileges of a resident, and entitled to vote in their municipal Borough elections. Either on account of feeble health or advanced life, Mr. Harnett was not an active participant as a soldier in the war of the Revolution, both heart and means were nevertheless enlisted in the cause and after Wilmington was occupied by the British, he was ousted from a sick bed and confined in their prison, where he died in consequence of their harsh and brutal treatment. Mr. Harnett, I believe left no descendants, and in after times, Hilton became the property and residence of Mr. William H. Hill, Esq. This gentleman was said to have possessed fine qualities of both head and heart. Genial of temper and fond of conviviality, he attracted many friends around him, and was always the life of his company. He was a leading spirit among the gentlemen of the Federal party when politics ran high, and represented the Wilmington district in Congress during the administration of the elder Adams.

ASHE'S "NOTES"

(The following include the "Notes" of Captain Samuel A. Ashe on Dr. John Hampden Hill's "Stories of the Old Plantations," and also is the property of Thomas W. Davis):

The patent for Stag Park was located after Burrington had been Governor, and he was out of office at the time; although, because of the tradition, it is probable that he and Moore had their trouble when he was surveying for the purpose preliminary to locating an old blank patent, issued in 1711, it is said, for 640 acres and changed by Burrington to 5000 acres. The tradition as I heard it was that when Burrington came to the land with his retinue of surveyors and chain bearers, Moore met him and told him that he had patented that land and warned him off; after some words they both drew swords and then "Colonel Swann who was the King's Officer," remonstrated with them, saying, "For shame gentlemen, you who hold such high positions should set an example of this kind to the people." And at his instance they put up their swords; and as Burrington turned off, Moore cried out to him, "Governor Burrington, I owe you nothing, but go up higher to Stag Park, and you will find there, a body of land not inferior to this."

There was no "Colonel Swann a king's officer" at that time, and it would seem that the incident must have occurred while Moore was Speaker of the Assembly and Burrington Governor, and that having made their surveys, the patents for the land were subsequently obtained. It would seem that Colonel Moore was more familiar with the lands on the Cape Fear than Burrington was, although the latter had made considerable explorations. It would also seem that they were familiar with Hilton's report, and indeed Lawson in his History of 1708 embraced in it Hilton's report; and thus these early settlers re-applied the names of "Stag Park," "Rocky Point," "Turkey Creek," etc., which Hawks with his usual want of careful accuracy located on the North West. Dr. Hill mentions that Hilton bestowed his name on the Bluff near the junction of the two branches. The report does not say so; but he named a river lower down Hilton. When that property was first taken up after Wilmington was settled, it does not seem to have been called Hilton. Mrs. Harnett conveyed it to Captain John Hill after the Revolution by the name of Maynard. After a year or two, Captain Hill sold it to his brother, William, and after the Hills owned it, it became known as Hilton.

Dr. Hill's inaccuracies about the original settlement having been made by Sir John Yeamans, I suppose you are aware; also as to his error as to the death of Burrington.

MOSELEY HALL

I think he misdescribes Moseley Hall, which in later times was the property of Mr. Sidbury; he putting it lower down the river than Green Hill. It was above Green Hill, next to the Neck. He says one of Governor Ashe's daughters married Governor Joseph Alston. It was Colonel Wm. Alston and their son was Governor Joseph.

When he comes to speak of John Swann at Swann's Point, he apparently is in error, in saying that it was John Swann's father who codified the laws; and I think he is in error in saying Mr. Fred Jones at Turkey Creek, Spring Garden, was a Virginian, and induced to settle on the Cape Fear by Mr. Swann, whose niece he married. I have always thought that John Swann Jones, who changed his name was the son of Fred Jones, Jr., a son of Tom Jones (who had married Sarah Swann and himself the son of the Chief Justice, Fred Jones). So he was not a Virginian and married his first cousin, and it was their child that John Swann left his property to; named for him, John Swann Jones.

THE OAKS

The Oaks that was destroyed by fire after it was bought by Mr. Duncan Moore and was rebuilt by him about 1816, was subsequently destroyed again. I visited the ruins in 1858 with a party of the Moore girls, and the traditions which they had about mahogany stair cases and other such splendors seemed to be justified by the ruins. Such parts as I saw recalled the finest residences of a city. They told me that the old house had a fish pond on top of it. I did not know that Major Duncan Moore had rebuilt it, but I now presume that as the original edifice had been destroyed by fire, he took that precaution of having a supply of water on the roof to prevent a similar destruction, which however, befell it. The house was situated some 250 yards from the railroad where it immerges from the river swamp. To the East of that point about the same distance, the main road comes from the ferry, and along there are entrenchments thrown up by the patriot troops to hold the British in check; as also at Bannerman's Bridge on the East side of the river, some ten miles further up, and which are easily traced to this day. Dr. Hill mentions that it was by a particular ordinance that Cornelius Harnett was made eligible as representative of the borough of Wilmington. That is an error. In the original Charter any person living that side of Smith's Creek, possessed of a brick or stone or frame house, with one or more brick chimneys, was made a voter and also eligible to be a member from the Borough. (See Sprunt Monograph No. 4, Page 57, and original Charter see Page 9.)

Another one of Tom Martin's feats was this; the young men were displaying their agility and he beat them all—so that they thought him a circus actor; and finally, he bantered them to jump over the house they were at in three jumps. It was a house with a piazza in front and rear. He procured a long pole and landed in one jump on the front piazza, another with the pole carried him over the ridge, and from the rear piazza, he safely landed to the ground, much to the surprise of everyone.

Late one evening, the Colonel sent his two sons, William and Tom, to hunt for several lost sheep; the sheep were not to be found, and a storm coming up, the boys took refuge in the Clayton vault. It became very dark; presently the boys heard something move at the lower end of the vault, and peering down, saw something white there. Their fears of ghost were at once aroused. Apprehensions and apparitions were in the ascendant. It was sometime before they mustered courage to explore, but nerving themselves, they groped down the vault hand in hand, and instead of Clayton's ghost, found the lost sheep they were in search of.

A narrow foot bridge, long and high crossed the creek by the new house, the pathway leading to Green Hill where General John Ashe's family burying ground was. The Colonel had in his old age a trick of his mind, as some others fond of talking have, of breaking off the topic and reverting to some subject that had previously been in mind. He was very much venerated. Once a visitor who had the highest reverence for him was spending some days with him. The Colonel had told him of the havoc an old white hawk had made with his poultry, what trouble he had given, and despite every effort they had made, they had never been able to kill him. He was very much wrought up about the hawk. He was tail and in his old age had lost his flesh, and his arms were long and his fingers long and bony. Shortly after telling about the hawk, he and his guest strolled over to see the graveyard at Green Hill, and passing by the Clayton vault, old Clayton became the subject of his discourse. As he told of Clayton's life, they reached the bridge and were up high above the stream on the narrow planks, and the Colonel was telling about Clayton, who had at first been a leading patriot, then deserted the Cause and turned tory, and went back to England; and his indignation rising, he grew quite earnest and animated. When suddenly he stopped and extending his long arm towards the sky and pointing with his bony finger, he exclaimed very earnestly, "Yonder goes that damned scoundrel now." His companion in amazement said "Where Colonel, where?" "Yonder, don't you see them?" With head thrown back and with great earnestness and gazing intently in the sky. "No," said his friend, still more amazed and somewhat startled, lest the Colonel had gone stark mad. "Why there he is, don't you see him? Look right there!" Still looking and features rigid, "Right there, there's the damned rascal, right there!" Still looking and expecting to see old Clayton, his friend had to say that he could see nothing. "Why there he is, that old white hawk I was telling you about." "Oh," said the other, now much relieved; and no longer straining his eyes to see Clayton's disembodied spirit, he quickly found the white hawk, to whom the Colonel's mind had reverted on observing him, leaving Clayton in the lurch for the time being.

Old Mr. Hardin, the Grandfather of the Mr. Hardin, your Druggist, who lived to be very aged, was fond of the Colonel whom he knew intimately, and often related to me several anecdotes. Mr. Hardin told me that he together with some eight or ten young men being at Rocky Point, the Colonel took them to the Vats and standing by the grave of Colonel Maurice Moore, told them what a wonderful man he was, and that everyone present except Mr. Hardin and another, was his descendant, and they should never forget about him. While Colonel Moore had interests elsewhere, his family resided at the Vats, his wife being a Porter, near their Porter and Lillington kin, the Swanns, Moseleys and Ashes, and Jones, I think.

One of Mr. Hardin's anecdotes was this: Captain Maule was courting at the house of Colonel John Porter, the Second, who was living on the Pamlico, courting the sister—when the Indian Massacre took place. Pompey, a slave, had an infant, John Porter, the Third (afterwards one of the incorporators of Wilmington), out in the yard. An Indian seized the child and was in the act of dashing out its brains against a tree, when Madam Porter (Sarah Lillington) ran out and so imperiously and resolutely faced the Indian and looked at him so fiercely, that she subdued him and rescued her child. Other savages rushing towards the house, Captain Maule said, "Colonel Porter there is no time to be lost between a bad situation and a worse," and with their firearms, they beat off the Indians and protected the women and family to a boat and made their escape to a vessel. Their house was burned by the Indians.

Mr. Hardin was very fond of recalling that saying, "There is no time to be lost between a bad situation and a worse." Colonel Ashe was very proud of his Porter blood; the father of his mother was that Mr. John Porter to whom Mr. Murray in 1738 wrote "I have observed in you a justness of thought and a generosity of temper that I would endeavor to imitate wherever I found it." (Sprunt Monogrtaph No. 4, Page 83).

The Colonel caused his son afterwards, Dr. Richard Porter Ashe of California, to change his name to Porter, and by that name I think he entered West Point; but later he preferred to resume his father's own name.

Colonel Ashe and Ezkiel Lane after the Revolution started life on their own account with slender means. They were friends and associated together in business, making tar, getting out shingles and so on. Eventually they rented the

Vats and farmed there in partnership, perhaps for more than ten years. I have seen their account books, kept with unusual neatness and precision, reminding me of General Washington's farm book. They made money, and one purchased the Vats from the Moores, and the other, Clayton Hall, the deed being made by one of the Prestons as executor of Clayton, I think. Mr. Walker Meares (married Claybrook Wright) had it for his brother, Dr. Buckey, I suppose, as Dr. Buckey was the owner of the place after Dr. McRee. The deed was composed of a half a dozen distinct pieces of paper, each eight inches wide; each part of the deed being written on a separate piece all fastened together with tape and wax and big seals; apparently prepared in England. Colonel Ashe bought Clayton Hall about 1800, about the time that he married. His wife was the sister of the wives of Wm. Bary Grove, Wm. Hay, and Sam Porter Ashe, all living at Fayetteville; and so Colonel Ashe later also moved to Fayetteville where he died in 1835. (See a remarkable obituary in the Wilmington newspaper of that date, Wilmington Library.)

Devil Ditch. Just before the railroad makes its curve and starts on a straight course of 45 miles, about a mile north of the depot, it crosses a trestle, which is the head of Devil Ditch—a ditch originally about 6 or 8 feet wide and 4 feet deep, running nearly to the main road, about a half a mile. The purpose of this ditch was evidently to conduct water from the upper part of the branch to a particular point, either in connection with rice fields, or to prevent too great an accumulation of water in a pond that was a little to the North of George Moore's residence. The tradition was that George Moore was rather hard on his negroes, and ordered that ditch to be cut in one day, and that night, the ditch was cut by the Devil himself—such a throwing up of earth, felling of trees and clearing away roots and rubbish never was seen before, and when the hands came out in the morning to do the work, it had all been finished by his Satanic Majesty the night before.

There was also a tradition that George Moore used to brand his Negroes as a punishment, and his wife after remonstrating with him about it in vain, took the irons and threw them into this pond.

The pond was called a fish pond; and perhaps it may have been stocked, but it was evidently used to flood the heavy ditch that surrounded the house on the North, the East and South sides. Whether this excavation was designed as a protection from insurrection or Indians, or whether in connection with rice culture, was uncertain, and it may have been designed as a means of promoting health to secure a better drainage. The house lot, Moore fields, after the late war on property owned by Bryan Brown, was just at the edge of the pine woods and second low ground. It was about a quarter of a mile south of where a branch crosses the main road near the end of Devil Ditch, and about sixteen miles from Wilmington, and it was about 250 yards east of the main road. Between the branch and the house was the fish pond, and there began this remarkable ditch, about 20 feet wide and about 20 feet deep. It ran south to the house yard, then east some hundred feet, then South about 150 feet, then West a hundred feet or more; and in the enclosed area, was where the house had stood; there being two large artificial hillocks on the right and left of the approach, to the house. It had the appearance of military outposts, but were probably rabbit warrens.

The Southern part of this ditch extended due East and was connected with the rice fields. Far to the North and South and East, lay the second low grounds, traversed by very extensive ditches and embankments, in some places 20 feet broad at the base and 10 or 15 feet high. They were the work of hundreds of laborers through several years, and they will remain monuments of George Moore's misdirected energies for a thousand years. All that low ground is more or less underlaid by limestone rock, too near the surface for the plough, and not eligible for rice fields; but here and there are considerable areas that are arable. The growth is heavy forest trees. Some of the rocks above the ground show indisputably that at no very remote period, that was an arm of the Sea, while the beds of sharks teeth at Clayton Hall were remarkable.

Across the Ditch to the North of the house, is the George Moore burying ground with many gravestones in it, but I never visited it, though often saw it across the ditch.

I think Mount Gallant was in my day owned by Dr. S.S. Satchell, in right of his wife, who I think was a Miss Moore.

HYRNEHAM

Colonel Maurice Moore, I think, gave the Hyrneham tract to his friend Colonel Hyrne. The date of the house was on the chimney. I have an indistinct impression that the date was 1752, but that is now hardly more than a mere conjecture. Indeed my impression has long been that Hyreham was mentioned by a traveler at a much earlier date. As far back as 1845, I think Hyrneham belonged to Mr. Bordeaux. It was burned some twenty years ago, and the date on the chimney can doubtless be ascertained from some of the Bordeauxs. As Dr. Hill says, the walls were near three feet thick, and in my day, it was a very hospitable mansion. Mr. Bordeaux's liquors being always on the sideboard. As Harry Watters was Colonel Hyrne's nephew, then old Mr. Watters must have married Colonel Hyrne's sister. Watters name does not appear among the graduates of the University.

One of DeKiser's daughters was the mother or grandmother of Warren Winslow. DeKiser trained a horse belonging to the young men of the neighborhood that somebody told me Dr. Hill had said, was the fastest horse in America.

The following is condensed from a statement of Mrs. Donald Bain, who was born about 1765: "My grandmother by my mother's side was a French lady by name. Francis Pycarp DeLapite, who left France in the reign of Louis XIV on account of her religion, being a Huguenot, went to England, where my mother was educated and where my grandmother married a Dr. John Green, an Englishman, and from there they came to America. My grandfather Green died not long after the arrival and my grandmother married a second time to another doctor by the name of Adams, who was uncle to Ex-President John Q. Adams and brother to the first President, John Adams. By him she had one son who was sent to Scotland for his education and died at the age of sixteen. His name was Roger. My grandfather by my father's side was Dr. Thomas Hall, who also came from England and married Miss Elizabeth Beever, my father married Lucy Ann Green, my mother; my father had a sister by name Elizabeth (Hall), who married Samuel Watters, grandfather to the present Joseph H. Watters, who also came from England. My brother Thomas Hall, had twelve children; my sister, Lucy Green Hall, married a Mr. Roger Moore, son of William Moore (the Moores also came from England).

My brother, John Hall, married Elizabeth Porter Grange, by whom he had three daughters, Lucy G., Sophie and Betsey Ann, and two sons, Thomas McLaine and William Roger. Thomas died in his 22nd year, and is buried at Pittsboro; William Roger married a Mrs. Anna Hall, widow of Captain William Hall (Miss Anna Laspier). Captain William Hall was my first cousin. Lucy married John Moore, who died soon afterwards. My brother William married Miss Lydia Daniel, by whom he had three sons and three daughters, John, William and Stephen, Julia, Mary Francis and Jane.

Julia married Joseph H. Watters; Mary Francis married Isham Blake; Jane married A.G. Steele, nephew of Blake, and both of Fayetteville. My brother Roger Hall, married Miss Mary Robeson of Fayetteville.

My father Thomas Hall, son of Dr. Thomas, and Elizabeth Beevers, had a brother William, who married a widow lady, Mrs. John Watters, who had a son by her first husband, William Watters. This William Watters married Mary Moore, a daughter of General James Moore.

My uncle, William Hall, had a son named William, whose first wife was Anna Ashe, daughter of General Ashe. She died and he married Phereby Williams, niece to Governor Williams. By this wife, he had three daughters; two died early and the other, Mildred, married Maurice Waddell, son of the late Hugh Waddell. His second wife died and for a third wife, he married Anna Laspier, by whom he left two sons and one daughter, Hamilton and Washington and Anna, the present Alfred Waddell's wife, and brother to Mr. Maurice Waddell.

My brother Thomas, was killed at Charleston in 1780. He was First Lieutenant in the North Carolina Brigade, age 20 years and six months.

(Note by S.A. Ashe.)

After the death of Captain William Hall, his last wife and widow, Anna Laspier, married William Roger Hall and had a large family. William Roger was her dead husband's nephew. It seems that whether the original Dr. Thomas Hall came to the Cape Fear or not, he had two sons to come, William Hall and Thomas, and they were on the Cape Fear before 1760. Governor Robert Daniel arrived in Charleston in 1690, Governor of North Carolina in 1703, of South Carolina 1716, died 1718, left two sons and three daughters; John Daniel, second son, moved to North Carolina, Lydia Daniel who married Wm. Hall and whose daughter Julia, married Joe Watters, was of that family, and I think that "old lady Robinson" as she was called, the Aunt of Caroline and Cornelia Jones, was of that family. One of these girls who married General Waddy Thompson, was one of the most beautiful women of the world. Judge Penn Mears was telling me about her the other day. General Thompson courted her at my father's house in 1850. Landgrave Smith came to South Carolina about 1688, and had a brother who went to New England. And from him the Adams descended.

Tales of the Cape Fear Blockade

being a turn of the century account of blockade-running
told by the

Hon. James Sprunt,

formerly purser of the Confederate States Steamer *Lilian*.

The Chase

Freed from the lingering chase, in devious ways, Upon the swelling tides, Swiftly the *Lilian* glides through hostile shells and eager foemen past; The lymx-eyed pilot gazing through the haze, And engines straining, "far hope dawns at last."

Now falls in billows deep the welcome night Upon white sands below; While signal lamps aglow Seek out Fort Fisher's distant answering gleams, The blockade runner's keen, supreme delight,— Dear Dixie Land, the haven of our dreams!

- James Sprunt.

Blockade Runner *Lilian* (same class) was:
Built by Messrs. Thompson, Glasgow
Launched in May of 1864
Made five successful runs through the blockade
Captured August 23,1864, on sixth run
Sent for adjudication to Philadelphia
Fitted out as a gunboat with four guns
Took part in the bombardment of Fort Fisher

Contents

INTRODUCTION

CAPE FEAR PRIVATEERS IN THE WAR OF 1861

By way of introduction, we present an account by Mr. Sprunt, printed in Wilmington in 1896 from TALES AND TRADITIONS OF THE LOWER CAPE FEAR, the book that he composed and had printed in six weeks (the good-old days of leisure)," as a compliment to Captain John W. Harper, of the steamer *Wilmington*, by one who treasures the memories of the Lower Cape Fear"...as does the artist-editor, from my experiences since I came to its banks after my separation from the United States Naval Reserve in 1946, having served my beloved country to put down the forces of tyranny then seeking control of the lives and souls of the human race.

"This little guide book" by our author has served the community as a source book for history ever since its publication. The Lower Cape Fear cherishes and maintains these traditions.

In that book it says: "When the war between the States commenced, the entire common navy was in possession of the Federal authorities, and the Confederates had no other resort than to enlist armed ships under letters of marque. Very soon quite a number of small vessels were put in commission, and reached the high seas by running the blockade; and in less than a month more than twenty vessels were taken and run into Southern ports.

The first vessel fitted out as a privateer in Wilmington was the steam tug *Mariner* during the summer of 1861. She was owned by a company of which the late Joseph H. Flanner was president, and was armed with one twenty-four pounder forward and two nine pounders aft, and under the command of Captain B.W. Beery. She made a cruise on the coast of North Carolina, captured one, perhaps two, vessels, and sent them into New Berne, when she returned to Wilmington. She was afterwards used during the spring and summer of 1862 by Confederate States Government as a guard boat on the Cape Fear River, and was under command of the late Captain Joseph Price, a Wilmington boy, who was well known and greatly esteemed by our citizens. She then made one trip through the blockade to Nassau and back to this port, but was captured on the next outward trip.

The United States Government tug *Uncle Ben* came to Wilmington in April 1861, and was taken possession of by the Confederate States Government. When the iron-clad *North Carolina* was built, the engines of the tug were taken out and used for that ship, the hull was sold and bought by a Mr. Power, of the firm of Power, Low & Co., who was engaged in the blockade business at that time. She was rigged as a schooner and armed with one twenty-pound Parrott gun and two nine-pound smooth bore guns. She went to sea as a privateer, cruised in the West

Indies for some months, capturing three or four vessels, but only succeeded in getting one into port, owing to the rigid blockade. She was finally sold in Nassau and was lost on Hatteras in the Winter of 1865. After the seizure of the *Uncle Ben* by the Confederate authorities, her name was changed to *Retribution*, and she was commanded by Captain Locke, of Nova Scotia, her first officer being Captain Joseph Price, of Wilmington. These two were the only privateers fitted out in Wilmington during our late Civil War. They did not accomplish very much, and much could have been expected of them, for they were ordinary tug-boats improvised for the occasion, and not suited to the hazardous business in which they were employed. But they did some damage, nevertheless, and those who managed and had charge of them are justly entitled to praise for the skill and intrepidity they displayed under very embarrassing and adverse conditions.

(The foregoing has been kindly furnished me by Colonel J.G. Burr.)

PREFACE.

From early youth I have loved the Cape Fear River, the ships and the sailors which it bears upon its bosom. As a schoolboy I delighted to wander along the wharves and watch the strangers from foreign lands, whose uncouth cries and unknown tongues inspired me with a longing for the sea, and for the countries far away whence they had come; in later years I heard the stories of the old time Cape Fear gentlemen, and treasured these memories of our brave and generous people; and now as I watch from my window the white sails glistening in the morning light, or as, when the evening shadows deepen, I gaze upon the wide expanse resplendent with the glory of the stars, I try to catch the vanishing lines of its history as the current sweeps along with its message to the sea.

But now the oft told tales of ante-bellum times are seldom heard. John Hampden Hill, George Davis, John S. James, A.J. deRosset, James G. Burr, and other treasurers of Cape Fear annals, have crossed over the river, and there are none to take their places. It is of more recent times that I write: of an epoch in our history stained with the best blood of Cape Fear gentlemen; of war and pestilence and famine; of indomitable courage and heroic fortitude; of privations and suffering; and of a strange traffic through a beleaguered city, which supplied the sinews of war long after the resources of the South had been exhausted; a traffic which will be unique in our history because the conditions which sustained it can never again occur.

As I close these pages and look westward across the river, the bright light falls on the yellowish green of the pasture land; and above its ceaseless current loom the Brunswick pines fringing the sky line with a somber hue. The old time planter with his retinue of slaves is gone. The wharves where the swift blockade runners were moored are rotting away, and thick vines cover the ruins of the old Confederate Cotton Press: but the harbour and the river are the same as when Yeamans came with the first settlers, or as when Flora MacDonald sailed past the town to the restful haven of Cross Creek; and the Dram Tree still stands to warn the outgoing mariner that his voyage has begun, and to welcome the incoming storm-tossed sailor to the quiet harbour beyond.

JAMES SPRUNT.

Wilmington, N.C. February 10th, 1902.

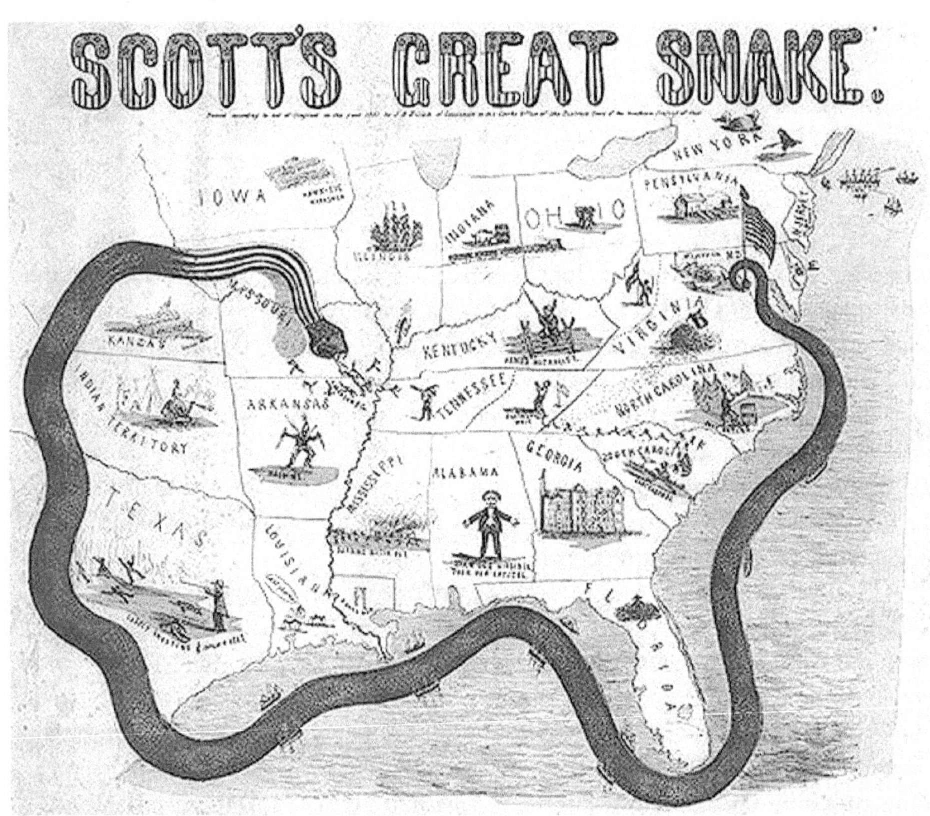

A contemporary illustration of Gen. Winfield Scott's "Anaconda Plan," wherein Union forces would blockade Southern ports, strangling the rebellion by denying the Confederacy supplies from overseas.

THE BLOCKADE.

On the nineteenth of April 1861, President Lincoln declared by proclamation, a Military and Commercial Blockade of our Southern ports, which was supplemented by the proclamation of the twenty-seventh of May, to embrace the whole Atlantic Coast from the capes of Virginia to the mouth of the Rio Grande. This was technically a "Constructive," or "Paper," Blockade, inasmuch as the Declaration of the Great Powers assembled in Congress at Paris in 1856 removed all uncertainty as to the principle upon which the adjudication of prize claims must proceed, by declaring that "Blockades, in order to be binding, must be effective; that is to say, must be maintained by a force sufficient really to prevent access to the enemy's coast." It was obviously impossible at that time for the Federal Government to enforce a blockade of the Southern Coast, measuring 3,549 miles and containing 189 harbors, besides almost innumerable inlets and sounds through which small craft might easily elude the four United States warships then available for service, the remaining 38 ships of war in commission being on distant stations.

Measures were, therefore, taken by the Navy Department to close the entrance of the most important Southern ports, notably those of Charleston and Savannah, by sinking vessels loaded with stone across the main channels or bars. Preparations were also made on a more extensive plan to destroy the natural roadsteads of other Southern ports and harbours along the coast by the same means; but, although twenty-five vessels were sunk in the smaller inlets, it does not appear that this novel method of blockade was generally adopted.

In the meantime, urgent orders had been sent recalling from foreign stations every available ship of war; and by December of the same year the Secretary of the Navy had purchased and armed 264 ships which, with their 2,557 guns and 22,000 men, rendered the "Paper Blockade" comparatively effective. A sorry looking fleet it was as compared with our modern navies; ships, barks, schooners, sloops, tugs, passenger boats—anything that would carry a gun, from the hoary type of Noah's Ark to the double-end ferry boat still conspicuous in New York waters.

"The Blockading Fleet," says Judge Advocate Cowley, "was divided into two squadrons; the Atlantic Blockading Squadron of 22 vessels carrying 296 guns and 3,300 men, and Gulf Blockading Squadron of 21 vessels carrying 282 guns and 3,500 men." This force was constantly increased as the two hundred specially designed ships of war were built by the Navy Department. The Squadron reached its highest degree of efficiency during the fourth year of the war by the acquisition of many prizes which were quickly converted into light draft cruisers and which rendered effective naval service, frequently under their original names.

USS Daylight, ***the first Federal blockader off the Cape Fear coast.***

THE BLOCKADERS

The first blockader placed upon the Cape Fear Station was one bearing the misnomer "Daylight," which appeared July 20,1861. Others soon followed, until the number of the blockaders off New Inlet and the main bar of Cape Fear River was increased to about thirty or more; these formed a cordon every night in the shape of a crescent, the horns of which were so close in shore that it was almost impossible for a small boat to pass without discovery. Armed picket barges also patrolled the bars and sometimes crept close in upon the forts. For a year or more the fleet was largely kept upon the blockading stations; then a second cordon was placed across the track of the blockade runners near the ports of Nassau and the Bermudas, the cruisers of which sometimes violated the international distance restriction of one league—three geographical miles—from neutral land. At last a third cordon was drawn on the edge of the Gulf Stream, by which the hunted and harassed blockade runner often became an easy prey in the early morning, after a hard night's run in the darkness during which no lights were visible to friend or foe; even the binnacle lamp being carefully screened, leaving only a small peep hole by which the ship was steered.

THE CRUISERS.

Some of the later cruisers were faster than the blockade runners, and were more dreaded than the blockading squadron; not only because of their greater speed, but chiefly because of the proximity of their consorts which kept them almost in sight, often to the discomfiture of their unhappy quarry, headed off and opposed in every direction. The prospective division of big prize money running into millions of dollars was, of course, the most exciting feature of the service on the Federal side. Occasionally there was comparatively trifling compensation, but greater enjoyment, in the capture of some small fry of blockade runners, consisting of pilot boats or large yawls laden with two or three bales of cotton and a crew of three or four youths, which sometimes came to grief in a most humiliating way. These small craft, upon one of which the writer was at sea for two weeks, were too frail for the risk of the longer voyages, and were usually projected from the small inlets, or sounds, farther south, which gave them a short run of about a hundred miles to the outer Bahama Keys, through whose dangerous waters they would warily make their way to Nassau. A boat of this description sailed over a Florida bar on a dark night under a favorable wind; but, failing to get out of sight of land before morning dawned, was overhauled at sunrise by a blockader and ordered to come alongside, where, with their own hands, these miniature blockade runners were obliged to hook on the falls of the Yankee's davits, by which they were ignominiously hoisted – boat, cargo and crew – to the captor's deck.

A contraband sailor.

The desertion of negro slaves from tide water plantations and their subsequent rescue as "Intelligent Contrabands" by the coasting cruisers formed an occasional incident in the records of their official logs; but it is a noteworthy fact, deserving honorable mention, that comparatively few of the trusted negroes upon whom the soldiers in the Confederate Army relied for the protection and support of their families at home were thus found wanting. A pathetic and fatal instance is recalled in the case of a misguided negro family which put off from the shore in the darkness, hoping they would be picked up by a chance gunboat in the morning. They were hailed by a cruiser at daylight, but in attempting to board her their frail boat was swamped, and the father alone rescued; the mother and children perished in the sea.

PORTS OF REFUGE.

The natural advantages of Wilmington at the time of which we write made it an ideal port for blockade runners, there being two entrances to the river; New Inlet on the north, and the Western, or main bar on the south of Cape Fear. "This cape," said Mr. George Davis, "is the southernmost point of Smith's Island, a naked, bleak elbow of sand, jutting far out into the ocean. Immediately in its front are the Frying Pan Shoals, pushing out still farther twenty miles to sea. Together they stand for warning and for woe; and together they catch the long, majestic roll of the Atlantic, as it sweeps through a thousand miles of grandeur and power from the Artic towards the Gulf. It is the play-ground of billows and tempests, the kingdom of silence and awe, disturbed by no sound save the sea-gull's shriek and the breaker's roar. Its whole aspect is suggestive, not of repose and beauty, but of desolation and terror. Imagination cannot adorn it; romance cannot hallow it; local pride cannot soften it; there it stands to-day, bleak and threatening and pitiless as it stood three hundred years ago when Grenville and White came near unto death upon its sands; and there it will stand bleak and threatening and pitiless until the earth and sea shall give up their dead. And as its nature, so its name, is now, always has been, and always will be, the "Cape of Fear."

***The blockade runner* Lilian.**

The slope of our beach for many miles is very gradual to deep water. The soundings along the coast are regular, and the floor of the ocean is remarkably even. A steamer hard pressed by the enemy could run along the outer edge of the breakers without great risk of grounding; the pursuer, being usually of deeper draft, was obliged to keep further off shore. The Confederate Steamer *Lilian*, of which I was then Purser, was chased for nearly a hundred miles from Cape Lookout by the U.S. steamer *Shenandoah*, which sailed a parallel course within half a mile of her and forced the *Lilian* at times into the breakers. This was probably the narrowest escape ever made by a blockade runner in a chase. The *Shenandoah* began firing her broadside guns at three o'clock, p.m., her gunners and commanding officers of the batteries being distinctly visible to the *Lilian*'s crew.

A heavy sea was running which deflected the aim of the man-of-war, and which alone saved the *Lilian* from destruction. A furious bombardment by the *Shenandoah*, aggravated by the display of the *Lilian*'s Confederate flag, was continued until nightfall, when by a clever ruse, the *Lilian*, guided by the flash of her pursuer's guns, stopped for a few minutes; then putting her helm hard over, ran across the wake of the war-ship straight out to sea, and, on the following morning, passed the fleet off Fort Fisher in such a crippled condition that several weeks were spent in Wilmington for repairs.

This principal seaport of North Carolina had become also the most important in the Southern Confederacy. Prior to the beginning of hostilities it had sustained a large traffic in naval stores and lumber, and now it was to be for a time the

Wilmington, North Carolina

chief cotton port of America. Before the war, its miles of tidy wharves had been lined, often three deep, with white-winged sailing vessels from near and far: there being only two steamers, the *North Carolina* and the *Parkersburg*, forerunners of the steam era which was to revolutionize commerce throughout the world.

A startling change in the aspect of the port was now apparent. The sailing vessels, even to the tiny corn crackers from Hyde County, had vanished: likewise, the two New York steamers. The long line of wharves was occupied by a fleet of nondescript craft the like of which had never been seen in North Carolina waters. At a cotton compress on the western side of the river near the Market Street ferry were cargoes for Nassau and Bermuda, while other new comers were busily discharging their anomalous cargoes of life-preserving and death-dealing supplies for the new Confederacy.

Dr. James Dickson

The good old town was sadly marred by the plagues of war and pestilence and famine; four hundred and forty-seven of a population reduced by flight to five thousand, had been carried off by the epidemic of yellow fever brought from Nassau by the steamer *Kate*; and hundreds more of the younger generation, who gave up their lives in the Confederate cause, had been brought to their final resting place in Oakdale Cemetery. Suspension of the civil law, neglect of sanitary precautions, the removal of nearly all the famine stricken women and children to safer places in the interior, and the coming of speculators and adventurers to the auction sales of the blockade runners' merchandise, as well as of lawless and depraved characters attracted by the camps and shipping, had quite changed the aspect of the whole community. The military post, including all the river and harbour defences, was under the command of Major General W.H.C. Whiting, a distinguished West Point engineer of great ability, well known and honoured in Wilmington, where he married and resided. He fell, mortally wounded, in the last Fort Fisher fight, and died a prisoner of war in a Northern hospital. His remains were brought home, and now rest in Oakdale beside those of his most estimable wife who recently followed him.

The distress of Wilmington during the yellow fever epidemic was described as follows by the late Doctor Thomas F. Wood in his biographical sketch of one of the heroes of that fearful scourge, Doctor James H. Dickson, who died at his post of duty.

"The month of September, 1862, was one of great calamity to Wilmington. The alarming forebodings of the visitation of yellow fever in a pestilential form had ripened into a certainty. Depleted of her young and active men, there was only a military garrison in occupation, and when the presence of fever was announced the soldiers were removed to a safer locality. The country people, taking a panic at the news of the presence of the fever, no longer sent in their supplies. The town was deserted, its silence broken only by the occasional pedestrian bound on errands of mercy to the sick, or the rumbling of the rude funeral cart. The blockade was being maintained with increased rigor. The only newspaper then published was *The Wilmington Journal*, a daily under the editorship of James Fulton, and its issues were maintained under the greatest difficulties, owing to the scarcity of paper and to sickness among the printers. All eyes were turned anxiously toward the physicians and those in authority, for help. To all the resident physicians, the disease was a new one; not one in the number had ever seen a case of yellow fever, and among them were men of large experience. The municipal authorities recognized their helplessness; the town was neglected, for it had been overcrowded with soldiers and visitors since the early days of the spring of 1861. The black pall of smoke from the burning tar barrels added solemnity to the deadly silence of the streets; designed to purify the air and mitigate the pestilence, it seemed more like fuliginous clouds of ominous portent, a somber emblem of mourning. Panic, distress , mute despair, want, had fallen upon a population then strained to its utmost, with the bleeding columns of its regiments dying the hills of Maryland with their blood, until the whole air was filled with the wail of the widow and orphan, and the dead could no longer be honored with the last tribute of respect.

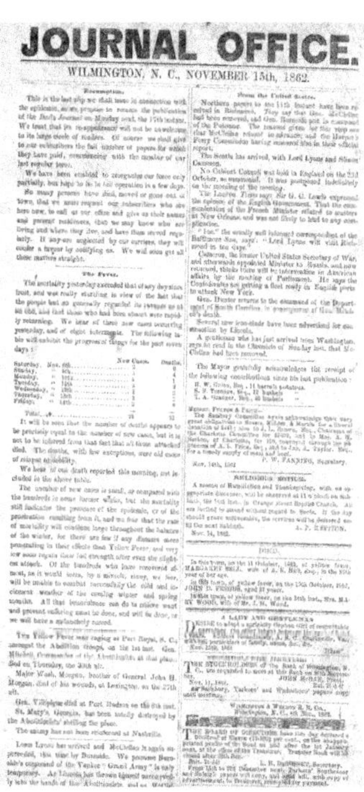

JOURNAL OFFICE.

WILMINGTON, N. C., NOVEMBER 15th, 1862.

A Journal *broadside*

The Wilmington Journal of September 29th, 1862, gave all its available editorial space to chronicle, for the first time, the character of the epidemic, and in a few brief words to notice the death of some of the more prominent citizens. One paragraph in the simple editorial notice ran as follows; "Dr. James H. Dickson, a physician of the highest character and standing, died here on Sunday morning of yellow fever. Dr. Dickson's death is a great loss to the profession and to the community." Close by, in another column, from the pen of the acting

Adjutant, Lieutenant VanBokkelen, of the 3d N.C. Infantry, numbering so many gallant souls of the young men of Wilmington, was the list of the killed and wounded from the bloody field of Sharpsburg.

Distressed and bereaved by this new weight of sorrow, Wilmington sat in the mournful habiliments of widowhood, striving, amidst the immensity of the struggle, to make her courageous voice heard above all the din of war, to nerve the brave hearts who stood as a girdle of steel about beleaguered Richmond.

"James Fulton, the well known editor of the *Journal*, the wary politican and cautious editor, striving to keep the worst from the world, lest the enemy might use it to our disadvantage, often ruthlessly suppressed from his limited space such matters as in these days of historical research might be of the greatest service. There were two predominant topics which eclipsed all the impending sorrow and distress: first, foreign intervention, for the purpose of bringing about an honorable peace; second, warnings to the State government of the inadequacy of the defense of Wilmington harbour against the enemy. The former topic was discussed with unvarying pleasure. The horizon of the future was aglow with the rosy dreams of mandates from the British and French governments which would bring independence to the Confederacy and peace and quietness to the numerous homes, from the sea to the mountains, where sorrow and death had hung like a pall. It is not strange, therefore, that the few publications that had survived the scarcity of printing material should have contained so little biographical matter. Comrades dropped on the right and on the left, but the ranks were closed up, the hurried tear wiped away, and the line pushed steadily forward. The distinguished physician, or general, or jurist, as well as the humble private, got his passing notice in the meager letters which a chance correspondent sent to one of the few newspapers, and in a short time he was forgotten in the fresh calamity of the day."

RESCUE OF MADAME DeROSSET.

We found at the ship-yard in Wilmington, while the *Lilian* was undergoing repairs, the noted blockade runner *Lynx*, commanded by one of the most daring spirits in the service, Capt. Reed. This officer has been described in a Northern magazine as a pirate, but he was one of the mildest mannered of gentlemen, a capital seaman, and apparently entirely devoid of fear. He had previously commanded the *Gibraltar*, formerly the first Confederate cruiser *Sumter*; and he brought through the blockade in this ship to Wilmington the two enormous guns which attracted so much attention at that time. One of them exploded, through a fault in loading; the other was used for the defense of Charleston, and rendered effective service.

A thrilling incident occurred in the destruction of the *Lynx*, a few weeks after we left her at Wilmington, which nearly terminated the life of a brave and charming little lady, the wife of Mr. Louis H. deRosset, and of her infant child, who were passengers for Nassau. At half past seven o'clock on the evening of September 26, 1864, the *Lynx* attempted to run the blockade at New Inlet, but was immediately discovered in the Swash Channel by the Federal cruiser *Niphon*, which fired several broadsides into her at short range, nearly every shot striking her hull and seriously disabling her. Notwithstanding this, Captain Reed continued his efforts to escape, and for a short time was slipping away from his pursuer; but he was again intercepted by two Federal men-of-war, the *Howquah* and the *Governor Buckingham*. Mrs. deRosset describing the scene a few days afterwards, said:

"Immediately the sky was illuminated with rockets; broadside upon broadside, volley upon volley, was poured upon us. The Captain put me in the wheel house for safety. I had scarcely taken my seat when a ball passed three inches above my head, wounding the man at the wheel next to me; a large piece of the wheel house knocked me violently on the head. I flew to the cabin, took my baby in my arms, and immediately another ball passed through the cabin. We came so near one of the enemy's boats that they fired a round of musketry, and demanded surrender. We passed them like lightning; our vessel commenced sinking! Eight shots went through and through below the water line. I stayed in the cabin until I could no longer keep my baby out of the water."

Mrs. deRosset

The *Howquah* then engaged the *Lynx* at close quarters, and her batteries tore away a large part of the paddle boxes and bridge deck. The *Buckingham* also attacked the plucky blockade runner at so short a range that her commander fired all the charges from his revolver at Captain Reed and his pilot on the bridge. The continual flashing of the guns brightly illuminated the chase and, escape being impossible, Captain Reed, much concerned for the safety of his passengers, headed his sinking ship for the beach. In the meantime Fort Fisher was firing upon his pursuers with deadly effect, killing and wounding five men on the *Howquah* and disabling one of the guns. The sea was very rough that night, and the treacherous breakers with their deafening roar afforded little hope of landing a woman and a baby through the surf; nevertheless, it was the only alternative, and right bravely did the heroine meet it. Through the breakers the *Lynx* was driven to her destruction, the shock as her keel struck the bottom sending her crew headlong to the deck. Boats were lowered with great difficulty, the sea dashing over the bulwarks and drenching the sailors to the point of strangulation. Madame deRosset, with the utmost coolness, watched her chance while the boat lurched and pounded against the stranded ship, and jumped gracefully to her place; the baby, wrapped in a blanket was tossed from the deck to her mother ten feet below, and then the fight for a landing began; while the whole crew, forgetful of their own danger, and inspired with courage by the brave lady's example, joined in three hearty cheers as she disappeared in the darkness towards the shore. Under the later glare of the burning ship, which was set on fire when abandoned, a safe landing was effected, but with great suffering; soaking wet, without food or drink, they remained on the beach until a message could reach Colonel Lamb at Fort Fisher, five miles distant, whence an ambulance was sent to carry the passengers twenty miles up to Wilmington. The baby blockade runner, Gabrielle, survived this perilous adventure, also an exciting run through the fleet in the Confederate steamer *Owl*; and she is now the devoted wife of Colonel Alfred Moore Waddell, Mayor of Wilmington.

WAR PRICES.

The prices of food and clothing had advanced in proportion to the depreciation of Confederate money; the plainest necessities were almost unobtainable—$50 for a ham, $500 for a barrel of flour, $500 for a pair of boots, $600 for a suit of clothes, $1,500 for an overcoat, and $100 a pound for coffee or tea, were readily paid as the fortunes of the Confederacy waned. Coffee was perhaps the greatest luxury, and was seldom used; substitutes of beans, potatoes and rye, with "long sweetening,"—sorghum, having been generally adopted. Within a mile or two unattractive spinsters of mature age, one of whom, in the other's absence, was asked by an old reprobate of some means in the neighborhood to marry him, a preposterous proposal which she indignantly rejected. Upon the return of the absent sister, however, she was made to feel that she had thrown away the golden opportunity of a life time; for, "Why," said the sister, "didn't you know he has a bag of coffee in his house?"

Another true incident will also serve to illustrate the comic side of the great crisis. Our evening meal consisted of milk, rye coffee, youpon tea, honey, and one wheaten biscuit each, with well prepared corn muffins and hominy ad libitum. These biscuits, however, were valued beyond price, and the right of each individual to them, as well as the plate upon which they rested, was closely guarded by the younger members of the family. One evening there appeared just before supper and itinerant preacher, who was made welcome to the best we had. Addressing himself with vigor to the tempting plate of biscuits, and ignoring the despised muffins, which were politely pressed upon him by our dismayed youngsters at his side, he actually devoured the entire dozen with apparent ease and great relish. Upon being informed at the hour of retiring that it would be inconvenient to serve his breakfast at daylight, when he desired to depart, he said, to our amazement, that, rather than disturb us in the early morning, he would take his breakfast then and there before going to bed.

INTERMEDIATE PORTS.

The chief intermediate neutral ports of refuge for the blockade runners from Wilmington were Nassau, upon the island of New Providence in the Bahamas, and St. George's and Hamilton, in the Bermudas. These towns were of small note before the Civil War began, but they became of great commercial importance as the traffic through the blockade increased. The distance from Cape Fear to Nassau, almost due south, is 570 miles, and to Bermuda, nearly due east, is 674 miles. The run to Nassau by a fast ship was 48 to 55 hours, and to Bermuda about 72 hours.

The inhabitants of Nassau had, with few exceptions, gained a precarious and questionable livelihood by wrecking, which in many instances was little short of piracy. Nature is so beautiful in the West Indies that the worthless, indolent negroes who largely composed the population subsisted daily upon fish and yams and tropical fruits, in great variety, at the cost of an hour's work. Left to themselves, they had relapsed into semi-barbarism, which may be said of the West Indies negroes of Congo origin in general. The American blacks, especially those of the South in their state of slavery, were infinitely superior, and their characteristics were kindly and peaceable, quite the reverse of those with whom

A blockade runner at anchor in the harbor at Nassau.

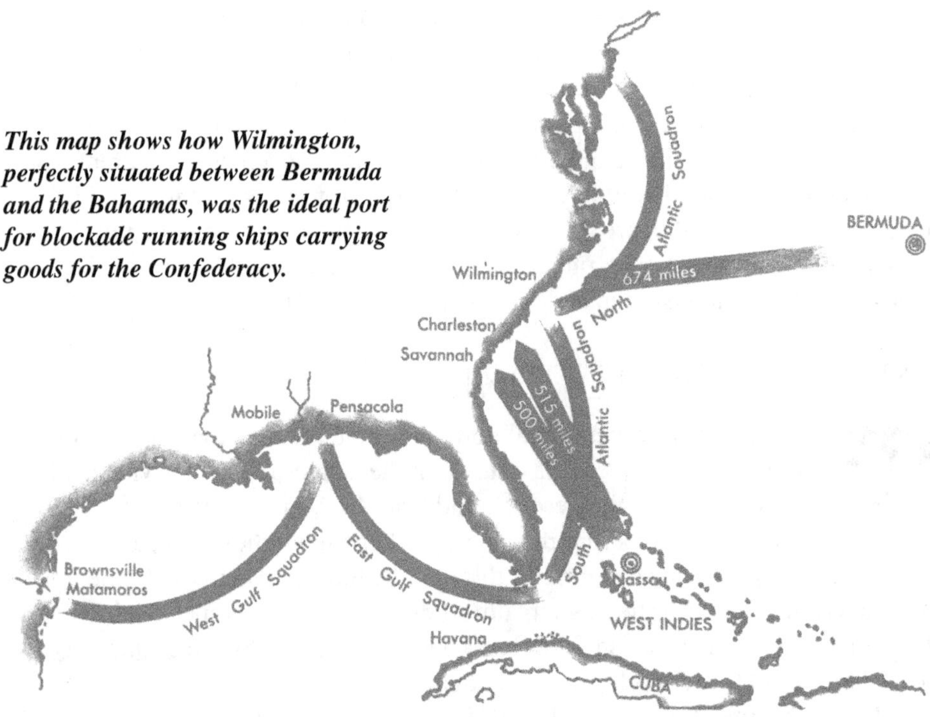

This map shows how Wilmington, perfectly situated between Bermuda and the Bahamas, was the ideal port for blockade running ships carrying goods for the Confederacy.

we had to deal in Nassau. The influx of speculators and adventurers, and good business men as well, from all parts of the world soon gave to Nassau, and also to Bermuda (whose population comprised a much better class of natives), a heterogeneous and motley aspect sometimes quite picturesque. The cost of respectable living became so exorbitant that the British government was asked for a larger allowance by the officers of the regiment quartered at Nassau, and also by the commander at the Bermudas. The enormous profits made by successful blockade runners quite turned their heads; and swaggering sailors with their pockets full of gold were as reckless in spending it upon their dissolute associates, as many of the officers and ship owners were in the indulgence of their more expensive tastes for wine and gambling at the Royal Victoria Hotel.

FINANCIAL ESTIMATES.

I have not been able to obtain an approximate estimate of the value of supplies brought by blockade runners into the Confederacy during the four years' war, nor the amount of the losses by ship owners who failed to make a successful voyage through the Federal fleet. I have, however, carefully computed the actual sum realized by the United States government from public sales of prizes, recorded by Admiral Porter in his *Naval History of the Civil War*, which aggregates $21,759,595.05; to which may be reasonably added $10,000,000.00 for prizes of my knowledge not included in this report, and $10,000,000.00 more for valuable ships and cargoes stranded or destroyed by design or accident while attempting to escape from the blockading squadron. This total of $42,000,000.00 represents only a part, perhaps one-half, of the capital invested. Many successful steamers ran up their profits into millions. A steamer carrying 1,000 bales of cotton sometimes realized a profit of a quarter million dollars on the inward and outward run, within two weeks. Cotton could be purchased in the Confederacy for 3 cents per pound gold, and sold in England at the equivalent of 45 cents to $1 a pound, and the profits on some classes of goods brought into the Confederacy were in the same proportion. It is probably within the bounds of truth to say that the blockade running traffic during the war, including the cost of the ships, amounted to about one hundred and fifty-millions of dollars, gold standard.

THE FAMINE STRICKEN CONFEDERACY.

A pathetic feature of the traffic in the last year of the war was the falling off in the demand for blockade goods in the South at a time when they were most needed by the people, and when they were most difficult to obtain, even by the employment of the latest designed blockade runners, the construction of which cost twice as much as that of the previous type. The sad truth is, the Confederates were no longer able to buy even the commonest necessities of life, and four-fifths of the women and children at home, as well as the soldiers in the field, were on the verge of starvation. Also, the demands of the Confederate Government for a larger proportion of the cargo space at reduced rates of freight had a depressing effect upon traffic; and many of the successful traders withdrew their ships, which, otherwise, would have had to face the hazard of almost certain capture or destruction. Mr. Tom Taylor, a conspicuous and celebrated leader in blockade running, who controlled a fleet of steamers, said that the Commissary General of the Confederacy in Richmond divulged to him early in the last year of the war that Gen. Lee's army had rations for only thirty days, and that there were no means of replenishing the commissariat unless Mr. Taylor could proceed to Nassau and bring relief within three weeks. Mr. Taylor had then in Wilmington his steamer *Banshee*, whose captain he telegraphed to prepare for sea and await his arrival. After an exciting and lengthy journey of three days and nights from Richmond to Wilmington by way of Danville, the Weldon road connection having been cut off, Mr. Taylor embarked upon the steamer *Banshee* on a most exciting and dangerous run to Nassau, and brought back a ship-load of provisions, which he landed in Wilmington within eighteen days after his departure from Richmond. It is an established fact, stated by both Southern and Northern authorities, that the *Banshee* saved the Army of

Northern Virginia from starvation. Mr. Taylor graphically describes this run as follows:

In the interim between our leaving Wilmington and our return, Porter's fleet had made an unsuccessful attack upon Fort Fisher, and this Federal commander was just then, at the time of our appearance upon the scene, concluding his attack and re-embarking his beaten troops. When morning broke and we were near the fort, we counted sixty-four vessels that we had passed through. After being heavily fired into at daybreak by several gunboats (the fort being unable to protect us as usual, owing to nearly all of its guns having been put out of action in the attack of two days previous), it was an exciting moment as we crossed the bar in safety, cheered by the garrison, some two thousand strong, who knew that we had provisions on board for the relief of their comrades in Virginia.

I shall never forget that trip. We sailed from Nassau at dusk on the evening before Christmas day, but were only just outside the harbor when our steam-pipe split and we had to return. As it was hopeless, on account of the moon, to make the attempt unless we could get away next day, I was in despair, and thought it was all up with my enterprise. After long trying in vain to find some one to undertake the necessary repairs, owing to its being Christmas day, I found at last a Yankee, who said: "Well, sir, it's only a question of price." I said, "Name yours," and he replied, "Well, I guess $400 for three clamps would be fair." I said, "All right, if finished by six o'clock." He set to work, and we made all arrangements to start. Shortly after six the work was finished, but the black pilot then declared he couldn't take her out until the tide turned, there being no room to turn her in the harbour. As it was a question of hours, I said, "Back her out." He grinned and said, "Perhaps do plenty damage." "Never mind;" said I, "try it;" and we did, with the result that we came plump into the man-of-war lying at the entrance of the harbour (officers all on deck ready to go down to their Christmas dinner), and ground along her side, smashing two of her boats in, but doing ourselves little damage. "Good-bye," I shouted; "A merry Christmas! Send the bill in for the boats." Away we went clear, and fortunate it was we did so, as we only arrived off Wilmington just in time to run through Porter's fleet before daybreak on the 28th of December.

The trip out was equally exciting, for I had as passengers General Randolph, ex-Secretary of State for War, who was going to Europe invalided, and his wife. I did not want to take them, as the Banshee *had practically no accommodation whatever, particularly for ladies. However, she had such a good character for safety, that they pleaded hard to be taken, and I at last consented, though I did not like at all the responsibility of having a lady on board. I was determined, however, to make Mrs. Randolph as safe as possible, so I told the stevedore to keep a square space between the cotton bales on deck, into which she could retire in case the firing became hot. And hot it did become. Running down with a strong ebb tide through the Smith's Island inlet channel, we suddenly found a gunboat in the middle of the channel on the bar. It was too late to stop, so we put at her, almost grazing her sides and receiving her broadside point blank. Mrs. Randolph had retired to her place of safety, but she told me afterwards that, alarmed as she was, she could not help laughing, when, after she had been there only an instant, my colored servant, who had evidently fixed upon the place as appearing to be most safe, jumped right on top of her, his teeth chattering through fear. How we laughed the next morning, and how poor Sam got chaffed! But he afterwards became quite a cool hand; and when we were running in, in daylight, in the* Will-o'-the-Wisp *and the shot were coming thick, Sam appeared on the bridge with his usual "Coffee, Sar!"*

After we had got rid of our friend on the bar, we were heavily peppered by her consorts outside, from whom we received no damage; but we fell in with very bad weather, and the ship was under water most of the time. Right glad I was to land my passengers, who were half dead through sea-sickness, exposure and fatigue.

DEFENSES.

The defenses of Oak Island, commanding the main bar of the Cape Fear river, were composed of Fort Caswell and Fort Campbell—the latter a large earth work situated about one mile down the beach from Fort Caswell—Battery Shaw, and some smaller earthworks. With reference to the principal fortification I have received the following official particulars from the Secretary of War:

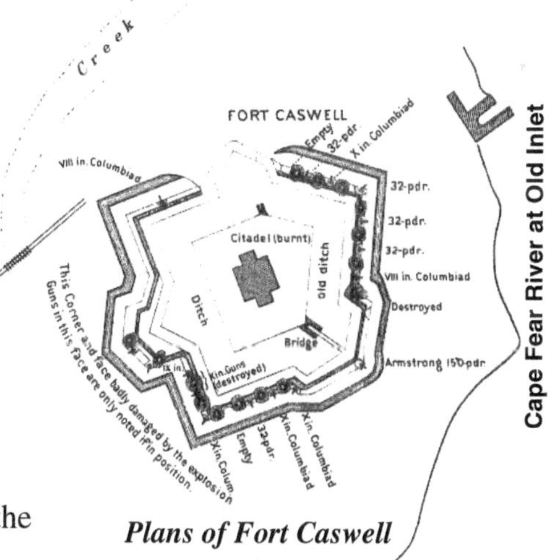

Plans of Fort Caswell

Fort Caswell, at the mouth of the Cape Fear River, North Carolina, was commenced in the year 1826, the first appropriation for its construction being under act of Congress approved March 2nd, 1825. It was reported as about completed by Captain Alexander J. Swift, United States Engineers, Oct. 20th, 1838, at a total cost of $473,402. From 1838 to 1857, for preservation of site, repairs &c., at Fort Caswell, and some repairs at Fort Johnston, the sum of $69,422.09 was expended, making a total to 1857 of $542,844.09. It was named Fort Caswell by War Department Order, No. 32 of April 18th, 1833.

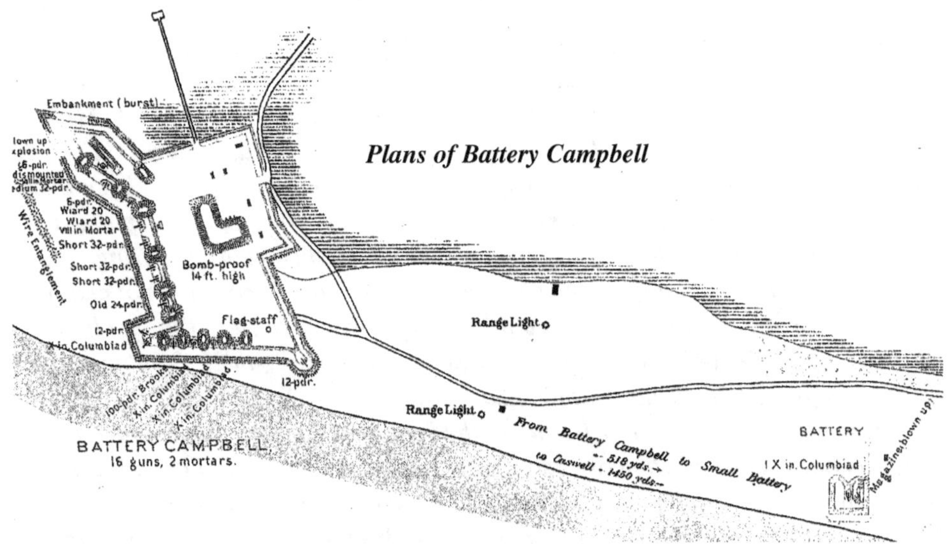

Plans of Battery Campbell

Fort Caswell was an enclosed pentagonal work, with a loop-holed scrap wall, flanked by caponieres; it was constructed for an armament of 61 channel-bearing guns, mounted en-barbette, and a few small guns for land defense. Capacious defensive barracks, called a citadel, occupied a large part of the parade.

It is a remarkable fact that, notwithstanding its exposed position to the Federal fleet, no general engagement occurred at Caswell during the four years' war. The fort was of great service, however, in defending the main bar and the garrison at Smithville, although the fighting was confined to an occasional artillery duel with the United States blockading fleet.

During the past three years the ruins of Fort Caswell have disappeared; and the General Government has erected on Oak Island, under the old name—in honor of the first governor of North Carolina—one of the strongest forts on the Atlantic coast, armed with far reaching disappearing batteries and equipped with the most approved appliances of modern warfare.

The New Inlet, which was more frequently used by the blockade runners, was protected for four years by Fort Fisher, a splendid creation of its gallant defender, Colonel Lamb, and which was styled by Federal engineers "The Malakoff of the South."

The plans of Fort Fisher were Colonel Lamb's; and as the work progressed they were approved by Generals French, Raines, Longstreet, Beauregard and Whiting, who were among the best engineers of West Point. It was built solely for the purpose of resisting the fire of a large fleet, and it withstood uninjured, as to armament, two of the fiercest bombardments in history. The land face of the works was 682 yards long, and the sea face was 1,898 yards long. The position commanded the last gateway between the Confederate States and the outside world. Its capture, with the resulting loss of all the Cape Fear River defenses and Wilmington, the most important entrepot of the Confederacy, effectually ended blockade running. Gen. Lee, recognizing the importance of Wilmington, sent word to Colonel Lamb that Fort Fisher must be held, or he could not subsist his army. The following description of the land face and sea face of Fort Fisher is given in Colonel Lamb's own words;

At the land face of Fort Fisher the peninsula was about half a mile wide. This face commenced about one hundred feet from the river with a half bastion, and extended with a heavy curtain to a full bastion on the ocean side, where it joined the sea face. The work was built to withstand the heaviest artillery fire. There was no moat with scarp and counterscarp, so essential for defence against storming parties, the shifting sands rendering its construction impossible with the material available.

The outer slope was twenty feet high and was sodded with marsh grass which grew luxuriantly. The parapet was not less than twenty-five feet thick, with an inclination of only one foot. The revetment was five feet nine inches high from the floor of the gun chambers, and these were some twelve feet or more from the interior plane. The guns were all mounted in barbette on Columbiad carriages, there being no casemated gun in the fort. Between the gun chambers, containing one or two guns each, there were twenty heavy guns on the land face; there were heavy traverses exceeding in size any known to engineers, to protect from an enfilading fire. They extended out some twelve feet or more in height above the parapet, running back thirty feet or more. The gun chambers were reached from the rear by steps. In each traverses was an alternate magazine, or bomb-proof, the latter ventilated by an air chamber. The passage ways penetrated traverses

This 150-lb. Armstrong gun was among the forty-seven cannons defending Ft. Fisher.

in the interior of the work, forming additional bomb-proofs for the reliefs for the guns.

As a defence against infantry there was a system of subterra torpedoes extending across the peninsula, five to six hundred feet from the land face, and so disconnected that the explosion of one would not affect the others; inside the torpedoes, about fifty feet from the berm of the work, extending from river bank to sea shore, was a heavy palisade of sharpened logs nine feet high, pierced for musketry, and so laid out as to have an enfilading fire on the center, where there was a redoubt guarding a sally port, from which two napoleons were run as occasion required. At the river end of the palisade was a deep and muddy slough, across which was a bridge, the entrance of the river road into the port; commanding this bridge was a napoleon gun. There were three mortars in the rear of the land face.

The sea face of Fort Fisher ran for a mile, down to New Inlet.

THE SEA FACE OF FORT FISHER.

The sea face for one hundred yards from the northwest bastion was of the same massive character as the land face. A crescent battery intended for four guns joined this. But it was converted into a hospital bomb-proof. In the rear a heavy curtain was thrown up to protect the chambers from fragments of shells. From the bomb-proof a series of batteries extended for three-quarters of a mile along the sea, connected by an infantry curtain. These batteries had heavy traverses, but were not more than ten or twelve feet high to the top of the parapets, and were built for ricochet firing. On the line was a bomb-proof electric battery connected with a system of submarine torpedoes. Farther along, where the channel ran close to the beach, inside the bar, a mound battery sixty feet high was erected, with two heavy guns which had a plunging fire on the channel; this was connected with the battery north of it by a light curtain. Following the line of the works it was over one mile from the mound to the northeast bastion at the angle of the sea and land faces, and upon this line 24 heavy guns were mounted. From the mound for nearly one mile to the end of the point, was a level sand plain scarcely three feet above high tide, and much of it was submerged during gales. At the point was Battery Buchanan, four guns in the shape of an ellipse commanding the inlet, its two eleven-inch guns covering the approach by land. An advanced redoubt with a 24-pounder was added after the attack by the forces on Christmas, 1864. A wharf for large steamers was in close proximity to these works. Battery Buchanan was a citadel to which an overpowered garrison might retreat and, with proper transportation, be safely carried off at night, and to which reinforcements could be sent under the cover of darkness."

THE CONFEDERATE NAVY.

If the Federal Government was unprepared for naval warfare at the beginning of the civil strife, the Confederacy was even less prepared, for it could not claim the ownership of a single ship. In a conversation shortly after the war, our distinguished naval officer, Captain John Newland Maffitt, said:

"The Northern navy contributed materially to the successful issue of the war. The grand mistake of the South was neglecting her navy. All our army movements out West were baffled by the armed Federal steamers which swarmed on Western waters, and which our government had provided nothing to meet. Before the capture of New Orleans, the South ought to have had a navy strong enough to prevent the capture of that city and hold firmly the Mississippi and its tributaries. This would have prevented many disastrous battles; it would have made Sherman's march through the country impossible, and Lee would have been master of his lines. The errors of our government were numerous, but the neglect of the navy proved irremediable and fatal.

John Newland Maffitt in Confederate naval uniform.

"Nobody here," he continued, "would believe at first that a great war was before us. South Carolina seceded first, and improvised a navy consisting of two small tug boats! North Carolina followed suit, and armed a tug and a small passenger boat! Georgia, Alabama and Louisiana put in commission a handful of frail river boats that you could have knocked to pieces with a pistol shot. That was our navy! Then came Congress and voted money to pay officers like myself, who had resigned from the Federal navy, but nothing to build or arm

CSS Merrimac

any ships for us to command. Of course, it woke up by and by, and ordered vessels to be built here, there and everywhere, but it was too late."

"And yet," said the Captain, with a momentary kindling of the eye, as the thought of other days came back to him, "The Confederate navy, minute though it was, won a place for itself in history. To the Confederates the credit belongs of testing in battle the invulnerability of ironclads, and of revolutionizing the navies of the world. The *Merrimac* did this; and, though we had but a handful of light cruisers, while the ocean swarmed with armed Federal vessels, we defied the Federal navy and swept Northern commerce from the seas."

Colonel Scharf, in his admirable *History of the Confederate States Navy* says: "In many respects the most interesting chapter of the history of the Confederate navy is that of the building and operation of the ships-of-war which drove the merchant flag of the United States from the oceans and almost extirpated their carrying trade. But the limitations of space of this volume forbid more than a brief review of the subject. The function of commerce-destroyers is now so well admitted as an attribute of war between recognized belligerents by all the nations of the world, that no apology is necessary for the manner in which the South conducted hostilities upon the high seas against her enemy; and, while the Federal officials and organs styled the cruisers 'pirates' and their commanders 'buccaneers,' such stigmatization has long since been swept away, along with other rubbish of the War between the States, and their legal status fully and honorably established. We have not the space for quotations from Prof. Soley, Prof. Bolles and other writers upon this point; but what they have said may be summed up in the statement that the government and agents of the Confederacy transgressed no principle of right in this matter, and that if the United States were at war to-day, they would strike at the commerce of an enemy in as nearly the same manner as circumstances would permit. The justification of the Confederate authorities is not in the slightest degree affected by the fact that the

Geneva Tribunal directed Great Britain to pay the Federal government $15,500,000 in satisfaction for ships destroyed by cruisers constructed in British ports.

"Eleven Confederate cruisers figured in the 'Alabama Claims' settlement between the United States and Great Britain. They were the *Alabama, Shenandoah, Florida, Tallahassee, Georgia, Chickamauga, Nashville, Retribution, Sumter, Sallie* and *Boston*. The actual losses inflicted by the *Alabama*, $6,547,609, were only $60,000 greater than those charged to the *Shenandoah*. The sum total of the claims filed against the eleven cruisers for ships and cargoes was $17,900,633, all but about $4,000,000 being caused by the *Alabama* and *Shenandoah*. The tribunal decided that Great Britain was in no way responsible for the losses inflicted by any cruisers but the *Alabama, Florida* and *Shenandoah*. It disallowed all the claims of the United States for indirect or consequential losses, which included the approximate extinction of American commerce by the capture of ships or their transfer to foreign flags. What this amounted to is shown in the 'Case of the United States' presented to the tribunal. In this it is stated that while in 1860 two-thirds of the commerce of New York was carried in American bottoms, in 1863 three-fourths was carried in foreign bottoms. The transfer of American vessels to the British flag to avoid capture is stated thus: In 1861, vessels 126, tonnage 71,673; in 1862, vessels 135, tonnage 64,578; in 1863, vessels 348, tonnage 252,579; in 1864, vessels, 106, tonnage 92,052. Commanders of the Confederate cruisers have avowed that the destruction of private property and diversion of legitimate commerce in the performance of their duty was painful in the extreme to them; but in their wars the United States had always practiced this mode of harassing an enemy, and had, indeed, been the most conspicuous exemplars of it that the world ever saw."

Since the foregoing was written by Colonel Scharf in 1887 there has been a growing aversion on the part of the principal commercial Powers to privateering. A recent press association dispatch from Washington says:

"The report from Brussels that former President Kruger is being urged to notify the Powers that unless they intervene in the South African contest he will commission privateers, is not treated seriously here. It is well understood, as one outcome of the war with Spain, that the United States government will never again, except in the most extraordinary emergency, issue letters of marque; and the same reasons that impel the government to this course would undoubtedly operate to prevent our government from recognizing any such warrants issued by any other nation, even were that nation in full standing.

"In the case of the Spanish war, both the belligerents by agreement refrained from issuing commissions to privateers, and it now has been many years since the flag of any respectable nation has flown over such craft."

About the beginning of the year 1862, the Confederate States Government began the construction of an iron clad ram, named *North Carolina*, on the west

CSS North Carolina, ***docked at Smithville (modern Southport).***

side of Cape Fear river at the ship yard of the late B.W. Beery; the drawings and specifications of the vessel having been made by Captain John L. Porter, Chief Naval Constructor of the Confederate States Navy, with headquarters at Portsmouth, Virginia.

The armament of the *North Carolina* consisted of one 10-inch pivot gun in the bow and six broadside guns of about 8-inch caliber. The timbers of the vessel were heavy pine and hard wood covered with railroad iron, giving the ram, when launched, the appearance of a turtle in the water.

The *North Carolina* was subsequently anchored for a long time off Smithville, now Southport, as a guard vessel commanding the entrance to the river at the main bar, until she was gradually destroyed by the toredo, or sea-worm, and sank at her moorings, where I believe she still remains.

The *Raleigh*, a vessel of like construction, was built later at the wharf near the foot of Church Street; and after being launched was completed at Cassidey's ship-yard.

Her construction and armament were similar to that of the *North Carolina*, but she was covered with heavy iron plates of two thicknesses running fore and aft and athwart ship.

I am indebted to a distinguished ex-Confederate officer for the following particulars of an expedition from Wilmington against the Federal blockading fleet off New Inlet Bar, in which the *Raleigh* took a conspicuous part; and which contrary to the hopes and expectations of our people, not only proved to be a dismal failure, but resulted in the loss of the *Raleigh*, which broke her back while trying to re-enter the river and sank in the middle of the narrow channel, proving afterwards a troublesome obstruction to the blockade runners at New Inlet.

The Star of the Confederacy was waning in the spring of 1864, a depreciated currency and the scant supply of provisions and clothing had sent prices almost beyond the reach of people of moderate means. In Richmond, meal was $10 per bushel; butter, $5 per pound; sugar, $12 per pound; bacon, hog round, $4 per pound; brogan shoes, $25 per pair; felt hats, $150; cotton cloth, $30 per yard: and it was a saying in the Capital of the Confederacy, that the money had to be carried in the market basket and the marketing brought home in the pocket book.

Early in May the condition of the commissariat had been alarming; but a few days' rations were left for Lee's army, and only the timely arrival of the blockade runner *Banshee* with provisions saved the troops from suffering.

Wilmington was the only port left to the blockade runners, and the blockade of the mouths of the Cape Fear had become dangerously stringent. Some twenty steamers guarded the two inlets, besides two outer lines of fast cruisers between this city and the friendly ports of Nassau and the Bermudas. On dark nights, armed launches were sent into the bar to report outgoing steamers by firing rockets in the direction taken by them. The ceaseless vigilance of the forts could scarcely make an exit for friendly vessels even comparatively free from danger. An hour after dark, Fort Fisher, having trailed its sea-face guns upon the bar, would ricochet its Columbiad shot and shell upon that point, so as to frighten off the launches; and then the blockade runners would venture out and take their chances of running the gauntlet of the blockading fleet.

In this emergency, Commodore Lynch, commanding the Confederate fleet in the Cape Fear River, determined to raise the blockade off New Inlet, the favorite entrance of the blockade runners.

The iron-clad ram *Raleigh*, already described, Lieutenant J.Pembroke Jones, commanding, and two small wooden gun-boats, *Yadkin* and *Equator*, were chosen for the purpose. Our late townsman, Captain E.W. Manning, chief engineer of the station, and the late engineer Smith, C.S.N., of Fayetteville, were in charge of the machinery of the *Raleigh*.

CSS Raleigh, ***one of two ironclads built at Wilmington shipyards.***

USS Niphon, ***one of the U.S. Navy ships in the Cape Fear Blockading Squadron.***

On the afternoon of May 6, 1864, the Commodore visited Fort Fisher, to take a reconnaissance, and obtain, as far as practicable, the co-operation of the fort. Seven vessels were at the anchorage at sundown; the *Tuscarora, Britannia, Nansemond, Howquah, Mount Vernon, Kansas* and *Niphon*. He arranged a distinguishing signal for his vessels—a red light above a white one, so that they would not be fired upon by the fort.

Fort Fisher had its sea-face guns manned after dark by experienced artillerists, and about eight o'clock the range lights were set at the Mound and the Confederate flotilla put to sea. The commander of the fort, Colonel William Lamb, with some of his officers, repaired to the ramparts opposite the bar and awaited the result.

Within thirty minutes after the vessels had disappeared from the vision of the anxious garrison, a few shots were heard from seaward, and some Coston blue lights were seen in the offing; then all was dark as Erebus and silent as the grave.

Speculation was rife among the Confederates who manned the guns. Had the foe been dispersed or destroyed? Why were no rockets sent up to announce a victory, to cheer the thousand hearts which beat with anxious hope within Fort Fisher?

A long night of waiting was spent without any sign save the occasional twinkle of a distant light at sea. The gunners were relieved at midnight, but all continued dark and silent.

At last day dawned, the breakers on the bar became visible, the *Raleigh* and her consorts appeared; and then outside of them, at long range, the enemy's fleet. Shots were exchanged after daylight between the combatants; one of the Federal vessels fired rapidly at the *Raleigh*, approaching as she fired, but, receiving a shot from the iron-clad through her smoke-stack, withdrew to a safer distance.

Then the seven blockaders came closer to the Confederate fleet, showing fight, and probably with the intention of trying to run the *Raleigh* down; but that vessel and her consorts headed for the fort and steamed slowly in, the enemy prudently keeping beyond the range of the guns of Fort Fisher.

It was with great disappointment that the garrison saw the *Raleigh*, *Yadkin* and *Equator* come over the bar and under the guns of the fort, leaving the blockading squadron apparently unharmed.

The *Yadkin* and *Equator* came safe into the river, but the *Raleigh*, after passing the mound and rounding Confederate Point, grounded on the rip at the mouth of the river. Efforts were made to lighten her and get her off, but the receding tide caused her to hog and break in two, on account of the heavy armor and, becoming a wreck, she subsequently sank and went to pieces. Little was saved from her, but the crew were not endangered, as the weather was calm.

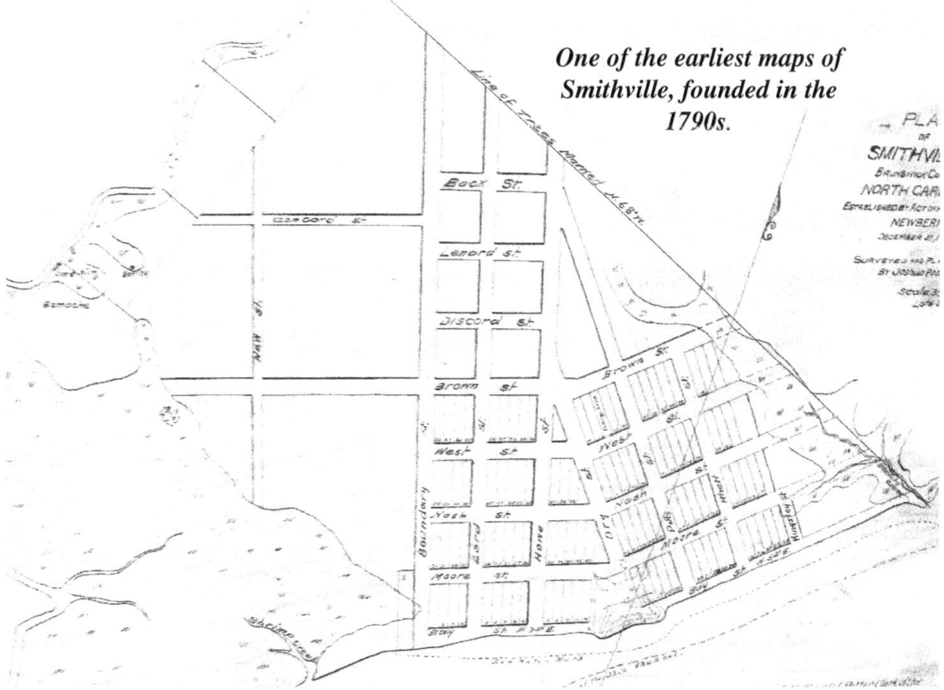

One of the earliest maps of Smithville, founded in the 1790s.

SMITHVILLE (SOUTHPORT.)

The staid old village of Smithville, situated on the Cape Fear between Fort Fisher and Fort Caswell, but nearer the latter, was in those days the center of busy military life. It was named in 1792, in honour of its distinguished citizen, Governor Benjamin Smith, who had served in his youth as Aide-de-camp of Washington and who afterwards became one of the most noted philanthropists, patriots and statesmen of his time. The village had been previously called Fort Johnston, a fortification named for the Colonial Governor, Gabriel Johnston, having been erected there about the year 1745 for the protection of the Cape Fear colony.

By authority of the Legislature, the name was changed to Southport, and it is but justice to the people that this apparent forgetfulness of their benefactor should be explained. Shortly before this, a number of prospectors, claiming abundant means and influence, promised to build a road, to be known as the "South Atlantic and Northwestern Railroad," in as direct a line as practicable from Smithville to Cincinnati; and suggested for the former a name more suitable for a commercial city. The towns folk were naturally filled with enthusiasm at the thought of the city which would arise at this terminus, and of the benefit to accrue to the whole State from the development of a deep water port. They more readily agreed to the change because the University of North Carolina had built a monument to Governor Smith in a building now used as a library, a more fitting tribute to his memory, they thought, than the name of an unimportant town. Now, after a lapse of fifteen years—the railroad having failed to materialize—they find themselves disappointed of all their hopes, and burdened with a meaningless name.

PILOTS.

This old military post with its obsolete guns was occupied by the N.C. State Troops at the beginning of the war, and was later strengthened by the Confederate engineers. Here was the headquarters of the Confederate General commanding; and here were the houses and homes of about 60 hardy pilots, whose humble sphere was suddenly exalted to one of dignity — that of the most important and responsible officers of the swift blockade-running steamers, which braved the dangers of a hostile fleet and crept in every night under the cover of darkness.

The story of the wonderful nerve of these pilots in the time of the Federal blockade has never been fully written; because the survivors are modest men, and time has obliterated from their memories many incidents of this most extraordinary epoch of their lives.

Amidst the impenetrable darkness, without lightship or beacon, the narrow and closely watched inlet was felt for with a deep-sea lead as a blind man feels his way along a familiar path; and often, when the enemy's fire was raking the wheel-house, the faithful pilot, with steady hand and iron nerve, would safely steer the little fugitive of the sea to her desired haven. It might be said of him, as it was told of the Nantucket skipper, that he could get his bearings on the darkest night by a taste of the deep-sea sounding lead.

THE BLOCKADE RUNNERS.

In the early stage of the war, blockade running was carried on in part by sailing vessels; for the blockade was not yet rigorous, and speed on the part of the venturesome had not become essential to success. The proclamation of the blockade had suspended legitimate commerce, and the owners of the cheap sailing craft which faced the extra hazard of war had, for a time, little to lose and much to gain in the venture. The inward cargoes were less valuable than those brought later by steam vessels, and they consisted of such necessary commodities as salt, sugar, molasses and other cheaper supplies. These cargoes were not then openly declared from neutral countries for a blockade port, their ostensible destination being the markets of the North; and when by chance an enterprising skipper suspiciously near the Carolina coast was overhauled by a cruiser, he was always ready with a plausible story of adverse winds or false reckoning. For a time such cases were allowed to withdraw with a warning. In later months all suspicious craft detected in the act of approaching a blockaded port were seized in the name of the United States, and sent in charge of a prize crew to a convenient Northern port for adjudication, which invariably resulted in their condemnation and sale. Attempts at re-capture were seldom made, precautions against such an event being always well taken; but there was an instance of rare heroism on the part of an obscure captain of a sailing vessel belonging to Charleston, which sent a thrill of emotion around the world wherever the story was told of the *Emily St. Pierre* and her brave commander.

A HEROIC CAPTAIN RECAPTURES HIS SHIP.

We learn from Chambers' *Journal* that in November 1861, the full-rig sailing ship *Emily St. Pierre*, William Wilson, master, sailed from Calcutta, India, for St. John, New Brunswick, with orders to call at Charleston, S.C. if that port was found open; but if it were blockaded, to proceed to the British flag. Her nominal owners were Fraser, Trenholm & Co., Liverpool, who were also the agents of the Confederate Government.

Upon approaching Charleston bar, twelve miles distant, on the morning of March 18, 1862, she was hailed by a Federal cruiser, *James Adger*, and ordered to heave to; Captain Wilson, accordingly, hauled up his courses, backed his main yard, and lay to. He was immediately boarded by a naval lieutenant and a force of twenty marines, who demanded his papers. These showed an innocent cargo, 2,000 bales of gunny bags, and her proper certificate of registration as a British vessel. Captain Wilson demanded permission to proceed towards his destination, Charleston being evidently blockaded; this the naval officer refused, and the two

USS James Adger

vessels proceeded to Charleston Roadstead, where at half past two Captain Wilson was ordered on board the flag ship of the blockading squadron, the *Florida*. Here he was kept for two hours in solitude and suspense; at the end of which Captain Goldsborough, the flag officer informed him that they had decided to seize the *Emily St. Pierre*, on the ground that the British certificate was not bona fide; that there were evidences that the ship was really of Charleston, and that the captain had not revealed his real intentions. Captain Wilson protested, but in vain; his crew was removed to the war ship, with the exception of the steward, named Matthew Montgomery, and the cook, a German named Louis Schelvin. The *Emily St. Pierre* was placed in charge of Lieutenant Stone of the United States Navy, a master's mate, an American engineer as passenger, and a prize crew of twelve men, with orders to proceed to Philadelphia for adjudication by the Admiralty Courts.

Captain Wilson was permitted to go as passenger on the prize to Philadelphia. The moment that he stepped again on board his vessel, he formed the resolution to recapture her and take her home. He was bold enough to think that it might be possible to recapture the ship, even against such odds. An unarmed man, aided by the questionable support of an Irish steward and a German cook, was pratically powerless against the fifteen of the crew. On the other hand, Captain Wilson was a brawny, big-framed Scotchman, (a native of Dunfrieshire), a thorough seaman, determined in resolve, cool and prompt in action. He called the steward and cook to him in his stateroom, and disclosed the wild project he had formed. Both manfully promised to stand by their chief. This was at half past four on the morning of the 21st of March, the third day out from Charleston. Captain Wilson had already formed his plan of operations, and had prepared to a certain extent for carrying it out. With the promise of the cook and steward secured, he lost no time; gave them no chance for their courage to evaporate, but proceeded at once, in the darkness and silence of the night, to carry out his desperate undertaking. He was prepared to lose his life or have his ship; this was the simple alternative. It was Lieutenant Stone's watch on deck, and the master's mate was asleep in his berth. The Scotch Captain went into the berth, handed out the mate's sword and revolvers, clapped a gag made of a piece of wood and some marline between his teeth, seized his hands, which Montgomery, the steward, quickly ironed, and so left him secure. The lieutenant paced the deck, undisturbed by a sound. Quickly another stateroom was entered, where the American engineer lay asleep. He also was gagged and ironed, silently and without disturbance. His revolvers and those already secured were given to the steward and the cook, who remained below in the cabin. Captain Wilson went on deck. Lieutenant Stone was still pacing the deck, and the watch consisted of one man at the helm, one at the lookout on the forecastle, and three others who were about the ship. For ten minutes Captain Wilson walked up and down, remarking on the fair wind, and making believe that he had just turned out. The ship was off Cape Hatteras, midway of their journey between Charleston and Philadelphia, the most easterly projection of the land on that coast. The difficult navigation thereabouts, with the cross-currents and a tendency to fogs, afforded the two captains subject for talk.

'Let her go free a bit, Captain Stone; you are too close to the Cape, I tell you, and I know.'

'We have plenty of offing,' replied the lieutenant; and then to helmsman: 'How's her head?'

'North-east by east, sir,' came the reply.

'Keep her so; I tell you it is right,' said the lieutenant.

'Well, of course, I'm not responsible now, but I'm an older sailor than you, Captain Stone, and I tell you, if you want to clear Cape Hatteras, another two points east will do no harm. Do but look at my chart; I left it open on the cabin table. And the coffee will be ready,' and Captain Wilson led the way from the poop to the cabin, followed by the commander.

"There was a passage about five yards long leading from the deck to the cabin, a door at either end. The Captain stopped at the first door, closing it, and picking from behind it an iron belaying-pin which he had placed there. The younger man went forward to the cabin, where the chart lay upon the table. 'Stone!' He turned at the sudden peremptory exclamation of his name. His arm upraised the heavy iron bolt in his hand, in low but hard, eager, quick words, the captain said: 'My ship shall never go to Philadelphia!' He did not strike, it was unnecessary. Montgomery had thrust the gag into the young lieutenant's mouth; he was bound hand and foot, bundled into a berth, and the door locked. Three out of fifteen were thus disposed of. There still the watch on deck and the watch below. Coming on deck from the cabin Captain Wilson called to the three men who were about, and pointing to a heavy coil of rope in the lazaret, ordered them to get it up at once—Lieutenant Stone's orders. They jumped down without demur, suspecting nothing, as soon as the Captain shoved the hatch aside. They were no sooner in than he quickly replaced and fastened the hatch. The three were securely trapped, in full view of the helmsman, whose sailor's instinct kept him in his place at the wheel.

'If you utter a sound or make a move,' said the Captain, showing a revolver, 'I'll blow your brains out;' and then he called aft the lookout man, the last of the watch on deck. The man came aft. Would he help to navigate the ship to England? No, he would not, he was an American. Then, would he call the watch? He would do that. And eagerly he did it, but the next moment he was laid low on deck and bundled unceremoniously into the lazaret with his three companions; the hatchway was replaced and secured, Captain Wilson standing on guard. Meanwhile the watch below had been called and were astir. When sailors tumble out they generally do so gradually and by twos and threes. The first two that came aft were quickly overpowered, one at a time, and bound. The third man drew his knife and dashed at the steward, who fired, wounding him severely in the shoulder. It was the only shot that was fired. Finding that the cook and steward, and Captain were all armed, the rest of the watch below quietly surrendered, and submitted to be locked in the round house, prisoners of the bold and resolute man, who, in the course of an hour had thus regained possession of his ship against overwhelming odds. For England! Yes, homeward bound in an unseaworthy ship; for a ship that is undermanned is unseaworthy to the last degree. It is worse than overloading. And here was our brave captain, three thousand miles from home, calmly altering the course the few points eastward he had recommended to the Lieutenant; homeward bound for England, his crew, a steward and a cook! Neither could steer, nor hand, nor reef. Brave-hearted Matthew Montgomery, the Irish steward, honest Louis Schelvin, the German cook, now is the time to show what savour of seamanship you have picked up amongst your pots and pans of the galley and the pantry! The first step was to wash and bandage the wounded shoulder of the man who was shot; the next, to put all the prisoners in the round house under lock and key. The Lieutenant was admitted to the captain's table under guard and on parole. The meal over, he was ushered into his stateroom and locked in. Once a day only—for the captain is captain and crew combined—bread and beef and water were passed to the prisoners in the round house; no more attention than was absolutely necessary could be spared to them.

Homeward bound! Captain Wilson had overcome his captors: could he overcome the elements? The glass was falling, the wind was rising, threatening a gale. The reeftackles were passed to the capstan, so that one man's strength could haul them. Then the wheel was resigned to the Irish steward and the German cook, whilst the Captain had to lie aloft and tie the reef-points; ever and anon casting a look behind and signaling to his faithful men how to move the wheel. Hours of hard work, fearful anxiety, before all is made snug to meet the fury of the coming storm. 'All is right at last,' thought the Captain, 'if everything holds.' Yes, if—. Everything did not hold. The tiller was carried away in the midst of the gale, and Capt. Wilson, brave heart as he was, felt the sadness of despair. He had been keeping watch day and night without intermission for many days, snatching an hour's sleep at intervals, torn with anxiety, wearied with work. It was but a passing faintness of the heart. The ship rolled and tossed, helmless, at the mercy of the sea. For twelve hours he wrought to rig up a jury-rudder, and at last, lifting up his heart in gratitude, for the second time he snatched his ship out of the hands of destruction; for the second time he could inform Lieutenant Stone that he was in command of his own ship. No longer was the ship buffeted at the mercy of the wild winds and the cruel Atlantic rollers, but her course was laid true and her head was straight—for England. For thirty days they sailed with westerly gales behind them. They made the land in safety, and the code signal was hoisted as they passed up the Channel. On the morning of the 21st of April, exactly one month since her course was altered off Cape Hatteras, the *Emily St. Pierre* threaded the devious channels which lead into the broad estuary of the Mersey; the anchor fell with a plunge and an eager rattle of the leaping cable, and the ship rode stately on the rushing tide. Much was made of Captain Wilson during the next few weeks. All England rang with applause of his brave exploit. Meetings were convened, presentations were made, speeches were delivered, to an extent that might have turned the head of a less simple and true-hearted man. Large sums of money were subscribed, of which plucky Matthew Montgomery and honest Lewis Schelvin, the cook, got their share. But probably the happiest and proudest moment of his life was when the Captain stood on deck on the day of arrival—his wife by his side, and near her the owner of the ship, Charles K. Prioleau, of Fraser, Trenholm & Co.,—whilst he narrated in simple words the story of his exploit. His big beard was torn and ragged, his eyes bloodshot with weariness and lack of sleep, his face haggard, weather-beaten and drawn; but he was a man of whom all Britain was proud—a man to inspire her with the faith that the race of heroes does not die."

THE *KATE'S* ADVENTURE.

In the spring of the year 1862, the Confederate Government, desiring to arrange for the importation of supplies for the War Department, and finding the principal ports of the South Atlantic Coast so well guarded by the blockaders that the new undertaking of blockade running was then considered extra hazardous, decided to use the smaller inlets, which were less carefully watched by the enemy; and dispatched the steamer *Kate* from Nassau with a cargo of ammunition to Smyrna, Fla., where an entrance was safely effected by that vessel, and the cargo immediately discharged and transported across the country to a place of safety.

The *Kate* was commanded by Captain Thos. J. Lockwood, of Smithville, on Cape Fear River, who was well known to our older pilots and seafaring people as a man of very superior skill and seamanship, and thoroughly familiar with the bars and inlets along the Southern coast.

A second voyage by the *Kate* had been completed, and the cargo successfully discharged and transported, before the movement was made known to the blockading squadron; but while the *Kate* was waiting for the return of Captain Lockwood from Charleston, whither he had proceeded to bring his family to the ship at Smyrna Inlet, a Federal man-of-war discovered her hiding place, which forced the chief officer of the *Kate* to proceed to sea at once, leaving the Captain behind. The Federal cruiser landed a boat's crew, and burned the house of Mr. Sheldon, the pilot who had assisted in bringing the *Kate* to an anchorage, shortly after which, Captain Lockwood at once determined to undertake the voyage with his family in this frail craft, and overtake the *Kate* at Nassau. The boat was only 16 feet long, and not at all well found for such a perilous voyage. After a short delay, the Captain, his brave wife, their two children and a hired boy, found themselves safe over the bar and headed for the Bahamas. The following account of this remarkable voyage was written by Mrs. Lockwood, and has been kindly furnished by her brother, Mr. McDougal:

After the baggage was safe on board, I was carried in a man's arms through the surf and placed in the boat, and we started over the sea in our frail little craft. A few yards from shore we discovered that she was sinking, but turned back in time to reach the beach, to which I was again transferred just as the boat went down. With some difficulty she was recovered, when it was found that the plug had come out of the bottom while drawing the boat over the beach. We soon found a remedy for this trouble, and proceeded to cross the gulf. On the following morning, the wind blew a gale. The waves dashed high over us all day, while the wind increased in fury. For fifteen hours we waited and prayed, thinking that every moment would be our last. About five o'clock in the evening, we discovered a reef, and steered along the rocks to find an opening, so that we might cross the line of breakers and get into calm water. Oakie told us to sit still and hold fast to the boat, as we must go over the rocks or sink. As each enormous wave came towards us it seemed to reach the sky and break over our frail craft, deluging us with water. For several moments in succession I would sit under these huge waver holding on with one hand and clasping my baby with the other. Breaker after breaker burst over us, and at the same time lifted the boat farther and farther on to the rocks, until at last we were plunged ahead into the smooth water of the bay beyond. By some means, I cannot tell how, we reached one of the vessels lying at anchor, when they lifted us all on board and carried us into the cabin. We could not walk for cold and cramp. On Sunday, the 23rd, the schooner upon which we had taken refuge sailed for Nassau, and on Monday we were landed on Elbow Cay, one of the Bahama Islands, the wind not being favorable for us to continue further that day. On the 25th, with a fair wind, we again proceeded towards Nassau, and arrived on Wednesday after being three weeks on the journey from Charleston.

Mr. McDougal adds to this journal, that he was then chief engineer of the steamer Kate, of 500 tons, in the Gulf Stream, about 150 miles from where Captain Lockwood was cruising in a little boat; and that the gale was so severe that this large vessel was obliged to lie to, and suffered considerable damage in consequence of the severity of the storm, and that it seems a miracle that a small boat like Captain Lockwood's should have lived through such a fearful gale.

FAMOUS BLOCKADE RUNNERS.

In the second stage of blockade running, when steam was at a premium, a number of walking-beam boats of excellent speed, which had plied regularly between Southern ports and which had been laid up since the proclamation, were bought by Southern business men, who became prominent in blockade running; and, after the removal of passenger cabins and conspicuous top hamper, they were placed in this dangerous traffic. Of these may be mentioned the steamer *Kate*, previously known as the *Carolina*, upon the line between Charleston and Palatka; the *Gordon* which was built to run between Charleston and Savannah; also the *Nina*, *Seabrook*, *Clinch*, and *Cecile*, which had also plied on the same line. The *Cecile*, loaded in Nassau with a cargo of powder, rifles, and stores for General Albert Sidney Johnston's army at Shiloh, struck a sunken rock off the Florida coast, and went to the bottom in ten minutes. The officers and crew escaped.

Two steamers which formerly ran between New Orleans and Galveston became prominent as Cape Fear blockade runners; the *Atlantic*, re-named the *Elizabeth*, and the *Austin*, which became the famous Confederate steamer *Ella and Annie*. In the early morning of November 9th, 1863, the *Ella and Annie*, under command of Captain F.N. Bonneau, of Charleston, was intercepted off New Inlet, near Masonboro Sound, by the United States steamer *Niphon*, which attempted to press her ashore. Several other cruisers preventing the escape of the *Ella and Annie*, Captain Bonneau at once resolved upon the desperate expedient of running the *Niphon* down. He accordingly ran his ship at reckless speed straight at the war vessel, and struck it with great force, carrying away the bowsprit and stem and wounding three of the men. The *Niphon*, by quick movement, avoided the full effect of the blow, and fired all her starboard guns into the *Ella and Annie*, wounding four of her men. As soon as the vessels came together the *Niphon* carried the *Ella and Annie* by boarding, and made her a prize. She afterwards became the United States flag ship *Malvern.*

The *Governor Dudley*, of the Wilmington and Charleston route before the completion of the Wilmington & Manchester Railroad, which had been put on the summer run between Charleston and Havana prior to the war, made one or two successful voyages through the blockade to Nassau.

A Nassau correspondent to the *New York Times* wrote on February 15th, 1862, that "on Tuesday last, 11th Feb., 1862, the old steamer *Governor Dudley* arrived from Charleston with 400 bales of cotton. The captain, fearing the cotton would go North if sold here, refused to take any price for it. After taking out a British register and changing her name to the *Nellie*, he left for Havana with a Nassau pilot on board to carry him across the (Bahama) Banks. He intends taking a return cargo to Charleston, and expects to be back here in about a month with more cotton. The *Nellie* is an old boat, nearly used up both in hull and machinery. Her speed is not over 8 or 10 knots, with a full head of steam." The other boats formerly comprising the Wilmington and Charleston line were probably too old for blockade running service. The *Wilmington* was sold to run on the river and gulf of St. Laurence. The *Gladiator* went to Philadelphia, and the *Vanderbilt*, having been sold to New Orleans, foundered in the Gulf of Mexico while running the blockade.

Another old friend, of the New York and Wilmington line, which was managed here by the late Edwin A. Keith, the *North Carolina*, rendered an important service to the Confederate Government by carrying through the blockade, as a passenger, the distinguished Captain James D. Bulloch, Naval Representative of the Confederacy in Europe during the war between the States. On Feb. the 5th, 1862, she completed the loading of a cargo of cotton, rosin and tobacco at Wilmington, under her new name, *Annie Childs*, and proceeded through the blockade by the main bar, arriving at Liverpool via Fayal, Madeira, and Queenstown, Ireland, early in March. Her supply of coal was quite exhausted when she sighted Queenstown, and she barely reached that port of call by burning part of her rosin cargo with spare spars cut into short lengths. Captain Bulloch said that she was badly found for so long a voyage, but she weathered a heavy north-west gale, and proved herself to be a fine sea boat. I am informed that she returned to other successful ventures in Blockade running under the name of *Victory*.

The fleet of runners was augmented by other old fashioned steamers, partly from Northern ports, bought by foreigners and sent via neutral ports, where they went through the process of "whitewashing," a change of name, ownership, registry and flag. A much greater number, however, came from abroad; a few of these formerly having been fast mail boats, but the majority freighters on short

The **Modern Greece,** *beached by Union pursuers.*

routes in Europe, bought at big prices for eager speculators, who were tempted by the enormous profits of blockade running.

A few of those of the better class became famous, as the North Carolina steamer *Advance*, before known as the *Lord Clyde*; the Confederate steamer, *R.E. Lee*, formerly the *Giraffe*; and the *Lady Davis*, previously the *Cornubia*. Some of the others were the *Alice*, *Fannie*, *Brittania*, *Emma*, *Pet*, *Sirius*, *Orion*, *Antonica*, *Hansa*, *Calypso*, *Duoro*, *Thistle*, *Scotia*, *City of Petersburg*, *Old Dominion*, *Index*, *Caledonia*, *Dolphin*, *Georgiana McCaw*, *Modern Greece*, *Ella*, *Hebe*, *Dee*, *Wave Queen*, *Granite City*, *Stonewall Jackson*, *Victory*, *Flora*, *Beauregard*, *Ruby*, *Margaret and Jessie*, *Eagle*, *Gertrude*, *Charleston*, *Banshee*, *Minna* and *Eugenie*, which were more or less successful.

The beach for miles north and south of Bald Head is marked still by the melancholy wrecks of swift and graceful steamers which had been employed in this perilous enterprise. Some of the hundred vessels engaged in this traffic ran between Wilmington and the West Indies with the regularity of mail boats, and some, even of the slowest speed,—the *Pet*, for instance—eluding the vigilance of the Federal fleet, passed unscathed twenty, thirty and forty times, making millions for the fortunate owners. One little beauty, the *Siren*, a fast boat, numbered nearly fifty voyages. The success of these ships depended, of course, in a great measure upon the skill and coolness of their commanders and pilots. It is noteworthy that those in charge of Confederate naval officers were, with one exception, never taken; but many were captured, sunk or otherwise lost, through no fault of the brave fellows who commanded them. The *Beauregard* and the *Venus* lie stranded on Carolina Beach; the *Modern Greece*, near New Inlet; the *Antonica*, on Frying Pan Shoals; the *Ella*, on Bald Head; the *Spunky* and the

Georgiana McCaw, on Caswell Beach; the *Hebe* and the *Dee*, between Wrightsville and Masonboro. Two others lie near Lockwood's Folly bar; and others, whose names are forgotten are half buried in the sands, where they may remain for centuries to come. After a heavy storm on the coast, the summer residents on Carolina Beach and at Masonboro Sound have occasionally picked up along the shore some interesting relics of blockade times, which the heaving ocean has broken from the buried cargoes of the *Beauregard*, *Venus*, *Hebe* and *Dee*. Tallow candles, Nassau bacon, soldiers' shoes, and other wreckage, comprise in part this flotsam yielded up by Neptune after nearly forty years' soaking in the sea.

The *Venus* was commanded by a prominent officer of the Royal Navy on leave of absence, Captain Murray-Aynsley, known by blockade runners as Captain Murray. He is now an admiral in the British Navy on the retired list. He was a great favourite with the prominent people, and especially with Colonel Lamb, of Fort Fisher, whose description of the veteran naval officer on the bridge of the *Venus*, running through the Federal fleet in broad daylight, hotly pursued by the enemy, with coat sleeves rolled up to his arm pits, but cool and defiant, is well worth recording.

The loss of the *Georgiana McCaw* is associated with a horrible crime—the murder of her pilot. When the ship was beached under the fire of the blockaders, Mr. Thomas Dyer did not go with the retreating crew who sought safety ashore; he seems to have been left behind in the rush. It was known that he had a large amount of money in gold on board, and it was thought that he remained to secure it. A boat returned for him, but found his bloody corpse, instead. His skull was crushed as by a blow from behind; there was no money on his person. Another man was found on board, but unhurt, who professed ignorance of his fellow. This person was the watchman, and it is said he carried ashore a large amount of money. He was arrested on suspicion, but there was no proof. He still lives on the river, but the cause of poor Byer's death will probably never be known until the Great Assize.

Examples of dash and daring on the part of noted Cape Fear blockade runners in this phase of their history could be multiplied, if the limited scope of this paper would permit of their narration; instances so thrilling that they still stir one's blood to recall them after an interval of nearly forty years. I shall, therefore, select from memory and from published accounts of others, whom I remember as participants, only a few exploits of the second and third years of the war; and, finally, some illustrations of the closing scenes, when only one venture in a dozen was successful, and when the multiplied arms of the new navy, like the deadly tentacles of the octopus, reached into every hiding place of these hunted fugitives of the sea, and gradually brought to an end this wonderful epoch in our commercial history.

Some Blockade Runners of the Cape Fear

CSS Ad-Vance

SS Badger

SS Banshee

SS Ella and Annie

SS Lady Davis

SS Pevensey

SS Lynx

SS Lilian

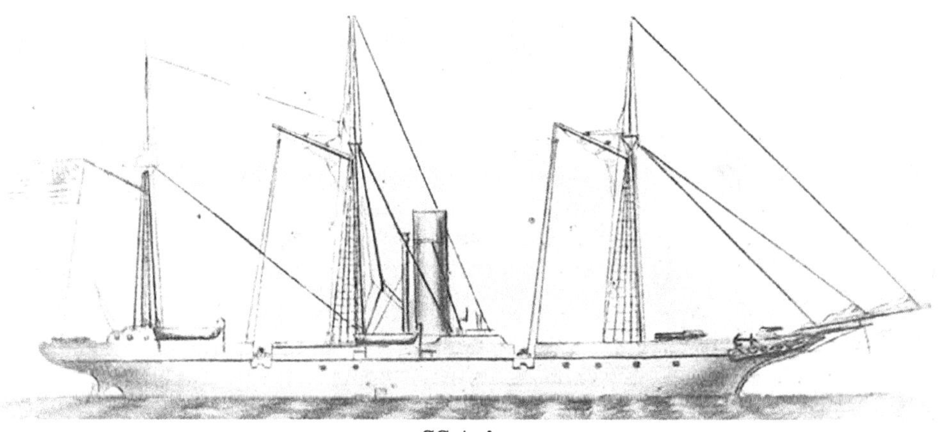

SS Aries

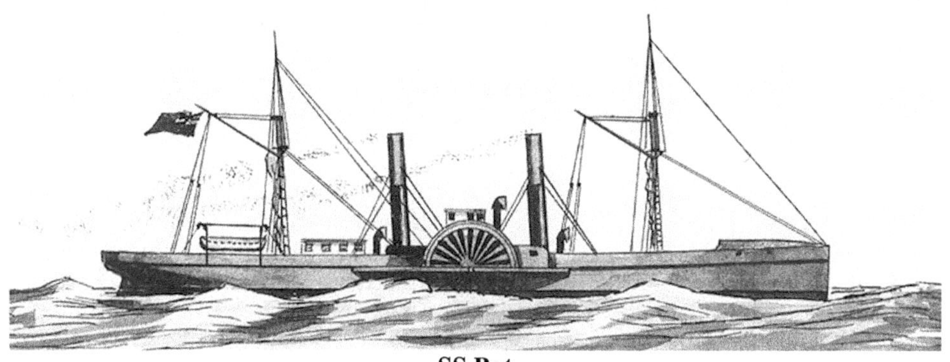

SS Bat

SS Chicora *(after the war, as a Canadian river ferry)*

SS Colonel Lamb

SS Dee

SS Fox

SS Lady Sterling

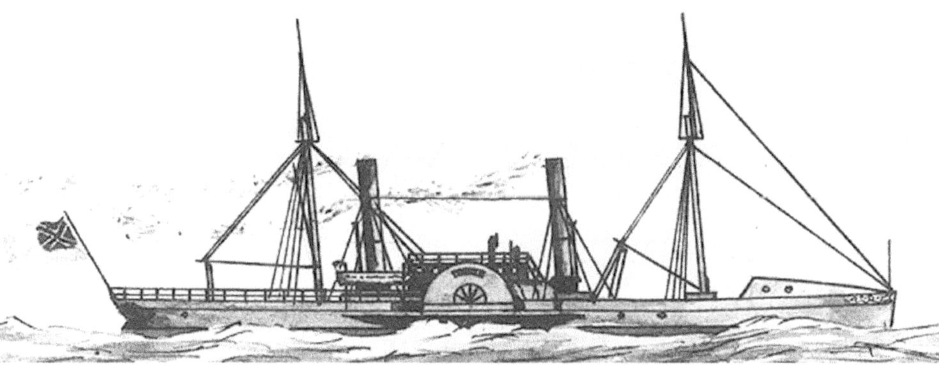

SS Let 'Er Rip (*later the* Wando)

SS Lizzie

SS Thistle

CSS Tallahassee

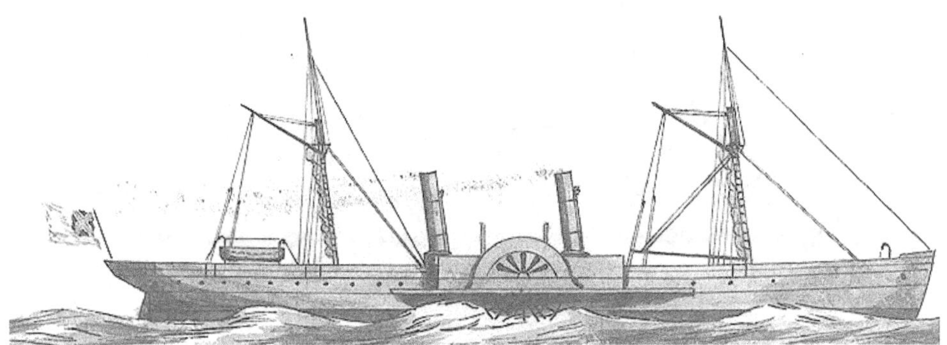

SS Giraffe

SS Emily St. Pierre *(right)*

A CLOSE CALL.

The following interesting narrative, which is true in all its details, was told to the writer by Mr. George C. McDougal, of Rosindale, N.C., who, by a clever expedient, kept out of Fort LaFayette, and made some forty voyages as chief engineer in the little steamer *Siren* before his former shipmates were released:

"The well known blockade-running steamer *Margaret and Jessie* left Nassau deeply laden for Wilmington, and made a good run across the North Carolina coast. About 12.00 meridian she was in the latitude of New Inlet, and she ran on the western edge of the Gulf Stream until sundown, when she headed for the beach and made land to the northward of the blockading fleet of the Caper Fear. While tracking down the beach, one of the cruisers sighted us, and sent up rockets, which made it necessary for us to run the remainder of the distance under fire from the whole line of the blockaders. Just as we got the lights in range at the Inlet and were about to head the ship over the bar, we distinguished a gunboat anchored in the channel under cover of the wrecked steamer *Arabian*. We immediately put the ship about, and, with the whole fleet trailing after us, ran off shore. At daylight none of our followers were in sight, but away off shore to the southward we sighted the armed transport *Fulton*; and as we could not cross her bow, Capt. Robert Lockwood, who commanded our ship, hauled to the northward and eastward, unfortunately driving us across the bows of all the cruisers which had run off shore in chase. We had to run the fire of five of these war ships as we crossed their bows and dropped them astern. During all this time, the *Fulton* kept the weather gauge of us; and after a hard day's chase from New Inlet to Hatteras, we were at last compelled to surrender late in the afternoon; as the *Fulton* seemed determined to run us down, there being hardly a cable's length between us when we hove to and stopped the engines. Before doing this, however, we were careful to throw the mail bags, government dispatches and ship's papers into the furnace of the fire room, where they were quickly consumed.

"While our ship's company was being transferred to the *Fulton*, the United States Steamer *Keystone State* and two other cruisers came up, and sent several boats' crews aboard the *Margaret and Jessie*, who looted her of all the silver, cutlery, glassware, cabin furniture, table cloths and napkins—doubtless, everything they could carry off in their boats. The *Fulton*, having sent a prize crew on board, took us in tow for New York, where, immediately on our arrival, we were confined in Ludlow Street Jail. Two days after, the officers and crew of the blockade runner *Ella and Annie* were brought in, she having been captured off Wilmington after a desperate resistance by her brave commander, Captain Bonneau.

SS Ella and Annie

During our incarceration we were visited frequently by Deputy United States Marshals, who tried to identify some of us, suspected of holding commissions in the Confederate service and of being regularly engaged in blockade running as distinguished from those less harmful members of the crew who would be only too glad to abandon further attempts on regaining their liberty. These officers were immediately assailed with questions from all quarters. 'What are you going to do with us here?' 'Are you going to let us out?' to which they would respond 'we cannot tell—the crew lists have been sent to Washington for inspection; you will have to wait until they are returned.' We were kept in this state of suspense for about three weeks, when a squad of Deputy Marshals came to the jail and mustered the entire company. We soon ascertained that the crew lists had come from Washington, and that we were to go down to the Marshals' office, where the names of those who were to be released were to be called out, and the unfortunate ones remaining prepared for a long term of imprisonment at one of the well known prison pens so dreaded by those who afterwards realized all their horrors. We were, accordingly, marched down to the Marshals' headquarters in Burton's old theatre, on Chambers Street, opposite the City Hall Park, where we were ordered to select our baggage and prepare to be searched for contraband articles. The entire office force of clerks had been drawn from their desks by curiosity to the other end of the large room, where the inspection was going on; and while my baggage was being examined by an officer I asked him if he knew who were to be released; to which he replied that he did not know, but that the list of those who would be released could be found in a large book on that desk, pointing with his finger to the other end of the room. When his inspection was completed he asked if I could read. I said, Yes, that I thought I could make out the names. Whereupon I walked with forced indifference to the desk, and found a big journal laid open upon it, containing the names of the men belonging to the *Ella and Annie*'s crew who were to be discharged. This did not interest me; and looking further down I saw, also, the names of those of my own ship who were to be released, but from the top to the bottom there was no George C. McDougal.

You may depend upon it, I felt very sad as Fort LaFayette loomed up in all its dreariness. My case was, indeed, hopeless. Looking furtively over my shoulder, I saw that the desk was so placed that my back shielded me from the eyes of the marshals at the moment, and also that the officers and clerks were very busy seeing what they could confiscate, each man for himself, out of the baggage of the unfortunate prisoners; and, feeling that no worse fate could overtake me, I slipped my hand cautiously along the desk, took up a pen, and imitating as closely as possible the character of the writing before me,inscribed my own name at the bottom of the list, and immediately returned to the crowd at the other end of the room. The Deputy asked me if I saw my name, to which I promptly responded, 'Yes.' ' Then you are all right,' said he, ' and will be turned out to-night.' Shortly afterwards, we were marched off to a neighboring place, to get our supper at the expense of Uncle Sam, after which the Chief Marshal and Judge Beebe appeared, and in due form separated those who were to be released from the unfortunate ones remaining. I waited, with feelings that can be imagined better than they can be described, as the names were read; and at last my own name was called without the detection of my expedient, which was, doubtless, owing to the fact that the room was badly lighted and darkness had already set in. Promptly responding to my name, I at once passed out into the night, leaving my commander, Captain Robert Lockwood, the Wilmington pilot, Mr. Charles Craig, and Billy Willington, our engineer, and several others of the *Margaret and Jessie* who, together with Captain Frank Bonneau, his Wilmington pilot, and his chief engineer, Alexander Laurence, were sent to Fort LaFayette, where they remained until about the end of the war.

"It may be interesting in this connection to recall the incident that led to the capture of the *Ella and Annie*, through the same gunboat's being anchored in the channel. Instead of turning backward and running out to sea, as we did, Captain Bonneau kept on his course, ordering his engineer to throw his throttle wide open and leave the engine room immediately, his intention being to run down the gunboat and take the consequences. The two ships came together with a frightful crash, and as they swung around, side by side, the gunboat got out lashings, and her boarders swarmed upon the *Ella and Annie*, and after a sharp resistance, succeeded in taking possession of her. The *Ella and Annie*'s crew was sent to New York, and the gunboat *Nyphon*, in a badly damaged condition, was sent to the Norfolk navy yard to be docked, as it was difficult to keep her afloat, owing to the effects of the collision. On Colonel Lamb's being asked subsequently to drive the gunboat out of the channel, he replied that is was impossible to do so, as she came in after dark and anchored under shelter of the wreck referred to and he could not get the range until the moon rose, when, of course, the gunboat steamed out to sea, the channel being no longer of any use to the blockade runners."

A NOTED ENGINEER.

John Niemyer, an old and trusted locomotive engineer on the Atlantic Coast Line, had been reading the writer's tales of the blockade in the *Southport Leader* with much interest, having himself served as one of the engineers of that remarkable boat, the *Siren*, which ran between Wilmington, Charleston and West Indies continuously for nearly two years of the war, with the regularity of a mail boat in time of peace. I repeatedly asked him for a blockade runner's yarn; and he gave me the following true story of a true man, which I shall put, as nearly as possible, in Mr. Niemyer's own words:

"I see you have been writing some stories about George C. McDougal, who was chief of the *Siren*. Why, he ought to have been captain, as well as chief engineer of that boat. He wasn't what you might call a scientific navigator, but he knew more about the ins and outs of blockade running, most likely, than any other man in the fleet. For years before the Wilmington, Columbia and Augusta Railroad was built, he had served as chief engineer of the steamboats plying between Wilmington and Charleston; and he knew every landmark ashore, and every hump and hollow under the water up and down the coast, from Hatteras to St. Augustine. He could tell the position of the ship by the revolutions of the engine nearly as accurately as our navigating officer with his sextant, chronometer and logarithms; and as for the bottom on a deep-sea lead, he was what you might call a specialist.

"The little *Siren* was an enchantress, sure enough. She didn't sing any, because we had to keep her very quiet. She must have hypnotized the Yankees, however, as they were never able to touch her. She was at first commanded by an Englishman, who dreaded the coast as the devil does holy water, and, when he fetched soundings, was always for running off again. On one occasion he made a bad land fall, and fearing he would get aground by following the beach, decided to run out to sea. The Boss, as we called McDougal, at once protested against such folly, which he said would surely lead to greater danger than if we continued towards Wilmington; besides which, the ship was short of coal, and could not possibly keep steam for more than twelve or fifteen hours longer. The captain, who was a deep-water navigator, refused to listen to him, however, and persisted in changing the course of the ship; whereupon McDougal quietly said that he felt it his duty under the circumstances to take the ship into his own hands, and that if the captain persisted in thus willfully risking the property of the owners and endangering the lives of all on board, he must take the consequences, as the *Siren* was bound to go into Wilmington that night, and no where else. The captain insisted that McDougal's proposal was contrary to all rules of navigation; but finding that his engineer was in earnest, and could easily command all the men on board, having their full confidence, he at last agreed, and, following the engineer's suggestions and having an excellent pilot, succeeded in making the harbor in safety.

"Captain J. Pembroke Jones, who was a passenger on board, at once sent ashore for his brother, in command at Fort Caswell, and there was quite a jollification in the cabin that night. Our captain had a good deal to say about his skill in bringing the ship into port, but he utterly failed to mention the part that his plucky engineer had taken, and McDougal was not a man to boast of his own exploits.

"But I started to tell you another story about the *Siren* and McDougal. We had successfully run the blockade and arrived at Nassau, where we immediately discharged and re-loaded. Between one and two o'clock p.m., the *Siren* got under way, and crossing the bar at Nassau headed up the northeast channel, bound for Wilmington. She was commanded on this occasion by Captain R—, a remarkably skillful navigator, but without any nerve in time of danger. It was his habit, whenever he got into a tight place, to leave the bridge and shut himself up in his cabin and trust to luck—which meant McDougal; for the latter generally took charge of the ship at once, and, with the assistance of a good man who was chief officer, always managed to get the boat out of difficulty, when R— would again assume command.

"On this occasion the weather was fair, and the sea as smooth as a pond. While we were tracking along Egg Island reef, which is a long, narrow shoal with shallow water inside, a Federal gunboat shot out from under the eastern end of the reef and headed for us. This was clearly contrary to international law, being within the limit of British jurisdiction; but it is a well known fact that the Federal blockading and cruising fleets had positive orders, after the second year of the war, to seize all suspicious vessels, no matter where found; and, if a foreign government set up a reasonable claim, to pay it without demur, the United States Government having determined that it was better to pay for such vessels than to permit them to reach the Confederacy. We know as well as they did that we were within the dominion of a British province. We also knew that this would not deter the Yankees from picking us up, if there were no British men-of-war in sight; and there was nothing for us to do, under the circumstances, but 'bout ship and run back for Nassau, which, in our position, appeared to be an impossibility. The little *Siren* was handicapped by a heavy cargo, and the gunboat gained on us rapidly. As soon as it became evident that we could not fetch Nassau, our pursuer opened fire upon us, under which our discomfited captain left the bridge, and took shelter in the cabin; and the first assistant engineer, Barbot, at once sung out to me, 'Niemyer, where's the Boss?' 'In his room, asleep,' said I. 'Rout him out quickly, then and tell him the Yankee is after us, is gaining rapidly, and has range of us, and the captain has left the deck.' I immediately ran to the chief's room and repeated Barbot's order, but before I could finish it the Boss was out on deck in his stocking feet; he took a quick look over the stern at the gunboat, another over the port side at the rocky and treacherous bottom which was clearly visible through the transparent water; then with half a dozen jumps, was on the bridge. I followed to see the outcome. He immediately hustled the Bahama pilot onto the paddle box with the order, 'Into the current immediately!' The pilot saw the danger of such a movement, which meant that the ship must run inside the reef and take the chances of getting out. He saw also that it was the only opportunity of escape, and he lost no time in following his instructions. The Boss then cried to Mr. Habnicht, our chief officer, who was a splendid seaman; 'Jump to the wheel, Mr. Habnicht. This is no child's play; we must make the most of it.' I then walked over to McDougal, and, touching him on the shoulder, pointed to a shell which was just bursting over us. He said, 'Don't bother about shells, but look to the water; if we strike one of those rocks, it will tear the whole bottom out of the ship.' I did look, and seeing the ugly rocks under the clear green water over which we were rushing at full speed, thought no more about the shells, but of the other dangers surrounding us. When the gunboat saw us go in among the rocks, she fired a parting shot, and having put about the ship, went back to the channel. I went below on duty, and soon got orders from the bridge, 'Stand by your engines'! and, at intervals, 'Slow down!' 'Stop!' 'Two turns back!' Then came the splash and rattle of the chain, and we were at anchor.

"On returning to the deck I found that we were lying in the prettiest harbor I ever saw, which probably never before embraced a ship of half our size. Our chief officer immediately sent a man aloft with the best glass in the ship, with orders not to lose sight of the gunboat; then ordered supper, with 'Be quick about it.' McDougal said to his first assistant, 'Barbot, get your fires in good trim, with plenty of coarse coal on the fire room plates. We have got to race for it to-night.' Shortly afterwards the mate went aloft to relieve the man in the cross-trees, and saw that the cruiser was playing off and on at the end of the reef, waiting to pick us up in the morning, well knowing that he had us in a trap. The Boss soon saw that our only chance lay in getting out of shoal water before darkness. The sun was in the meantime getting low. Orders were given to weigh anchor, and the ship proceeded very slowly towards the outlet, in order not to excite our pursuer's suspicions; the ships having each other's bearings, and each watching to see if the other moved. As soon as we got outside of the shoal we kept still again until the sun went down. In two hours the moon began to show above the horizon, and, to our great joy, we had our pursuer clearly defined under the moon's rays, while we were in comparative darkness. Now orders were given for full speed across the channel to Abaco, and you may be sure that Barbot got all out of the engines that was possible. We had been warned the day before by a passing schooner that two cruisers were waiting to shake off, before we could reach the western ocean. We soon sighted 'Hole in the wall' light, and made straight for deep water. Three hours afterwards we hauled up the ship off Elbow Key, and day broke without a sail in sight. We then eased down the engines and dropped into the homeward track for Wilmington. Our captain, in the meantime, had resumed charge.

"For some time before the war ended the Federals had blockaded both ends of the route. The United States Corvette *Junietta* anchored off the bar at Nassau, and was kept well informed as to the movement of Confederate steamers in port. The outlying gunboats would run down the channel in the night within a few miles of Nassau, and send a boat to the Corvette for news and instructions for cutting off blockade runners ready to leave; so that it was almost as difficult to get in and out of Nassau as it was to pass the coastline blockade.

"The *Siren* differed from the other blockade runners in this respect: she never waited for more favourable conditions, but took them as they came. On one occasion she ran into Charleston at night, and the next morning disclosed six blockade runners lying loaded and anchored in the Ashley river. We dropped to the wharf, discharged our inward cargo, loaded the outward cargo of cotton, and went straight to Nassau; came back, and found the same six ships anchored in the same places. We made a second voyage, and on our return found them still lying there; a third voyage and there they remained, waiting for an opportunity to go out. On our fourth return voyage three of the long waiting blockade runners had slipped out, and on our fifth two more had gone. On our sixth and last voyage the remaining one, called the *General Whiting*, had finally departed. Thus the *Siren* made six round voyages, clearing for her owners over $1,000,000.00 in gold, while the *General Whiting* lay at anchor waiting for a chance to go out. The *Siren*'s cargoes into the Confederacy were, of course, very valuable, and cannot be properly estimated. The outward cargo consisted of from 650 to 750 bales of cotton. This cotton cost the equivalent of six cents in coin, and sold in Nassau for 45 and 50 cents in coin; making a clean profit of $200 a bale, which multiplied by four thousand bales in the six voyages showed a gain during that time to the owners of $800,000 in gold."

DISTINGUISHED COMMANDERS OF BLOCKADE RUNNERS.

One of the most distinguished commanders of the blockade-running steamers was Captain Roberts (so-called), of the twin-screw steamer *Don*, a quick, handy little boat, admirably adapted to the trade. I had the pleasure of knowing him personally through frequent intercourse with his signal officer, a fine fellow, named Selden, from Virginia; and we were both much impressed with the superior bearing and intelligence of this remarkable man, who afterwards became famous in the war between Russia and Turkey as Hobart Pasha, Admiral-in-Chief of the Turkish navy.

"Captain Roberts" was the Honourable Augustus Charles Hobart Hampden (son of the Earl of Buckinghamshire), Post Captain in the Royal Navy, and for a time commander of Queen Victoria's yacht *Victoria and Albert.* He had seen service in the war against Emperor Nicholas in 1854, under the great British Admiral Sir Charles Napier, when he commanded *H.M.S. Driver*; and, after the general order, "Lads, sharpen your cutlasses!" boarded the Russian warships before Cronstadt, stormed the seven forts which guarded the entrance to that harbor, and sailed up the Neva even to St. Petersburg itself. In 1865, having made several runs into Wilmington during his absence from England on leave, he returned home; and, fretting under the dull routine of service ashore, accepted the command of the entire Turkish Navy at the outbreak of the war with his old antagonists, the Russians. He died in 1886 Admiral-in-Chief of the Turkish Navy, and was buried in the English cemetery at Scutari. The *Daily Telegraph*, of London, said of him: "Altogether, Augustus Charles Hobart was a remarkable man; bluff, bold, dashing and somewhat dogged. There was in his composition something of the medieval 'condottiere,' and a good deal more of that Dugald Dalgetty whom Scott drew. Gustavus Adolphus would have made much of Hobart; the great Czarina, Catherine II, would have appointed him Commander-in-chief of her fleet, and covered him with honours, even as she did her Scotch Admiral Gleig, and that other yet more famous seadog, king of corsairs, Paul Jones. It would be unjust to sneer at Hobart as a mercenary. His was no more a hired sword than were the blades of Schomberg and Berwick, of Maurice de Saxe and Eugene of Savoy. When there was fighting to be done, Hobart liked to be in it—that is all. Of the fearless, dashing, adventurous Englismen, ready to go anywhere and do anything, Hobart was a brilliant, representative type."

Charles Hobart-Hampden

The following incident is from his blockade sketches:

"On my return to Wilmington I found that my vessel was ready for sea, so I took charge of her, and we went down the river. We had to undergo the same ordeal as before in the way of being smoked and searched. This time there were no runaways discovered; but there was one on board, for all that, who made his appearance, almost squashed to death, after we had been twenty-four hours at sea. We then anchored under Fort Fisher, where we waited until it was dark; after which, when the tide was high enough on the bar, we made a move, and were soon rushing out to sea at full speed. There was a considerable swell running, which we always considered a point in our favour.

"By the way, writing 'swells' puts me in mind of a certain 'swell' I had on board as passenger on this occasion, who, while in Wilmington, had been talking very big about 'hunting,' which, probably, he supposed I knew nothing about. He used to give us long narratives of his own exploits in the hunting field, and expatiated on the excitement of flying over ditches and hedges, while, apparently, he looked upon blockade running and its petty risks with sublime contempt. Soon after we crossed the bar on our way out, a gentle breeze and swell began to lift the vessel up and down, and this motion he described as 'very like hunting.' Just after he had ventured this remark, a Yankee gun-boat favoured us with a broadside, and made a dash to cut us off. This part of the fun, however, my friend did not seem to think at all 'like hunting;' and after having strongly urged me to return to the anchorage under the protecting guns of the fort, he disappeared below, and never talked—to me, at least—about hunting again.

"But to return to my story:—there was, as I said before, a considerable swell running outside; which was fortunate for us, as we almost ran into a gun-boat lying watching unusually close to the bar. It would have been useless to turn round and endeavor to escape by going back; since, if we had done so, we should inevitably have been driven on to the beach, and either captured or destroyed. In such a predicament there was nothing for it but to make a dash past and take the gun-boat's fire and its consequences. I knew we had the legs of her, and, therefore, felt more at ease in thus running the gauntlet than I otherwise should have done; so on we went at full speed. She fired her broadside at about fifty yards distance, but the shot all passed over us, except one, that went through our funnel. The marines on board of her kept up a heavy fire of musketry as long as we were visible, but only slightly wounded one of our men. Rockets were then thrown up as signals to her consorts, two of which came down on us; but, luckily, made a bad guess at our position, and closed with us on our quarter, instead of our bow. They also opened fire, but did us no injury. At the moment there was no vessel in sight ahead; and, as we were going at a splendid pace, we soon reduced our dangerous companions to three or four shadowy forms, struggling astern without a hope of catching us. The signaling and firing had, however, brought several other blockaders down to dispute our passage, and we found ourselves at one moment with a cruiser on each side within pistol shot of us; our position being that of the meat in a sandwich. So near were the cruisers, that they seemed afraid to fire, from the danger of hitting each other; and, thanks to our superior speed, we shot ahead and left them without their having fired a shot.

"Considering the heavy swell running, there was the merest chance of their hitting us; in fact, to take a blockade runner in the night, when there was a heavy swell or wind, if she did not choose to give in, was next to impossible. To run her down required the cruiser to have much superior speed, and was a dangerous game to play; for vessels have been known to go down themselves while attempting this feat.

"Then again, it must be borne in mind that the blockade-runner had always full speed at command, her steam being at all times well up and every one on board on the lookout; whereas the man-of-war must be steaming with some degree of economy and ease, and her lookout men had not the excitement to keep them always on the *qui vive* that we had.

"I consider that the only chances the blockading squadron had of capturing a blockade-runner were the following, *viz*; in a fair chase in daylight, when superior speed would tell; or by chasing her on shore or driving her in so near the beach that her crew were driven to set fire to her and make their escape—in which case a prize might be made, through perhaps of no great value; or by frightening a vessel with guns and rockets during the night into giving up. Some of the blockade-runners showed great pluck, and stood a lot of pitching into. About sixty-six vessels left England and New York to run the blockade during the four years' war, of which more that forty were destroyed by their own crews or captured; but most of them, before they came to grief, made several runs, and in so doing paid well for their owners.

"I once left Bermuda in a blockade-runner shortly before the end of the war, in company with four others, and ours was the only fortunate vessel of the lot. Of the other four, three were run ashore and destroyed by their own crews, and one was fairly run down at sea and captured.

" I saw an extraordinarily plucky thing done on one occasion, which I cannot refrain from narrating. We had made a successful run through the blockade, and were lying under Fort Fisher, when as daylight broke we heard heavy firing, and as it got lighter we saw a blockade-runner surrounded by the cruisers. Her case seemed hopeless; but on she came for the entrance, hunted like a rabbit by no end of vessels. The guns of the fort were at once manned, ready to protect her as soon as her pursuers should come within range. Every effort was made to cut her off from the entrance of the river, and how it was she was not sunk I cannot tell. As she came on we could see N—, her commander, a well known successful blockade-runner, standing on her paddle-box with his hat off, as if paying proper respect to the men-of-war. And now the fort opened fire at the chasing cruisers, from whom the blockade-runner was crawling, being by this time well in shore. One vessel was evidently struck, as she dropped out of range very suddenly. On came the Old J—, one of the fastest boats in the trade, and anchored all right; two or three shots in her hull, but no hurt. Didn't we cheer her! The reason of her being in the position in which we saw her at daylight was, that she had run the time rather short, and daylight broke before she could get into the river; so that, instead of being there, she was in the very center of the blockade fleet. Many men would have given in, but old N— was made of different stuff.

"It is not my intention to inflict on my readers any more anecdotes of my own doings in the *Don*; suffice it to say that I had the good luck to make six round trips in her, in and out of Wilmington, and that I gave her over to the chief officer and went home to England. On arriving at Southhampton, the first thing I saw in the *Times* was a paragraph headed, 'The Capture of the *Don*.' Poor little craft! I learned afterwards how she was taken, and I know she died game.

"The officer to whom I gave over charge was as fine a specimen of a seaman as well can be imagined—plucky, cool, and determined; and, by the way, he was a bit of a medico, as well as a sailor; for, by his beneficial treatment of his patients, we had very few complaints of sickness on board. As our small dispensary was close to my cabin, I used to hear the conversations that took place between C— and his patients. I will repeat one.

C—'Well, my man, what's the matter with you?'

Patient—'Please, sir, I've got pains all over me.'

C.—'Oh, all over you, are they? That's bad!'

Then, during the pause, it was evident something was being mixed up, and I could hear C—say: 'Here, take this, and come again in the evening.' (Exit patient). Then C—said to himself : 'I don't think he'll come again; he has got two drops of the croton. Skulking rascal, pains all over him, eh!' I never heard the voice of that patient again; in fact, after, after a short time we had no cases of sickness on board. C—explained to me that the only medicine he served out, as he called it, was croton oil; and that none of the crew came twice for treatment.

"Never having run through the blockade as the commander of a vessel (though he was with me all the time and had as much to do with our luck as I had), he was naturally very anxious to get safely through. There can be no doubt that the vessel had lost much of her speed, for she had been very hardly pushed on several occasions. This told sadly against her, as the result will show. On the third afternoon after leaving Nassau, she was in a good position for attempting the run when night came on. She was moving stealthily about, waiting for the evening, when suddenly, on the clearing up of the weather, which had been hitherto thick and hazy, she saw a cruiser unpleasantly near to her, which bore down under steam and sail; and it soon became probable that the poor little *Don*'s twin screws would not save her this time, well and often as they had done so before.

"The cruiser, a large full-rigged corvette, was coming up hand over hand, carrying a strong breeze, and the days of the *Don* seemed numbered, when C— tried a ruse worthy of any of the heroes of naval history.

"The wind, as I said, was very fresh, with a good deal of sea running. On came the cruiser, till the *Don* was almost under her bows, and shortened sail in fine style. The moment the men were in the rigging, going aloft to furl sails, C— put his plan into execution. He turned his craft's head to the wind, and steamed deliberately past the corvette at not fifty yards' distance. The latter, with great way on, went nearly a quarter of a mile before she could turn.

"I have it from good authority, that the order was not given to the marines on the man-of-war's poop to fire at the plucky little craft who had so fairly out-manoeuvred the cruiser, for out-manoeuvred she was, to all intents and purposes. The two or three guns that had been cast loose during the chase had been partly secured, and left so while the men had gone aloft to furl sails, so that not a shot was fired as the *Don* went past.

"Shortly after she had done so, however, the cruiser opened fire with her bow guns, but with the sea that was running this could do no harm, the guns being without any top weights. The *Don* easily dropped the corvette with her heavy spars astern, and was soon far ahead; so much so that when night came on the cruiser was shut out of sight in the darkness."

IN QUARANTINE.

In the steamer *Lilian*, already referred to, we had on one occasion safely eluded the blockading fleet at Cape Fear bar, and, after several narrow escapes from the squadron in the Gulf Stream, reached St. George's, Bermuda, on the morning of the fourth day, and at once discharged our cargo, hoping to get away in time for another run while we had a few hours of darkness.

We had hardly received the half of our inward cargo of gunpowder and commissary supplies, when we were visited by the harbor physician, who alleged that we had a case of smallpox on board, and peremptorily ordered us to the quarantine ground, where he informed us that we must remain for twenty-one days. The place was about two miles out of port, among some uninhabited rocks, which made the usual dreariness of a quarantine station more distressing. In vain our captain protested that he was mistaken, that the case to which he referred was a slight attack of malarial fever, combined with other symptoms which were not at all dangerous (which subsequently proved to be true). The doctor was unrelenting. If we did not proceed at once, he said, he would report us to the Governor at Hamilton who would send *HMS Spitfire*, then on the station, to tow us out; and after we had served our quarantine, we would be arrested for resisting authority. Finding remonstrance of no avail, our captain agreed to get away as soon as possible; but before we could make preparation a tug was sent alongside which towed us out, *nolens volens,* and left us at anchor

The captain of the **Lilian** *keeps a watch out for Union warships.*

among the sea gulls, with only ten days' provisions for a three weeks' quarantine.

Being ex-officio the ship's doctor, I began at once to physic the unfortunate sailor who had unwittingly brought us into this trouble; and, although my knowledge of the pharmacopoeia did not go beyond cathartic pills and quinine, I soon had him on his feet, to join all hands for inspection by the quarantine officer, who came off to windward of us every day, and at a respectable distance bawled out his category of questions which were required by law.

We were daily warned that if any of our officers or crew were found on shore or on board any vessels in the harbor, the full extent of the law would be meted out to them, and we were given to understand that twenty-one days' quarantine was a mere bagatelle compared with the punishment which would follow any attempt to evade these restrictions. Notwithstanding this, we came to a unanimous decision at the end of three days, that we would prefer the risk of capture at sea to such a life in comparative security; and it was accordingly resolved by the captain that, if any of us were plucky enough to take his gig and a boat's crew to St. George's and secure from a shipwright on shore some castings required by the chief engineer, we would proceed towards Wilmington without further preparation, and without the formality required by law.

Being comparatively indifferent as to the result, albeit somewhat confident of success, I at once volunteered. Our captain consented to my proposal, and amid a good deal of chaffing from several Confederate officers who were with us as

passengers, I started with our second engineer and five trustworthy men for shore.

We were careful to start shortly after the visit of the health physician, so that our absence would not be noticed when all hands were turned out; and, as we approached the harbor, I was gratified to observe that we were entirely unnoticed. We landed about half a mile below town, and, leaving the men with the boat, which I ordered them to keep concealed, I proceeded with the engineer to dispatch our business, which delayed us several hours.

At last we were ready to return, and, finding our men unmolested, we proceeded down the harbor towards the ship *Storm King*, which had recently left the China trade to carry C.S. Government cotton from the Bermuda rendezvous to Liverpool. Passing under her quarter, we were excitedly hailed by her captain, to whom I was well known personally, with the intelligence that a quarantine boat had just left our ship, and that we were probably discovered, as its course had been suddenly changed for us while we were pulling down the bay.

Thinking to elude the pursuer, if such it proved to be, I steered for the rocks along shore, the men giving way at the oars with a will; but we soon saw that we were closely watched and that the fears of our friends were fully realized, for the well known yellow flag was borne by a boat now clearly in pursuit of us. Finding escape cut off, we at once returned to the *Storm King* and entreated the captain to secrete us on board, and if the health officer boarded him, to profess ignorance of us altogether. This the good fellow agreed to do; and, my men having been set to work as if they were part of the crew, I was, with the engineer, at once secreted and locked in one of the many state rooms then vacant.

We had hardly settled ourselves in the berths, determined that if the worst came we would cover our heads and draw the curtains, when we heard the measured sound of oars approaching the gangway near the room in which we were hiding, and a moment later the hail, "*Storm King*, ahoy!" "Aye, aye, sir, what do you want?"

"You have on board a boat's crew from the steamer *Lilian*, in quarantine, who have left contrary to law; I demand their surrender."

"But I protest Doctor, there are no such people on my ship."

"What a consummate liar old McDonald is!" groaned the engineer, sweltering under two pairs of blankets.

"Aha!" exclaimed the health officer at this moment, "we have here the captain's gig alongside, and here is the name *Lilian* on the stern. How is this?"

"Oh!" replied the imperturbable McDonald, "we picked her up adrift this morning—I am glad to know the owner."

"A very unlikely story, Captain, and we shall have to search," quoth the doctor; and then we heard several persons ascending the ladder; followed by further expostulations on the part of our friend the captain, evidently of no avail, for the party immediately entered the saloon and proceeded with their search.

Door after door was opened and shut, and, as they gradually approached our hiding place, I looked up at Sandy McKinnon, the Scotch engineer, who presented a most ludicrous and woeful sight, the perspiration streaming down his fat cheeks.

With anxious hearts we waited for the worst, and at last it came. A heavy hand wrenched our door knob, and an impatient voice demanded that the door be unlocked. The steward protested that the room was vacant and that the key was lost, which only seemed to increase the officer's determination to enter. High words ensued; the captain, with a heartiness which excited our admiration, but increased our fears, poured a volley of abuse upon the unlucky doctor, who was apparently discharging his duty, and at times I fancied that they almost came to blows. This was at last quelled by a peremptory demand that the ship's carpenter be sent for to force the door. The steward at this juncture produced the key, which he averred had just been found in another lock; and, while he fumbled at our door, I thought I heard the sound of suppressed laughter on the outside, but dismissed the idea as absurd.

A moment after the door opened, and, before our astonished vision, were ranged our good friends and shipmates, Major Hone, of Savannah, Captain Leo Vogel, of St. Augustine, Sergeant Gregory, of Crowels, and Eugene Maffitt, who, with Captain McDonald and several of his friends, were fairly shrieking with laughter at our sorry plight. We had been completely sold. The whole scheme was planned on board our own ship immediately after our departure; and Captain McDonald was privy to the arrangement, which he so successfully carried our.

The voices which, in our fright, we supposed came from Her Majesty's officers were feigned by our own people, who made the most of the joke at our expense. The trick was too good to keep; and, when the good doctor came next day to discharge us from quarantine, all traces of sickness having disappeared, no one enjoyed the fun more than he, although he said it might have resulted seriously enough. Having received the remainder of our cargo, we proceeded to sea; and, when about five miles from land, we sighted a rakish war steamer, which proved to be the Confederate Corvette *Florida*, to which we delivered important dispatches by an order from Major Norman Walker, the Confederate Agent in Bermuda.

CAPTAIN WILKINSON.

One of the most intelligent and successful commanders in the blockade-running fleet was Captain John Wilkinson, who entered the U.S. Navy as a midshipman in 1837, and, after an honourable and distinguished career, tendered his services to the Confederacy upon the secession of his native State, Virginia.

Having received a commission in the C.S. Navy, he served in various responsible positions, until ordered upon special service in command of the C.S. Steamer *R.E. Lee*.

In his interesting book entitled *Narrative of a Blockade Runner*, with reference to the citizens of Virginia who resigned their commissions in the old service, he says:

"They were compelled to choose whether they would aid in subjugating their State, or in defending it against invasion; for it was already evident that coercion would be used by the general government, and that war was inevitable. In reply to the accusation of perjury in breaking their oath of allegiance, since brought against the officers of the army and navy who resigned their commissions to render aid to the South, it need only be stated that, in their belief, the resignation of their commissions absolved them from any special obligation. They then occupied the same position towards the government as other classes of citizens. But this charge was never brought against them until the war was ended. The resignation of their commissions was accepted when their purpose was well known. As to the charge of ingratitude, they reply, their respective States had contributed their full share towards the expenses of the general government, acting as their disbursing agent; and, when these States withdrew from the Union, their citizens belonging to the two branches of the public service did not, and do not, consider themselves amenable to this charge for abandoning their official positions to cast their lot with their kindred and friends. But, yielding as they did to necessity, it was nevertheless a painful act to separate themselves from companions with whom they had been long and intimately associated, and from the flag under which they had been proud to serve."

With reference to his experience in blockade running at Wilmington, Captain Wilkinson continues:

"The natural advantages of Wilmington for blockade running were very great, owing chiefly to the fact that there are two separate and distinct approaches to Cape Fear River; i.e. *either by 'New Inlet' to the north of Smith's Island, or by the 'western bar' to the south of it. This island is ten or eleven miles in length; but the Frying Pan Shoals extend ten or twelve miles further south, making the distance by sea between the two bars thirty miles or more, although the direct distance between them is only six or seven miles. From Smithville, a little village about equidistant from the two bars, both blocking fleets could be distinctly seen; and the outward bound blockade runners could take their choice through which inlet to run the gauntlet. The inward bound blockade runners, too, were guided by circumstances of wind and weather; selecting that bar over which they would cross after they had passed the Gulf Stream, and shaping their course accordingly. The approaches to both bars were clear of danger, with the single exception of the 'Lump' before mentioned; and so*

regular are the soundings that the shore can be coasted for miles within a stone's throw of the breakers.

"The facts explain why the United States fleets were unable wholly to stop blockade running. It was, indeed, impossible to do so: the result to the very close of the war proves this assertion; for, in spite of the vigilance of the fleet, many blockade runners were afloat when Fort Fisher was captured. In fact, the passage through the fleet was little dreaded; for, although the blockade runner might receive a shot or two, she was rarely disabled; and, in proportion to the increase of the fleet, the greater we knew would be the danger of its vessels' firing into each other. As the boys before the deluge used to say, they would be very apt to 'miss the cow and kill the calf.' The chief danger was upon the open sea, many of the light cruisers having great speed. As soon as one of them discovered a blockade runner during daylight, she would attract other cruisers in the vicinity by sending up a dense column of smoke, visible for many miles in clear weather. A cordon of fast steamers stationed ten or fifteen miles apart, inside the Gulf Stream, and in the course from Nassau and Bermuda to Wilmington and Charleston, would have been more effective in stopping blockade running than the whole United States Navy concentrated off these ports. It was unaccountable to us why such a plan did not occur to good Mr. Welles, but it was not our business to suggest. I have no doubt, however, that the fraternity to which I then belonged would have unanimously voted thanks and a service of plate to the Honourable Secretary of the United States Navy for this oversight.

Capt. John Wilkinson

"I say, inside the Gulf Stream; because every experienced captain of a blockade runner made it a point to cross 'the stream' early enough in the afternoon, if possible, to establish the ship's position by chronometer, so as to escape the influence of that current upon his dead reckoning. The lead always gave indication of our distance from the land, but not, of course, of our position; and the numerous salt works along the coast, where evaporation was produced by fire, and which were at work night and day, were visible long before the low coast could be seen. Occasionally, the whole inward voyage would be made under adverse conditions. Cloudy, thick weather and heavy gales would prevail so as to prevent any solar or lunar observations, and reduce the dead reckoning to mere guess-work. In these cases, the nautical knowledge and judgment of the

captain would be taxed to the utmost. The current of the Gulf Stream varies in velocity and, within certain limits, in direction; and the stream itself, almost as well defined as a river within its banks under ordinary circumstances, is impelled by a strong gale towards the direction in which the wind is blowing, overflowing its banks, as it were. The counter current, too, inside of the Gulf Stream is much influenced by the prevailing winds.

"Upon one occasion, while in command of the R.E. Lee, *formerly the Clyde-built iron steamer* Giraffe, *we had experienced very heavy and thick weather, and had crossed the Stream and struck soundings about midday. The weather then clearing, so that we could obtain an altitude near meridian, we found ourselves at least forty miles north of our supposed position, and near the shoals which extend in a southerly direction off Cape Lookout. It would be more perilous to run out to sea than to continue on our course, for we had passed through the off-shore line of blockaders, and the sky had become perfectly clear. I determined to impersonate a transport bound to Beaufort, a port which was in possession of the United States forces and the coaling station of the fleet blockading Wilmington. The risk of detection was not very great, for many of the captured blockade runners were used as transports and dispatch-vessels. Shaping our course for Beaufort, and slowing sown, as if we were in no haste to get there, we passed several vessels, showing United States colors to them all. Just as we were crossing the ripple of shallow water off the 'tail' of the shoals, we dipped our colors to a sloop-of-war which passed three or four miles to the south of us. The courtesy was promptly responded to; but I have no doubt her captain thought me a lubberly and careless seaman to shave the shoals so closely. We stopped the engines when no vessels were in sight; and I was relieved from a heavy burden of anxiety as the sun sank below the horizon, and the course was shaped at full speed for Masonboro Inlet.*

"The staid old town of Wilmington was turned 'topsy-turvy' during the war. Here resorted the speculators from all parts of the South, to attend the weekly auctions of imported cargoes; and the town was infested with rogues and desperadoes, who made a livelihood by robbery and murder. It was unsafe to venture into the suburbs at night, and even in daylight there were frequent conflicts in the public streets, between the crews of the steamers in port and the soldiers stationed in the town, in which knives and pistols would be freely used; and not unfrequently a dead body with marks of violence upon it would rise to the surface of the water in one of the docks. The civil authorities were powerless to prevent crime. ' Inter arma silent leges!' The agents and employes of different blockade running companies lived in magnificent style, paying a king's ransom (in Confederate money) for their household expenses, and nearly monopolizing the supplies in the country market. Towards the end of the war, indeed, fresh provisions were almost beyond the reach of everyone. Our family servant, newly

arrived from the country in Virginia, would sometimes return from market with an empty basket, having flatly refused to pay what he called 'such nonsense prices' for a bit of fresh beef or a handful of vegetables. A quarter of lamb, at the time of which I now write, sold for $100; a pound of tea for $500. Confederate money which in September, 1861, was nearly equal to specie in value, had declined in September, 1862, to 225; in the same month in 1863 to 400; and before September, 1864, to 2,000!

"Many of the permanent residents of the town had gone into the country, letting their houses at enormous prices; those who were compelled to remain kept themselves much secluded, the ladies rarely being seen upon the more public streets. Many of the fast young officers belonging to the army would get an occasional leave to come to Wilmington; and would live at free quarters on board the blockade runners, or at one of the numerous bachelor halls ashore.

"The convalescent soldiers from the Virginia hospitals were sent by the route through Wilmington to their homes in the South. The ladies of the town were organized by Mrs. deR. into a society for the purpose of ministering to the wants of these poor sufferers; the trains which carried them stopping an hour or two at the station, that their wounds might be dressed and food and medicine supplied to them. These self-sacrificing, heroic women patiently and faithfully performed the offices of hospital nurses.

"Liberal contributions were made by companies and individuals to this society; and the long tables at the station were spread with delicacies for the sick, to be found nowhere else in the Confederacy. The remains of the meals were carried by the ladies to a camp of mere boys—home guards—outside of the town. Some of these children were scarcely able to carry a musket, and were altogether unable to endure the exposure and fatigue of field service; and they suffered fearfully from measles and typhoid fever. General Grant used a strong figure of speech when he asserted that 'the cradle and the grave were robbed, to recruit the Confederate armies.' The fact of a fearful drain upon the population was not exaggerated. Both shared the hardships and dangers of war, with equal self devotion to the cause. It is true that a class of heartless speculators infested the country, who profited by the scarcity of all sorts of supplies; but this fact makes the self sacrifice of the mass of the Southern people more conspicuous; and no State made more liberal voluntary contributions to the armies, or furnished better soldiers, than North Carolina.

"On the opposite side of the river from Wilmington, on a low, marshy flat, were erected the steam cotton presses and there the blockade runners took in their cargoes. Sentries were posted on the wharves day and night, to prevent deserters from getting on board and stowing themselves away; and the additional precaution of fumigating the outward bound steamers at Smithville was adopted; but, in spite of this vigilance, many persons succeeded in getting a

***The North Carolina-owned steamer* SS Advance (*or* Ad-Vance).**

free passage abroad. These deserters, or 'stowaways' were in most instances sheltered by one or more of the crew; in which event they kept their places of concealment until the steamer had arrived at her port of destination, when they would profit by the first opportunity to leave the vessel undiscovered. A small bribe would tempt the average blockade-running sailor to connive at this means of escape. The 'impecunious' deserter fared more hardly, and would usually be forced by hunger and thirst to emerge from his hiding place while the steamer was on the outward voyage. A cruel device, employed by one of the captains, effectually put a stop, I believe,—certainly a check,—to this class of stowaways.' He turned three or four of them adrift in the Gulf Stream, in an open boat, with a pair of oars, and a few days' allowance of bread and water."

STEAMER *ADVANCE*.

In the latter part of the year 1863, I embarked at Wilmington on the North Carolina Steamer *Advance*, bound for St. George's, Bermuda, to join at that port another blockade runner to which I had been assigned to duty. The Advance was commanded by Captain Crossan, of the old navy, with Captain Wylie, a hearty, whole-souled Scotchman, as sailing master. The purser was Mr. Joseph H. Flanner, a well-known Wilmington merchant and agent of the State; Captain George Morrison was chief engineer; J.B. Smith, a lad of nineteen, three years older than myself, was signal officer; and George Snow, of Raleigh, was a fellow passenger, with a short furlough for a frolic through the blockade. We three lads were assigned quarters in the main sleeping-cabin below deck, which had been used for general passengers in the old country while the ship, as the *Lord Clyde*, sailed on her former peaceful voyages.

It was my first separation from home; and, as we prepared to turn in for the night by the light of a carefully screened lamp, I was deeply impressed by the moral courage of young Smith, who, in the presence of several onlookers evidently careing nothing for these things, quietly got out his little Testament, read the evening lesson, and then upon his bended knees commended his soul and body to Him who has the confidence of those afar off upon the sea. That simple act of worship, under circumstances peculiarly trying to a young man, not only strengthened me for my duty then, but made an impression for good which has never been effaced.

This article, written by Mr. Smith, is copied from the *Guilford Collegian* of November, 1896:

"One beautiful afternoon in the summer of 1863 the steamship *Advance*, the famous blockade runner belonging to the State of North Carolina, with cargo of cloth, blankets, shoes, and other supplies for the North Carolina State troops in the Confederate Army, steamed out of the port of St. George's Bermuda. Her graceful bow headed for the port of Wilmington, N.C. which was at that time closely guarded by a blockading squadron, composed of the fleetest gunboats in the Federal Navy, to prevent the very purpose we had in view—that of taking in supplies for the Confederate army. I was serving as signal officer on the ship, being a lad of nineteen years of age.

"We had a smooth run of two days and three nights, always keeping a sharp lookout for Federal cruisers, which were kept in these waters to intercept any vessel suspected of contraband traffic. Not being permitted to carry an armament of any kind, our safety depended upon our vigilance and the speed of our ship. To be on the safe side, we would avoid any vessel carrying steam, the smoke being visible before its rigging loomed in sight.

"On the afternoon of the second day out, as usual, all hands were called up and told off by the first officer to their respective boats. It was the purpose of our captain, Thomas Crossan, if about to be captured to scuttle the ship, and by means of the ship's boats to endeavor to make our way ashore.

"What a motley sight our crew presented! With the exception of our sailing master, our officers were Southerners, but the crew was composed of men of every nationality, adventurers attracted to this most dangerous service by the tempting offer of enormous bounties and wages paid in gold or silver.

"On account of my youthfulness I was much petted by the officers, especially by the sailing master, who was a bluff, typical Scotchman. Heaven bless him! Though by no means of exemplary habits himself, he watched over and guarded me against the temptations to which I was exposed as carefully as a father could have done. He always assigned me to his boat; but Kit Morse, our Wilmington pilot, counted the most skillful pilot and surfman on our coast, would always whisper to me: 'Never mind, Smith, if ever we do have to take to the small boats, you just step in my boat, take a seat by Kit Morse, and if any boat can live through the surf, I will land you safe on North Carolina grit.' This always placed me in a quandary, in which obedience to orders and personal safety struggled for the mastery.

"It was the intention of our captain to make the coast of North Carolina at some point about twenty-five miles above Fort Fisher, at New Inlet to the Cape

Fear River, then to steam down the coast and run in about 3 a.m., which would be flood tide on the bar (our ship being so deeply laden we could not get over the bar except at high water). Owing to our having run off our course to dodge steamers, we made Hatteras lighthouse about 1 a.m., and although we steamed down the coast under full head of steam, daylight found us some twenty-five miles above Fort Fisher, and brought to view the Federal blockading fleet of five vessels, stretching in a line abreast of Masonboro Sound, and standing off about three miles at sea. The closest scrutiny with the aid of our glasses failed to show any sign of life on their decks. But we knew they always kept up full head of steam. The captain called Mr.Morse, the pilot, Mr. Morrison, the chief engineer, and myself to him, and said: 'We have either to run off the coast with chance of a long chase from those fellows out there,' pointing to the Federal vessels, 'and try to get in to-night, or, under cover of the fog and smoke from the surf and salt works hanging over the coast line, try to slip by them.' Then, after a minute's pause, said, with a sparkle in his calm blue eyes, and with compressed lips, 'I am going to take the risk of running by them. Mr. Morrison, be ready to give her all steam possible. Smith, stand by to signal Colonel Lamb to man his guns to protect us. Pilot, take charge of the ship; put her in, if possible; if not, beach her.'

"An extra hand was sent to the wheel, and as I, with my signal flag in hand, took my stand on the starboard side of the quarter deck, to the right of the pilot, he said, 'Smith, old boy, we are in for it.' We steamed on at a moderate speed, hugging the shore line as close as possible to keep under cover of mingled fog and smoke, which stretched like a veil along the coast.

"Scanning intently the line of blockaders, I began to flatter myself we were unobserved until we were off Masonboro, and abreast of the line of blockaders, when up went a signal from the flagship of the squadron, and in a moment each vessel, having slipped her cable, was in motion under full steam. One steamed in shore to our rear, three came bearing obliquely on our port beam, and one, the *Connecticut*, the fleetest of the squadron, steamed to head us off, and we saw that we were in a trap that had been set for us. 'Full speed ahead!' the pilot signaled the engineer, and the bonny ship bounded forward like a racer. 'Up with the colors!' spoke the captain, and the Southern Cross fluttered in the morning breeze from our flagstaff astern.

"Intense excitement prevailed among the sailors and firemen off duty as they gathered on the forward deck, on which, from our position, we had full view. Among them our chief cook, 'Frenchie" who was wont to boast a cap carried off his head by a Russian bullet at Sebastapol.

"Smith,' said the Pilot, 'twenty miles to Fort Fisher.' A puff of smoke, and a cannon ball from the *Connecticut* skipped the crest of the waves to the forward but short of our ship. I recognized it as a gentle hint to round to and surrender.

The motley crowd on deck, supposing it to be the extent of the *Connecticut's* ability to coerce, gave vent to their feelings in a suppressed cheer. Alas, for the hopes! The last spark of which was soon quenched. The *Connecticut*, our course not being changed, sent the next shot whistling between our smoke stacks, across the three-mile strip of land into the Cape Fear River, as I afterwards learned. 'Oh, good God!' said Frenchie, as he darted for shelter towards the forecastle, but was intercepted by a shot across our bows.

"The firing from the fleet had now become general, and amid the whistle of shot and bursting of shell all about us the pilot said with a smile: 'Smith, look at Frenchie dodging about like a partridge in a coop.' Just then the signal station highest up the beach hove in sight, and my time for action had arrived, which required me to become oblivious to the terrors menacing destruction and death; and, by waves of my signal flag spell out, letter by letter, this message to Colonel Lamb, commandant at Fort Fisher: 'Colonel Lamb: Have guns manned to protect us. Signed Crossan, Captain *Ad-Vance*.'

"No one can imagine how glad I was at the close of my message to catch the shore operator's reply of 'O.K.' My official responsibility being now ended, the peril that environed us burst upon me with full force. Fifteen miles to Fort Fisher! For fifteen miles to be subjected to such an ordeal, or to that of being dashed to pieces in that fearful surf which mingled its ominous warning with the reverberating roar of the pitiless cannon. I tried to read my destiny in the imperturbable countenance of my companion, a wave of whose hand could consign me to a Northern prison, or perchance to a watery grave. As well seek to penetrate the secrets of the Sphinx as the thoughts of Kit Morse. Yet I knew he loved me, thought of my safety even with this great responsibility resting upon him; for once, as the fragments of shell were falling all about us, he pushed me under the lee of the sailing master's cabin, saying, 'Smith, that may keep a piece from striking you.' How slow we seemed to be running! People ashore likened our speed to that of a bird seeking safety by flight. Minutes to us seemed hours, yet slowly, so slowly as scarcely to be perceptible, we were gradually forging ahead of all except the *Connecticut*, which was running in a straight line for the inlet, to cut us off, while we had to follow the curves of the shore. On sped the chase! In the press for speed the *Connecticut* fired only from her starboard guns.

"We had now reached the last curve of the shore which projected out seaward and would have to be turned before we could enter the inlet. This the pilot traced with his finger and said calmly: 'Smith, that will bring us in a hundred yards of the *Connecticut*. I wonder why Lamb doesn't fire.'

"Bang! went a gun from the shore battery, and a Whitworth shell bored through the hull of the rear vessel, being in point blank range. Suddenly the vessel to the rear gave up the chase and steamed seaward. Not so with that dreaded Connecticut which seemed right across our bows, with our ship as a shield to protect her from the guns of the fort.

"How fast we were approaching her! Every motion of her gun crew became plainly visible, even that of the gunner, as he pulled the lanyard and sent that fearful missile of destruction aimed at our water line, but buried in a wave twenty feet short.

"'That got us,' said the brave pilot to me. Then, with a quick wave of his hand and a cheery voice of command, 'Over, hard over!' The wheel rolled under the willing hands of the brave steersman; and, with the speed of a chased stag, and the grace of a swan, the bonnie craft rounded the point, and entered the inlet. The guns of Fort Fisher belched flames of fire, and we were safe."

IMPROVED SHIPS AND NOTABLE CAPTAINS.

The last year of the war evolved a superior type of blockade runners of great speed, many of which were commanded by celebrated men of nerve and experience. Of these may be mentioned at random and from memory: the *Lilian*, Captain Maffitt; the *Little Hattie*, Captain Lebby; the *Florie*, named for Captain Maffitt's daughter; the *Agnes E.Fry*, commanded by that noble but unfortunate naval officer, Captain Joseph Fry; the *Chicora* still running in Canadian waters; the *Let Her Rip*, the *Let Her Be*; also the fleet of three-funnel boats, one of which, the *Condor*, was commanded by the famous Admiral Hewitt, of the British navy, who won the Victoria Cross in the Crima, and who was knighted by Queen Victoria for his distinguished services as Ambassador to King John of Abyssinia. When this steamer was stranded off Fort Fisher, the celebrated Confederate spy, Mrs. Rose Greenhow, who was a passenger, entreated Captain Hewitt to send her ashore through the breakers, fearing that she would suffer death if captured by the Federals. Captain Hewitt refused, saying he would protect her; she insisted; at last he consented, and she was drowned in the attempt. Her body was picked up on the beach the next day by Mr. Thomas Taylor. The *Falcon* was commanded for one voyage by Hobart

Capt. Robert Halpin

Pasha; the *Flamingo*, the *Ptarmigan*, and the *Vulture* were also of three-funnel type.

Another notable British officer who ran the blockade was the gallant Burgoyne, who was lost in the iron-clad *Captain* in the Bay of Biscay, which vessel he commanded on that unfortunate voyage.

Admiral (formerly Captain) Hewitt

Captain Carter was a notable naval officer of the Confederacy, and he commanded the blockade runner *Coquette*.

Captain Thomas Lockwood, a North Carolinian, was, perhaps, the most noted of the commercial class. His last command was the celebrated steamer *Colonel Lamb*, named for the defender of Fort Fisher. This was the largest, the finest, and the fastest of all the ships on either side during the war. She was a paddle steamer built of steel, 281 feet long, 36 feet beam, and 15 feet depth of hold. Her tonnage was 1,788 tons. At the time she was built, 1864, she was the fastest vessel afloat, having attained on her trial a speed of $16^{3/4}$ knots, or about nineteen miles, an hour. Captain Lockwood made several successful runs in this fine ship, and escaped to England at the close of the war. The *Colonel Lamb* was sold to the Greek Government; and subsequently, under another name, was blown up while in the Mersey loaded with war supplies. Other fast boats were the *Owl*, *Bat*, *Fox*, *Dream*, *Stag*, *Edith*, *Atlanta*, *Virginia*, *Charlotte*, *Banshee*, and *Night Hawk*.

Another merchant commander of distinction was Captain Halpin, who was very skillful and successful, and who afterwards commanded the famous leviathan, *Great Eastern*, while she was engaged in laying the Atlantic cable.

CAPTAIN MAFFITT.

Among the devoted band of United States Navy officers whose home and kindred were in the South at the outbreak of the war, and who resigned their native State, there was none braver or truer than our own Captain John N. Maffitt, who, yielding to necessity, severed the strong ties of a service under the old flag, in which he had long distinguished himself; and not only relinquished a conspicuous position directly in the line of speedy promotion the rank of Admiral, but sacrificed at the same time his entire fortune, which was invested in the North, and which was confiscated shortly afterwards by the Federal government.

The story of the life and service of this modest hero has never been written. After the capture of the forts and the closing of the ports of Wilmington and Charleston in January, 1865, Maffitt, in command of the steamer *Owl*, and unaware of the situation, ran into each port in quick succession, escaping from the fleet in each exploit as by a miracle, although under a heavy and destructive fire. While running out of Charleston harbor when escape seemed impossible. The entire manuscript of his history of the cruise of the *Florida*, which warship he had so long successfully commanded, was, by an unfortunate misunderstanding on the part of a subordinate, sent to the bottom of the sea, along with the Confederate mail and other valuable papers. Some years after, with the assistance of his accomplished wife, he prepared for publication a number of historical manuscripts, which are still preserved by his widow, in the hope that they may be of pecuniary value to the survivors of the family. Captain Maffitt wrote, also, a story of naval life in the old service, entitled "Nautilus," as well as a number of articles for the *Army and Navy Magazine*, entitled "Reminiscences of the Confederate States Navy." His paper on the building of the ram *Albemarle* by Captain Cook, and the gallant officer's subsequent attack upon the Federal fleet in Plymouth Sound, which is copied entire by Colonel Scharf in his *History of the Confederate Navy*, has been pronounced one of the finest descriptions relative to the war between the states. It was my privilege to be numbered among his personal friends from the time he honoured me, a lad of seventeen years, with his recommendation for the appointment as purser of his own ship, the Confederate ram *Albemarle* at Plymouth. This friendship was unbroken until the close of his eventful life, the sacrifices and services of which should ever be held in grateful remembrance by our Southern people.

Capt. John Newland Maffitt

When President Davis wrote for Maffitt's war record for reference in his book, *Rise and Fall of the Confederate Government*, the modest commander gave more prominence to Lieutenant Read's exploits than to his own. When, a few years ago, I had the honor of frequent interviews with Mrs. Davis at

Maffitt's **CSS Florida** *crashing through Atlantic swells.*

Narragansett, Captain Maffitt was referred to repeatedly by that distinguished lady, who assured me that he was always held in high esteem by Mr. Davis and herself; and she pleasantly recalled some very amusing stories of Maffitt's gallantry and fine humor which made him such a universal favourite.

In a year after my appointment to the *Lilian*, I had the misfortune to be captured at sea, after an exciting chase of five hours, by the Federal cruisers *Keystone State*, *Boston*, *Gettysburg*, and two others unknown, in which our ship was disabled under a heavy fire by shot below the water line. I was held a prisoner on board the United States Steamer *Keystone State*, whose commander, Captain Crosby, a regular in the old navy, treated me most courteously. Upon the invitation of the paymaster, I messed with the superior officers in the wardroom; where I heard frequent bitter allusions to Captain Semmes and to other prominent Confederates, but never a word of censure for the genial Maffitt, the mention of whose name would provoke a kindly and amused smile, as some of his pranks in the old times would be recalled by those who had not learned to regard him as a foe.

The following passages taken from Admiral Porter's *Naval History of the Civil War*, confirm the personal observations of the writer with reference to Maffitt's reputation in the old navy:

"Maffitt was a different kind of man from Semmes. A thorough master of his profession, and possessed of all the qualities that make a favorite naval commander, he became a successful raider of the sea; but he made no enemies among those officers who had once known him and who now missed his genial humor in their messes. He was a veritable rover, but was never inhuman to those whom the fortunes of war threw into his hands; and he made himself as pleasant while emptying a ship of her cargo and then scuttling her, as Claude Duval when robbing a man of his purse, or borrowing his watch from his pocket."

Porter describes in almost flattering terms Maffitt's superior skill and daring in fitting out the *Florida* under most adverse conditions, and then, by way of explanation, says:

"It may appear to the reader that we have exhibited more sympathy for Commander Maffitt and given him more credit than he deserved. It must be remembered that we are endeavoring to write a naval history of the war, and not a partisan work. This officer, it is true, had gone from under the flag we venerate, to fight against it; but we know that it was a sore trial for him to leave the service to which he was attached, and that he believed he was doing his duty in following the fortunes of his State, and had the courage to follow his convictions. He did not leave the Untied States Navy with any bitterness, and, when the troubles were all over, he accepted the situation gracefully. What we are going to state of him shows that he was capable of the greatest heroism, and that, though he was on the side of the enemy, his courage and skill were worthy of praise."

He then recounts the wonderful story of Maffitt's perilous run through Commander Preble's fleet off Mobile in broad daylight, with a crew decimated by yellow fever, and he himself scarcely able to stand, owing to its prostrating effects:

"The *Florida* approached rapidly, her smoke pipes vomiting forth volumes of black smoke and a high pressure of steam escaping from her steam pipe. As she came within hailing distance, the Federal commander ordered her to heave to, but Maffitt still sped on, having sent all his men below, except the man at the wheel, and returned no reply to the hail. Preble then fired a shot ahead of the *Florida*, still supposing her to be some saucy Englishman disposed to try what liberties he could take, though the absence of men on deck should have excited suspicion. He hesitated, however, and his hesitation lost him a prize and the honor of capturing one of the Confederate scourges of the ocean. Preble had his crew at quarters, however, and, as soon as he saw that the stranger was passing him, he opened his broadside upon her, and the other two blockaders did the same. But the first shots were aimed too high, and the *Florida* sped on towards the bar, her feeble crew forgetting their sickness and heaping coal upon the furnace fires with all possible rapidity. Every man was working for his life, while the captain stood amid the storm of shot and shell perfectly unmoved, keenly watching the marks for entering the port, and wondering to himself what his chances were for getting safely in.

" During the whole war there was not a more exciting adventure than this escape of the *Florida* into Mobile Bay. The gallant manner in which it was conducted excited great admiration, even among the men who were responsible for permitting it. We do not suppose that there ever was a case where a man, under all the attending circumstances, displayed more energy or more bravery.

"And so the *Florida* was allowed to go on her way without molestation, and Maffitt was enabled to commence that career on the high seas which has made his name one of the notable ones of the war. He lighted the seas wherever he passed along, and committed such havoc among American merchantmen, that, if possible, he was even more dreaded than Semmes. We have only to say that his being permitted to escape into Mobile Bay, and then to get out again, was the greatest example of blundering committed throughout the war. Every officer who knew Maffitt was certain that he would attempt to get out of Mobile, and we are forced to say that those who permitted his escape are responsible for the terrible consequences of their want of vigilance and energy.

"Preble's failure to sink the *Florida*—for nothing else would have stopped Maffitt—brought him into disgrace with the Navy department, although he proved in his report of the affair that every means at his command had been used to intercept the bold Confederate; and shortly afterwards the Secretary of the Navy, supported by a majority of naval officers, recommended the dismissal of Commodore Preble from the navy, which was carried into effect September 20, 1863.

"Preble repeatedly demanded an investigation, which was refused; but he ultimately got his case before Congress, and was restored to the list February 21, 1864, with the grade of rear admiral.

"At the close of the war Captain Maffitt was summoned by a court of inquiry, demanded by Preble, to testify as to the facts of his exploit in entering Mobile Bay, in which he said:

"I can vouch for his (Preble's) promptness and destructive energy on the occasion of my entering Mobile Bay. The superior speed of the *Florida* alone saved her form destruction, though not from a frightful mauling. We were torn to pieces—one man's head taken off and eleven wounded; boats, and standing and running-rigging shot away, also fore gaff. Four shells struck our hull, and had the one (nine inch) that grazed our boiler and entered the berth deck (killing one and wounding two) exploded, every man belonging to the steamer would have been killed; as I had only the officers on deck until about to cross the bar, when I made some sail, and one man was wounded in the rigging. We had about fourteen hundred shrapnel shots in our hull, and our masts were pitted like a case of smallpox. The damage done her was so great that we did not get to sea again for over three months."

DR. HOGE'S ADVENTURE.

One of the interesting events connected with blockade running had to do with this great and good divine. There was, throughout the Confederacy, a deplorable lack of Bibles, and, in fact, of all religious literature. This was due to the scarcity of paper and of materials for printing and binding, all the industrial energies of the Confederacy being devoted to the great work of self-defense. Dr. William J. Hoge, the brother of Dr. Moses D. Hoge and father of Dr. Peyton H. Hoge, conceived the idea of laying this need before the Christians of Great Britain and asking for a ship-load of Bibles, tracts and other religious publications. He wrote to Dr. R.L. Dabney and Dr. M.D. Hoge of his plan. The latter hailed with delight the suggestion, but advised the going of a personal representative as likely to prove more successful. He consulted the other ministers of Richmond, and members of the Confederate Cabinet, and they heartily approved of the plan.

Capt. Louis M. Coxetter

A swift steamer was soon to sail from Charleston, and Dr. William J. Hoge, after consenting to go, found it impossible to prepare in time; so Dr. M.D. Hoge, hastily securing the proper credentials, himself started on the journey.

He ran the blockade from Charleston on the *Antonica*, commanded by Captain L.M. Coxetter. Of this he wrote: "Our run through the blockading squadron was glorious. I was in one of the severest and bloodiest battles fought near Richmond; but it was not more exciting than that midnight adventure, when, amid lowering clouds and dashes of rain, and just wind enough to get up sufficient commotion in the sea to drown the noise of our paddlewheels, we dashed along, with lights all extinguished, and not even a cigar burning on the deck, until we were safely out and free from the Federal fleet."

From Nassau he went to Havana on a small schooner, and from there on a British steamer to Southampton.

His visit was a complete success. From Nassau more than 1,200 copies of the Holy Scriptures were obtained. When he reached England, through the kind co-operation of the distinguished James M. Mason, he was introduced to Lord Shaftesbury. The latter secured a hearing before the British Foreign Bible Society. This society, though he desired to purchase, generously donated to this cause 10,000 Bibles, 50,000 Testaments, and 250,000 copies of the Gospels and Psalms. He also secured from the Tract Society a large gift of their publications. Of these books, going in on various blockade runners, more than three-fourths reached the Confederacy in safety, and were a mighty blessing to the soldiers.

His return was hastened by the sad news, found in a Northern paper, of the death of one of his children, he did not for some time know which. Hastening home, he sailed for Halifax, and from there to Bermuda. Thence he sailed for Halifax, and from there to Bermuda. Thence he sailed on the blockade runner *Advance*, formerly the *Lord Clyde*. The accompanying description of his entrance into the Cape Fear we copy from Dr. Peyton H. Hoge's *Moses Drury Hoge: Life and Letters.*

"Sunday morning, October 11th, was a day of cloudless beauty. Dr. Hoge came early on deck to find the Advance *sailing merrily southward, with the Federal fleet in full view. Dr. Hoge became anxious.*

'What are you going to do, Captain?'

'I am going to Wilmington today.'

'But, surely, you are not going to attempt it in broad daylight.'

'Why not?'

'Well, for one reason, the Confederate government cannot afford to lose this ship; and, for another, there are some of us on board who do not wish to be captured, and I am one of them.'

'Oh! You will not be captured, and this ship will not be lost.'

"Still they bore on; but as yet there was no movement in the Federal fleet. It is probable that they were deceived by the boldness of the steamer's approach, and took her for some transport or supply vessel. When she was nearly opposite the entrance, the helm was put hard to port, and all steam put on as she made the inlet.

"The mask was now thrown off, and three Federal vessels gave chase. She had a good start; but, if they could not catch her by steam, perhaps they could with gunpowder, and soon the shells were shrieking through her rigging. Any moment might decide her fate, but still she sped on untouched. The situation was critical and uncomfortable. But now the pursuing vessels came within range of the Confederate guns, and Fort Fisher opened fire. The pursuit slackened, and the pursuers fell off. Almost the next instant the Advance *was stuck fast on a shoal; had it happened a moment sooner, they would have been lost. The captain came to Dr. Hoge, and besought him to lead them in a service of thanksgiving; and on that Sabbath morning, in sight of the baffled enemy and the protecting fort, passengers and crew assembled on deck and stood with bared heads beneath their own blue Southern skies, while he lifted his heart to God in thanksgiving and praise for their deliverance. Yet the danger was not quite over. If they did not get free by night, there was risk of their being boarded under*

cover of darkness. But with the rising tide they were afloat again in the early afternoon, and that night they slept in Wilmington."

CLOSING SCENES.

The closing scenes of blockade-running were described by Colonel Scharf in his *History of the Confederate States Navy*, as follows:

" The military and naval expeditions against Wilmington in December 1864, and January 1865, resulted in the capture of the forts and the closing of the port. Eight vessels left the port of Nassau between the 12th and 16th of January, one of which took four one-hundred-pounder Armstrong guns; and at the time of their sailing there were over two and a half million pounds of bacon stored at Nassau awaiting transportation. The confidence reposed in the defense of Wilmington continued unabated on the part of the blockade-runners, and the *Charlotte*, the *Blenheim*, and the *Stag*, all British steamers, ran in after the fall of Fort Fisher, and were captured by the Federal cruisers in the river. The blockade-runner *Owl*, Captain John N. Maffitt, C.S.N., in command, succeeded in passing over the bar near Fort Caswell, and anchored at Smithville on the night the forts were evacuated; and immediately returned to Bermuda, arriving on the 21st, and carrying the news of the fall of Fort Fisher and the end of blockade-running at Wilmington. Her arrival was timely, stopping the *Maud Campbell*, *Old Dominion*, *Florence*, *Deer* and *Virginia*. Most, if not all, of these steamers now turned their prows toward Charleston, the last harbor remaining accessible; and, though the fall of that city was impending, yet a cargo might be safely landed and transported along the interior line to the famishing armies of the Confederate States. To that end Captain Wilkinson determined to make the effort; but it was the part of prudence to ascertain, positively, before sailing, that Charleston was still in our possession. This intelligence was brought by the *Chicora*, which arrived at Nassau on the 30th of January; and on February 1st, the *Owl*, *Carolina*, *Dream*, *Chicora* and *Chameleon* sailed within a few hours of each other for Charleston.

"The effort was a brave and gallant one, but was ineffectual. The *USS Vanderbilt* intercepted the *Chameleon*, and, after an exciting chase, was dodged by the fast sailing vessel under the cool seamanship of the gallant Wilkinson. Turning on the *Vanderbilt*, the *Chameleon* again attempted to reach Charleston; but having lost a day in escaping from the *Vanderbilt*, and, being retarded by unfavorable weather, she did not reach the coast near Charleston bar till the fifth night after leaving Nassau. The blockading fleet, reinforced from that off Wilmington, now closed every practical entrance; but it was not until after assurances from the pilot that entrance was impossible, that Captain Wilkinson 'turned away from the land, and our hearts sank within us, while conviction forced itself upon us that the cause for which so much blood had been shed, so many miseries bravely endured, and so many sacrifices cheerfully made, was about to perish at last.' The *Chicora*, more fortunate than the *Chameleon*, ran into Charleston, but finding that city evacuated, ran out, despite the effectiveness of the blockade, and reached Nassau on the 28th. The *Fox*, less fortunate, ran into Charleston in ignorance of its capture, and was seized by the Federal cruisers.

"Captain John N.Maffitt, C.S.N., in *Owl*, left Havana about the middle of March, within 'a quarter of an hour' after the *USS Cherokee* steamed out of the harbour. Passing Morro Castle, the *Owl* hugged the coast towards the west, followed by the *Cherokee*, the chase continuing for an hour or more. The *Owl* had speed, and Maffitt had the seamanship to 'throw dust into the eyes' of his pursuer by changing her coal from hard to soft; thus clouding the air with dense black smoke, under cover of which the *Owl* turned on the *Cherokee*, and, steaming away to the stern of the cruiser, disappeared in the darkness of night and storm."

EXPERIENCES ON THE *LILIAN*

The author's adventures as purser of the *Lilian*, are briefly presented in the following account from various sources. In giving his own experiences in connection with the first time that he ran the blockade inwards by sea, he writes; "Early in 1864 I started from Richmond, in Virginia, and making my way across the Potomac, reached New York via Washington…and upon the twentieth day after I left Richmond I landed at Liverpool. After passing nearly four months in Europe, half in England and half in Rome, I started again from Liverpool for "Secessia," where in truth, my heart, touched by the splendid courage of her sons…remained…Upon 15 May 1864, I started from Queenstown for Halifax, Nova Scotia, on board the Cunard royal mail steamship *China,* passing on from Halifax to Bermuda in a small commercial steamer—how she did roll!—belonging to the same great steamship company.

On arrival at Bermuda—as lovely a little group of islands as eye could rest upon—I found that the same good luck which throughout the war attended my blockade-running efforts, did not desert me on this occasion.

Two ships, the *Lilian* and the *Florie,* lay in Hamilton harbor when I entered it on the last day of May 1864. They seemed like a couple of beautiful steam yachts of about 500 tons, but without rigging. They were painted a dull, leaden grey color, to make them as invisible as possible at sea. Their engines were, of course, in tip-top order; plentiful supplies of Welsh steam coal brought out from England, enabled them to fill their bunkers just before starting. The weather was beautiful and everything and everything portended a swift and successful trip.

The only question still to be decided was to which of the two should I commit my fortunes. Both were to start for Wilmington next day, 1 June, and each claimed to be faster than the other. The same company owned both, and bets had been freely made by their respective crews as to which would reach Wilmington first. The *Lilian* was commanded by Captain Maffitt, an officer of the United States Navy before the war, who, however, being a North Carolinian, had followed his State when she seceded from the Union. I knew that Captain Maffitt was a favorite of General Lee, who was always glad to relieve the strain upon his mind by listening to his old friend's sea yarns, and one glance at his resolute, straightforward face made me determine that I would go with him. He was, in truth, a fine specimen of a Carolina sailor, and the more I saw of him during our short three days and four nights voyage, the more I liked him.

We started in the evening almost abreast of the *Florie,* our sister ship, with which we kept company until darkness fell. The sea was like a mill dam. What wind there was blew from the right quarter, and during that first night, our little company of passengers, eight in number, enjoyed themselves as Englishmen and Americans always did when there was a spice of danger and adventure in the job upon which they had embarked. The cool sea breeze was delightfully refreshing after the hot coral rocks of Bermuda, and no vigilant Yankee steamer, such as the *Rhode Island,* from whose too strenuous attentions many a blockade-running vessel had suffered on putting forth from Bermuda, seemed to be in pursuit. We all slept like tops, and when morning came a fairer sight than that which presented itself never had met my eyes at sea. Not a vessel was anywhere visible to the lookout perch, aloft in the crow's nest, the *Florie* had disappeared, the sea sparkled in the glorious sunshine, and lots of flying fish, the first that I had ever seen, emerged from the ocean, and after a short, sharp flight of two or three hundred yards dropped again into the billowy depths. I confess that I was never tired of watching them, much to Captain Maffitt's amusement, who had seen more than enough of flying fish when in command of the *Oreto,* afterwards the *Florida,* with which he audaciously ran into Mobile in broad daylight, and although cut to ribands by the heavy short-distance fire of the blockaders, got safely through without being sunk, and moored his little vessel at Mobile wharf, more than thirty miles distant from Fort Morgan, the Confederate fort which guarded the entrance to Mobile Bay and kept the blockaders at a respectful distance.

Returning to the 'airy, fairy *Lilian,'* we had got about 350 miles away from Bermuda, when Captain Maffitt's quick eye discerned a sail upon our port bow, enveloped in a dense canopy of smoke. She lay in a part of the ocean continually swept by Federal cruisers, and our wily captain well knew that nowhere was more guile displayed by both belligerents than in connection with blockade-running. The vessel might very likely prove a trap to lure the *Lilian* on to her destruction, but after carefully scrutinizing her through his glasses, Captain Maffitt came to the conclusion that she might be on fire. Time was ineffably precious to us, but after generously exclaiming. "No luck can betide a vessel which leaves a comrade in distress at sea!" our humane captain ordered our course to be altered, and bore down upon the stranger. She was soon made out to be a Federal cruiser, emitting a dense white cloud with her Cumberland coal and beating rapidly eastward in pursuit of another outward bound delinquent. The *Lilian's* helm was therefore changed and she resumed her original course.

Meantime the fine weather had deserted us, and the noon of our third day out was so dull and dark that it was impossible to take an observation. It was generally believed by the captain and his officers that ere day dawned on the following morning it was possible that we might make a run into Wilmington, and onward we pressed. The *Lilian's* sharp bow seemed to cleave the waves like a razor, and the exhilaration of flying through the water at a speed which defied pursuit, raised our spirits to such a pitch, that Charles Mackay and Henry Russell's famous old song, "There's a Good Time Coming, Boys!" burst in chorus from our lips,followed by such familiar Confederate war strains as—

Frank Vizetelly

"Then let the big guns roar as they will,
We'll be gay and happy still;
Gay and happy, free and easy,
We'll be gay and happy still."

By the way, poor Frank Vizetelly used to substitute for the third line "Free and easy, fat and greasy," the last words being only too suggestive of his own appearance on a hot Summer day.

Before long, however, the captain silenced our ill-timed mirth, and soon our position, as we drew nearer and nearer to the land, became too excited to admit of irrelevant ebulitions.

It was impossible at such a moment to withhold one's admiration from the fitness of the vessel under our feet for the purpose for which she had been built, and also for the perfection of the system under which she was handled, and which experience had already shown to be necessary to give her and her consorts every chance of success. When night fell, not a single light was visible in any part of the ship, and no one under any circumstances was allowed to smoke, lest his cigar or cigarette or pipe might be seen by a lookout on board of one of our vigilant enemies. Steam was blown off under water, our coal made no visible smoke, and our feathering paddles no noise; our hull rose only a few feet, out of the water; our only spars were two short lower masts with no yards, and only a small crow's nest in the foremast. The forward deck was constructed in the form of a turtle back to enable the *Lilian* to go through a heavy sea. Our start from Bermuda was so well timed that a moonless night and high tide were secured for our running into Wilmington. For the rest, we trusted to our speed, which as will shortly be seen, saved our vessel next day from capture, and ourselves from the distinguished honor of passing a few months as prisoners in the Old Capitol, or in a fort off Boston or Baltimore harbor. The blockading vessels, too, were admirably managed. No lights were carried by them except on board one vessel, that in which the Flag-Admiral sailed. She changed her position every night, and the absence of strong lights on shore, discernible two or three miles away from Fort Fisher, greatly augmented the difficulty of hitting New Inlet, a narrow channel leading into the Cape Fear river. Moreover, the vessels which maintained the blockade were provided with calcium or other incandescent lights, which they flashed forth on the slightest provocation, and also with rockets which they let off in the direction of a blockade-runner was taking,—talking to each other, in fact, with colored lights at night as effectually as they did with signals by day.

It will readily be imagined that during our third night out from Bermuda, going to bed was far from our thoughts. The night wore rapidly away; 2 o'clock, 3:30 came, but no eye peering through the thick gloom could descry the light on top of the mound at Fort Fisher. Then, as morning dawned, Captain Maffitt stopped his engines and prepared to lay to for the day between the outer and inner cordon of blockaders. It was too much to hope that for sixteen or seventeen hours of broad daylight we could escape observation in that cruiser-haunted neighborhood; nevertheless from four in the morning till 1:30 p.m., we were unmolested. Then the tall masts of a big steamer, her immense paddle wheels and lofty, black hull hove in sight from the direction of Wilmington, going at full speed, and by the keen eyes on board her, the little *Lilian* was instantly described. Before we could get up steam fully, our gigantic enemy drew uncomfortably near, and orders were given to have all the mail bags dropped with weights attached to them, into the all devouring ocean. Several shots flew over our heads or dropped by our side, but going at such a pace it is not easy to hit a little vessel with projectiles fired from the unstable platform of a pursuer going fifteen knots an hour through a lumpy sea.

Presently our beautiful little craft began to answer in earnest to the driving power within her, as a thoroughbred horse gallantly responds to the spur of his rider. As the pressure of steam ascended from fifteen pounds to twenty, from twenty to twenty-three, from twenty-three, to twenty-six, and as the revolutions of the paddle mounted from twenty-six to twenty-eight, from twenty-eight to thirty-three per minute, the little vessel flew out to sea swift as a startled wild duck. Before two and a half hours had passed the hull of the big Yankee was invisible and her top-gallant sails a mere speck on the distant horizon. As, however, she and doubtless others of her sisters lay between us and Wilmington, it became necessary to run around them. Our helm accordingly was changed and as the sun dropped into the sea our pursuer, though a long way off, still hung upon our rear. There was nothing for it but to stick to our course; but such had been the speed of our flight that the inside blockading squadron was clearly sighted by us before the close of the day. Grim and forbidding enough in all conscience the black hulls looked and so close did they lie to each other that it seemed hoping against hope to expect that a little craft like ours would pass unscathed between them or among them, taking the fire of two or three broadsides at little more than pistol range, or that she could eventually escape destruction at the hands of such formidable antagonists. But in command we had a captain who, in broad day, had braved the worst that the blockaders off Mobile could do to the little *Oreto,* without being scared or sunk. It is at such moments that you realize how paramount is the influence of a dauntless chief upon all around him; and it is felt more in so confined a space as the deck of a ship than in a great battle on land. Nevertheless, we could not but perceive—indeed, Captain Maffitt's anxious face plainly told us so—that our position was far from comfortable, pursued as we were by a vessel a few miles off to the rear, which clearly saw us, and, swiftly approaching a powerful squadron of heavily armed blockaders, which had not yet caught sight of the *Lilian's* two masts, but might do so at any moment.

Fortunately for us, before we got close in, night fell. The crews on board the blockaders were taking their evening meal as we approached them, and I suppose the lookouts were not quite so sharp as they undoubtedly became before the end of the war. Not a moment was lost by Captain Maffitt, or by our excellent pilot, a Wilmington man, when the darkness had fairly settled upon the face of the deep. Silently, and with bated breath we crept slowly in, passing blockader after blockader so close that at every moment we expected a brilliant light to flash forth, turning night into day, and followed by a hurricane of shot and shell, which might easily have torn the little *Lilian* to pieces. It was destined, however, that upon this occasion she was not to receive her baptism of fire, for the shots sent after her by her big Yankee pursuer hardly deserve the name. Just as we approached the big mound, close to which Fort Fisher stands, a dark spot was discerned on the bar. It was a Federal launch groping for secrets, or perhaps sinking rocks and other obstructions into the channel immediately under the fire of Fort Fisher's guns. I am afraid that if Captain Maffitt had seen her a little earlier he would have run her down. As matters stood, the launch escaped and those on board were either too much scared to fire a musketry volley into us, or reluctant to do so, as Fort Fisher would doubtless have opened upon them, and, as I had many subsequent opportunities of ascertaining, her guns were seldom fired without effect upon any object within range.

Another moment, and we lay safe and sound before the mound, eagerly asking for news from within the Confederacy, and as eagerly questioned in our turn for news from without. The welcome extended to us by Colonel Lamb, commandant of the fort, and one of the most lovable men in existence, was so hearty that he made us regard entering the mouth of the Cape Fear River as tantamount to returning home. Moreover the *Florie* had not yet arrived, which raised the spirits of the Lilianites to fever heat.

(Mr. Sprunt later sailed from Wilmington as purser on the *North Heath,* and while he was in Bermuda he had been left behind when he fell sick in that harbor. Late in the summer, as he writes, the *Lilian* that he loved came into port where he was.)

In the summer of 1864, the Confederate steamer *Lilian*, which had repeatedly reached the Confederacy under command of the gallant Captain John N. Maffitt, arrived at St. George's Bermuda, after a successful run from Wilmington, with cargo of cotton, which was immediately transferred to the clipper ship *Storm King,* for Liverpool. I was then a lad of about 17 years of age, and had been left behind sick by my ship, the steamer *North Heath,* which was subsequently loaded with stone and sunk in the channel of the Cape Fear River by the Confederate authorities, as an obstruction to the Federal fleet then threatening an invasion. Fortunately for me, the purser of the *Lilian*, an Englishman, having decided that he had enough of the perils of blockade running, tendered his resignation, and I, having been previously recommended by Capt. Maffitt, was at once appointed in his place. Much to the regret of our officers and men, Captain Maffitt was ordered home to take command of the ram *Albemarle,*and a skipper of greatly inferior ability succeeded him on the *Lilian*. Our ship was one of the finest of the large fleet of vessels then engaged in blockade-running, and had been specially designed and built for good service, with a speed of fourteen knots an hour, which in those days was considered very fast. Under the direction of Major Norman Walker, the Confederate agent and Quartermaster at St. George's, we soon completed our cargo of arms and ammunition, blankets, bacon, flour, etc., and with a full crew of forty-eight men, proceeded towards Wilmington, about 720 miles distant.

Shortly after getting under way, I began paying the crew the usual bounty money from several kegs of silver dollars which had been rolled on board at the last moment, during which I noticed from the sullen manner of nearly our whole complement of firemen that trouble was brewing. Just as our pilot was leaving us, the firemen on duty struck work, and without any reasonable excuse, demanded to be put ashore. We soon ascertained that it was simply a plot to "jump the bounty money," and the ship was put about and steered a straight course for the harbor, lying within which was the clipper ship already referred to. Running close aboard, our captain hailed him, "*Storm King* ahoy! Will you bring your officers and help us out with some mutineers?" "Aye, aye, sir, we will," came back the prompt response. In a few moments they were with us, and joined our captain, chief and second officer in an immediate attack upon the malcontents, who had retreated to the forecastle. Each man who refused to work was then unceremoniously knocked down, dragged out, and put in irons, and in an almost incredibly short time we were steaming away to sea again. A few hours meditation in the calaboose without food or water, and the dread of further punishment when we reached the Confederacy, brought the unruly firemen to their senses and to their work.

As night drew on we were out of sight of land, and with horizon clear of cruisers, began the usual precautions against chase or capture. The cabin lights were most carefully screened by heavy curtains across the port holes, and even the binnacle lamp was tightly covered, leaving only a small peephole the size of a silver dollar, for the guidance of the quartermaster at the wheel. (Mr. Sprunt relates that he took the wheel, on occasion.) We saw and passed in darkness, several vessels, being invisible to them, and at dawn carefully avoided all those which appeared to be under steam; one of the greatest dangers being the proximity of a hostile vessel at daybreak, or upon the clearing of a fog. On the morning of the second day we sighted several United States cruisers, but successfully evaded them. At noon of the third day we found ourselves in a heavy sea, about fifty miles to the northeastward of Cape Lookout, and as we approached nearer the land, we sighted a large man-of-war to windward, which speedily bore down upon us and soon got us within range of his heavy guns. Owing to the swell which kept our paddles rolling out of water, we could not run away, and for several hours both vessels steamed a parallel course, so nearly together that I could see the men at the guns, their broadside batteries raking us fore and aft every minute. Nothing but the heavy seaway upon which we bobbed up and down like a cork, thereby defeating their aim, saved us form destruction. We were truly in a bad position which was made worse by the collapse of one of our boilers, reducing our speed from twelve to eight knots, and by the abject fear of our panic-stricken engineers and stokers, who came up in a body and begged the captain to surrender at once. But he had no notion of such a thing, and having fortified himself with a bottle of brandy and a big navy revolver, was quite prepared to hold his own against all odds, and roundly swore he would shoot the first man who shirked his duty, a threat which they evidently took in earnest, as they immediately went below to make the best of it. I had never been under fire before, and I confess the situation was painfully distressing to me. Every time the big, conical shells like nails kegs came tumbling over the rail, with their diabolical wailing shriek, my knees became unmanageable and smote together in a most demoralizing way. I thought every moment would be the last, but after a while this desperate feeling was overcome, and I was comparatively indifferent to the firing which, strange to say, did us very little damage. Our pursuer gradually forced us nearer the breakers, along which we dashed with fore and aft sails set, thereby steadying our ship and making better speed. The cruiser being of much deep draft, kept well off shore and continued a constant and heavy fire which did no harm, the shells passing well over us and landing in the surf. Our captain expecting to strike bottom, ordered lifeboats lowered to the rail, and the crew to take their stations the moment the ship was stranded.

I greatly admired the pluck of several officers of the Confederate cruiser *Georgia*, who were returning home as our passengers, and who amused themselves by measuring with their sextants the distance between the contending ships, and by noting with their watches the time between the flash of the guns and the passing of the projectiles. They were so sure of capture, however, that they unfortunately threw overboard some valuable rifles and other personal property which might have been saved. I threw the Confederate mail bag into the furnace, by order of the captain as he seemed to think it was quite useless to risk the lives of our crew any longer.

As the sun went down, however, we were inspired with some hope of escape, which increased as night drew on and it became apparent that the cruiser was hauling off a little, evidently fearing shoal water in the darkness. Of course we were careful to make no lights, and later on we were overjoyed to see that he was firing wildly and forging farther ahead. When it became too dark for him to see us, he burned Drummond lights and sent up rockets, hoping to attract other cruisers to his assistance, but none responded; and then our captain determined upon a bold movement. Lowering our sails, we came to a full stop and anxiously awaited the result. To our great joy, the enemy continued on his course, firing from his broadside guns under his quarter unobserved, leaving him firing at the breakers, the roar of which had overcome the sound of our paddles as we crossed his wake and sped onwards towards New Inlet.

And now a new and perhaps greater danger confronted us. By a careful computation it was ascertained that in our crippled condition we could not possibly reach the bar before daylight, but as our reduced speed would not save us in a chase, our captain resolved to run the gauntlet of the blockaders rather than risk capture at sea during the next day. We passed a very anxious night, watching with the utmost solicitude our unsatisfactory progress as we labored through a heavy sea towards our dangerous destination. At the first streak of dawn we were off Masonboro Sound, and soon after distinguished through the haze no fewer than eight blockaders apparently waiting to gobble us up. To our astonishment, however, they took no notice of our approach, as our ship was painted the exact color of the sand dunes along the beach, which we hugged as closely as we dared, and steered straight for the fleet, through which we passed without a gun being fired; and when we anchored off Fort Fisher it was broad daylight. We learned afterwards that the blockaders had not observed us until we were quite near the bar, and then they believed, until it was too late, that we had come to join the fleet; a steamer of our description being then due. We received a hearty welcome from the boarding officer at Fort Fisher, and steamed up towards Wilmington shortly afterwards. While passing Fort Anderson, a gun was fired, but having received no intimition at Fort Fisher that we would be detained on the river, we continued our course, which was immediately arrested by another gun sending a round shot through our rigging. We were boarded by Lieutenant McNair (still known as crazy Mac) who laughingly remarked that his next shot would have sunk us, as his orders were to stop all vessels passing the port, for inspection. After this function was completed, we continued our course to Wilmington, where we were boarded by the quarentine physician, the late Dr. William George Thomas, who was greatly interested and amused by my description of our exciting adventure. Our ship was consigned to Messrs. DeRosset & Brown, the collector of the port at that time being Major Henry Savage. We discharged cargo at a wharf near the foot of Chestnut street and dropped down to the Clarendon Iron Works for repairs, which caused a detention of three weeks.

During this time several changes were made in our crew. The engineers were discharged and sent through the blockade as passengers on another steamer, and several stokers who had behaved badly during the chase were summarily dealt with. When ready for our outward freight, we were laden with 1,250 bales of cotton at the Confederate cotton press, which stood on the west side of the river below the ferry, and which was subsequently destroyed by fire, together with a large quantity of cotton. The unbroken brick chimney still stands like the leaning Tower of Pisa, a conspicuous relic of an extra ordinary era in the foreign trade of Wilmington.

It was almost a universal custom of the officers of blockade-runners to smuggle a few bales of cotton for their personal benefit along with the cargo—but I had received strick orders from our new captain not to take any on my account, nor to permit any one else on board a single bale. I was simple enough to follow his instructions, not withstanding the fact that he, with characteristic duplicity, had a dozen bales put on board secretly at night for himself. I was not sorry a few days after to see this sharp adventure go overboard with the rest of the deck load to lighten the ship during an exciting chase by a Federal cruiser.

The bales were bound with rope, and axes were used to cut them asunder when pitched over the rail, in order that they would fall to pieces in the sea before being picked up by the pursuers at their leisure.

Sometimes the wake of a blockade-runner could be traced for miles by floating bales of cotton which were thrown over in an emergency. I remember, while a prisoner on board the United States steamer *Keystone State,* seeing the crew pick up as many as a hundred bales in the Gulf Stream, which were held together by the bagging only.

On 22 August, 1864, the *Lilian* hauled out from the cotton press on the west side of the Cape Fear, and anchored in the stream, ready for her sixth voyage through the blockade. The Federal squadron, flushed with numerous captures of prizes, had become more aggressive and the cordon of watchful blockaders more closely drawn than ever before.

In addition to the ships of war, numerous armed launches patrolled the bar and river under cover of the darkness. These scouting barges proved to be to the alert blockaders what the sacred crackling geese were to the sleeping Romans, for they lay in the track of incoming and outgoing steamers, and at the constant risk of being run down, gave quick and timely warning to the enemy of any approaching vessel, by burning Drummond lights and by firing their rockets and howitzers after the phantom steamers, as they loomed up and quickly disappeared in the gloom. It was said that occasional captures were made of timid blockade-runners by these small fry, but only such as were open to the charge of cowardice took any notice of their hail beyond an immediate attempt to run them down.

Extraordinary preparations had been made for a successful voyage. In addition to the usual cargo of about 1,200 bales of cotton, we had five Cape Fear pilots on board, four of whom were passengers, going out for as many new steamers awaiting them in Bermuda. Two of the five survive, the other three have run their last course and "crossed the bar." Young Tom Grissom, our ship's pilot, fearless and daring to the last, was lost during a memoramble gale some years ago.

After the usual precautions against spies and stowaways by the cruel test of fumigation, and farewell tokens to the thirsty officers from the forts, we were at last free to face the music with which we were usually greeted in our attempts to get outside. While feeling our way cautiously in the darkness, and before we reached the first line of blockaders, a large barge appeared close aboard from which came the warning cry, "Heave to, or I'll sink you." Instantly our helm went hard a-port in the pilot's eagerness to run him down. The barge was too wary, however, as striking our sponsons with an unsuccessful cast of his grapping irons, he fired his signal rocket almost simultaneously with his bow gun and quickly dropped astern. The silence was now broken by the order, "Full

The blockade runner **Lilian** *dashes between Union warships off Cape Fear.*

speed ahead!" followed by a blinding glare of pyrotechnics from every ship in the squadron, and by a pandemonium of artillery both deafening and confusing. I can never forget the antics, on this occasion, of our second steward, old Mickey Mahoney, who, calling upon all the saints in the calendar for deliverance, tumbled headlong down the companionway, with such groans and shrieks of terror, that we thought the poor fellow had gone mad.

The cannonading was a repetition of the Kilkenny cat fight, as the shells crashing over us were apparently doing more damage to the fleet than to us. Boom Boom! Went their heavy ordinance, with such rapidity and recklessness that we drove at our best speed without serious damage, and in half an hour had left them all behind except one of their fastest ships which pursued us until nearly daylight when we returned to the station.

After the storm, the calm. Next morning dawned upon a scene so quite, so peaceful, that the events of the night seemed but an ugly dream which passed away with the darkness. The sea, like glass, with not a ripple upon its surface, dense white clouds above the horizon reflecting the glory of the sun resplendent in the east; the watch on deck tranquil and motionless, with naught to disturb the profound stillness save the monotonous rumble of our feathered paddles as the staunch little ship sped on her course toward the distant Bermudas.

How annoying it was to the captain when his belated slumbers, after a night at poker, were disturbed in the early morning by the usual holy-stoning and washing-down-decks which Chief Officer Carrow was so particular. On one occasion when, having finished breakfast, we were strolling about the quarter-deck, and a rooster got out of the coop near the captain's stateroom, crowed and crowed, until with a savage oath the skipper burst out of the door in his pajamas with a big navy revolver and chased that rooster all over the ship in a rage that fairly choked us with laughter.

To some of us, the danger of yellow fever, which was then raging in St. George's was more dreadful than that of the blockade. Among the hundreds of its victims some weeks later were many gallant Southerners, including our genial friend and fellow townsman, Captain Robert Williams purser of the *Index.* At eight bells, which was announced from the bridge, but never struck unless in port, the lookout in the crow's nest aloft aroused the sleepy company with his shrill cry of: "Sail ho!" "Where away?" responded the skipper. "Two points on the starboard bow, sir." At first only a thin thin haze was visible; then the spars and hull of an unmistakable cruiser gradually came into view, showing a decided inclination for closer acquaintance.

Again the warning cry from aloft: "On deck there. Another steamer on the starboard beam. He rises fast, sir, and is heading for us!" Almost immediately a third steamer appeared dead ahead. Our course was then changed to bring two steamers abeam and one astern, and a few minutes later two more steamers joined in the chase from the port bow. We had run into the Gulf Stream squadron, the second cordon of gunboats in the track of the blockade runners one day out, by which many were picked up at daybreak who, having escaped the previous night, found themselves under the guns of a cruiser in the haze of the morning. Hopeful and fairly confident of our ability to outstrip the three pursuers, we had run up a new Confederate flag in the face of our enemies, which soon was made the target of their artillerists, and carried away in the beginning of the fray. The shrieking shells from three directions which passed far ahead of us in line shots, proved very soon our inability to get away; nevertheless, our Captain determined to attempt an escape by running between the two nearest ships, *Keystone State* and *Gettysburg*, thus getting them within the danger line of their own fire, as well as that of our pursuers.

The *Lilian's* engines were already going at such speed that it was impossible to stand the heat of the fire room more than a few minutes at a time, while she tore through the water like a thoroughbred on a race course. As we rapidly approached the two ships in close action, it seemed as if we were running into the jaws of destruction. Their firing was frightfully accurate; the spray from the falling and plunging shells flying over the rail and into our faces. Old *Boston* dragging behind; managed to make himself both heard and felt as he blazed away with his heavy bow chaser. After about three hours of this hot work, a conical shell from the *Gettysburg* pierced us in the starboard bow just below the waterline, which sent a sharp quiver through the entire ship and caused such a rush of water into the forehold that our speed was immediately slackened, and the *Lilian* for the first time refused the helm. Ineffectual efforts were made to stop up the hole with blankets, and within another half hour of keen suspense, cam the reluctant last order, "Hard a-port! Stop her!" and the little vessel lay motionless like a dying stag surrounded by his dog-foes. A barge from the *Gettysburg* was quickly alongside, joined later by one from the *Keystone State,* and a Federal officer, making his way to the bridge and to our sullen and disgusted commander, formally declared the *Lilian* a prize to the United States, and the ship's company prisoners of war.

BIBLIOGRAPHY

For those interested in the history of the Blockade stationed by the United States government to close the ports of the Confederate States of America, and the ships that ran through that blockade:

- Abbott, Willis J. *BLUE JACKETS OF '61*. New York, 1886.
- Almy, John J. *INCIDENTS OF THE BLOCKADE*. Washington, 1892.
- Ammen, Daniel. THE NAVY IN THE CIVIL WAR—ATLANTIC COAST. New York,1905.
- Ashe, S.A. *HISTORY OF NORTH CAROLINA, Vol.II*. Raleigh, 1925.
- Bradlee, Frances B.C. *BLOCKADE RUNNING DURING THE CIVIL WAR*. Essex, Mass., 1925.
- Boynton, C.B. *THE HISTORY OF THE NAVY DURING THE REBELLION*. New York, 1868.
- Possibly the most valuable study of blockade running is that of James D. Bulloch, *THE SECRET SERVICE OF THE CONFEDERATE STATES IN EUROPE; or, How the Confederate Cruisers Were Equipped.* 2 vols. London, 1883, reprinted in New York (with instruction by Philip Van Doren Stern), 1959.
- Carse, Robert. *BLOCKADE*. New York, 1958.
- Clark, Walter. *HISTORIES OF THE SEVERAL REGIMENTS AND BATTALIONS FROM NORTH CAROLINA IN THE GREAT WAR 1961-1865*. Goldsboro, N.C. 1901, printed by the State and still in print from the State Library, Raleigh, N.C. Vol V has blockade-running material.
- Cochran, Hamilton. *BLOCKADE RUNNERS OF THE CONFEDERACY*. Indianapolis, 1958.
- Curtis, Dr. Walter G. *REMINISCENCES OF WILMINGTON AND SMITHVILLE*. Southport, 1900.
- DeRosset, W.L., ed. *PICTORIAL AND HISTORICAL NEW HANOVER COUNTY AND WILMINGTON N.C.* Wilmington, 1938.
- Dowd, Clement. *LIFE OF ZEBULON B. VANCE*. Charlotte, 1897.
- Eisenschiml, Otto and E.B. Long. *AS LUCK WOULD HAVE IT*. Indianapolis, 1948.
- Howell, Andrew J. *THE BOOK OF WILMINGTON*, 1930.
- Lefler, Hugh T. *NORTH CAROLINA HISTORY TOLD BY CONTEMPORARIES*. Chapel Hill, N.C. 1948.

- Maffitt, Emma M. *THE LIFE AND SERVICES OF JOHN NEWLAND MAFFITT*. New York, 1906.
- Moore, Frank, ed. *THE REBELLION RECORD*. New York, 1863.
- Moore, Louis T. *STORIES OLD AND NEW OF THE CAPE FEAR REGION. WILMINGTON*,1956.
- McKoy, Henry Bacon.*WILMINGTON, N.C.—DO YOU REMEMBER WHEN*. Greenville, S.C., 1957.
- Oliver, W.H. *BLOCKADE-RUNNING BY THE STATE OF NORTH CAROLINA*, 1863-4. Newbern, 1895.
- Porter, Adm. D.D. *INCIDENTS AND ANECDOTES OF THE CIVIL WAR*. New York, 1886; *THE NAVAL HISTORY OF THE CIVIL WAR*. New York, 1886.
- Roberts, A.C.H. *NEVER CAUGHT*. London, 1867.
- Robinson, Wm. M.,Jr. *THE CONFEDERATE PRIVATEERS*. New Haven, 1928.
- Sands, F.P.B. *THE LAST OF THE BLOCKADE AND THE FALL OF FORT FISHER*. Washington, 1902.
- Scharf, J.T. *HISTORY OF THE CONFEDERATE STATES NAVY*. New York, 1887.
- Semes, Raphael. *CRUISE OF THE ALABAMA AND THE SUMTER*. 1864; *MEMOIRS OF SERVICE AFLOAT DURING THE WAR BETWEEN THE STATES*. Baltimore, 1869.
- Soley, J.R. *THE BLOCKADE AND THE CRUISERS*. New York, 1897.
- Sprunt, James. *TALES AND TRADITIONS OF THE LOWER CAPE FEAR, 1661-1896*. Wilmington, 1896.
- Sprunt, James. *CHRONICLES OF THE CAPE FEAR RIVER*, 2nd edition. Raleigh, 1916.
- Stick, David. *GRAVEYARD OF THE ATLANTIC*. Chapel Hill, N.C., 1952.
- Thornton, Mary L. *A BIBLIOGRAPHY OF NORTH CAROLINA*. Chapel Hill,1958.
- Watson, William. *THE ADVENTURES OF A BLOCKADE RUNNER*. London, 1892.
- Wiley, B.I. *THE COMMON SOLDIER IN THE CIVIL WAR*. New York, 1952.
- Wilkinson, J. *THE NARRATIVE OF A BLOCKADE RUNNER*. New York,1877.
- Yates, Richard E. THE CONFEDERACY AND ZEB VANCE. Tuscaloosa, Ala.,1958.

A Colonial Apparition.

A STORY OF THE CAPE FEAR.

By
JAMES SPRUNT.

READ BEFORE THE SOCIETY OF
COLONIAL DAMES OF
NORTH CAROLINA.

ORIGINALLY PUBLISHED BY
Harper's Steamboat Line.

WILMINGTON, N.C.
MORNING STAR ELECTRIC POWER PRESSES
1909

A Colonial Apparition.

A biting storm of sleet and snow is seldom seen in Wilmington. For many years the winter season passed with scarcely frost enough to chill the poor, and then a Christmas season came that will long be remembered for the rigor of its cold.

For several days a blizzard had prevailed along the far Northwest, and when the weather warning came, the signal lights—a white above a red—increased the apprehension of a storm.

The week began with dismal, rainy days, black clouds, and bitter cold, and when complacent home-blessed people heard the moaning wind sing dolefully or rush with sudden, smothering fury down the chimney flues, they yawned beside their cheerful fires and made some commonplace remarks about the suffering poor.

At night a gale blew fiercely, some fifty miles an hour. The driving rain was congealed into stinging sleet which smote the cheeks like showers of needles. The dreary lonesome streets bore striking contrast with brighter seasons in the past.

With sudden burst, the howling storm would seize some luckless passenger and bend him double, while his splintered umbrella went flying into space. The second day the havoc of the storm was shown by prostrate fences in the streets, broken branches, tin signs, and chimney pots, with not a few old buildings unroofed and torn as by a hurricane.

To those who watched and prayed for some loved toiler on the sea, the news of many wrecks along the coast came like a knell of doom. The telegraphic wires were down; but every tardy mail brought word of savage storms which crushed the life from many shipwrecked sailors from Hatteras to Cape Fear.

How few of those accustomed to everlasting hills can comprehend the awful fury of a storm at sea when broken, helpless ships are tossed in air, where stricken and beaten with maddening fury, they plunge a moment later into the seething hollows, and the foundering fabrics, with their haggard, hopeless crews, sink to rise no more!

The church's prayer for those in peril on the sea is often said unthinkingly; but as the daily record came of shattered ships and drowning men, there went from many hearts a silent invocation for those in such extremity.

The crews on board the lightships never before had seen such fury in the storm. The one on Frying Pan was staunch and safe enough, and rode without a strain through previous gales; but now she leaped upon the wild and sloping sea like some mad animal, and standing for a moment with her bowsprit heavenward, plunged into the foaming chasm of the hollow waters, and vanished in the smother, which seemed to hold her down. The mushroom anchors held until the strain broke the heavy iron chains, and then she drifted in the whirl far out to sea.

The Southport pilots called to mind the frightful gale of April 12, 1877, when five brave men went down, while all that courage, coolness and good seamanship could do, did not avail.

The coast guard looked upon the saddest sights. They saw dismasted staggering vessels, with shreds of canvas, impelled by rushing seas to imminent destruction on the beach. The acts of heroism performed on such occasions would fill a volume; and those who know the service of life-savers have often thought the compensation small.

The third day showed a subsidence of the storm. The glass at times was steadier, but still the mercury stood at 29, denoting heavy gales. The temperature was much below the freezing point. Distressed, bewildered cattle suffered greatly and many died from cold. The wildest birds were dazed and tamed and came for food about the city doors. Beneath a pile of wood was found twelve lifeless frozen partridges, their heads arranged within a circle, as is their nature when asleep. The cruel sufferings of the poor and homeless shut out the thoughts of Christmas gaiety, and made the favored ones more kindly to the needy.

The Southport mail boat, *Wilmington*, made her daily runs without a break, although at times the gale would seize and bend her in its grasp, until her upper rail was partly hidden in the foam; but Captain Harper knew his craft and kept her well in hand. With steady stare ahead and vice-like grip upon the wheel, he safely steered her up and down, without an accident.

The 24th brought weather indications of a change; but such a storm dies slowly, and often comes again in gusts, as if unwilling to depart. The boat was timed to sail at 5 o'clock, and long before the warning whistle blew, the Southport party came well laden with big parcels for the holidays. With plank hauled in, the rail secured and hawser neatly coiled, the stately steamer shaped her course. But the double bells were rung, a little rivet broke away from thousands of its kind and soon caused trouble with the furnace fires. There was a pause; then a parley through the speaking tube revealed the fact that nothing less than six hours' work would "mend the kettle" in the engine room. Without assistance from the shore and helplessly adrift, the Captain promptly anchored in the stream. He also told the passengers the truth; and asked them to refrain from visits to the engine room, as everything was being done to make another start.

On similar occasions the average engineer will seldom rule his spirit, and, when beset by senseless queries, is apt to profane. The chief on board the *Wilmington* was a model of his kind. To one inquirer anxiously obtrusive he said the boat had caught a catfish in the strainer which broke the suction valve; and, to a lady who would know the worst, he answered that a rat was in the cylinder; to a third, a pompous man, he confidentially whispered that she had lost her centres and that the oilers were in the bilges looking for them. A later messenger was sent by the uneasy passengers, who said on his return that Mr. Platt looked dangerous when he invited him to call again next week. Meantime, a friendly tug appeared and towed the hapless steamer to her landing berth.

The wind and snow increased as darkness came, and all the passengers save one debarked for better quarters on the shore. At nine o'clock a furious sleet intensified the bitter cold. The snow-clad streets at 10 o'clock were quite deserted, save here and there a market man might be seen scuttling homeward-bound. Then, disappointed tradesmen put up their shutters in despair; and even noisy revelers retreated with their blatant horns.

The clouds were black and angry looking; and the frequent flashes of lightning—unusual at this season—revealed the awful grandeur of the scene. Sometimes the flaring area lights flickered and went out, leaving the wharf as black and dismal as the sky and then a tipsy raftsman would break the silence at the dock with lusty cries of "boat ahoy," which brought at length the tired, reluctant ferryman with his twinkling lantern glimmering through the gloom. A ragged, drunken wretch ejected from a neighboring bar, blinked stupidly below the hanging light and stumbled into darkness.

Along the western shore the lightwood fires on timber rafts reflected wretched shelters of rough boards, with scant-clad, shivering countrymen hugging the shifting blaze. Upon the eastern side were glowing anchor lights of vessels waiting at the wharves, while moving lamps upon the stream described the passage of small boats to safer points ashore.

Left with his lonely passenger, the Captain's social quality prevailed. With mainbrace spliced, tobacco pouch and pipes, an hour was spent in cheerful chat, from which the skipper learned some pleasant tales of old Colonial times.

"Do you remember having read of the extraordinary meeting between Sir William Berkeley, Governor of Virginia, and William Drummond, our first Colonial Governor of North Carolina in 1677?" said the stranger.

The Captain admitted that he did not recall it, and asked if the salutations had been similar to the alleged remark of the Governor of South Carolina to the Governor of North Carolina, that it was a long time between drinks.

"Far from it," replied McMillan, for such was the stranger's name. "He gave him neither drink nor shelter, but said in the almost inconceivable cruelty of his wicked heart: 'Mr. Drummond, you are very welcome; I am more glad to see you than any man in Virginia. 'Fore God, Mr. Drummond, you shall hang in half an hour.' "

"What your honor pleases," was the calm reply; for our brave Governor had long believed that Berkeley would kill him without the formalities of judge or jury.

"Is it possible," said the Captain, "that such a crime could be committed without severest punishment, and did he really hang him?"

"Alas! such was the case," said McMillan. "Drummond was a man of the noblest impulses. Of him the historians generally have said that he was of most estimable character, unsullied integrity and great ability. He had retired from office several years previously, having served as Governor three years and having joined himself to the so-called Bacon rebellion, was hounded by Berkeley to his death. He was a Scotsman and a Presbyterian."

"There was another Scots Governor of the Province," said Captain Harper, "a man closely identified with the lower Cape Fear, for whom the first military fort on the river was named."

"You allude, no doubt, to Gabriel Johnston," said Mr. McMillan. "He served for sixteen years and his was the best administration of Colonial times."

"Yes, he seems to have influenced the movement of the Scots to this Province after their oppression by the English. I have read that his interest in his suffering countrymen nearly cost him his official place."

"Undoubtedly an attempt was made to turn the home government against him," said McMillan; "but the Governor clearly established his innocence of the charge of disloyalty to his King, and proved that his feelings were aroused by a natural affection for his fellow countrymen."

"The clannish feeling of the Scots has been frequently remarked in Wilmington, and especially in the upcountry where the greater number of immigrants found their new homes," said the Captain.

"I remember a story of old Kenneth Murchison, the grand-father of the present proprietor of Orton, who lived in Cumberland county on a road which in his day was frequented by travelers. Some belated strangers applied for food and shelter for the night, but the old gentleman's house was already full and he said it was impossible, that further entreaty was useless. He was obdurate, but just as the disappointed and weary travelers were turning away, they fired their last shot. "But, Mr. Murchison, you must know we are Scotsmen, and surely you would never turn a fellow-countryman from your door?"

"A weel," said he, "ye are none the better for thot; but ye may bide." And they did, greatly to their enjoyment.

The late British Vice Consul at Wilmington was often imposed upon by wandering vagabonds, and he admitted to me that some Scotsmen were utterly unworthy and degenerate, and yet the most abandoned wretch that ever tramped the streets had always found the Consul easy prey if he could only speak the Scottish dialect."

"I have read a laughable story," said McMillan, "of the dismay of the Wilmington people when McNeill arrived in 1739 with his 500 wild Highlanders, whose strange cries and uncouth manners so startled the inhabitants that he was hauled up before a magistrate who required of him a bond for their good behavior."

"And yet," said Captain Harper, "those wild and uncouth strangers were not lacking in good sense. The Gaelic language which is spoken yet among the older of that class was music to the ears of those who followed the survivors of Glencoe. Poor as they were, they yet denied themselves the commonest necessities at times, in order that they might provide for the education of their children. It has been said that they served their God and generation well; and 'tis common proof that their descendants have maintained the love of truth and liberty which brought their fathers to this favored land. When Flora McDonald came in 1774, some of her old-time friends and fellow countrymen were well advanced as leaders of the colony. At Wilmington a ball was given in her honor and many compliments were paid the beautiful protector of 'Bonnie Prince Charlie'."

"Indeed she was worthy of it," replied McMillan, "for she had acquired in Edinboro all the graceful accomplishments of the best society of her day, to which was added such personal courage and striking beauty that her influence among the Scots was almost unbounded. Tradition says that her presence was superb. In the Scotch counties of upper Cape Fear her name is still held with much the reverence paid that of a patron saint.

"Some years ago an eccentric person in the settlement claimed to be a lineal descendant of Flora, and in order to substantiate his claim, he always wore a pair of immense ruffles. He would never bemean himself by working with his hands, considering manual labor beneath the dignity of a person so highly connected. He became so poor in consequence that he sometimes went bare-footed, but he was never seen without the ruffles."

"How was it possible," asked the Captain, "for the English under the Duke of Cumberland to over-run Scotland and utterly defeat such a fighting race as they had ever proved themselves in other wars?"

"You were never further from the truth of history, my friend, than in believing that the English overcame Scotland at Culloden. The Wizard of the North has said:

" 'A primitive people, residing in a remote quarter of the empire, and themselves but a small portion of the Scottish Highlanders, fearlessly attempted to place the British crown on the head of the last scion of those ancient kings whose descent was traced to their own mountains. This gigantic task they undertook in favor of a youth of 21, who landed on their shores without support of any kind, and threw himself on their generosity. They assembled an army in his behalf. Their speech, their tactics, their arms, were alike unknown to their countrymen and to the English. Holding themselves free from the obligations imposed by common law or positive statute, they were yet governed by rules of their own, derived from a general sense of honor, extending from the chief to the lowest of his tribe.

With men unaccustomed to arms, the amount of the most efficient part of which never exceeded 2,000, they defeated two disciplined armies commanded by officers of experience and reputation, penetrated deep into England, approached within ninety miles of the capital and made the crown tremble on the King's head; retreated with like success when they appeared on the point of being intercepted between three hostile armies; checked effectually the attack of a superior body detached in pursuit of them; reached the North in safety and were only suppressed by a concurrence of disadvantages which it was impossible for human nature to surmount.

"All this has much that is splendid to the imagination, nor is it possible to regard without admiration, the little band of determined men by whom such actions were achieved, or the interesting young Prince by whom their energies were directed'."

"It was a heroic struggle against most fearful odds," said the Captain. "I have been told that their subsequent punishment was barbarously extreme."

"Nothing more devilish could have been devised. The unfortunate ones who came to Wilmington had witnessed the execution of one out of every twenty of their companions; the remaining nineteen were banished to America. Many of the leaders were tortured beyond description. Among the subsequent executions was that of a young man, James Dawson, a familiar name in Wilmington, whose betrothed wife desperately resolved to attend the horrid ceremonial. I have read in Scott that she beheld her lover after having been suspended for a few minutes on the gallows, but not dead, (such was the barbarous sentence) cut down, disemboweled and mangled by the knife of the executioner. All this she bore with apparent fortitude; but when she saw the last scene finished by throwing young Dawson's heart in the fire, she drew her head within her carriage, repeated his name and expired on the spot."

"I recall an expression of Victor Hugo in his account of the Paris deviltries of 1793, which seems to apply in this case," said the Captain—"the words 'these were times when men were more like wolves than they are now'."

"Your information interests me greatly," he continued. "We shall have steam in half an hour: can you beguile the time with something new to me about the river history?"

"Have you ever heard of the execution of the Scottish Highlanders at Brunswick during the American Revolution?" asked McMillan.

"The subject is entirely strange to me," replied the Captain, "pray proceed."

"My great-grandfather," continued Mr. McMillan, "was William McMillan, of Edinboro, who enlisted with the Camerons in the Rebellion of '45; and after Culloden, was compelled to leave his country.

"He was fortunate in being personally acquainted with Governor Gabriel Johnston, of North Carolina, who kindly and cordially invited him to make his home among the Cape Fear Scotsmen already settled on the lands now known as Robeson county.

"At first he stopped at Waddell's Ferry, and in the course of time became imbued with the spirit of the Whigs, who held among their number not a few whose wounded spirits had never healed since the oppression of their countrymen. The daring exploits of the Tory, Colonel David Fanning, whose rapid marches and reckless bravery were equal to any emergency, had become the talk and the terror of many who knew how cruel and how desperate was this scourge of the enemy.

"On the 13th of September, 1781. Col. Fanning and Col. McNeill, with a small force, entered Hillsboro by different routes at dawn, taking the town by surprise. In a few moments they seized Governor Burke and his entire suite with other prominent inhabitants numbering forty or fifty persons whom they conducted with great celerity to Wilmington, where they were lodged in jail by Major Craig, the British commandant of that town. This remarkable feat, one of the most memorable in the history of North Carolina, involved the destiny of my ancestor and of many others whose homes lay in the track of this evil-minded man. Fanning appears also to have been remarkable for the facility and accuracy with which he obtained information respecting every person and everything within the range of his operations, therefore, it is not surprising that my great-grandfather fell into his hands together with two other Highland Whigs who had been marked as doomed men, because of their so called treason in violating the oath, reluctantly given, which bound them to a hostile sovereign.

After delivering Governor Burke and party into the hands of Major Craig at Wilmington, Colonel Fanning continued his march to the town of Brunswick, now a ruin on Orton Plantation, in whose harbour lay several British ships of war, and also an old prison hulk which was anchored in the bay a greater distance from the wharves, just opposite the Sugar Loaf. To this gloomy, loathsome, floating cell my ancestor and his companions were at once consigned, whence, after agonizing dread and fruitless efforts to escape, they were brought again on the shore, put through the mockery of a trial and sentenced by Fanning to immediate execution. The hour was 1 o'clock and the unfortunate Scotsmen were given but few moments for their preparations for the end.

While the unwilling soldiers were being drawn by lot for their obnoxious duty, the thoughts of these brave men who were to sacrifice their lives for American independence, turned sadly to the old familiar scenes in far off bonnie Scotland, then to the loved ones in the new home among the pine trees of Carolina, where they had fondly hoped to live and die in peace. The place of execution was near the ruins of Governor Tryon's palace at Russelboro between King Roger's house at Orton and the town of Brunswick. A pine tree, to which the victims were bound, still marks the memorable spot where these two nameless martyrs' dust is now reposing.

"At length a platoon of soldiers of the line drew up before the doomed but fearless men and, at the word, discharged their pieces simultaneously; two quivering bleeding bodies were drawn aside and then McMillan was brought forward and unbound a few paces from the tree. He was a powerful man, and years before had been the champion of a curling club who 'put the stone' with strength like that of Samson, and like Samson he sent an earnest agonizing prayer to Heaven for help so needful in such extremity. Held firmly by two stalwart guards, he drew his muscle to its utmost tension and quickly smote one of them senseless at his feet, the other seized him round the waist and bore him to the ground. But the desperate prisoner with almost superhuman strength broke clear away, and, though covered by a dozen muskets whose contents pierced his clothing yet leaving himself unarmed, he ran with the speed of a frightened deer into the friendly shelter of the neighboring woods, and setting his face to the northwest continued with varying speed from 2 o'clock in the afternoon a distance of seventy miles, reaching his home in Robeson at daylight, the following morning.

"He long survived the troublous times and died in 1800.

"The Orton people hold an old tradition that on stormy nights ghosts of these two Scotsmen sometimes walk abroad, and also row a phantom boat in search of vessels bound for foreign parts.

"An aged negro who had lived for more than seventy years upon the place, is quite familiar with the tale, and showed a curious friend of mine the execution tree, well known in olden times and often talked about. It bore some rude inscription, long since obliterated by the hand of time."

McMillan's weird, uncanny tale impressed the Captain strongly and made him strangely silent. The moaning wind and crackling sleet against the window sash conspired to chill the cheerful flow of ready conversation and made them dread the dangerous run through storm and darkness at so late an hour, for it was now near midnight.

Just then the mate appeared bearing a message from the engineer that steam was ready. The Captain glanced above the wheel and tapped the aneroid, which indicated twenty-nine and a half—a very ugly record; but mail-boats cannot choose their weather, and so were given the orders:

"Haul in the gang plank! Let go the bow line! Ease the stern line! Let go all! Haul in!" Buffeted by the wind and hail, the boat swung out upon the ebbing tide and started on her long-delayed return. On dark and cloudy nights the river lights are of little use, so dim and insufficient is their glow, and on this night they seemed almost obliterated in the thick and dismal weather which prevailed. At times, the Captain slowly felt his way without a guiding mark, while Peter Jorgensen, the watchful mate, kept the lead line going constantly.

"Three fathoms!" shouted Peter: "by the mark, two half! Mark two! Now one fathom, sir! She is shoaling fast!" A moment more they reached the lights at Clarendon too late for luck: for the widened river caught the full force of the gale, which driving the boat, sent her hard aground. Although the tide was running downward fast, the shifting wind came round a point or two and helped the backing engine to put her off again.

Once more they started, but at slower sped and groped their way along the narrow channel as a blind man often does upon familiar paths.

"Of all the nights I ever saw in ups and downs for twenty years I never saw the match of this." said Captain Harper to his friend.

"I ran the blockade off your bar in several steamers during our late war, was under fire for twenty hours and narrowly escaped; a Federal cruiser sank us off the coast, and captured all our crew. I have seen many heavy gales at sea; but I never saw in all my life such a dismal, fearful night as this," replied the lonely passenger.

"The heavy gloom increases," said the anxious Captain. "I fear we are astray again. Can you see any lights ahead? The snow is blinding—we should be off the lower jetties. I'll give a spoke or two a'port!"—but at this moment the wheel refused to move—"Here's worse luck still," he cried, "the rudder chains are jammed."

"We are out of the channel, sir!" shouted the watchful Peter Jorgensen from the deck below; "she shoals again!—two fathoms! one, three, quarters! by the mark one, a half one fathom! We're on the lower jetty, sir!" And ere the full stop gong sounded in the engine room, ship went crashing over the soft timbers of the State obstruction, which had not felt a keel in nearly seventy years. It is sad to say, the Captain swore, and sadder still, he kept on swearing. The Presbyterian passenger concurred in every oath, but did not give expression to his rage.

"Thank you," he said, as Harper turned apologetically; "the provocation's great." This sally soon restored the Captain to his calm and normal temperament.

The tide was at low-water slack, and every effort exerted to twist her off, made matters worse. After carefull search, no damage was apparent: then lights were set, and fires reduced, until the turning of the tide which would float her clear. All hands, save Peter Jorgensen, were glad to seek the comfort of the furnace fires. He, only, walked the upper deck despite the cruel weather: his thoughts reverting to the father land and to the Christmas seasons of the past.

As he stood below the sheltering upper deck and pictured to his mind the scenes of his early home in distant Denmark, he seemed to see the "Jule Aften" preparation for the feast of rice which always comes before the sacred service of the following holy day.

Then, filled his contemplative mind, the memories of the simple sports and homely games of village men and women; and music and dancing and drinking everywhere, but nothing to excess. And, too, the early prayers at Church before the Christmas dawn: familiar faces of friends of long ago and those of dearer memory, filled his eyes and made a swelling in his throat. A sudden icy gust of wind awoke him from his dream.

When he turned to walk again he saw the standing figure of a man clad in rough, dripping garments, with hair and beard unkempt and flecked with snow, and a faced distorted with agonizing dread. His right hand grasped the weather rail; the other pointed east by south towards Big Sugar Loaf.

"How came you here? What do you want?" said Peter, drawing nearer with hand outstretched to touch him. No answer came.

"Who are you?" shouted Peter, "are you mad?" And as he reached to seize him, his hand fell on the empty air—the man was gone!

A moment later, when Peter reached the pilot house, his face was ashy and his legs were limp from fright. The Captain gave an angry glance, and turning to McMillan, said: "The man is drunk."

"I am not drunk," declared the terror stricken mate. "I have not touched a drop this night. I—have—seen—a ghost!" And then with frightened looks he told them of the apparition.

"Now I know for a certainty that you are drunk," said Captain Harper. "Who ever saw a ghost? McMillan, did you ever see a ghost?"

"I doubt not Mr. Jorgensen has supernatural causes for his alarm. A Scotsman born is often charged with native superstition. I know of things in my experience beyond the range of our so called Philosophy. But let us search for Peter's ghost, and then discuss the cause of his disordered mind."

"Well said," replied the Captain; "call all hands!"

"Excuse me, Captain," said the shivering mate; "I would not for a present of the ship look on that awful face again."

With an angry exclamation of disgust, the Captain reached the speaking tube and ordered up the crew. Each man was questioned, and all declared that none other than those present had been on board that night.

"Now," said the Captain, "let every man attend me while I search the boat."

McMillan joined the party and every nook and corner, up and down, was closely scrutinized with safety lamps, in vain.

The skipper still looked vexed; but when he saw the drawn and anxious face of his devoted mate, he seemed quite ill at ease. In vain he questioned and cross-questioned the unhappy man.

"Did you see this person approaching you?" said he.

"I did not, sir," the mate replied.

"I was standing on the lee side near the turn of the after cabin and my thoughts were not excited; I was thinking of my home in Denmark. A sudden gust of icy wind swept around the deck. I thought the wind was shifting from northeast; and, when I turned to walk around the bend, I saw the figure standing on the port quarter outside the rail and grasping it with one hand, while with the other it pointed down the river. At first, I thought it had climbed on board and was trying to get over the rail. When I spoke it made no answer; I then advanced to touch it, but it was not there."

"Did it seem to try to speak to you?" enquired McMillan.

"I cannot tell," said Jorgensen. Its lips did not move, neither did any sound come from its mouth; but, O, that fearful face; I can never forget it."

"What did it indicate—did it seem to have a fit?"

"I will tell you what it seemed to me," said Peter. "If your only child was drowning before your eyes and you were powerless to save it; and if you suddenly saw some one standing near whom you knew was equal to its rescue, I think you would have done as that ghost did. I say it was a ghost—a human being could not vanish before my eyes like that."

"The night is dark; perhaps you were asleep and only dreamed of what you saw."

"A man who was asleep, sir—you will pardon me—could not walk in such bitter cold and hold a lantern in his hand as I did then."

"Was it burning brightly, and did you see the features of the figure? Had you ever seen such a face before?"

"I was standing within a yard of the stranger," said Peter. "My lamp shone clearly three times as far. Besides, the ship's lights from the after cabin made the deck quite visible."

"The whole thing is utterly incomprehensible," said Captain Harper, and if ghosts are taking their walks aboard tonight, we may see troops of them before we get out of this confounded mess.

"We lie quite near the dead Colonial town of Charlestown, built by the Yeaman's colony, which came in 1665. They numbered some eight hundred, and when they abandoned it for other parts, they left a hundred of their number in the graveyard near. Perhaps this is their calling night; in which event, look out for further company. How is the tide, Mr. Jorgensen?"

"It has been running up for quite two hours," said Peter. "She is already lifting a little, sir."

The Captain sharply scanned the weather glass, which had risen steadily; the snow and sleet had ceased; the gale was abating, but the wind was still high and it came in gusts, veering several points at intervals. The temperature had also risen from 18 to 22 degrees. In less than an hour the constant motion of the screw had slowly eased the steamer from the ragged timber; then, with hopeful courage, they made another start towards their destination.

With the widening of the river, they encountered a heavy sea which kept the forward deck awash and made the little boat roll heavily. Sea birds dashed past them on graceful curving wing; their hoarse cries mingling with the sound of the whistling wind and splashing waves; their movement scarcely visible until quite near at hand. Suddenly, attracted by the wheel house lights, a blinded gull came crashing through the glass and fell quivering and bleeding at the Scotsman's feet.

"The foul fiend is abroad this night," cried McMillan in great agitation. "Beware of further trouble, Captain: this is the worst of all bad omens."

The Captain was more hopeful, and having passed Big Island light in safety, was heading for the Angel stake light number nine, off Lilliput.

"If you keep a sharp lookout," said he, "you may see another ghost. Old Admiral Frankland, of the Royal Navy, owned the plantation, Lilliput, just off our starboard bow; and he, also, may be on a cruise tonight in company with the other spooks."

"I have heard," said McMillan, "that this old rice plantation was really owned by Sir Thomas Frankland, in 1750. Perhaps, you know that he was a great grandson of Oliver Cromwell, and that he also held the high distinction of an Admiral of the White."

As the lights of Kendal and of Orton were safely passed, remarks were made about the ancient reputation of these fine plantations, famous in history by the lives of Eleazer Allen, of Kendal, and the lordly King Roger Moore, who founded Orton—the grandest of the old Colonial homes. Below old Orton light the river broadens to at least three miles, and here a squall struck the boat, and made her pitch and roll quite lively in the heavy swell.

"There," said the Captain, pointing to the western shore, "is one of the most interesting ruins in America. Beyond that fringe of timber, was Tryon's palace, which minute men from Brunswick and from Wilmington surrounded and demanded the surrender of the King's Commissioner—and mark you, this first overt act preceding the war of Revolution occurred ten years before the Declaration of American Independence; nine years before the battle of Lexington; and nearly eight years before the Boston Tea Party, of which so much is made in story books. The Boston men disguised themselves as Indians; but Ashe and Waddell scorned such subterfuge. After seizing the British warship's rowing barge, they placed it on wheels, and, having formed their men in marching order, with it moved in triumphal procession to Wilmington.

"The Boston incident is a famous one; but who has heard of this far more daring deed? Perhaps that lonely spot, which should be the Mecca of every lover of liberty, is unknown to many of our nearest neighbors."

The words were scarcely uttered, when they were startled by a human cry coming from the direction of the further shore. McMillan stepped out upon the slanting deck and holding to the upper rail, gazed anxiously into the darkness whence the cry had come. Sometimes the rolling vessel would almost pitch him into the boiling waters which threw up gleams of phosphorescent light, leaving a track of radiance for many miles astern and then, the flying spray, ripped from the heaving water by the rushing bow, would shoot above the pilot house and drench him to the skin.

The incessant shrieking of the wind, the many noises of the splashing waves, the deep and thunderous roar of bellowing surf on Carolina Beach confused and troubled him. Meantime a sharp blast from the steamer's whistle had brought the mate up to the Captain's side.

"Did you hear a hail just now?"

"I did, sir," answered Peter, "and it sounded like a syren whistle."

"Impossible," said Captain Harper; "more likely some poor cast-a-way, Hark! there it is again."

Instantly reaching for the signal wire he rang full stop, and as the steamer sank into the hollow troughs, he blew three quick and piercing blasts.

For several moments the steamer rose and fell upon the waves, and then there came borne on the howling wind an awful, agonizing shriek which brought McMillan to the wheelhouse—a look of terror in his face.

"On deck," shouted the Captain.

"Aye, aye, sir," came the answer from below. "What sound was that?"

"We do not know sir. It seemed to come from off the Sugar Loaf."

"We cannot send assistance; our boat would never live in such a sea," said Captain Harper to the mate. "Station your men at once with casting lines both fore and aft. Take your position well forward in the eyes, and hail me when you see the cause of this distress. McMillan, you can help me at the wheel if you will hold her steady while I look about."

At once the orders were obeyed and every head was bent with eager gaze towards the old Colonial anchorage, where, strange to say, the prison ship had been moored far back in revolutionary times.

"What is the so called Sugar Loaf?" McMillan asked.

"It is the highest elevation on the river banks," said Captain Harper; "a steep and shining bluff of sand which can be seen for many miles. It was a noted Indian settlement in olden times."

"Then it is possible." McMillan said, "that some wild animal on shore has made the cry we heard."

"It is a desert place," replied the Captain; 'there are no such wild creatures there. The sound we heard is on the water—there it comes again!"

Above the moaning wind, which came in fitful gusts and died away like voices in the distance, there rose again that cry for help beginning with a shriek and ending with a wailing sound as of mortal agony.

"On deck there," shouted Captain Harper—"what do you see?"

"We cannot make it out, sir," responded Peter from his station. 'I think we are drifting out of the channel sir."

Again three blasts came from the steamer's whistle, and with her head towards the stake light No. 1. on Midnight shoal, the Captain gave the signal for dead slow ahead, which kept the vessel from the shoaling water dangerously near.

A repetition of the scream drew all attention toward the place, whence it seemed to come.

While Peter's eyes were straining in the darkness, a hand was laid on his shoulder which made him start and utter a cry of terror. He, turning, saw the Engineer, who shouted:

"Look yonder, man!—just off the weather bow!" And as he looked, the word was passed to others, and immediately all were striving for a better point of view.

The squall had ceased, but it left a heavy swell; the clouds were moving slowly in broken drifts; the stars came out and with their faint light made dimly visible the distant shore—now blotted out by passing shadows, and anon, revealed in vague and hazy outline.

Upon the troubled water, two cable lengths abeam, appeared an object like a boat surrounded by a phosphorescent glow above which played a pale and lambent light, which gradually approaching nearer, revealed an ancient rowing barge so foul with barnacles and slimy seaweed that Peter thought she might have been afloat a hundred years.

The Captain rubbed his eyes, and looked again. Then turning to McMillan, said: "You seem to be acquainted with supernatural things; for all the river ghosts have come with you tonight. There's something weird about that thing, and I am not inclined to wait."

"They must be mortal men in trouble," he replied, "for spirits could not howl like that."

"There comes that awful hail again," said Captain Harper, now thoroughly excited; "and it is not from yonder object; it seems to permeate the air."

"On deck, there!"

"Aye, aye, sir," said Peter Jorgensen.

"Stand by and throw that barge a line."

An inarticulate reply denoted Peter's fright. The barge was now a cable's length away. There was no sound of oars; but in a minute more the frightened people on the *Wilmington* beheld two tall, gaunt, human forms, in tattered Highland dress, from which emerged their bare and boney legs in heavy chains, expending to their scarred and bloody wrists. As the battered hulk with its strange occupants drew nearer, McMillan saw depicted in their sad and weary faces the deep marked lineaments of settled disappointment and distress. Their bands uplifted in beseeching attitude, their worn and yearning faces, recalled to his excited mind the story of the prison ship with all its scenes of cruelty and woe.

For several minutes—which seem hours to those on board—the Captain stood awe stricken at the sight, but suddenly, with trembling voice, he shouted to the mate, "Stand by and heave those men a line."

As Peter came with shaking limbs, the barge was lifted on a swelling wave which hurled it almost to his arms; and as he heaved the rope across the rotten hulk, the fabric and its gruesome, voiceless crew was gone. All eyes were turned upon the wierd, uncanny sight, and when the strange thing melted into the gloomy shadows of the night, the hopeless mystery appalled and silenced every one on board.

Without a word the course was laid again, and hardly had the ship resumed her speed, when from the darkness just ahead came once again that shrieking, wailing sound. Again the boat was put half speed, as Peter shouted, "Starboard! Hard-a-starboard, sir; we are running down a wreck."

The Captain quickly turned the helm and narrowly escaped collision with a mass upon the waves which proved to be a vessel bottom up—to which was clinging two poor, wretched seamen, disabled and exhausted with the cold. A cheerful hail assured the men of coming safety as Captain Harper, with dexterous hand, steered near enough to pass a line by which the wretched creatures came on board.

As Peter held his lantern to the face of one of the rescued seamen who had fainted on the deck, he raised both hands and shrieked to the Captain: "This is the man who came on board when we were run ashore!"

The skipper and McMillan quickly scanned the stranger's face, which proved the accuracy of Jorgensen's description.

"How could this be?" said Captain Harper.

"His spirit was abroad in search of help," replied McMillan. "I've read and heard of similar phenomena."

"Then how do you explain the phantom of the barge?" "I dinna ken," replied the Scotsman, and then was silent.

The cast-a-ways were promptly warmed and fed, and then they told a thrilling story of distress. Their vessel was a schooner bound from Nassau for a Northern port, when the gale had wrecked them off the coast. Bearing up for Wilmington, they fell into a heavy sea which shifted their scant ballast and rolled the vessel on beam ends.

In peril of their lives, the crew had worked hard to cut away the broken spars and rigging; but all their efforts to right the vessel failed. The captain, mate and three men of the crew were washed away; the other two clung to the hulk, which drifted on the rising tide into the river—an extraordinary incident, but not unparalleled. The two survivors, though growing weaker from exposure every hour, had continued to shout together in hope of rescue from the shore.

When asked if they had seen the *Wilmington* before, one said he had been partly unconscious for a time and thought he saw a steamer coming to their aid; but he could not for a moment recall the scene described by Peter Jorgensen.

Once more the steamer made her way towards her destination. At Federal Point they saw the first faint streaks of early dawn; and while McMillan's mind dwelt on the sacred story of lowly Bethlehem in the far off East, the brightness of the morning star grew paler in the radiance of the dawning Christmas day.

The Southport wharf was reached at last; the boat was berthed and moored in silence. So hushed and beautiful the day appeared after the terrors of the dreadful night; and as the weary toilers separated for their holiday, their hearts were full of thankfulness.

As Captain Harper trudged through crunching snow and reached the higher level of Fort Johnston of Colonial times, he turned at the gateway of the ancient garrison to gaze upon a scene of loveliness. Below the sleeping, snow-bound village lay Battery Island, shimmering in the morning glory like a field of floating ice, while sunbeams danced along the rippling waters of the bay, reflecting rainbow tints upon the ice-clad spars of anchored vessels outward bound.

Around Cape Fear, old Neptune's racers rushed with crested manes, ever charging and reforming for the fray. Above it all, secure, serene and beautiful, old Bald Head Light House pierced the blue, amidst a wilderness of snow. Beyond Smith's Island rose the ocean's murmur like the dreamy roaring of a seashell to the listening ear, while away upon the heaving bosom of the sea, the bell buoy rocked and rang in ceaseless harmony. A little stormtossed coaster neared the wharf and lowered her glistening sails, while chuckling blocks gave out a pleasant sound. Then puny waves appeared, and seemed to whisper, as they gently kissed the welcome shore.

Along the shining beach from Caswell to Fort Fisher the tossing breakers rose and fell in the sheen of the rising sun, and from the deeps the mystic voices of the sea joined in the song of the angels, "Glory to God in the Highest, on Earth Peace, Good Will to Men."

Before the Harper cottage gate a robin sang his joyous note, and when the Captain bent above the cradle of his motherless boy, the sleeping baby stirred and smiled; perhaps he too, had heard the angels in the sky.

Index

More James Sprunt from Dram Tree Books

Chronicles of the Cape Fear River: 1660-1916

(ISBN 0-9723240-5-4 • $34.95 • 732 pgs • Trim 6x9 • Trade Paperback • Illustrated)

Blockade runner, philanthopist, business man and historian - James Sprunt was all of that and more. He once owned the famous Orton Plantation and Wilmington's Dudley Mansion. His family cotton business was the largest exporter of the fiber in the world. He was also a life-long lover of the Cape Fear. This book is Sprunt's signature history of the place that he loved more than any other. If you love the Cape Fear and North Carolina's history, then you absolutely must have this unique and all-encompassing history of the region!

Derelicts:

An account of ships lost at sea in general commerce traffic and a brief history of blockade runners stranded along the North Carolina coast 1861 - 1865

(ISBN 0-9723240-9-7 • $17.95 • 200 pgs • Trim 9 1/4 x 6 1/4 • Trade Paper • Illustrated)

There is a reason sailors call the waters off the North Carolina coast "Cape Fear" and "Graveyard of the Atlantic." In this reprint of a book first published in 1920, celebrated North Carolina historian James Sprunt tells the stories of the ships and men that met their doom in the pitiless depths off Tar Heel beaches. Illustrated for the first time, this account of the dangerous blockade running trade - which the author knew from first-hand experience, is a riveting tale that has the power to thrill even today.

Get yours today at fine bookstores, or at

www.dramtreebooks.com

www.ingramcontent.com/pod-product-compliance
Lightning Source LLC
LaVergne TN
LVHW020534100826
845148LV00010B/1463

* 9 7 8 0 9 8 1 4 6 0 3 6 9 *